REGIONAL PLANNING
IN AMERICA
Practice and Prospect

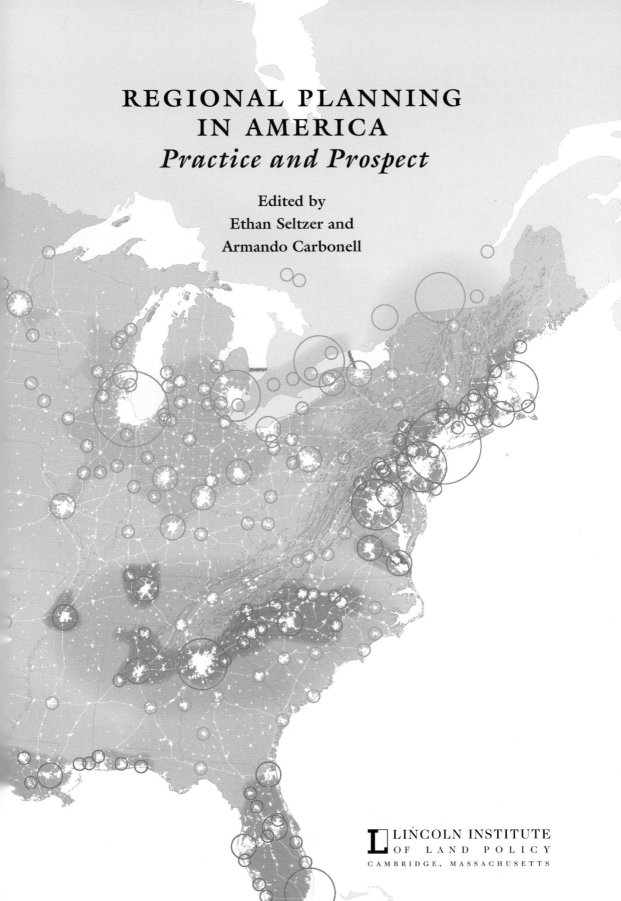

REGIONAL PLANNING IN AMERICA
Practice and Prospect

Edited by
Ethan Seltzer and
Armando Carbonell

LINCOLN INSTITUTE
OF LAND POLICY
CAMBRIDGE, MASSACHUSETTS

Library of Congress Cataloging-in-Publication Data

Regional planning in America : practice and prospect / edited by Ethan Seltzer and
Armando Carbonell.
    p. cm.
 Includes index.
 ISBN 978-1-55844-215-3
 1. Regional planning--United States. 2. Sustainable development--
United States. I. Seltzer, Ethan. II. Carbonell, Armando, 1951-
 HT392.R4184 2011
 307.1'20973--dc22

                        2011003403

Designed by Peter M. Blaiwas, Vern Associates, Inc., Newburyport, Massachusetts

Composed in ITC Galliard. Printed and bound by Puritan Press, in Hollis,
New Hampshire

MANUFACTURED IN THE UNITED STATES OF AMERICA

Cover image: Map adapted from The United Regions of America, as mapped by the National
Resources Board in 1935 to identify 16 regions for national planning purposes across the 48
contiguous states. National Resources Committee. 1935. *Regional factors in national planning.*
Washington, DC: Government Printing Office.

Title page image: Map of emerging U.S. megaregions, courtesy of Regional Plan Association.

CONTENTS

LIST OF FIGURES, TABLES, AND BOXES

Figures

Tables

Boxes

CHAPTER 1

PLANNING REGIONS

Ethan Seltzer and Armando Carbonell

We live in regions—territories defined by function and only rarely by jurisdiction. The places where we work, live, shop, recreate, and socialize constitute a territory that seldom corresponds to a single town or city. Getting our food, water, and energy, quite apart from cars, computers, and tools, often involves global supply chains, and we may send our sewage and solid waste to jurisdictions and communities miles from our doorsteps.

In fact, as the earth's human population has become predominantly urban, some have argued that metropolitan regions, rather than individual cities, states, and nations, will become the keystones for both local and national economies. According to this view, competitiveness will rely on metropolitan and even megaregional networks and flows. Still, there are reasons other than economic competitiveness to employ a regional view for meeting the challenges of this age.

Sustainability and sustainable development have received an enormous amount of attention in recent years. Making choices today in a manner that does not foreclose choices for those who will follow speaks directly to those broader systems that overlap into the functional territories we know as regions. How we manage the development and use of land, energy, water, and other resources immediately calls on the overlapping territories that comprise whole ecosystems. In an interconnected, sustainable world, there is no "away" to which waste can be consigned or where unbridled extraction can take place. In a sustainable world, everything is connected to everything else, and people are called on to act accordingly.

In a perfect world, institutions for governance would match the territories within which we live. The dynamics of ecosystems, cultures, and societies would occur in territories closely aligned with one another. Concerns for present-day competitiveness or future sustainability would play out within territories where natural and social systems, and institutions for managing these shared places, would all act with respect to the same territory of interests, and the impacts of those actions and decisions would be understood and elicit responses in logical and ethical ways.

For many reasons, this kind of functional alignment is hard to find. Further, for most of us, regions are mere abstractions. We experience trust, community, and empowerment at a more human scale—the block, neighborhood, or city. Achieving the sustainability we say we seek requires bridging the gaps between the scales at which we experience place and act effectively.

Over time, as connections between places and activities change, what might have begun as a closely aligned set of systems in a shared territory loses the definition and meaning associated with a single place. We become invested in a set of institutional relationships that change more slowly, particularly for governance, and that commitment becomes capitalized as part of a political economy of place. Over time, boundaries, as inadequate as they may be or will become, are associated with property values, and changing those boundaries becomes not just a governance challenge but a profound economic challenge as well.

No matter how much sense it may make to reshuffle jurisdictional boundaries to better approximate actual patterns of daily life, those boundaries take on cultural meaning associated with values. Issues of race and class are closely associated with jurisdictional boundaries and politics throughout the United States (Dreier, Mollenkopf, and Swanstrom 2001; Orfield 1997; Pastor, Benner, and Matsuoka 2009). Proposing a change in boundaries quickly becomes an attack on long-held (though not necessarily laudable) beliefs, making institutional realignment for purposes of sustainability and economic competitiveness not just an administrative challenge, but a fundamental question of cultural change requiring the public resolution of conflicting values.

Thus we are stuck between two clear and compelling notions: on one hand the allegiance of individuals, communities, economies, and cultures to the jurisdictional status quo; and on the other the logic of better matching planning and governance to the actual scale of activities. We may live in regions, but we plan and govern through jurisdictions. The history of American urban planning over the past 100 years has largely been written as a story of individual jurisdictional initiatives.

That is not to say that serious efforts toward regional realignment have not been made. From time to time, we have attempted to change the pattern, most notably in the 1930s. However, the inertia of jurisdictional planning and the resistance to a role for regional interests has produced a less than stellar record for regional planning in the United States.

In 1933, Evelyn Brooks and Lee Brooks reviewed five years of planning literature, one of the first such reviews for this then-young field. Of 927 titles reviewed, 237 had to do with regional planning and 119 with national planning, reflecting both the challenges of the times and the ambitions for regional planning. The issues raised in their review are familiar to planners today.

> It is impossible to consider regional planning apart from city planning and the details of communication, highways, airways, traffic, zoning,

and the like. It also includes the whole problem of beautification in metropolitan and rural areas where the assault on ugliness and waste is gathering momentum. (Brooks and Brooks 1933, 434)

They go on to ask, "Is there any clear evidence that regional planning is a going concern rather than a mere academic occupation?" (Brooks and Brooks 1933, 435). Their conclusion is that, indeed, the plans then in place and the trends toward metropolitan planning in both the United States and Europe combined to paint a convincing picture for the role and efficacy of regional planning. Nonetheless, they condemned what they saw as a flow of propaganda in the form of plans, constituting little more than wishful thinking on the part of vested interests and academics rather than useful and scientific planning.

Similarly, writing 40 years later, Martha Derthick (1974, 3) noted:

There has never been a sustained movement for regional organization that left its impress across the United States. Regionalism . . . is one of those ideas that grips a few minds or much of an academic discipline, as it gripped sociologists and planners in the 1930s and economists and planners in the 1960s, but then disappears for a while. It has been much subject to intellectual fad and fashion.

Derthick challenged the notion that regionalism expressed through regional planning would ever emerge as a pragmatic approach to managing the habitation and growth of urban places and regions. Why? Largely because of its history of failed attempts and her concern that regions were poor substitutes for states. If it were just a question of facts and data, regional planning would win the day. It is not, however, and never has been. Local control and the aspiration to maintain local institutions for planning and resource management are desires that are not easily displaced.

Leora Waldner (2008, 697) goes further, asserting that regional governance is meant to be ineffective, and therein lies the reason for which regional planning and (weak) governance has salience:

US regional governments are ineffectual by design, as they are given very little land-use power, no tax base, no direct representation, and no constitutional base. . . . Thus, in their role as a think tank, they may have an implied moral obligation to promulgate best practices and innovative land use policies. . . . [I]t appears worthwhile for COGs to produce these plans, despite the likelihood of repeated conformance failures.

Whether regional governance is ineffective by design or by nature, this book takes up the ongoing challenge of linking regional lives to local institutions through planning. Regionalism and regional planning make sense, but in most cases not enough to cause us to change the ways we govern ourselves and plan and act together.

Nonetheless, a quick scan of news headlines across U.S. communities reveals a host of issues that are regional in nature. Traffic congestion is a problem in every metropolitan region in the country, and the failure of purely local approaches has led to new initiatives to reconsider past practices and craft regional solutions. Many communities in the Southeast, Southwest, and in some parts of the Midwest have encountered water supply issues that bring into sharp focus the need for better regional planning and implementation. In the Pacific Northwest recovery efforts for anadromous fish species have involved all landscapes—urban, rural, working, and wild.

Though the practice of planning in the United States has evolved to have a largely local outlook, decision makers, planners, and citizens keep coming back to regional planning because they recognize that contemporary challenges to quality of life are beyond the scope of what a single jurisdiction can manage. There is a need for planning that matches the inescapable regionalism of real patterns of daily life in major population centers. A pressing need also exists for planning that matches the scale of the systems upon which sustainability, certainly, and in some cases survival depend.

This book seeks to address the lack of a strategic and optimistic embrace of regional planning by focusing on U.S. practice and the ways that it can help to advance sustainability and quality of life. We believe that regional planning is not optional and that, like it or not, no local planning effort can meaningfully address local concerns without understanding and acting on them in a regional context. Local communities already engage regions through planning across the United States, whether intentionally or not. With the other contributors to this volume, we hope to enable decision makers and planners to make more productive and strategic use of regional planning by showing how it can respond to their desire to build a better future for their communities. This book offers a gateway to regional planning directed at the challenges and opportunities we face locally and as a nation.

WHAT DO WE MEAN BY REGION?

Any discussion of regional planning, the reasons for doing it, or the way in which it gets done, has to start with a clear understanding of what we mean when we refer to a region. According to Douglas Kelbaugh (1996, 8), "*region* is an ambiguous term." He notes that to planners it means something large, but to architects it refers to something smaller than the global international scale at which capital, projects, and contemporary ideas about architecture are developed.

In the United States regionalists in the early part of the twentieth century distinguished between regions defined as sections that are distinct from the nation or the "whole," and regions defined explicitly by what they contributed to the nation (Odum and Moore 1938). Politically, sections were viewed as inevitable while regions were not (National Resources Committee 1935).

Defining a region involves a combination of overlapping and interconnected characteristics along with the purposes for planning. Such characteristics can include ecological or biophysical features or systems, economic and political conditions or relationships, social and cultural traditions, or frequently, some combination of all of these. A single factor, multiple factors, multiple jurisdictions, or administrative convenience can be used to identify a region.

The fundamental principle, though, is that regions are composed of overlapping factors that together describe shared interests and dynamics. When multiple factors are involved, the overlap is most apparent at the center of the region, and least so at its edges, where the multiple territories for overlapping concerns may or may not be coterminous. This also means that regional planning occurs most often with respect to functions and relationships rather than jurisdictions. In other words, the definition of a region has less to do with determining where its outer boundary is situated, and more with creating a case for shared interests.

Defining the region is an extraordinarily important—and delicate—task. Define the region too narrowly, and dynamics essential to the success of the plan may be beyond the reach of the places and partners involved. Define it too broadly, and local jurisdictions that states and the federal government have charged with planning may view regional planning as threatening a loss of local control and autonomy.

A region defined without respect for its role in a broader world makes plan implementation a zero-sum game boxed in by old animosities and contests. Planners who define the region without respect to local and regional identity risk cutting themselves off from the essential role that this identity plays in motivating citizens and decision makers to act on behalf of the territory.

How the region is defined for regional planning, therefore, is a central planning and policy question in itself. Establishing the region's definition identifies the nature of the planning questions and the key constituents for that planning. Defining a region is not necessarily a simple or mechanical act, however. Unlike city- and other jurisdiction-based planning, regional planning lacks the institutional authority found at those other scales and occurs in and for a territory where the center is clearly identified but the edges remain fuzzy. In a world of absolute boundaries, a fuzzy edge is difficult to maintain. Douglas Powell (2007, 21), writing about critical regionalism, has stated:

> Region, then, is not a thing in itself, a stable and bounded object of study. My assertion here is that just as "community" is for Raymond Williams "a warmly persuasive word to describe an existing set of relationships, or the warmly persuasive word to describe an alternative set of relationships," "region" is always at some level an attempt to persuade as much as it is to

describe. Because the "set of relationships" intersecting at any one point on the landscape is potentially unsummarizable by any one account, all versions of region are necessarily partial, and hence an attempt to persuade, at the very least, of the validity of their own particular definitions.

Further, the definition for a planning region used at one time may vary considerably at another. Often, it must. Because charters, specific regulatory or taxing powers, or delegations of authority from state or federal legislation sustain few regional institutions, regional planning proceeds with no guarantees for ongoing implementation, monitoring, assessment, and subsequent planning.

City or county planning speaks specifically to the relationships among community and property interests, and in so doing becomes a part of what creates and maintains property value over time. This central role in the creation and maintenance of property value ensures a continuing role for local planning that is seldom associated with regional planning in the United States.

WHAT IS REGIONAL PLANNING?

Planning, regional or otherwise, is a basic human activity. Uniquely among species, human beings have been endowed with the abilities to think about the future, sort out desired from undesired alternatives, and create strategies for choosing and advancing those futures. In this sense, planning, regardless of its scale, generally occurs through a familiar process.

Artur Glickson (1955, 11) noted, "It is obvious that Regional Planning is not an invention of our days, but a practice of old times." Though much of what we discuss when we talk about planning in the United States is associated with the emergence of city planning in the early years of the twentieth century, Greg Hise (2009) similarly reminds us that regional planning predates those origins of city planning and is associated with the ways that the federal government contemplated national development in the nineteenth century. He notes that historic accounts of planning in America typically regard regional planning as episodic, emerging briefly from time to time and then vanishing, despite the fact that planners consistently describe their practice in regional terms. Hise makes this observation as a challenge to the way that scholars have marginalized regional planning in the American planning experience, and poses it as a challenge to our historic and current understanding of the necessary role for regional planning as an integral part of all planning.

Robert Fishman (2007), writing about the history of national planning in the United States, points out that although its citizens do not regard planning as a federal responsibility or authority, it is, in fact, an important part of the history of both the nation and its planning. He reminds us that these initiatives were regional in scale: the Gallatin Plan of roads and canals in 1808; the development of transcontinental railroads; the large landscape focus of the conservation movement; the great dam and water projects in the West; the federal interstate highway system; and, perhaps, the development of high-speed passenger rail nationwide. They exemplify regional planning as an organizing principle at key points in U.S. history, beginning well before the practice and profession of city planning emerged here.

John Friedmann and Clyde Weaver (1979) sketch the history of regional planning in the United States as coming into its own approximately 50 years after the Civil War. In their analysis, the impacts of rapid urban industrialization, the close of the frontier, the rise of the conservation movement, and the South's persistent dependency on national support for development served as catalysts for the emergence of regional planning early in the twentieth century. They identify alternating periods of "territorial integration," the "common bonds of social order forged by history within a given place," and "functional integration"—action born of mutual self-interest—as descriptive of the swings in purpose of regional planning since that time (Friedmann and Weaver 1979, 7).

Early efforts in the period from 1925 to 1935 were characterized by the work of Lewis Mumford, Benton MacKaye, and other individuals, and by the Regional Planning Association of America (RPAA). Friedmann and Weaver (1979) considered this the initial period of territorial integration for regional planning, which was focused on the development of a new cultural regionalism developed in harmony with the characteristics and assets of the natural landscape.

Fishman (2000) points out that this early twentieth century regional planning had a huge impact on regional planning thought and practice for the next 100 years. He describes an epic battle between the "metropolitanists," those who viewed the task to be the planning and development of urban regions in a manner that sustained the primacy of central cities and their economies, versus the "regionalists," led by Mumford and others associated with the RPAA, who advocated for the decentralization of the city and its functions. The profound city-suburb split implied in the regionalist view came to dominate metropolitan politics after World War II. Fishman concluded, however, that later in the century the subsequent synthesis of the urbanism of Jane Jacobs with the environmentalism of Ian McHarg created a new lease on life for regional planning.

Friedmann and Weaver also identify a later stage of this initial territorial integration in the years from 1935 to 1950. The earlier idealism had been tempered by politics and by the suspicion that there was something unsound if not subversive in the regionalist efforts. This period was marked by a more practical, less idealistic regionalism. Comprehensive river basin development and the scientific application of planning to problems of regional underdevelopment marked the practice of regional planning during this time. David Lilienthal (1944, xxi), director of the Tennessee Valley Authority (TVA), described himself and his colleagues as "dreamers with shovels," who were engaged in realizing the promise of New Deal liberalism in underdeveloped Appalachia.

However, even the practical application of regional planning to problems of underdevelopment was too much for those who saw it as a threat to a political order dominated by states and localities. In Friedmann and Weaver's assessment, the development of new spatial planning techniques and the emergence of what became known as regional science during the period from 1950 to 1975 moved regional planning even further away from its idealistic roots. Spatial systems planning and the attempted management of specific resource and capital flows became its primary tasks. Most of this activity was focused on urbanization in developing countries although, as with the TVA, some attention continued to be paid to the problems of underdevelopment in the United States and other developed nations.

Friedmann and Weaver then identify a second period of territorial integration that arose after 1975 as issues of urban sprawl, coupled with the environmental movement, led to a new interest in regional, and particularly metropolitan, planning. This is what Fishman (2000) has termed a period of new "life" for regional planning in America. The synthesis of powerful ideas gleaned from Jane Jacobs and Ian McHarg and the current literature on regional planning seem to confirm that we are continuing along this path.

In this volume, Gerrit-Jan Knaap and Rebecca Lewis identify a range of metropolitan planning efforts, which seem to be increasing in frequency throughout the nation. Smart growth (Daniels 2001; Krueger and Gibbs 2008); sustainability (Condon and Teed 2006; Haughton and Counsell 2004); equity (Clark and Christopherson 2009; Pastor and Benner, this volume); large landscape conservation (Chester 2006; McKinney and Johnson 2009); economic development (Levine 2001); rural development (Morrison 2006); and climate change (Read, Shenot, and McGalliard 2010) are on the growing list of regional planning applications being studied, discussed, and pursued in the United States. Add in the experience from Great Britain and Europe, and regional planning now is clearly a central part of planning practice.

Unlike the neat derivation of eras proposed by Friedmann and Weaver, however, it is also clear that regional planning today carries with it all of the trends and characteristics of its prior incarnations. Functional integration is clearly present in the way that regional planning is being conceived. Douglas Porter and Allan Wallis (2002), for example, examine what they call ad hoc regionalism—regional planning and governance efforts that arise not just in the absence of formal governing institutions, but because of a desire to avoid formal arrangements and to respond effectively to perceived threats to quality of life. Thomas Barth (2001), in fact, observes that ad hoc alliances are increasingly welcome because they don't have the capacity to threaten existing institutional relationships, and they exist only when acceptable to those already assured a place at the table.

Similarly, the voices of the bioregionalists, echoing Mumford, MacKaye, Odum, and the RPAA, are still with us. The arguments on behalf of habitation and planning informed by the underlying ecology of the landscape that Kirkpatrick Sale (2000) and Robert Thayer, Jr. (2003) provide would be familiar to those early regionalists. Like McHarg (1994; Steiner, this volume), Richard Forman (2008) proposes a planning method that is based on landscape ecology and provides the same sort of blend of science and planning proposed by MacKaye (1991) some 90 years before. Rather than bringing the curtain down on one approach and welcoming another, we tend to see the whole of the U.S. experience reflected in what regional planning and regional planners address today. In this sense, there may be less distance than we think between the so-called utopian idealists of the early twentieth century and our contemporary results-oriented pragmatists.

What are the key characteristics of present-day regional planning? In any era or for any reason, regional planning starts from a unique position. Rather than encompass a territorial interest that is sharply bounded and represented (or at least claimed) by an institution that holds general governmental powers and responsibilities, it is carried out over a territory that, at least when that planning takes place, is found to share enough characteristics to assert its existence as a region. Fundamentally, rather than planning within boundaries, regional planning addresses issues across boundaries.

In fact, regional planning can be defined as planning that tackles issues that no single jurisdiction or implementing agency can address or manage effectively on its own. That is, regional planning deals with issues that occur in territories comprised of more than one jurisdiction, where interjurisdictional strategies are mandatory, not elective. As a consequence the nature of regional planning in the United States must be viewed as profoundly collaborative.

Theories about collaborative planning have been well described in recent years. Patsy Healey (2003, 116) states that it "is about strategic approaches to the governance of place." She goes on to describe it as a means for melding different governance structures with each other in order to govern and plan for the whole effectively. Judith Innes and David Booher (2010) go further in describing a regional planning process for resource management. They conclude that informal relationships—those neither defined legally nor embodied formally in institutions—play an important role in enabling the various interests to arrive at collaborative outcomes. Formal governance structures must also interact with each other in ultimately productive ways.

T. H. Morrison (2006, 150) reviews collaborative and institutional theories and suggests that the kind of collaborative institutional behavior described by Healey, Innes and Booher, and others is ". . . not necessarily about voluntary and consensual participation but about positional relationships between actors in a network of governance. . . . [R]egional institutional integration is shaped not only by relationships of power but also by social constructions. Any integrative initiatives, therefore, will always be deeply conflicted and contested." She proposes that planners need to proceed from a shared understanding of common circumstances rather than "manufacturing" an organization or boundary—a key principle for collaborative planning processes.

These fundamental themes from collaborative planning theory are reinforced by much of the contemporary literature on regional planning and regionalism. Matthew McKinney and Shawn Johnson (2009), in their book *Working
Across Boundaries,* write about the governance gap at the regional level, where
no institutions are charged with dealing with transboundary issues. Echoing
the collaborative planning theorists, they point to creating a shared sense of the
need for action and fashioning a collaborative path that links diverse interests in
order to achieve goals in a regional setting.

Kevin Morgan (1997, 492) writes about "learning regions" that are organized via networks as means by which to overcome traditional tensions between
markets and the state. "Over the past few years in particular," he notes, "we
have witnessed the spread of a new paradigm, variously referred to as the network or associational paradigm. Whatever the shortcomings of this new paradigm, it is clearly fuelled by the pervasive belief that 'markets' and 'hierarchy'
do not exhaust the menu of organizational forms for mobilizing resources for
innovation and economic development."

In applying the new regionalism idea to smaller metropolitan areas, James
Visser (2004, 52) writes that "new regionalism promotes regional action through
governance, defined as the use of interorganizational collaboration rather than
hierarchical regional government to resolve area-wide public problems." Though
he concludes that institutionally weak regionalism is unlikely to achieve new
regionalist objectives for equity and participation, nonetheless it is still better and
more constructive than a status quo of destructive interlocal competition.

Kathryn Foster and William Barnes (2009, 3) define regional governance as
"deliberate efforts at collective action in environments of multiple governmental
jurisdictions. . . . [By this definition, regional governance:]

- crosses borders, by definition jurisdictional, and also often sectoral and
  functional;

- is almost always a problem-solving or goal-seeking activity;

- encompasses, but is not limited to, the institutional tools that are used to
  establish and implement regional action;

- is not a single jurisdiction that encompasses an entire region. As a single jurisdiction, local governance would by definition not cross jurisdictional boundaries. Because no such entity exists in the United States, we exclude this option as
  a 'straw man' and a distraction in the regional governance discussion.

- is not 'no government' or a 'market' governance because that system, if it
  exists somewhere, would not be intentional or deliberate action. Here again,
  no such entity exists in the United States."

They go on to describe regional governance as occurring through a coalition of interests.

It is tempting to describe regional planning as a collaborative enterprise simply because so few regional institutions throughout the United States are able to respond to regional needs or conditions, but defining regional planning as a transboundary exercise also necessitates a collaborative approach. Regional planning—as the management of issues or action on behalf of goals that cross boundaries in regions—must be recognized as a collaborative enterprise in which the challenges for planning and planners start with the presentation of shared concerns.

The purposes for regional planning depend on one or a combination of several motivations. Plans can arise because they are mandated; conditions require that they be made; or communities elect to create them in order to advance shared goals. In the first instance, required regional planning is most often associated with access to or the use of resources from the federal government at the local or regional level. Coordination and efficiency are often the reasons for these regional planning requirements, as exemplified by transportation planning carried out by metropolitan planning organizations.

The second reason comes into play because conditions that require regional planning are often associated with natural or man-made disasters that far exceed the boundaries of single jurisdictions. Securing adequate water resources for growing communities and economies, salmon-recovery planning in the Pacific Northwest, or efforts to create greater resilience along the Gulf Coast are examples of regional planning instigated because conditions and issues require a regional response.

Finally, regional planning may be pursued because it is the best or possibly only strategy for seeking commonly held goals. Recent examples of metropolitan planning in Portland (Oregon), Salt Lake City, and Sacramento combine elements of the first two motivations, but they also took on regional form and scale because the communities involved chose to do so.

Regional planning for large-scale landscapes, such as the Yellowstone-to-Yukon effort, often arise not because of a requirement but rather a desire to fit future planning to the scale of the resource at stake (McKinney, Scarlett, and Kemmis 2010). The utilization of regions as the basis for planning and action that will counter persistent societal inequities is another strategy being elected by those who see little progress or prospect for these issues solely on the part of local jurisdictions, particularly in metropolitan areas.

When they engage in regional planning, what do planners do in practice? To MacKaye (1991), along with more contemporary authors, regional planning emerges from the real relationships created across landscapes by people and communities. As such it offers the best chance to create a useful fit between human and nature, built and unbuilt, urban and rural, and present and future. McHarg's 1969 book *Design with Nature* integrated ideas about ecology, fitness, fit, and the pressing need to respond to global challenges into a method for ecological, regional planning that formed the foundation for much of what we know of regional planning practice today.

More recently, Innes and Booher (2010, 35) described the practice of collaborative planning in terms that directly address the networked, boundary-crossing nature of contemporary planning practice that has been advanced by Healey and others. They propose that true collaborative planning emerges from practices that elicit what they call "collaborative rationality."

> Three conditions are critical to whether a collaborative process can be collaboratively rational, productive of socially valuable outcomes, and adaptive to the opportunities and challenges of its unique and changing context. These conditions include full diversity of interests among participants, interdependence of the participants, who cannot get their interests met independently, and engagement of all in face to face authentic dialogue meeting [Jürgen] Habermas' basic speech conditions.

Innes and Booher's DIAD theory of planning—*D*iversity of participants, recognized *I*nterdependence of interests, and *A*uthentic *D*ialogue in the process—provides a means for articulating a theoretical basis for regional planning practice in line with our expectation that regional planning is distinguished by its boundary-crossing nature and the need for planners to be able to engage interests whose institutional context most often encourages just the opposite.

CONTEMPORARY REGIONAL PLANNING PRACTICE

The state of our world and the realities of contemporary daily life make the case for robust regional planning, and our concern here is with what regional planners actually do. With regional planning practice in the United States settling into a new century, and the challenges that face communities and institutions requiring boundary-crossing collaboration like never before, it is time to assess what we know about regional planning practice in anticipation of an approaching, new era of conscious regionalism.

Many would agree that one of the contemporary innovators for U.S. regional planning was Ian McHarg. As Frederick Steiner reminds us in chapter 2, McHarg's work has helped to spawn much of what we now take for granted: environmental impact statements, landscape ecology, and the application of the natural sciences to a planning framework previously dominated by concerns with institutions, investment, and politics. What we now know as environmental planning and sustainable development were profoundly affected by his work. Further, as a public intellectual, McHarg's legacy includes roles for planners that move from behind the technical and analytical tasks that, during his time, circumscribed the field.

Today, the practice of regional planning is bracketed by two key concerns: governance and participation. In chapter 3, Kathryn Foster takes up the topic of governance. She builds a convincing case for governance being the bedrock challenge for regional planning and presents governance as the means by which autonomous actors organize and act for a shared purpose. With a disjunction between the institutional landscape on one hand and the actual landscape of activities and systems on the other, Foster identifies ways that regions have stepped up to the challenge of creating effective governance mechanisms. In her interpretation, regional planning does not necessarily take up topics different than those encountered by planners at the local or state levels. The requirement of explicitly engaging the governance dilemma, however, does make the practice of regional planning uniquely challenging. Moreover, Foster provides guidelines for effective regional planners and planning in this context and suggests that the way forward will either include changes in local powers or the creation of new regional relationships and authorities.

Continuing the theme of the disjunction between the scale for the issue and that utilized for governance, in chapter 4 Manuel Pastor and Chris Benner present the region as the proper scale at which to address and advance issues of equity in society. Particularly with the emergence of interest in sustainable development at all levels of government, new concern about social justice and equity as critical planning objectives are entering the discussion of planning practice in this country. According to the authors, equity is best addressed at a regional, often metropolitan scale, and they document the emergence of new social movements that champion regional planning for purposes of fulfilling the promise of a more equitable society. Because of its scale, however, planning at the regional level runs the real risk of becoming inauthentic. Pastor and Benner suggest ways that planners can work effectively at the regional level in order to advance equity concerns and to make real sustainability possible.

In chapter 5 Deborah and Frank Popper turn our attention to one of the longest-standing regional development efforts in the United States: that of the frontier. They review the history of the idea of the frontier and the planning that has occurred on its behalf, noting that far from having disappeared, the U.S. frontier persists and continues to be a national project. They conclude that though the nation's frontier planning is deeply flawed, working out its deficiencies could be beneficial both for the future of the frontier and for creating more effective regional development planning practice in this country. As in the preceding chapters, the authors identify the need for new institutional relationships as a critical factor going forward.

Timothy Beatley's examination of regional planning for environmental quality and management, in chapter 6, presents ideas about environmental planning and natural resources, one of the more familiar themes in American regional planning. He goes beyond notions of environmental systems and ecological planning to consider what a true green regionalism might be. Drawing on examples from throughout North America and Europe, he presents regional planning as a possible vehicle for creating the robust sustainability that is needed and often sought in communities across the country today.

In chapter 7, Gerrit-Jan Knaap and Rebecca Lewis examine the ways that regional planning is addressing the challenges of metropolitan growth management. They note that planning for growth at this scale is not new to planning in the United States and chronicle the overwhelming influence that planning for transportation systems has had on the emergence of regional urban form and metropolitan planning practice. Though they are profoundly optimistic about the emerging role for this country's metropolitan planning, particularly at this time, they warn that implementation remains an enormous challenge. Generally speaking, the interest in and willingness to plan at the metropolitan scale has yet to be matched by a widespread willingness to act as a region in order to implement those plans. The authors issue a call for institutional reforms that will enable successful planning and the effective use of plans to proceed in the decades ahead.

John Fregonese and C. J. Gabbe, in chapter 8, continue the theme of metropolitan planning and its practice by reflecting on their work to engage residents of a region in its planning. It is no easy task to engage a large, diverse group of people in planning aimed at a territory they all share but often don't recognize as being part of their community or that might be viewed as being at odds with their community. Whereas Foster presents regions and regional planning from the perspective of institutions, Fregonese and Gabbe bring it back to the scale of the household and the neighborhood. Based on their practice throughout the United States, they provide a description of what they have done to engage broad, often disinterested audiences in regional planning. Their method involves starting with an examination of values, some shared and some contested. Without grounding planning in the values and culture of the region, in all of its diversity, they believe that regional planning will almost certainly produce plans of little consequence or lasting influence.

Also on the theme of regional development and competitiveness, Robert Yaro presents the work in which he and others are engaged in order to advance the state of the art for megaregional planning, in both national and global contexts. In chapter 9 he identifies emerging national interest in high-speed passenger rail service as requiring a megaregional scale of thinking and acting. Simply stated, high-speed rail works best for trips of 150 to 600 miles, which requires planning on a scale that, though subnational, most often entails multiple states and more than one metropolitan area.

Finally, in chapter 10, we return to the questions that prompted this book:

- What makes regional planning different from other forms of planning?

- What do regional planners need in order to excel?

- How is regional planning evolving through practice?

Even though regional planning processes don't appear to be much different from those used at other scales, their context has a profound impact on the timing and strategies used to make such plans, the ways they are used, and the skills needed by planners. We conclude with a discussion of the prospects for regional planning in the United States, particularly in the context provided by the insights contributed by the chapters' authors.

We are unapologetic fans of the regional approach and optimists when it comes to envisioning the future for regional planning in this country. Some people may suggest that being any kind of optimist with respect to regional planning is tantamount to being an idealist, but we come to this view as both planners and inhabitants of regions. Our view is grounded in practice, and we believe that through practice the challenges of effective regional planning can be worked out. It is to the prospects for the practice of regional planning in the United States and to its practitioners, now and in the future, that we address this work.

REFERENCES

Barth, Thomas. 2001. The role of ad hoc regional alliances in managing growth. *Public Works Management Policy* 6(2):114–125.

Brooks, Evelyn C., and Lee M. Brooks. 1933. Five years of planning literature. *Social Forces* 11(3):430–465.

Chester, Charles. 2006. *Conservation across borders: Biodiversity in an interdependent world.* Washington, DC: Island Press.

Clark, Jennifer, and Susan Christopherson. 2009. Integrating investment and equity: A critical regionalist agenda for a progressive regionalism. *Journal of Planning Education and Research* 28(3):341–354.

Condon, Patrick, and Jackie Teed, eds. 2006. *Sustainability by design: A vision for a region of 4 million.* Vancouver, BC: Design Centre for Sustainability, University of British Columbia.

Daniels, Tom. 2001. Smart growth: A new American approach to regional planning. *Planning Practice and Research* 16(3/4):271–279.

Derthick, Martha. 1974. *Between state and nation: Regional organizations of the United States.* Washington, DC: Brookings Institution.

Dreier, Peter, John Mollenkopf, and Todd Swanstrom. 2001. *Place matters: Metropolitics for the twenty-first century.* Lawrence: University Press of Kansas.

Fishman, Robert. 2000. The death and life of American regional planning. In *Reflections on regionalism,* ed. Bruce Katz. Washington, DC: Brookings Institution.

———. 2007. 1808–1908–2008: National planning for America. Prepared for the America 2050 Project, Regional Plan Association, New York (8–13 July).

Forman, Richard T. T. 2008. *Urban regions: Ecology and planning beyond the city.* New York: Cambridge University Press.

Foster, Kathryn A., and William R. Barnes. 2009. Reframing regional governance for research and practice. Paper presented at Annual Conference of Association of Collegiate Schools of Planning, Crystal City, VA.

Friedmann, John, and Clyde Weaver. 1979. *Territory and function: The evolution of regional planning.* Berkeley: University of California Press.

Glickson, Artur. 1955. *Regional planning and development: Six lectures delivered at the Institute of Social Studies, The Hague, 1953.* Publication of the Netherlands Universities Foundation for International Cooperation, The Hague. Leiden: A. W. Sijthoff's Uitgeversmaatschappij N.V.

Haughton, Graham, and Dave Counsell. 2004. Regions and sustainable development: Regional planning matters. *The Geographical Journal* 170(2):135–145.

Healey, Patsy. 2003. Collaborative planning in perspective. *Planning Theory* 2(2):101–123.

Hise, Greg. 2009. Whither the region? Periods and periodicity in planning history. *Journal of Planning History* 8(4):295–307.

Innes, Judith E., and David E. Booher. 2010. *Planning with complexity: An introduction to collaborative rationality for public policy.* New York: Routledge.

Kelbaugh, Douglas. 1996. Five points of a critical regionalism. *On the Ground* 2(2):8–11.

Krueger, Rob, and David Gibbs. 2008. "Third wave" sustainability? Smart growth and regional development in the USA. *Regional Studies* 42(9):1263–1274.

Levine, Joyce N. 2001. The role of economic theory in regional advocacy. *Journal of Planning Literature* 16(2):183–201.

Lilienthal, David E. 1944. *TVA: Democracy on the march.* New York: Harper.

MacKaye, Benton. 1991. *The new exploration: A philosophy of regional planning.* (Orig. pub. 1928.) Harpers Ferry, WV: Appalachian Trail Conference; Urbana-Champaign: University of Illinois Press.

McHarg, Ian L. 1994. *Design with nature,* 2nd ed. (Orig. pub. 1969.) Garden City, NY: Natural History Press/Doubleday.

McKinney, Matthew J., and Shawn Johnson. 2009. *Working across boundaries: People, nature, and regions.* Cambridge, MA: Lincoln Institute of Land Policy.

McKinney, Matthew J., Lynn Scarlett, and Daniel Kemmis. 2010. *Large landscape conservation: A strategic framework for policy and action.* Cambridge, MA: Lincoln Institute of Land Policy.

Morgan, Kevin. 1997. The learning region: Institutions, innovation, and regional renewal. *Regional Studies* 31(5):491–503.

Morrison, T. H. 2006. Pursuing rural sustainability at the regional level: Key lessons from the literature on institutions, integration, and the environment. *Journal of Planning Literature* 21(2):143–152.

National Resources Committee. 1935. Regional factors in national planning and development. Washington, DC: U.S. Government Printing Office. www.archive.org/details/regionalfactorsi1935unitrich

Odum, Howard W., and Harry E. Moore. 1938. *American regionalism: A cultural-historical approach to national integration.* New York: Henry Holt and Company.

Orfield, Myron. 1997. *Metropolitics: A regional agenda for community and stability.* Washington, DC: Brookings Institution Press; Cambridge, MA: Lincoln Institute of Land Policy.

Pastor, Manuel, Chris Benner, and Martha Matsuoka. 2009. *This could be the start of something big: Social movements for regional equity and the future of metropolitan America.* Ithaca, NY: Cornell University Press.

Porter, Douglas R., and Allan D. Wallis. 2002. *Exploring ad hoc regionalism.* Cambridge, MA: Lincoln Institute of Land Policy.

Powell, Douglas Reichert. 2007. *Critical regionalism: Connecting politics and culture in the American landscape.* Chapel Hill: University of North Carolina Press.

Read, Anna, Christine Shenot, and Ted McGalliard. 2010. Getting smart about climate change. Washington, DC: International City/County Management Association, Smart Growth Network.

Sale, Kirkpatrick. 2000. *Dwellers in the land: The bioregional vision,* 2nd ed. Athens: University of Georgia Press

Thayer, Robert L. Jr. 2003. *LifePlace: Bioregional thought and practice.* Berkeley: University of California Press

Visser, James A. 2004. Voluntary regional councils and the new regionalism: Effective governance in the smaller metropolis. *Journal of Planning Education and Research* 24:51–63.

Waldner, Leora. 2008. Regional plans, local fates? How spatially restrictive regional policies influence county policy and regulations. *Environment and Planning B: Planning and Design* 35:679–700.

CHAPTER *2*

PLAN WITH NATURE
THE LEGACY OF IAN McHARG

Frederick Steiner

Ian McHarg formulated an ecological approach to planning, most notably at
the regional scale. He advocated that ecology be given equal weight to the
traditional social and economic concerns of planning. In this way, McHarg's
approach can be viewed as a precursor to contemporary ideas about sustainability, which seek to balance environmental, equity, and economic goals. Consequently, regional planners owe a great debt to McHarg. It's worth revisiting his
life and career as a means for providing a context for regional planning practice
in the United States today.

This chapter first sets the stage by reviewing McHarg's life and the precedents to his ecological planning method, and the importance and limits of that
method are discussed. His legacy and impact are explored by reviewing his influence on environmental impact assessment, geographic information system (GIS)
technologies, national- and global-scale planning, landscape and urban ecology,
sustainable development, new regionalism, and landscape urbanism.

McHARG'S LIFE

Ian L. McHarg was born in Clydebank, a shipbuilding town northwest of
Glasgow, Scotland, on 20 November 1920. During his youth, he explored the
rugged coastal terrain of western Scotland. Hiking and American jazz were his
teenage passions. McHarg also took a deep interest in religion and worked for
the Associated Scottish Newspapers as a copy boy and editor's boy.

In 1936, McHarg became intrigued by landscape architecture. He with-
drew from high school to become a pupil-apprentice to Donald A. Wintersgill,
a landscape architect with the Glasgow firm Austin and McAslan, Ltd. He also
enrolled in the Glasgow College of Art and the West of Scotland Agriculture
College.

He enlisted in the British Army in May 1938 and was mobilized into the
regular army on 2 September 1939, at the onset of World War II. McHarg
distinguished himself during the war, rising through the ranks from private to
major. As a commando in the Second Parachute Squadron, McHarg participated in campaigns in North Africa, Italy, France, and Greece. In Italy, he led

Ian McHarg (standing) with his family, ca. 1929

Source: Ian L. McHarg Papers, The Architectural Archives, University of Pennsylvania.

Ian McHarg at 16, with his brother and sisters, 1936.

Source: Ian L. McHarg Papers, The Architectural Archives, University of Pennsylvania.

the reconstruction of the Acquedotto Pugliese during 1943. This aqueduct helped provide water supplies to Allied troops as well as Italian citizens. In 1945, McHarg won the competition to design the British military cemetery in Athens.

After the war, McHarg decided to enter the Master of Landscape Architecture (MLA) program at Harvard University. This presented a challenge since he had neither a high school diploma nor an undergraduate degree. Still, Harvard admitted him. Early in his days there, McHarg met Pauline Crena de Iongh, a Radcliffe College student from a prominent Dutch family. She and McHarg married in 1947 and later had two sons, Alistair and Malcolm.

In his four years at Harvard, McHarg earned both bachelor (1949) and master of landscape architecture (1950) degrees. The atmosphere at Harvard at that time encouraged cross-disciplinary collaboration, due in large part to the modernist German Bauhaus model that influenced instructors in the architecture department. McHarg

Officers of the Second Parachute Squadron dressed in civilian garb in Ramsbury, Wiltshire, 1945. McHarg, then a captain, is in the back center.

Source: Ian L. McHarg Papers, The Architectural Archives, University of Pennsylvania.

took advantage of opportunities offered in architecture and city and regional planning, which permitted him to collaborate with three architecture students on a plan for downtown Providence, Rhode Island. In 1951, McHarg earned a master of city planning degree from Harvard, receiving the distinction after he had returned to Scotland.

In Scotland, McHarg discovered he had tuberculosis, and he almost died at the Southfield Colony for Consumptives in Edinburgh. Fortunately, he went for treatment to Hotel Belvedere in Leysin, Switzerland, where he regained his health. The contrast between what he called the "dank" conditions in the Scottish hospital and the clean Swiss sanatorium instilled an interest in the relationship between health and the built environment that would have a lasting influence on McHarg's approach to design and planning.

Ian McHarg with psychologist Erich Fromm on the set of "The House We Live In," October 1960.

Source: Ian L. McHarg Papers, The Architectural Archives, University of Pennsylvania.

From 1951 to 1954, McHarg worked as a planning officer for Scotland's Department of Health. During this time, he offered lecture courses in landscape architecture at Edinburgh College of Art and Glasgow College of Art. In 1954 G. Holmes Perkins, his former Harvard professor and then dean of the University of Pennsylvania (Penn) Graduate School of Fine Arts, invited McHarg to Philadelphia. He was appointed assistant professor of landscape architecture and city planning with the charge to create a Department of Landscape Architecture at Penn. The school had offered an undergraduate program in landscape architecture since 1924, but McHarg established the MLA degree and the graduate department. In 1959, he introduced the "Man and Environment" course, which became one of the most popular at Penn. McHarg invited prominent designers, theologians, and scientists to the class to discuss the relationship between people and their environments.

This course led to the CBS television series "The House We Live In," which McHarg produced and hosted from 1960 to 1961. His numerous guests included

Figure 2.1 **Development Principles from the Plan for the Valleys, Maryland**
Source: Design with Nature *(McHarg 1969, 87); reproduced with permission of John Wiley & Sons, Inc.*

Development principles are as follows:

VALLEY WALLS WITHOUT FOREST COVER Such lands should be prohibited to development and should be planted to forest cover. When they are covered with the appropriate distribution of mixed hardwoods to an average height of 25 feet they may be considered as below.

VALLEY WALLS IN FOREST COVER These walls, exclusive of slopes of 25% or greater, should be developed in such a manner as to perpetuate their present wooded aspect. The maximum density permitted for development should be 1 house per 3 acres.

WALLS AND SLOPES OF 25% OR GREATER Valley walls, and all slopes of 25% or greater should be prohibited to development and should be planted to forest cover.

WOODED PLATEAU Forest and woodland sites on the plateau should not be developed at densities in excess of 1 house per acre.

PROMONTORY SITES On specific promontories, in wooded locations, the density limitations can be waived to permit tower apartment buildings with low coverage.

OPEN PLATEAU Development should be largely concentrated on the open plateau.

BASIC AMENITY

GEOLOGY

UNFORESTED PLATEAU

FORESTED PLATEAU

VALLEY WALL

VALLEY FLOOR

PHYSIOGRAPHIC SECTION

Loren Eiseley, Eric Fromm, Julian Huxley, Luna Leopold, Margaret Mead, Lewis Mumford, Paul Tillich, and Arnold Toynbee. The ideas about people and their environments generated in both the Penn course and the television series influenced McHarg's teaching and burgeoning practice.

With planner-architect David Wallace, he founded the firm Wallace-McHarg Associates in Philadelphia in 1962. Their first two projects were the Plan for the Valleys and the Baltimore Inner Harbor Plan, both in Maryland (figure 2.1). McHarg led the innovative Plan for the Valleys, which addressed a bucolic Maryland landscape threatened with suburban sprawl and the construction of an interstate highway. The plan pioneered concepts such as the transfer of development rights, protection of environmentally sensitive areas, and conservation-based clustered village settlements. In 1965, Wallace and McHarg expanded their practice to include landscape architect William Roberts and architect Thomas Todd in their team, which they renamed Wallace, McHarg, Roberts and Todd (WMRT).

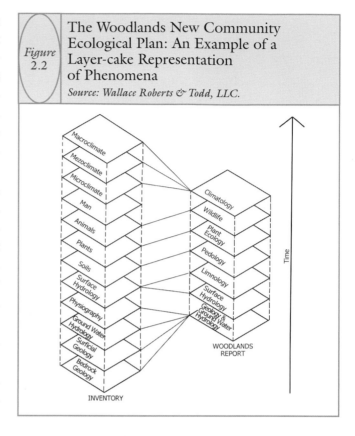

Figure 2.2

The Woodlands New Community Ecological Plan: An Example of a Layer-cake Representation of Phenomena
Source: Wallace Roberts & Todd, LLC.

At Penn, McHarg began to explore and expand his ideas about using ecology as a basis for design and planning. Grants from the Rockefeller and Ford Foundations permitted him to engage in further exploratory studies, and the growing WMRT practice allowed him to apply these theories and reflect on their utility. For example, his work in the late 1960s on siting highway routes, through which he recommended what basic data should be collected to determine the environmental impacts of proposed projects, laid the groundwork for national environmental impact assessment policy and procedures (figure 2.2).

Meanwhile, McHarg became more prominent as a public personality. President Lyndon Johnson appointed him to the White House Task Force on Conservation and Natural Beauty in 1966, and Secretary of the Interior Steward Udall invited him to serve on the American Institute of Architects' Potomac Planning Task Force from 1965 to 1967.

At the urging of Russell Train, then president of the Conservation Foundation, and noted ecologist Raymond Dasman, McHarg started to pull together

Design with Nature cover, 1969

his theories about an ecological approach for design and planning in 1966, then tested several ideas in various articles and speeches. He hosted "Multiply and Subdue the Earth," a PBS documentary filmed in 1968 and broadcast the following year. Also in 1969, he published the results of his explorations in his classic book *Design with Nature*. In it McHarg advocated an approach to design and planning grounded in an understanding of ecological systems and human values. He suggested how such knowledge should be applied to the planning of regions, such as the Potomac River Basin. The widely influential book was a National Book Award finalist and went on to be translated into French, Italian, Japanese, and Spanish.

   Design with Nature appeared at a time of great environmental awakening, when few environmental books were available and even fewer addressed design and planning. With the nationwide Earth Week celebrations of April 1970, book sales skyrocketed and McHarg was in high demand for speaking

Ian McHarg in his University of Pennsylvania office, circa 1979

Source: Ian L. McHarg Papers, The Architectural Archives, University of Pennsylvania. Photograph by Becky Young.

engagements. Student applications increased when he created Penn's Master of Regional Planning degree as a larger-scale complement to the landscape architecture degree. McHarg lost his wife Pauline to cancer in 1974, making that a sad time for him personally. But the "Environmental Decade," as the 1970s were called, was also productive for McHarg, both as a scholar and a practitioner. Among the important projects with which he was involved as part of WMRT were community plans for The Woodlands near Houston (1970–1974), the Amelia Island resort community in Florida (1971), and the new Nigerian capital Abuja (1978–1979). Other projects included the design of the Pardisan environmental park in Tehran (1973–1975; figure 2.3) and the plan for the Toronto Central Waterfront (1976; figure 2.4). He also completed regional ecological studies and plans for Minnesota's Twin Cities

Figure 2.3	Habitat Cross-sections for Pardisan Environmental Park in Tehran, Iran, 1973–1975
	Source: Wallace Roberts & Todd, LLC.

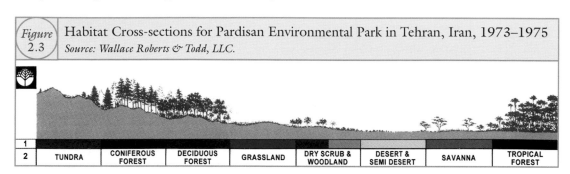

| | TUNDRA | CONIFEROUS FOREST | DECIDUOUS FOREST | GRASSLAND | DRY SCRUB & WOODLAND | DESERT & SEMI DESERT | SAVANNA | TROPICAL FOREST |

Figure 2.4	Environmental Resources of the Toronto Central Waterfront, 1976
	Source: Wallace Roberts & Todd, LLC.

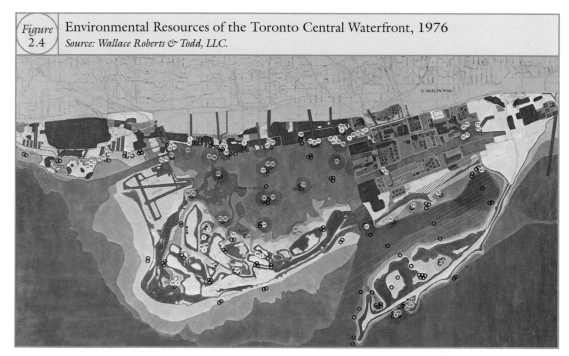

By synthesizing data from diverse sources, this map shows relationships (e.g., between sources of contamination and water pollution) that should be taken into consideration in the planning and design of the Toronto waterfront. Original shoreline and historic rivers (now buried in sewers) are shown in blue.

(1969); Denver (1971–1972 and 1978); Wilmington and Dover, Vermont (1972); Lake Austin in Texas (1976–1977); Toledo, Ohio (1977); Detroit (1978); and northwestern Colorado (1978). Important transportation studies included those for Wilmington, Delaware (1973); Easton, Pennsylvania (1973); and Washington, DC (1977).

These projects broke new ground in the areas of community design and regional planning. For example, The Woodlands is widely regarded as the most successful new town in the United States planned at that time. During the early 1970s (and again in the 1990s), McHarg worked with the U.S. Environmental Protection Agency (EPA) on a comprehensive plan for environmental quality that envisioned a nationwide, computer-based, ecological mapping system. Through this body of work, McHarg did much to advance the organic tradition of regional planning.

For instance, The Woodlands was intended to establish an alternative, organic development model for the Houston metropolitan region. In the 1970s, developer George Mitchell recruited WMRT to prepare the ecological plan for The Woodlands, north of Houston (figure 2.5). The Woodlands was the most socially and ecologically ambitious new community plan of the decade (see Forsyth 2002; 2003; 2005).

In 1977, McHarg married Carol Smyser, and they had two sons, Ian and Andrew. McHarg resigned from WMRT in 1979, and it continues today as Wallace Roberts & Todd. He continued to teach at Penn long after stepping down as department chair and later retired in 1986; he also was a visiting professor and guest speaker at universities throughout the world. From the 1980s on, however, he devoted much of his considerable energy to advocating national and global

Figure 2.5	The Woodlands New Community Ecological Plan: The Results of "Typical" Urbanism
	Source: Wallace Roberts & Todd, LLC.

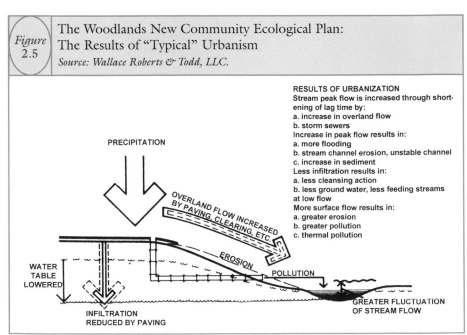

RESULTS OF URBANIZATION
Stream peak flow is increased through shortening of lag time by:
a. increase in overland flow
b. storm sewers
Increase in peak flow results in:
a. more flooding
b. stream channel erosion, unstable channel
c. increase in sediment
Less infiltration results in:
a. less cleansing action
b. less ground water, less feeding streams at low flow
More surface flow results in:
a. greater erosion
b. greater pollution
c. thermal pollution

PRECIPITATION

OVERLAND FLOW INCREASED BY PAVING, CLEARING, ETC.

WATER TABLE LOWERED

EROSION

POLLUTION

INFILTRATION REDUCED BY PAVING

GREATER FLUCTUATION OF STREAM FLOW

systems for mapping environmental and social information through computing technologies.

He remained active as a lecturer and writer through his seventies and published two more books: *A Quest for Life* (1996) and *To Heal the Earth* (with Frederick Steiner 1998). In *A Quest for Life*, McHarg recounts his life's story from his boyhood in Scotland through his career in Philadelphia, peppering the story with amusing anecdotes about human nature. He received

Housing and open space at The Woodlands, Texas
Source: Photograph © Frederick Steiner.

the National Medal of Art in 1990 and the Japan Prize in 2000, as well as honorary doctoral degrees from Amherst College (1970), Lewis and Clark College (1970), Bates College (1978), and Heriot-Watt University in Edinburgh (1998). Ian McHarg died in Chester County, Pennsylvania, on 5 March 2001.

PRECEDENTS: ON THE SHOULDERS OF GIANTS

Ian McHarg identified his mentors as Loren Eiseley, Walter Gropius, Lewis Mumford, and G. Holmes Perkins. At Harvard, McHarg had marinated in the modernism espoused by Gropius and his Bauhaus colleagues, and he would remain committed to the modernist notion that knowledge should lead to action to better the human condition. Through Mumford, however, McHarg grew increasingly skeptical of the modernist universal style for design. With Mumford, McHarg rejected the one-size-fits-all

Loren Eiseley
Source: Photograph © Frank Ross, 1960; University of Pennsylvania Archives.

International Style. Instead, both men believed that designs for both architecture and landscape should respond to their regions' ecologies.

Holmes Perkins and Loren Eiseley were academic mentors. As dean of Penn's Graduate School of Fine Arts, Perkins hired McHarg to revamp the landscape architecture program and create a graduate degree. Having taught regional planning at Harvard, Perkins supported McHarg's goal to establish a

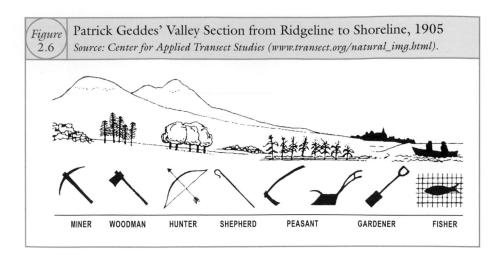

Figure 2.6 Patrick Geddes' Valley Section from Ridgeline to Shoreline, 1905
Source: Center for Applied Transect Studies (www.transect.org/natural_img.html).

MINER   WOODMAN   HUNTER   SHEPHERD   PEASANT   GARDENER   FISHER

regional planning program to bridge and expand the city planning and land-scape architecture fields. As Penn's provost, Eiseley inspired McHarg intellectually and helped lead him to deeper explorations into relationships between people and nature. As the well-known author of influential books such as *The Immense Journey* (1957) and *Darwin's Century* (1958), Eiseley also provided McHarg a role model as a public intellectual.

Mumford also introduced McHarg to fellow Scotsman Patrick Geddes. McHarg's approach to planning can be viewed as an elaboration of Geddes' advocacy of surveys as guiding plans as well as his use of transects to show natural conditions associated with human presence (figure 2.6). Relatively later in life, McHarg also became strongly influenced by the work and ideas of Charles Eliot. He frequently noted the importance, both to his own thinking as well as to regional planning more generally, of Eliot's pioneering ecological inventories of Mount Desert Island in Maine and the innovative Emerald Necklace Plan he had developed for Boston with Frederick Law Olmsted.

IMPORTANCE AND LIMITS OF THE ECOLOGICAL PLANNING METHOD

The most significant statement of McHarg's ideas comes from *Design with Nature*. In his insightful, personal history of landscape planning, Carl Steinitz (2008, 69) illustrates that many of the tools and techniques advocated by McHarg have significant precedents. In the eighteenth century, Humphry Repton used before-and-after drawings, and Jean-Marie Morel advocated that design be used to manage "the natural processes of the landscape" to take "advantage of the natural processes of the site, its terrain, hydrology, vegetation, and drainage."

In the nineteenth century, John Claudius Loudon promoted "a landscape plan for the entire region of London," Peter Joseph Lenné designed a regional plan for Berlin, and Horace W. S. Cleveland created a regional park system for the twin Minnesota cities of Minneapolis and St. Paul (Steinitz 2008, 70). In the late 1800s Olmsted and Eliot developed their regional Emerald Necklace for Boston and Eliot (1902) reports the Olmsted office's use of hand-drawn overlays, a technique also employed for analysis by Warren H. Manning in the early twentieth century (Steinitz 2008). As early as the 1930s British geographers were also recognizing landscapes as systems, "with complex elements that are connected to each other" (Steinitz 2008, 72). By the 1940s overlays and sieve mapping[1] had become common regional planning techniques, with L. B. Escritt showing "how to make overlays and how to use them to analyze the landscape for particular purposes" (Steinitz 2008, 72).[2]

Even though McHarg addressed each of these ideas in *Design with Nature,* his approach continued to be viewed as revolutionary because it made four advances: (1) he provided a compelling case for the need for planning and designing with nature in order to face significant environmental challenges; (2) he also created a synthesis of various techniques into a unified, replicable method; (3) he advanced ecology as a theory for planning and design; and (4) he became an outspoken catalyst for action. McHarg not only helped spread awareness of environmental challenges facing society, he also proposed design and planning solutions that would tackle those issues from the standpoints of practitioner, teacher, and public intellectual.

After the publication of *Design with Nature,* McHarg continued to promote ideas based on precedent, but with his own contributions. As he was developing his ecological planning method at Penn, Howard Fisher, Carl Steinitz, and Peter Rogers were laying the foundation for computer-based mapping systems (figure 2.7). Their students—Jack Dangermond of Environmental Systems Research Institute (ESRI) among them—would use McHarg's

Figure 2.7	An Early Example of GIS at Harvard
	Source: Steinitz and Rogers (1970); The MIT Press.

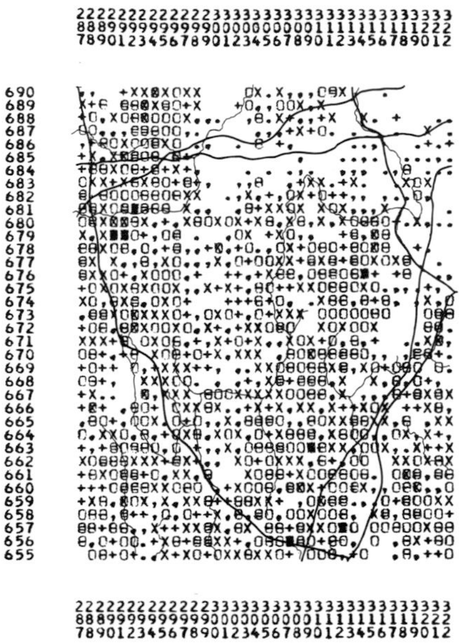

Figure 14
Attractiveness for natural open space.

$$y = 4.34 + .33x_1 + .23x_2 - .44x_3 - .36x_4$$

where

y = attractiveness for natural areas
4.34 = intercept
x_1 = forests, percentage of area
x_2 = major water type
x_3 = poor agriculture, percentage of area
. 0 = lowest attractiveness
■ 9 = highest attractiveness

---

1. Sieve mapping is used to determine which opportunities and constraints may be applicable when considering development or conservation projects. It involves creating a series of overlay maps that are then consulted in order to rule out certain areas for development based on a variety of environmental criteria such as wetlands, prime agricultural land, important habitats, and flood zones. Whatever land is not ruled out through this process is identified as suitable for development or, conversely, for preservation.

2. See also the work of Christopher Tunnard, as reported in Jacques and Woudstra (2009).

ideas about map overlays organized ecologically to refine and advance the development of GIS.

McHarg also promoted national ecological inventories, especially to the EPA. National-level planning has precedents in Albert Gallatin and Thomas Jefferson's infrastructure plan of 1808; Theodore Roosevelt's New Nationalism begun in 1908; and Warren Manning's 1923 national landscape plan (Fishman 2007; Peirce, Johnson, and Peters 2008; Steinitz 2008). Manning's proposals had racist overtones, however, as Robin Karson (2007, 43) notes: "Some of the ideas Manning put forward were extreme even for their day, skewed by nativist ideology, particularly notions of geographic determinism that led to xenophobic recommendations, such as relocation of ethnic types." But if McHarg was aware of these earlier attempts, he did not acknowledge them. Rather, his inspiration appears to have come from the NASA images of Earth.

While McHarg helped usher in many important advances through his ecological planning method, his work had its limits, too. His approach required massive amounts of data, which could be quite expensive to collect. Furthermore, Herrington (2010) calls into question McHarg's use of science, specifically his outdated interpretations of evolutionary and ecological theory. McHarg often suggested that his method was based on *ecological determinism,* a term that recalls the discredited, even racist *environmental determinism* espoused by some early twentieth–century geographers who suggested that characteristics of people and human behavior are narrowly defined by their surroundings.

Still, McHarg held a "genuine reverence for existing ecologies" as a basis to direct future urban development (Weller 2009, 176). James Corner has referred to his method as a "tyranny of positivism" (1991, 117). While this positivism is effective in identifying the best areas to develop and to conserve, it falls short on deriving the ideal nature of urban development. According to Richard Weller (2009, 171), "McHarg's method remains proficient at identifying where not to develop, [but] it is not necessarily good at determining *how* or *what* to develop." Subtleties in the definitions of *environment* (surroundings) and *ecology* (interactions) imply that determinism based on how we interact differs from the environmental determinism of the past. In addition, because McHarg clearly viewed people as parts of ecological systems, he saw that our actions through planning and design may be viewed as agents of determinism. The more consistently our actions align with natural processes, the theory goes, the greater the chance that they will succeed.

LEGACY AND IMPACT
McHarg's ideas have endured and been expanded upon in the areas of environmental review and assessment, GIS technologies, national- and global-scale planning, landscape and urban ecology, sustainability, new regionalism, and landscape urbanism.

Environmental Impact Assessment

The publication of *Design with Nature* coincided with the passage of the National Environmental Policy Act (NEPA), which was signed into law by President Richard Nixon on New Year's Day 1970. A key provision of NEPA was to require federal agencies to conduct environmental impact assessments for their proposed actions and projects. In the 1960s McHarg had directed projects that became the basis for this requirement, and *Design with Nature* provided guidance for such reviews. McHarg, with WMRT, prepared some of the first environmental impact statements (EIS) (figure 2.8).

In 1965, based on environmental analysis, McHarg prepared an analysis of alternative routes for Interstate 95 between New Jersey's Delaware and Raritan Rivers. With its use of environmental information to generate planning

Figure 2.8 Analyses of Six Aspects of the Environmental Situation in Areas of New Jersey Being Considered for Interstate 95
Source: Design with Nature *(McHarg 1969, 36); reproduced with permission of John Wiley & Sons, Inc.*

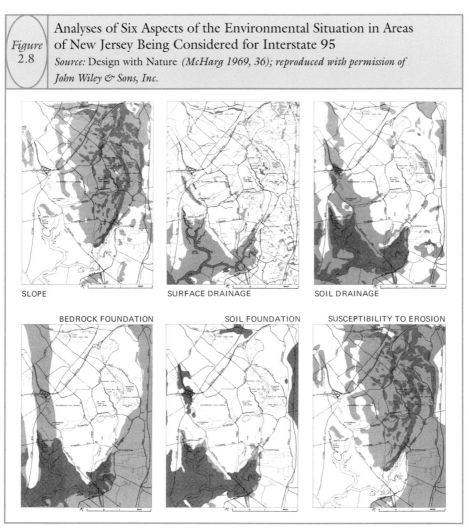

SLOPE   SURFACE DRAINAGE   SOIL DRAINAGE

BEDROCK FOUNDATION   SOIL FOUNDATION   SUSCEPTIBILITY TO EROSION

These analyses of environmental information for alignment options for Interstate 95 in New Jersey were precursors to environmental impact assessment.

alternatives, this routing study was an important precursor to EIS. McHarg documented it in *Design with Nature*. Among the many early EIS prepared by WMRT, two of the most influential are those for The Woodlands near Houston and the Metro subway system in Washington, DC. For the latter, each partner at WMRT was responsible for one of the lines of the Metro; McHarg was the principal in charge of the Green Line.

Geographic Information System Technology

McHarg grounded his approach for landscape intervention in ecology. He argued that ecology should inform the schemes of designers and planners by helping them to understand interactions among natural phenomena and landscape patterns. His approach is based on collecting data in a chronological order. That is, regional climate helps shape the geology of a place, which in turn affects other abiotic processes such as physiography and hydrology, and they then influence specific soils and microclimates. These abiotic processes combine in ways that provide niches for plant and animal communities. McHarg suggested that information about these processes can be mapped and overlaid in what he called a "layer cake" model, which can be used to determine opportunities in and constraints against potential land uses and, thus, balance the requirements of conservation and development. As a result, the suitability of land uses can be presented to local decision makers.

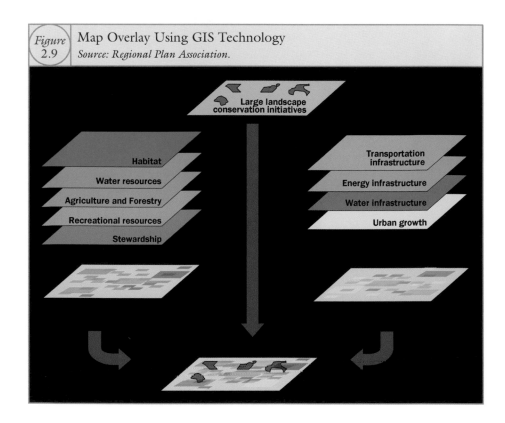

Figure 2.9 | Map Overlay Using GIS Technology
Source: Regional Plan Association.

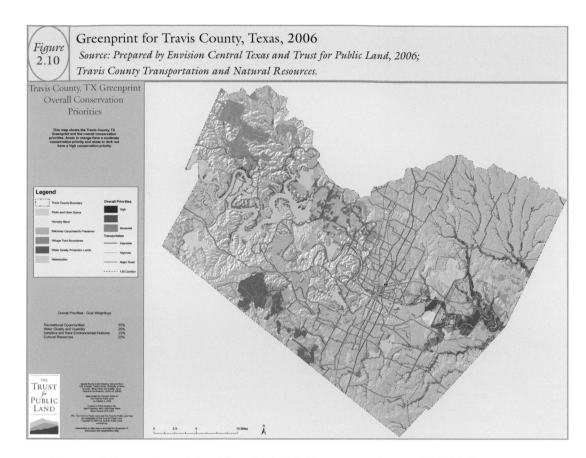

Figure 2.10

Greenprint for Travis County, Texas, 2006
*Source: Prepared by Envision Central Texas and Trust for Public Land, 2006;
Travis County Transportation and Natural Resources.*

The multilayered model with which McHarg experimented, initially using transparent mylar overlays, evolved through GIS technology (figure 2.9). GIS and other new technologies provide landscape architects, city planners, architects, and engineers with the ability to intervene in landscapes to address the pressing issues facing communities and regions. For instance, to ameliorate urban heat island effects, the amount of black asphalt should be reduced in streets and parking lots, more shade should be created, and more trees and other plants added. GIS and visualization programs present tools for planning that determine where such interventions would have the most positive impacts.

The Trust for Public Land subsequently created greenprinting, a tool used to balance conservation and development at a large landscape scale. This tool was developed to assist community leaders in identifying the most important areas for conservation. Greenprinting uses GIS technology to map and rank lands for conservation based on local priorities (figure 2.10). The resulting GIS-based greenprints can be used in growth management plans and for open space purchase efforts. Greenprinting allows local decision makers to consider important sustainability concerns, such as social equity, in addition to environmental factors. For example, the distribution of open space and recreational areas can be considered in ways that will grant all income groups equal access.

Figure 2.11	China's Integrated National Ecological Security Pattern
	Source: Kong-Jian Yu, Peking University College of Architecture and Landscape Architecture.

Planning at National and Global Scales

Ian McHarg generated big ideas. As he witnessed the growing application of those ideas through GIS and visualization technologies, he realized that they could be used at the national and even global scales. In the early 1990s, McHarg and several colleagues produced a prototype database for a national ecological inventory, which built on an earlier proposal for a national inventory that he had prepared for the EPA during 1972 and 1973. EPA Administrator (and McHarg admirer) William K. Reilly commissioned the study, and the prototype was submitted to the EPA in 1993. McHarg and his colleagues proposed an extensive inventory at three scales—national, regional, and local.

Scholars at Peking University have mapped China's landscapes at the national, regional, and local scales along the lines suggested by McHarg. At the national level, Kong-Jian Yu and his colleagues focused on "ecological security" (Yu et al. 2009). Their maps (figure 2.11) are based on critical natural processes, which they define as headwater conservation, soil erosion prevention, stormwater management, flood control, desertification mitigation, and biodiversity conservation.

Similarly, Frederick Steiner and Robert Yaro (2009) built on McHarg's work for their proposed national landscape assessment for the United States

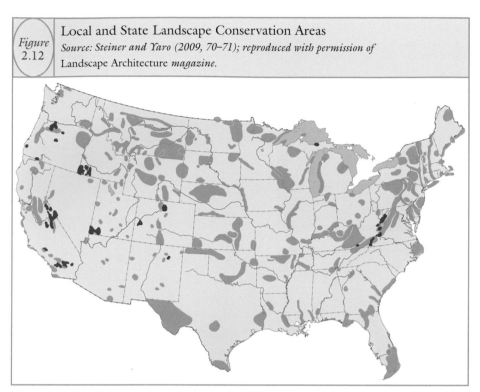

Figure
2.12
Local and State Landscape Conservation Areas
Source: Steiner and Yaro (2009, 70–71); reproduced with permission of
Landscape Architecture *magazine.*

In 1987, a National Park Service team comprised of Joan Chaplick, J. Glenn Eugster, Margaret Judd, Cecily Corcoran Kihn, and Suzanne Sutro produced a national map that documented landscape conservation efforts then under way in the continental United States (in dark green; areas protected by the 2009 Omnibus Appropriations Act in red).

(figure 2.12). Their approach includes four components: geological, hydrological, and ecological protection areas; cultural protections areas; resource production protection areas; and natural hazard protection areas.

McHarg used an early NASA image of Earth from space on the back cover of *Design with Nature*. Not surprisingly, he suggested increasing the scale of ecological inventories to encompass the whole planet. Beyond Earth, Mark Kerr (2004) applied McHarg's sieve mapping method to identify possible human habitat sites on Mars.

Landscape Ecology and Urban Ecology

McHarg advocated the use of ecology based on the state of the science at the time and urged that humans be considered part of ecological systems. Concurrently, ecologists were advancing similar ideas, which have since matured in the science's subfields of landscape ecology (figure 2.13) and urban ecology. Richard Forman and Michel Godron (1981; 1986) are responsible for defining the field of landscape ecology and illustrating its potential for planning. They explain:

Edge Structure: A Landscape Ecology Concept Useful in Regional Planning
Source: Dramstad, Olson, and Forman (1996, 28); reproduced with permission of Island Press.

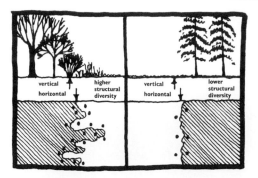

E1. Edge structural diversity
Vegetative edges with a high structural diversity, vertically or horizontally, are richer in edge animal species.

E2. Edge width
Edge width differs around a patch, with wider edges on sides facing the predominant wind direction and solar exposure.

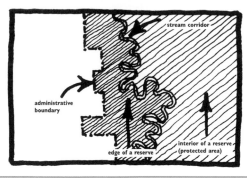

E3. Administrative and natural ecological boundary
Where the administrative or political boundary of a protected area does not coincide with a natural ecological boundary, the area between the boundaries often becomes distinctive, and may act as a buffer zone, reducing the influence of the surroundings on the interior of the protected area.

Landscapes as ecological units with structure and function are composed primarily of patches in a matrix. Patches differ fundamentally in origin and dynamics, while size, shape, and spatial configuration are also important. Line corridors, strip corridors, stream corridors, networks, and habitations are major integrative structural characteristics of landscapes. (Forman and Godron 1981, 733)

Forman has expanded the field to address regions and planning. His particular interest addresses the ecology of landscapes and regions beyond the city (Forman 1995; 2008). Meanwhile, ecologists have also begun to refocus their science inside the city.

The U.S. National Science Foundation (NSF) initiated the long-term ecological research (LTER) program in 1980 to support research on such phenomena, and it now supports a network of 26 LTER projects. The LTER mission
is to document, analyze, and understand ecological processes and patterns that
change over long temporal and large spatial scales. Until 1997, these LTERs
were located outside urban regions. After an intense competition, however, the
NSF selected the contrasting U.S. cities of Phoenix and Baltimore to be the
first urban LTERs. Baltimore has a longer European settlement history and is
located in a humid, coastal region. Although the Phoenix region was home to
ancient native settlements, it has grown rapidly only since World War II and is
located in a desert.

The Baltimore LTER aims to understand the metropolitan region as an ecological system. The team of cross-disciplinary researchers in the Baltimore Ecosystem Study explores complex interactions among built and natural environments
with ecological, social, economic, and hydrological processes (Cadenasso et al.
2003; Felson and Pickett 2005; Pickett et al. 1997; 2007). The Baltimore LTER
attempts to advance both ecological research and environment policy.

> Our finding that urban riparian zones experiencing hydrologically induced
> drought are not sinks for nitrate, but in fact may be nitrate sources,
> helped lead policy makers concerned with the water quality of the Chesa-
> peake Bay to reduce their reliance on stream corridor tree planting as a
> primary mitigation strategy. (Pickett et al. 2007, 51)

In addition, the Baltimore LTER team has suggested how science can be
used in urban landscape design (Cadenasso and Pickett 2008).

The Central Arizona–Phoenix LTER also includes an interdisciplinary team
of researchers at Arizona State University. They study the interactions of ecological and socio-economic systems in a rapidly growing urban environment and
especially have advanced our understanding of land use change on ecological
patterns and processes (Grimm and Redman 2004; Grimm et al. 2000; 2008;
Lewis et al. 2007; Peters et al. 2008). Such understanding is important because
cities in the southwestern United States continue to grow rapidly in an environmentally sensitive context.

In addition to the formal NSF-backed urban LTERs, other U.S. scholars
are advancing urban ecology research across disciplines, most notably in the
Puget Sound region in the Pacific Northwest (Alberti 2008; Alberti and Marzluff 2004; Alberti and Waddell 2000; Marzluff et al. 2008). The Puget Sound
group from the University of Washington has contributed to our understanding
of ecological resilience in urban ecosystems.

> In cities and urbanizing areas fragmentation of natural habitats, sim-
> plification and homogenization of species composition, disruption of

hydrological systems, and alteration of energy flow and nutrient cycling reduce cross-scale resilience, leaving systems increasingly vulnerable to shifts in system control and structure. (Alberti and Marzluff 2004, 241)

The ability for urban areas and landscapes to rebound from disaster is termed *resilience*, from the Latin *resilire* meaning to spring back or rebound. Resilience is a concept and a theory that holds growing appeal in the disciplines of ecology and planning. When rising from traditional concepts in ecology, resilience emphasizes equilibrium and stability. The United Nations defines resilience as the ability to absorb disturbances while retaining the same basic structure and ways of functioning, the capacity for self-organization, and the capacity to adapt to stress and change.

Concepts of resilience have emerged from what is called "new ecology," which focuses on nonequilibrium and the adaptability of ecological systems. The latter is appropriate "to urban ecosystems, because it suggests that spatial heterogeneity is an important component of the persistence of adaptable metropolitan regions" (Pickett and Cadenasso 2003, 34). Cities are anything but stable and predictable systems.

As a result of urban-based ecological studies, urban ecology is emerging as a field that emphasizes an interdisciplinary approach to understanding the drivers, patterns, processes, and outcomes associated with urban and urbanizing landscapes. Marina Alberti (2008) conceives of urban ecosystems as complex, coupled human-natural systems in which people are the dominant modifiers, which thus produces hybrid social-ecological landscape patterns and processes. Some urban ecology research focuses on the impacts of habitat fragmentation on suburban and urban housing development patterns for avian species' productivity (Marzluff et al. 2007). Other research focuses on the integration of scientific analyses into growth management strategies (Robinson, Nowell, and Marzluff 2005).

An emerging emphasis in urban ecology research is on the unintended social outcomes resulting from environmental planning efforts in urban places. Particular attention is paid to economically vulnerable people (Dooling 2008). These diverse research agendas are united in their recognition that urban ecosystems are characterized by complexity, heterogeneity, and hybridity. Urban ecosystems are best analyzed within an interdisciplinary approach, and such analyses are intended to close the gap between scientific research and policies aimed at creating sustainable urban environments. Such an interdisciplinary approach can be viewed as an extension of McHarg's planning studies at WMRT and Penn.

As these more comprehensive efforts continue, urban ecology has been advanced in the United States through more focused research, most notably around habitat conservation plans at the metropolitan-region scale advocated by former Secretary of the Interior Bruce Babbitt (2005). Examples of such planning include the Balcones Canyonlands Conservation Program in Austin,

Texas; the Sonoran Desert Conservation Plan in Pima County, Arizona; and San Diego's Multiple Species Conservation Program (Layzer 2008).

For example, the San Diego program resulted from cooperation between the U.S. Fish and Wildlife Service and the California Department of Fish and Game. Its goal is to create a 172,000-acre preserve network of biological core areas and wildlife corridors (Layzer 2008). The plan represents a large-scale application of landscape ecology, which, like urban ecology, emphasizes an understanding of nodes, corridors, and matrices (Forman 1995; Forman and Godron 1986).

Sustainability

The concept of sustainable development can be traced back to the first half of the twentieth century when the innovative forester Gifford Pinchot pioneered an approach to managing natural resources based on multiple use and sustained yield. McHarg's advocacy for the integration of cultural and natural systems may also be viewed as a precursor. It gained much broader attention in 1987 when the World Commission on Environment and Development (the Brundtland Commission) of the United Nations issued its well-known report entitled *Our Common Future,* commonly referred to as the Brundtland report. It noted that the present generation should consider the consequences of their actions on future generations and defined *sustainable development* as "development that meets the needs of the present generation without compromising the ability of future generations to meet their own needs" (UN WCED 1987, 8).

Critics argue either that sustainable development goes too far or that it does not go far enough. Sustainable development seeks to balance the "three *Es*"— environment, economics, and equity. Laissez-faire economic determinists argue that the market will create development with the greatest good. More environmentally inclined scholars argue that we must go beyond sustaining the planet— that is maintaining what is—and create new organic forms of human settlement. For example, John Lyle (1994) advocated a regenerative approach to planning and design.

Still, we need to begin by sustaining what we have. The design and planning of the built environment has much to contribute to that goal. As noted by Philip Berke (2008, 404), "there is a growing consensus in scientific and technical evidence that greening urban form has significant effects on advancing sustainable development."

In a vacuum of early twenty-first-century leadership by the federal government in the United States, several of the country's cities, most prominently New York, Chicago, Seattle, and Portland are undertaking greening efforts that are based on principles of sustainability (Birch and Wachter 2008). Local governments are not adopting sustainable development as a comprehensive framework, however. Rather, "cities are adopting sustainability initiatives in a piecemeal, ad hoc manner" (Saha and Paterson 2008, 21). Still, mayors of

---

| Box 2.1 | New York City's Sustainability Goals
Source: City of New York (2010, 6). |

LAND

- *Housing*
  Create homes for almost one million more New Yorkers while making housing more affordable and sustainable

- *Open Space*
  Ensure that all New Yorkers live within a 10-minute walk of a park

- *Brownfields*
  Clean up all contaminated land in New York

WATER

- *Water Quality*
  Open 90 percent of our waterways for recreation by reducing water pollution and preserving our natural areas

- *Water Network*
  Develop critical back-up systems for our aging water network to ensure long-term reliability

TRANSPORTATION

- *Congestion*
  Improve travel times by adding transit capacity for millions more residents

- *State of Good Repair*
  Reach a full "state of good repair" on New York City's roads, subways, and rails for the first time in history

ENERGY

- *Energy*
  Provide cleaner, more reliable power for every New Yorker by upgrading our energy infrastructure

AIR

- *Air Quality*
  Achieve the cleanest air of any big city in America

CLIMATE CHANGE

- *Climate Change*
  Reduce global warming emissions by more than 30 percent

several cities are providing leadership, and these efforts have received support from the Obama administration through initiatives such as its Sustainable Communities Planning Grant Program. New York City Mayor Michael Bloomberg's December 2006 challenge to his fellow citizens to pursue 10 key goals for a sustainable future is an example of this kind of city-level leadership. It focused on land, water, transportation, energy, air, and climate change concerns (box 2.1).

In 1991, Austin, Texas, initiated its Green Building Program, which evolved from its Energy Star program created in 1985. As the first comprehensive sustainable building program in the United States, the Austin program is designed to encourage such techniques in residential, multifamily, commercial, and municipal construction. Projects qualify for the program through a rating system, and Austin Energy, the city's public utility, assists participants with using this program and making choices regarding building materials and systems.

Austin's efforts influenced the development of the U.S. Green Building Council's (USGBC) Leadership in Energy and Environmental Design (LEED) program. The Natural Resources Defense Council initiated the development of LEED in 1994, involving a broad group of environmentalists, architects, engineers, developers, builders, and product manufacturers. LEED provides a system of standards for environmentally sustainable construction and addresses six major areas:

- sustainable sites;

- water efficiency;

- energy and atmosphere;

- materials and resources;

- indoor environmental quality; and

- innovation and design process.

While these areas continue to evolve, they form the basis by which buildings are certified for energy and environmental efficiency and are based on a scoring system consisting of prerequisite standards and additional credits. Both new construction and existing building renovations are eligible for LEED certification, which occurs at four levels—certified, silver, gold, and platinum—depending on the number of points the project scores. In addition to certifying buildings, the USGBC also accredits individuals, thus qualifying them to help with LEED rating buildings.

LEED is a system in progress, and it continues to be improved by the USGBC. Although it has done much to advance green building in the United States, there are gaps in its scope. For example, for sites surrounding buildings, LEED encourages the use of native plants and water conservation. While a good start, much more can be done to improve design at the site scale. In response, the Sustainable Sites Initiative was launched to address areas outside buildings and consider the impact of developments on soils, hydrology, plants, materials, and human well-being (Steiner 2008a). The designers of the Sustainable Sites Initiative explicitly build on the ideas of McHarg and Lyle.

New Regionalism

New urbanist architect Peter Calthorpe (1993; Calthorpe and Fulton 2001) has also advanced new perspectives on regionalism. With planner John Fregonese, Calthorpe first put his theories into practice in Portland, Oregon, then in Salt Lake City, Utah. Through their leadership in Envision Utah, Calthorpe and Fregonese developed new tools for scenario planning.

The success of Envision Utah spawned similar efforts across the United States, including Envision Central Texas. Initiated in 2001, the project created a common vision for the progressive city of Austin and its more politically conservative surrounding jurisdictions. Five rapidly growing counties comprise the Envision Central Texas region. Fregonese Calthorpe Associates led the visioning exercise, which extensively involved the community through public workshops, test-site charrettes, a regional survey, and leadership training. Using GIS technology, four growth scenarios were designed that combined public preferences with land use and transportation models. More than 12,500 local citizens responded to the survey that detailed these scenarios. Based on the survey results and other research, a preferred vision was released in May 2004. Implementation of the vision has occurred since then, focusing on seven critical issue areas:

- transportation and land use integration;
- economic development coordination;
- housing and jobs balance;
- density and mixed uses;
- open space funding plan;
- social equity; and
- recognition of best practices.

Envision Central Texas has contributed to the approval of a new commuter rail line, municipal and county bond approvals for new open space and affordable housing, and a regional greenprint with the Trust for Public Land. In partnership with the School of Architecture of the University of Texas at Austin, Envision Central Texas developed a web-based "quality growth toolbox," an online interactive site consisting of more than 100 planning techniques to assist public officials and the private sector in using the best practices to manage growth.

As Calthorpe and Fregonese have developed scenario-based visions for regions across the nation, Carl Steinitz and his Harvard colleagues have advanced a compatible approach for landscape futures (Kepner et al. 2004; Shearer 2005; Steinitz 1990; Steinitz et al. 1996; 2000; 2003). The Steinitz team has been involved in several regional planning studies, such as those for Camp Pendleton and associated military installations in Southern California and the San Pedro River basin in Arizona and northern Mexico, which integrate landscape ecology and GIS technology with scenario planning.

Allan Shearer and his colleagues (2006, 362) explain their approach to scenario planning as a process "to help manage the inherent uncertainties of decision-making [by comparing] the potential consequences of planned actions against alternative future contexts." In their work in Southern California, the process consisted of three steps:

[1] the development of a geographic information system (GIS) technology to characterize the existing landscape in terms that are salient to biodiversity;

[2] the creation of a set of scenarios that explored critical uncertainties which might drive development and a correlated set of alternative futures that map the resulting development with 500,000 and 1,000,000 new residents; [and]

[3] the development of a set of hydrologic and biologic process models that allow possible future impacts to be assessed and compared to current conditions. (Shearer et al. 2006, 360)

In his development scenarios for the metropolitan Perth region, Richard Weller (2009) offers an Australian approach to scenario planning that is clearly grounded in McHarg's work. While intended as "realistic development options, . . . more than anything they are intended to incite more creative debate about what Perth might become in 2050" (Weller 2009, 19). This goal to incite recalls McHarg's view that planners should be catalysts for change.

Another new approach to regional visioning evolved from a planning studio at Penn taught by Robert Yaro, Armando Carbonell, and Jonathan Barnett (Lincoln Institute, RPA, and Penn 2004). It identified 10 megaregions that will receive approximately 80 percent of the population and economic growth in the United States by 2040. The studio was inspired by large-scale thinking in the European Union, such as the Blue Banana, as well as the Northeast Megalopolis identified by geographer Jean Gottman (1961).

The Blue Banana concept was developed in 1989 by a team of French geographers led by Roger Brunet. It refers to a corridor of western European

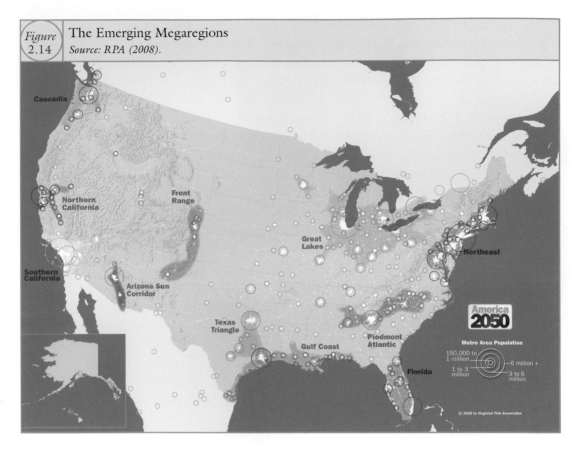

Figure 2.14 The Emerging Megaregions
Source: RPA (2008).

cities from Liverpool to Milan (with Paris located centrally) that forms the industrial backbone of the continent and provides home to some 90 million people. The Blue Banana influenced European policy makers' perceptions of development and planning, and Yaro, Carbonell, and Barnett found the concept helpful for their teaching as they sought to adapt it for North America at the same time as they worked to update Gottman's megalopolis.

In addition to teaching at Penn, Yaro directs the Regional Plan Association (RPA), and Carbonell chairs the Lincoln Institute of Land Policy's Department of Planning and Urban Form. Together, they and others continue to refine and expand the megaregion concept through the America 2050 project (RPA 2006). According to the RPA, the five major categories of relationships that define megaregions are:

- environmental systems and topography;
- infrastructure systems;
- economic linkages;
- settlement patterns and land use; and
- shared culture and history.

As Yaro, Carbonell, and others advanced megaregions, scholars formerly at Virginia Tech's Metropolitan Institute refined the "megapolitan" scale (Lang and Dhavale 2005; Lang and Knox 2008; Lang and LeFurgy 2007; Lang and Nelson 2007a and 2007b). Robert Lang introduced this scale for areas between traditional metropolitan areas and a megaregion. A megapolitan area combines at least two existing metropolitan areas, will have a total of more than 10 million residents by 2040, derives from contiguous metropolitan and micropolitan areas, constitutes an organic cultural region with a distinct history and identity, occupies a similar physical environment, links centers through major transportation infrastructure, forms an urban network via goods and service flows, creates usable geography suitable for large-scale regional planning, lies within the United States, and consists of counties as the most basic unit (Lang and Dhavale 2005).

With several Arizona State University (ASU) researchers, Lang pursued a more detailed assessment of one megapolitan megaregion: the Arizona Sun Corridor, which stretches northwest from Mexico's border with the United States on the south to Nevada on the north (Gammage et al. 2008). This megaregion is centered in the Tucson-Phoenix metropolitan area, and by 2040 it is likely to double in population from 5 million to 10 million. The ASU team noted that the Sun Corridor needed to be viewed as a place and planned in a coordinated fashion. They also observed that "the Sun Corridor can become a world leader in understanding the challenges of sustainability faced by humankind." To do so, the ASU team concluded, a "bold willingness to face climatic challenges" is required (Gammage et al. 2008, 50). As America 2050 leaders continued to refine the concept, the Sun Corridor was added as its eleventh megaregion (figure 2.14).

The Brookings Institution also has promoted megapolitan and megaregional research, most notably in its Mountain Mega study (Lang, Sarzynski, and Muro 2008; figure 2.15). Led by Lang, the Brookings researchers noted that states in the southern Intermountain West (Arizona, Colorado, Nevada, New Mexico, and Utah) are experiencing the fastest population growth in the nation. In fact, "the southern Intermountain West has grown nearly three times faster than the United States as

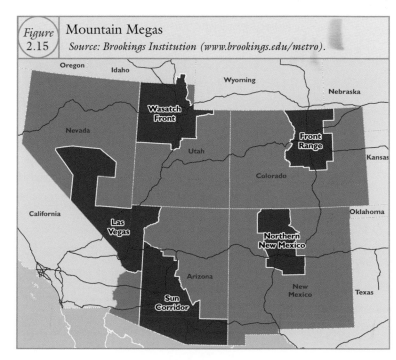

Figure 2.15 Mountain Megas
Source: Brookings Institution (www.brookings.edu/metro).

a whole over the past two decades" (Lang, Sarzynski, and Muro 2008, 11). As a result, the researchers proposed five megapolitan areas in which to coordinate planning for this growth. In addition to the Arizona Sun Corridor, the Colorado Front Range, Utah's Wasatch Front, Greater Las Vegas, and northern New Mexico were put forth as "Mountain Megas." The megaregion/megapolitan concept offers a new geographic unit of analysis and a new scale for planning.

Landscape Urbanism

New regionalism represents a movement led by planners and architects that also involves geographers, demographers, and policy makers. Landscape urbanism, which, like new regionalism, had its origins at Penn, is a more design-based approach. The term was coined by Charles Waldheim who, as a Penn architecture student in the 1980s, was influenced by landscape architecture professors Ian McHarg and James Corner.[3] Landscape urbanists' most prominent advocates, including Waldheim, Corner, and Chris Reed, are former students of McHarg's later years at Penn. This final generation of McHarg's students was more critical than those who flocked to Penn after the first Earth Week in 1970. Still, he encouraged these young architects and landscape architects to take on urban design as a project in human ecology. This younger generation sought a more urban design–based approach than their mentor, however. Their focus was on the design more than the nature in McHarg's theory. Landscape urbanists suggest that landscape should replace buildings and transportation systems as the principal organizing structure in urban design. Networks and complexity are emphasized in order to establish frameworks for urban change. But what came with this emphasis was the transformation of urban natural systems into entirely artificial ones, and former urban parks became urban theme parks.

Landscape urbanism blurs disciplinary boundaries—architecture, landscape architecture, planning, civil engineering, law, historic preservation, and real estate all intermingle. It is possible to see landscape urbanism as a dynamic outcome of the blending of ecological and economic determinism.

Landscape urbanism remains a relatively new concept with few realized works. The Fresh Kills project in the Staten Island borough of New York City provides an example of a project that is moving toward realization (figure 2.16). Fresh Kills covers some 2,200 acres and formerly was the largest landfill in the world. Much of the debris from the 11 September 2001 terrorist attacks on the World Trade Center was deposited there. The plan by James Corner Field Operations (JCFO) suggests how the landfill can be converted into a park that will be three times larger than Central Park. The 30-year plan involves the restoration of a large landscape and includes reclaiming much of the toxic wetlands that surround and penetrate the former landfill. In addition to landscape architecture,

---

3. See Almy (2007); Corner (1991); Corner and MacLean (1996); McHarg (1969; 1996); McHarg and Steiner (1998); Mostafavi and Doherty (2010); Steiner (2008b); and Waldheim (2006).

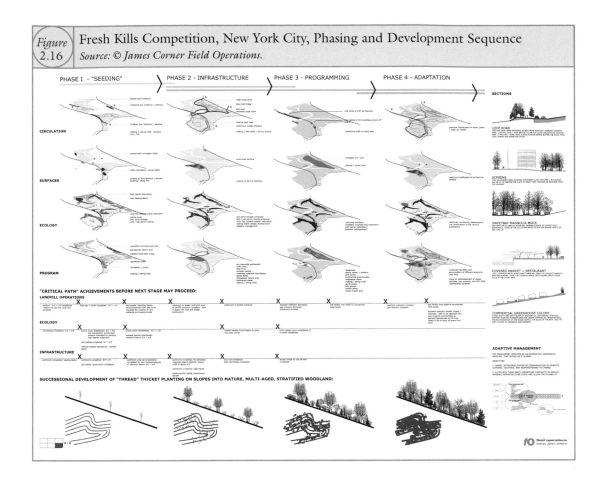

Figure 2.16 | Fresh Kills Competition, New York City, Phasing and Development Sequence
Source: © James Corner Field Operations.

the master plan required the expertise of architects, planners, ecologists, traffic engineers, soil scientists, and hydrologists. A key innovation is that, in its design, JCFO has eschewed a set end state and instead embraced long-term change and a more dynamic, flexible framework of possibilities that are grounded in an initial "seeding."

Another example of recent landscape urbanism is the High Line Project in Manhattan (figure 2.17). The RPA and the Friends of the High Line advocated for an abandoned rail line weaving through 22 blocks in New York City to be converted into a 6.7-acre park. They promote the 1.45-mile-long corridor as a recreational amenity, a tourist attraction, and a generator of economic development. In 2004, the Friends of the High Line and the City of New York selected JCFO and Diller Scofidio + Renfro to design the project. They proposed a linear walkway that blurs the boundaries between paved and planted surfaces while suggesting evolutions in human use plus plant and bird life. The first section opened with widespread public acclaim in June 2009, with the second section projected to open in 2011. The High Line design suggests a model for how abandoned urban territories can be transformed into community assets and follows directly on the worldwide redevelopment of brownfields begun during the 1980s and 1990s (JCFO et al. 2008).

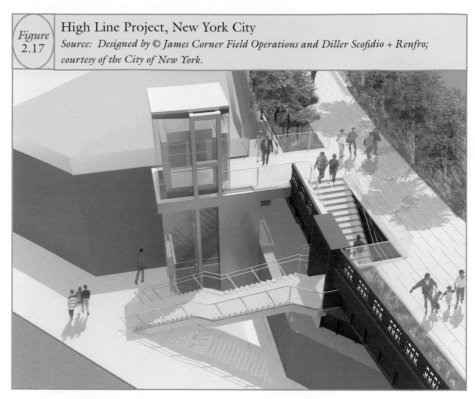

The High Line's dramatic curve westward along 30th Street is augmented by an access point with stairs intersecting the structure and rising up through it.

The High Line, New York City

Source: Photograph © Frederick Steiner.

As JCFO advances landscape urbanism on the ground, others continue to refine the concept theoretically by means of competitions and proposals. For instance, Chris Reed and his colleagues at Stoss Landscape Urbanism presented many fresh ideas in their proposal for the Lower Don Lands design competition organized by the Toronto Waterfront Revitalization Corporation in 2007 (figure 2.18). The site covers 300 acres of mostly vacated, former port lands just east of downtown Toronto. Stoss's approach considered flood protection, habitat restoration, and the naturalization of the Don River's mouth. The firm also proposed new development areas and an integrated transportation system. Canadian ecologist Nina-Marie Lister joined the Stoss team, and her contribution is evident in proposals for restoring the fish ecology, part of a broader strategy to "re-ignite dynamic ecologies" (Reed 2007, 198). The approach suggested restoration and renewal strategies for both the Don River and Lake Ontario. The river marsh was envisioned as a breeding ground for fish. The Stoss team followed McHarg's strategy by including knowledgeable environmental scientists from the region, and they incorporated current urban ecological knowledge into the overall plan. Presently, a key gesture in such projects is inclusion of large-scale development as a means of paying for the project.

Reed observes that McHarg's broader regional planning lessons are at the base of all that Stoss does. The firm looks to understand large-scale systems first and allow them to inform and even structure proposals in order to develop schemes that engage and inaugurate ecological and social dynamics. Stoss departs from McHarg in the ways it allows multiple functions to be hybridized or to occupy the same territory simultaneously. McHarg's approaches brought people closer to nature. For example, his plan for The Woodlands successfully used storm drainage systems to structure the master plan, thus making water an organizing principle (McHarg 1996; McHarg and Steiner 1998; Steiner 2006). Protected hydrologic corridors form green ribbons weaving through the urban fabric of The Woodlands. In contrast, Stoss and other landscape urbanists are interested in people and nature occupying the same space—and in constructing new urban ecologies that tap into social, cultural, and environmental dynamics that play off one another. This is much like E. O. Wilson's (1998) concept of consilience insofar as urban natural and human systems interact with and alter

Figure 2.18 Lower Don Lands Proposal, Toronto, Ontario, Canada
Source: © Stoss Landscape Urbanism.

A hybridized river and river marsh—carefully structured with a full range of surfaces, from armored to porous—give rise to a new habitat for fish and wildlife and to a new type of green city.

one another, producing an energetic synthesis in the process. To this, landscape urbanism adds the often unfathomable flows of cultural and economic data, updating if not negating McHarg's original vision.

PROSPECTS

Through the dual lenses of nature and culture, we can begin to use our increased knowledge about our surroundings to take the actions necessary to halt suburban sprawl, protect prime farmlands and environmentally sensitive areas, redirect development and investment to existing cities, and green those cities to reduce their urban heat islands in the process. We need to design with nature to heal the earth.

As Ian McHarg recommended, "Let us plan to save lives, to protect the environment, to achieve savings from appropriate ecological planning, to improve prediction and placement, and to improve the human condition" (McHarg and Steiner 1998, 71).

He opened a new way for us to see the world. His approach for interpreting the play between natural and cultural systems has become the dominant visualization technology of our time, just as Brunelleschi's experiments with linear perspective have dominated architectural visualization for nearly 600 years. Ian McHarg provided a roadmap for applying ecological information to the way we interpret, plan, and shape our surroundings. This became his quest, his principal contribution.

His vision did not stay put. Advancing technologies, such as GIS and remote sensing from space, help us see the world in new ways and improve our ability to assess the impacts on the built environment of proposed policies and projects. These technologies enable us to view the world at many scales, from the local to the global. Meanwhile, ecologists advance our understanding of urban and landscape systems.

Ian McHarg in his office at Penn, 2000
Source: Photograph © William Thomas Cain, Cain Images.

We can employ technology and knowledge to help us plan a better world—one that is more sustainable certainly, but also more regenerative and resilient. The windows to the future opened by McHarg have sparked new approaches for regional planning and urban design.

Designing with nature becomes designing and planning with regional nature, urban nature, and human nature in this post-McHargian world. As we move ahead, we need to envision places where people are not separate from nature, but rather integral parts of the natural world.

ACKNOWLEDGMENTS

This chapter is derived from parts of three earlier works that appeared in *Log*, *Ciudades*, and *Shaping the American Landscape*. I appreciate the contributions made by the editors of these publications: Charles Birnbaum, Stephanie Foell, Gavin Keeney, and Juan Luis de las Rivas.

REFERENCES

Alberti, Marina. 2008. *Advances in urban ecology.* New York: Springer Science.

Alberti, Marina, and John M. Marzluff. 2004. Ecological resilience in urban ecosystems: Linking urban patterns to human and ecological functions. *Urban Ecosystems* 7:241–265.

Alberti, Marina, and Paul Waddell. 2000. An integrated urban development and ecological assessment model. *Integrated Assessment* 1:215–227.

Almy, Dean J., ed. 2007. *On landscape urbanism. CENTER 14.* Austin: Center for American Architecture and Design, University of Texas at Austin.

Babbitt, Bruce. 2005. *Cities in the wilderness: A new vision for land use in America.* Washington, DC: Island Press.

Berke, Philip R. 2008. The evolution of green community planning, scholarship, and practice. *Journal of the American Planning Association* 74(4):393–407.

Birch, Eugenie L., and Susan M. Wachter, eds. 2008. *Growing greener cities: Urban sustainability in the twenty-first century.* Philadelphia: University of Pennsylvania Press.

Cadenasso, Mary L., and Steward T. A. Pickett. 2008. Urban principles for ecological landscape design and management: Scientific fundamentals. *Cities and the Environment* 1(2).

Cadenasso, Mary L., Steward T. A. Pickett, Kathleen C. Weathers, and Clive Jones. 2003. A framework for a theory of ecological boundaries. *BioScience* 53(8):750–758.

Calthorpe, Peter. 1993. *The next American metropolis: Ecology, community, and the American dream.* New York: Princeton Architectural Press.

Calthorpe, Peter, and William Fulton. 2001. *The regional city.* Washington, DC: Island Press.

City of New York. 2010. *PlaNYC Progress Report 2010.* Mayor's Office of Long-Term Planning & Sustainability. www.nyc.gov/html/planyc2030/downloads/pdf/planyc_progress_report_2010.pdf

Corner, James. 1991. Discourses on theory II: Three tyrannies of contemporary theory and the alternative of hermeneutics. *Landscape Journal* 10(2):115–133.

Corner, James, and Alex MacLean. 1996. *Taking measures across the American landscape.* New Haven, CT: Yale University Press.

Dooling, Sarah. 2008. Ecological gentrification: Re-negotiating justice in the city. *Critical Planning* 15:51–58.

Dramstad, Wenche E., James D. Olson, and Richard T. T. Forman. 1996. *Landscape ecology principles in landscape architecture and land-use planning.* Washington, DC: Island Press.

Eiseley, Loren. 1957. *The immense journey.* New York: Random House.

———. 1958. *Darwin's century.* Garden City: Doubleday.

Eliot, Charles. 1902. *Charles Eliot, landscape architect.* Boston: Houghton Mifflin.

Felson, Alexander J., and Steward T. A. Pickett. 2005. Designed experiments: New approaches to studying urban ecosystems. *Frontiers in Ecology and the Environment* 3(10):549–556.

Fishman, Robert. 2007. 1808–1908–2008: National planning for America. New York, America 2050, Regional Plan Association.

Forman, Richard T. T. 1995. *Land mosaics: The ecology of landscapes and regions.* Cambridge, UK: Cambridge University Press.

———. 2008. *Urban regions: Ecology and planning beyond the city.* Cambridge, UK: Cambridge University Press.

Forman, Richard T. T., and Michel Godron. 1981. Patches and structural components for a landscape ecology. *BioScience* 31(10, November):733–740.

———. 1986. *Landscape ecology.* New York: John Wiley & Sons.

Forsyth, Ann. 2002. Planning lessons from three U.S. new towns of the 1960s and 1970s: Irvine, Columbia, and The Woodlands. *Journal of the American Planning Association* 68(4):387–417.

———. 2003. Ian McHarg's Woodlands: A second look. *Planning* (August):10–13.

———. 2005. Evolution of an ecoburb. *Landscape Architecture* 95(7):60, 62, 64, 65, 66–67.

Gammage, Grady Jr., John Stuart Hall, Robert E. Lang, Robert Melnick, and Nancy Welch. 2008. *Megapolitan: Arizona's Sun Corridor.* Tempe, AZ: Morrison Institute of Public Policy, Arizona State University.

Gottman, Jean. 1961. *Megalopolis: The urbanized north-eastern seaboard of the United States.* New York: Twentieth Century Fund.

Grimm, Nancy B., and Charles L. Redman. 2004. Approaches to the study of urban ecosystems: the case of central Arizona-Phoenix. *Urban Ecosystems* 7:199–213.

Grimm, Nancy B., Charles L. Redman, J. Morgan Grove, and Steward T. A. Pickett. 2000. Integrated approaches to long-term studies of urban ecological systems. *BioScience* 50:571–584.

Grimm, Nancy B., Stanley H. Faeth, Nancy E. Golubiewski, Charles R. Redman, Jianguo Wu, Xuemei Bai, and John M. Briggs. 2008. Global change and the ecology of cities. *Science* 319:756–760.

Herrington, Susan. 2010. The nature of McHarg's science. *Landscape Journal* 29(1):1–20.

Jacques, David, and Jan Woudstra. 2009. *Landscape modernism renounced: The career of Christopher Tunnard (1910–1979).* Oxford, UK: Routledge.

JCFO (James Corner Field Operations), Diller Scofidio + Renfro, Friends of the High Line, and City of New York. 2008. *Designing the High Line: Gansevoort Street to 30th Street.* New York: Friends of the High Line.

Karson, Robin. 2007. *A genius for place: American landscapes of the country place era.* Amherst: University of Massachusetts Press.

Kepner, William G., Daruis J. Semmons, Scott D. Bassett, David A. Mouat, and David C. Goodrich. 2004. Scenario analysis for the San Pedro River: Analyzing hydrological consequences of a future environment. *Environmental Monitoring and Assessment* 94:115–127.

Kerr, Mark E. 2004. A site selection technique for Martian habitats. *American Institute of Physics Conference Proceedings* 699(1):1000–1006.

Lang, Robert E., and Dawn Dhavale. 2005. *Beyond megalopolis: Exploring America's new "megapolitan" geography.* Alexandria, VA: Metropolitan Institute at Virginia Tech.

Lang, Robert E., and Paul K. Knox. 2008. The new metropolis: Rethinking megalopolis. *Regional Studies* 41(1):1–14.

Lang, Robert E., and Jennifer B. LeFurgy. 2007. *Boomburbs: The rise of America's accidental cities.* Washington, DC: Brookings Institution.

Lang, Robert E., and Arthur C. Nelson. 2007a. Beyond the metroplex: Examining commuter patterns at the "megapolitan" scale. Working paper. Cambridge, MA: Lincoln Institute of Land Policy.
———. 2007b. The rise of the megapolitans. *Planning* 73(1):7–12.

Lang, Robert E., Andrea Sarzynski, and Mark Muro. 2008. *Mountain megas: America's newest metropolitan places and a federal partnership to help them prosper.* Washington, DC: Metropolitan Policy Program, Brookings Institution.

Layzer, Judith A. 2008. *Natural experiments: Ecosystem-based management and the environment.* Cambridge, MA: MIT Press.

Lewis, David B., Nancy B. Grimm, Tamara K. Harms, and John D. Schade. 2007. Subsystems, flowpaths, and the spatial variability of nitrogen in a fluvial ecosystem. *Landscape Ecology* 22:911–924.

Lincoln Institute of Land Policy, Regional Plan Association, and University of Pennsylvania School of Design. 2004. *Toward an American spatial development perspective.* Philadelphia: Department of City and Regional Planning, University of Pennsylvania.

Lyle, John. 1994. *Regenerative design for sustainable development.* New York: John Wiley & Sons.

Mandala Collaborative/Wallace, McHarg, Roberts and Todd. 1975. *Pardisan: Plan for an environmental park in Tehran.* Philadelphia: Winchell Press.

Marzluff, John M., John C. Withey, Kara A. Whittaker, M. David Oleyar, Thomas M. Unfried, Stan Rullman, and Jack DeLap, 2007. Consequences of habitat utilization by nest predators and breeding songbirds across multiple scales in an urbanizing landscape. *Condor* 109(3):516–534.

Marzluff, John M., Eric Shulenberger, Wilfried Endlicher, Marina Alberti, Gordon Bradley, Clare Ryan, Ute Simon, and Craig ZumBrunnen, eds. 2008. *Urban ecology: An international perspective on the interaction between humans and nature.* New York: Springer Science.

McHarg, Ian L. 1969. *Design with nature.* Garden City, NY: Natural History Press/Doubleday.
———. 1996. *A quest for life: An autobiography.* New York: John Wiley & Sons.

McHarg, Ian L., and Frederick R. Steiner, eds. 1998. *To heal the Earth: The collected writings of Ian L. McHarg.* Washington, DC: Island Press.

Mostafavi, Mohsen, and Gareth Doherty, eds. 2010. *Ecological urbanism.* Baden, CH: Lars Müller Publishers.

Peirce, Neal R., Curtis W. Johnson, and Farley M. Peters. 2008. *Century of the city: No time to lose.* New York: Rockefeller Foundation.

Peters, Debra, Peter M. Groffman, Knute J. Nadelhoffer, Nancy B. Grimm, Scott L. Collins, William K. Michener, and Michael A. Huston. 2008. Living in an increasingly connected world: A framework for continental-scale environmental science. *Frontiers in Ecology and the Environment* 6:229–237.

Pickett, Steward T. A., and Mary L. Cadenasso. 2003. Integrating the ecological, socioeconomic, and planning realms: Insights from the Baltimore ecosystem study. In eds. Laura Musacchio, Jiango Wu, and Thara Johnson. *Pattern, process, scale, and hierarchy: Advancing interdisciplinary collaboration for creating sustainable urban landscape and communities.* Tempe: Arizona State University.

Pickett, Steward T. A., William R. Burch Jr., Shawn E. Dalton, Timothy W. Foresman, J. Morgan Grove, and Rowan Rowntree. 1997. A conceptual framework for the study of human ecosystems in urban areas. *Urban Ecosystems* 1(4):185–199.

Pickett, Steward T. A., Kenneth T. Belt, Michael F. Galvin, Peter M. Groffman, J. Morgan Grove, Donald C. Outen, Richard V. Pouyat, William P. Stack, and Mary L. Cadenasso. 2007. Watersheds in Baltimore, Maryland: Understanding an application of integrated ecological and social processes. *Journal of Contemporary Water Research & Education* 136(June):44–55.

Reed, Chris. 2007. *StossLU.* Seoul, KR: C3 Publishing Co.

Robinson, Lin, Joshua P. Nowell, and John M. Marzluff. 2005. Twenty-five years of sprawl in the Seattle region: Growth management responses and implications for conservation. *Landscape and Urban Planning* 71(1):51–72.

RPA (Regional Plan Association). 2006. *America 2050: A prospectus.* New York.

———. 2008. The emerging megaregions. (America 2050 map). New York. www.america2050.org/ images/2050_Map_Megaregions2008_150.png

Saha, Devashree, and Robert G. Paterson. 2008. Local government efforts to promote the "three e's" of sustainable development. *Journal of Planning Education and Research* 28:21–37.

Shearer, Allan W. 2005. Approaching scenario-based studies: Three perceptions about the future and considerations for landscape planning. *Environment and Planning B* 32:67–87.

Shearer, Allan W., David A. Mouat, Scott D. Bassett, Michael W. Binford, Craig W. Johnson, and Justin A. Saarinen. 2006. Examining development-related uncertainties for environmental management: Strategic planning scenarios for Southern California. *Landscape and Urban Planning* 77:359–381.

Steiner, Frederick, ed. 2006. *The essential Ian McHarg: Writings on design with nature.* Washington, DC: Island Press.

———. 2008a. Setting our sights higher and wider. *Urban Land Green* 3(1, Spring):76–79.

———. 2008b. The ghost of Ian McHarg. *Log* 13/14:147–151.

Steiner, Frederick, and Robert Yaro. 2009. A new national landscape agenda. *Landscape Architecture* 99(6):70–77.

Steinitz, Carl. 1990. A framework for the theory applicable to the education of landscape architects (and other environmental design professionals). *Landscape Journal* 9(2):136–143.

———. 2008. Landscape planning: A brief history of influential ideas. *Journal of Landscape Architecture* (Spring):68–74.

Steinitz, Carl, Robert Anderson, Hector Arias, Scott Bassett, Mary Cablk, Michael Flaxman, Tomas Goode, Robert Lozar, Thomas Maddock III, David A. Mouat, Winifred Rose, Richard B. Peiser, and Allan W. Shearer. 2000. *Summary report: Alternative future for the Upper San Pedro River Basin, Arizona, U.S.A., and Sonora, Mexico.* Cambridge, MA: Graduate School of Design, Harvard University.

Steinitz, Carl, Hector Arias, Scott Bassett, Michael Flaxman, Tomas Goode, Thomas Maddock III, David A. Mouat, Richard B. Peiser, and Allan W. Shearer. 2003. *Alternative futures for changing landscapes. The Upper San Pedro River Basin in Arizona and Sonora.* Washington, DC: Island Press.

Steinitz, Carl, Michael W. Binford, Paul Cote, Thomas Edwards Jr., Stephen Ervin, Richard T. T. Foreman, Craig W. Johnson, A. Ross Kiester, David A. Mouat, Douglas Olson, Allan W. Shearer, Richard Toth, and Robin Wills. 1996. *Biodiversity and landscape planning: Alternative future for the region of Camp Pendleton California.* Cambridge, MA: Graduate School of Design, Harvard University.

Steinitz, Carl F., and Peter Philip Rogers. 1970. *A systems analysis model of urbanization and change: An experiment in interdisciplinary education.* Cambridge, MA: MIT Press.

UN WCED (United Nations World Commission on Environment and Development). 1987. *Our common future.* Oxford, UK: Oxford University Press.

Yu, Kong-Jian, Hai-Long Li, Di-Hua Li, Qing Qiao, and Xue-Song Xi. 2009. National scale ecological security patterns. *Acta Ecologica Sinica* 29(10):5163–5175.

Waldheim, Charles, ed. 2006. *The landscape urbanism reader.* New York: Princeton Architectural Press.

Weller, Richard. 2009. *Boomtown 2050: Scenarios for a rapidly growing city.* Crawley, Western Australia: University of Western Australia Publishing.

Wilson, E. O. 1998. *Consilience: The unity of knowledge.* New York: Alfred A. Knopf.

CHAPTER **3** A REGION OF ONE'S OWN

Kathryn A. Foster

Suppose that growing up you had to share a bedroom with a sibling. You and your sibling each had your own bed, dresser, and bedside lamp, but the rest of the space was common ground: the floor, the closet, the radiator, windows and shades, entrances and exits. Also shared were several key facilities, including the laundry hamper, clock radio, and record player. Your parents expected you to keep the place hazard-free and hygienic, beyond which you had age-appropriate latitude over the domain. They also expected you to maintain in-room order, harmonizing sufficiently well with your sibling to keep domestic peace.

As anyone who has shared bedroom space knows, such an arrangement requires negotiation of virtually every room-related decision: the amount of light, volume of noise, allocation of closet space, temperature of the room, whether doors are open or shut. Sometimes siblings agree (parents may not enter!), but many choices are disputed.

Confronted with such space-sharing challenges, you and your equally empowered sibling must devise a workable plan for in-room governance. One approach is to compete over resources and authority. For an older, stronger, or otherwise dominant sibling, competition may be a preferred governance approach, while for a theoretically equal but practically weaker sibling, fighting it out will hold little appeal. Alternatively, you and your sibling could bargain collaboratively to reach resolutions. "You may listen to the radio, but not until I finish my homework." "I'll let the cat in if you turn up the heat." Another approach to room governance would be to cede authority to a third-party arbiter—in this case let's call this party Mom or Dad—whose determination rules. Mom or Dad might simply reassert the basic rules for health and safety and direct you to work it out yourselves. Other parents or third-party authorities might assume a more active role, making and enforcing room decisions and mandating sibling action.

Sharing a bedroom and sharing a region are not altogether different enterprises. In each, autonomous players with common interest in the territory, but often different preferences, capacities, and perspectives, must agree on goals and standards, manage resources, determine fair and efficient processes for getting along, resolve disputes, make and enforce collective decisions, and steward the shared space sufficiently well to sustain it for future users. Thus, as with sharing a room, sharing a region is an exercise in governance—*how autonomous actors organize and act for shared purposes.*

Regional planning means planning for shared space. Unlike planning for a single jurisdiction, whether a small municipality or a large state or nation, regional planning requires planners to cross jurisdictional borders. Regions are "of the many," shared territories containing multiple independent units, each with power to plan and act for part, but not all, of the whole. There is no region of one's own.

This chapter trains a practical, contemporary lens on regional planning governance in the United States. It notes that despite a growing and increasingly pressing set of regional challenges, regional governance complicates regional responses. An easy-to-say regional governance solution remains hard to accomplish, in part because of fundamental institutions—norms, rules, and regularized practices of governance—within which regional planning happens. Nonetheless, as indicated by an audit of regional planning governance for six well-regarded efforts, U.S. regions routinely succeed in organizing and undertaking regional planning, albeit in various ways. Regardless of differences, however, these and other regional planning efforts have in common their need to answer three key governance questions: By what authority? Exercised by whom? and In what territory? The chapter ends with some speculations about alternative regional planning governance pathways and a proposal for a regional governance ethos to guide current and future regional planners.

CONTEMPORARY REALMS FOR REGIONAL PLANNING

As the twenty-first century unfolds, regional planners confront both chronic and newly familiar areas of planning practice, each with complex governance structures and relations. Climate change, homeland security, public health, shrinking regions, broadband access, economic globalization, immigration influxes, obsolescent infrastructure systems, the suburbanization of economic insecurity, and emerging challenges of megaregional development now inhabit the regional planning menu. They join traditional regional planning fare such as environmental quality, transportation mobility, housing choice and affordability, and growth management.

While getting governance right for these challenges is difficult, it is imperative for regional planners and leaders to do so. Successfully securing borders against those who would do harm, mitigating the effects of warmer and more volatile climate conditions, diffusing public health threats that pass across political boundary lines, and generally understanding and preparing for environmental and man-made risks and vulnerabilities demand highly effective cross-border coordination, communication, and action. Immigration, major infrastructure development, and globalization also require common—or at least compatible—policy and practices, unified decision making, and often a pooling of resources to achieve desired outcomes.

Many emerging realms of regional planning look to higher-level international, federal, state, and provincial governments for guidance and resources. Yet local and regional planners cannot wait for outside directives and support before planning and acting responsibly to address cross-border concerns. Setting goals, building relationships, navigating alternative perspectives, addressing tradeoffs, effectively articulating need, shoring up weak intraregional links, and brokering cross-border, cross-function, and cross-sector tensions are governance-based skill sets essential for today's regional planners.

THE REGION AS GOVERNANCE

The centrality of governance in regional planning is embedded in the etymology of the word *region,* which comes from the Latin *regere,* to direct or rule. Flexibly demarcated to reflect the fortunes of its ruler or regent, the region in its early formulation encompassed the tracts and fields under unitary rule (or, more directly, under the regent's regiment). While a region's boundaries shifted continually to reflect gained and lost territory, as long as the regent was in favor its governance was singular and clear.

Today regions have largely lost both such flexibility of boundary adjustment and the singularity of rule. They may be defined by:

- natural features, such as watersheds, special resource areas, or climatic zones (e.g., the Chesapeake Bay Watershed, which encompasses 64,000 square miles of urbanized and undeveloped territory across parts of six states and the District of Columbia);

- human-drawn, political-administrative boundaries crafted from municipal, county, or state building blocks (Omaha Metropolitan Area, defined by the U.S. Office of Management and Budget as eight counties in Nebraska and Iowa); or

- territories of cultural or linguistic characteristics ("Ecotopia," the politically progressive, environmentally conscious coastal region between Alaska and Northern California [Garreau 1981]).[1]

Within these and other regions are hundreds of autonomous actors, not only local and sometimes state governments with specific powers to plan and act, but also private and civic organizations, whose decisions further shape the activities and outcomes in that place.

---

1. In an earlier conception of this enviro-cultural region, Ernest Callenbach (1975) describes a fictional environmental and social haven in the Pacific Northwest. Joel Kotkin (2010) recently used the term to connote the nation's "greenish left coast" encompassing San Francisco north through Seattle.

The Problem

At the crux of the regional planning governance problem is a territorial mismatch between the scale of a regional problem and that of a political organization to address it. Common regional concerns—where to locate the metropolitan airport; how to improve lake and stream quality; what to do about traffic, workforce development, or affordable housing—do not fall neatly within local jurisdictional lines. When environmental, social, and economic activities transcend local political borders, they cause externalities and generate coordination problems that defy solution by a single local unit.

The equivalence principle of governance holds that the territory of decision making should equal both the territory affected by the decision and the territory financing that decision. By this logic, the decision-making unit that deliberates and determines the location and use of a new metropolitan airport would include all territories affected by and paying for—or realizing the proceeds from—such a decision. Lack of equivalence leads to outcomes that are less efficient, fair, and accountable than if a match between the problem space and the decision space were attained.

This challenge of matching region-scale management to region-scale problems might be trivial, but for a legal reality. Under the country's federal system, legal authority is structured at the national, state, and local levels. The Constitution divides authority between the federal and state levels, outlining federal powers in the Constitution and its amendments and reserving to the states all powers not specifically delegated to the federal level. Through their enabling laws and charters, states in turn may delegate authority and powers to local governments, including municipalities, townships, counties, and special districts. Whether one views the amount of delegated local planning authority as too little (Barron, Frug, and Su 2004; Frug 2010) or too much (Rusk 1999), the practical point is that local leaders tend to hold authority dearly and cede it sparingly.

Given strong and fiercely guarded local planning powers, even when regional residents and planners agree on the benefits of region-scale management, in practice creating a strong regional planning governance system is hard to do. It necessarily entails collaboration on regional matters, reaching consensus on goals and priorities, coordinating service delivery and resolution of intraregional disputes, strategic planning for infrastructure and environmental assets, and presenting a common front to higher-level governments.

As Neal Peirce (1993, 32) summarized the dilemma:

> The . . . great disability of American citistates is their common lack of coherent governance—either formal or informal. The result is that fundamentally *public* decisions, on every question from air quality to transportation to solid waste disposal to assuring a competent work force for the future, are reached in piecemeal, often haphazard fashion—or worse still, are never made at all. [Emphasis in original]

The Solution

In theory, the solution to the regional planning governance problem is as simple as the challenge is difficult. For every regional planning problem, a society could create and empower a regional decision-making entity that has boundaries neatly matched to the territory affected. The resulting regional jurisdiction would be free of internal borders and thus of cross-border coordination and externality problems.

This solution implies a system of overlapping, problem-delineated entities, each of which addresses a particular regional issue. In fact, regions often do rely on districts and authorities managing a particular issue such as flood control, public transit, or sewer provision. In addition, independent local governments often collaborate, more or less formally, to tackle common problems. Ad hoc partnerships may address sporadic regional issues, such as a military base closing.

Problems with the Solution

Even while they sport one or more regional planning authorities and ad hoc partnerships, however, why do many regions stop shy of fully embracing the simple solution?

One answer lies in the fact that having multiple problem-based jurisdictions simply replicates the burdens of multiple local jurisdictions. Functional silos, each with authority over just one element of the regional system—water, sewer, transit, housing, or air quality, for example—create coordination and externality problems of their own. Moreover, the territory for many regional issues, including metropolitan growth boundaries, coastal zones, and social services may shift continually in response to demographic, economic, and environmental trends. To maintain governance equivalence for legal entities with firm borders would require constantly changing jurisdictional boundaries, a prospect that is both costly and chaotic.

A political impediment to forming and empowering regional authorities also exists. Regional power must be delegated or ceded from federal, state, or local units, each with its own interests that are not necessarily compatible with a strong regional governance outcome. Regional planning governance thus confronts intergovernmental balance of power and the necessity of political negotiation.

Despite these challenges, the U.S. federal government routinely asserts the national interest in state and local planning. The Environmental Protection Agency, Department of Housing and Urban Development, Bureau of Land Management, Department of Transportation, and Army Corps of Engineers are among the agencies that may intervene in housing finance, national park formation, clear air regulations, construction of interstate highways, and the like. Each federal intervention requires negotiating state and local interests and determining that the issue is sufficiently ripe for federal involvement (Whitfield and Hart 2000).

States encounter a similar dynamic when they supplant local government authority. Florida, Georgia, Hawaii, Maryland, New Jersey, Oregon, Vermont, and Washington have all famously been active in centralizing power at the state level or creating strong regional planning bodies (DeGrove 2005). Other states have been reluctant to supersede local planning powers aggressively and have encouraged local entities to craft local solutions to regional challenges.

Local interests likewise need compelling motivations to cede powers voluntarily to a regional authority. Even when local actors willingly collaborate, as they do through a council of governments, metropolitan mayors' caucus, or intergovernmental service agreement, relations may sunder when local interests conflict with regional ones (Greenblatt 2008).

Business and civic interests, which operate comfortably at the regional scale, have been consistently fervent proponents of regional authority (Foster 1997). Peter Calthorpe and William Fulton's (2001) review of innovative regional planning efforts across the United States credits in part nongovernmental groups with propelling visioning, planning, lobbying, and marketing of regional plans in those areas. Among their examples are 1000 Friends of Oregon in Portland, Envision Utah in Salt Lake City, Seattle-based environmental activists, New York City's Regional Plan Association (RPA), the Center for Neighborhood Technology and Commercial Club in Chicago, and the Greenbelt Alliance in the San Francisco Bay Area. Robert Mason's (2008) investigation of recent regional land use efforts likewise highlights citizen-led, government-assisted planning. Elinor Ostrom (1990; 2005), winner of the 2009 Nobel Prize for Economics, has devoted her career to understanding how voluntary collaboration and rule making can resolve common property problems, an argument that gives nongovernmental players the central role in regional operations.

Regardless of the direction of empowerment, however, regional planning activity requires sign-off from public sector entities. A regional planning agenda that lacks sanction from voter endorsement or approval from elected or appointed bodies empowered to act on the community's behalf is destined to be a toothless tiger, the chronic lament of regional planning governance in the United States.

INSTITUTIONS OF REGIONAL PLANNING GOVERNANCE

When our two siblings negotiate how to achieve a workable strategy for room sharing and its desired outcomes, they do so within the context of basic institutions. These institutions—the rules and regularized practices, norms, and values of how we do things here—condition the siblings' choices for in-room governance.

Institutions shape regional planning governance similarly. They may largely account for why some states or localities assume control over regional operations while others do not. They may also provide further understanding of the different package and balance of mandates, incentives, and laissez-faire nonactions that shape regional planning processes and programs. Although seemingly stable and established, these ever-changing and contested institutions are objects of reform that often may be slow moving or stunningly abrupt.

Two types of institutions matter to this discussion: General institutions are the codes and cultural norms that shape regional planning in the United States and distinguish it from planning in other countries. Specific institutions reflect the history, heritage, economy, political culture, geography, and social relations that differentiate one place from another within the United States. These rules and practices help account for why regional planning governance in Washington, Texas, or Virginia—or, for that matter, Seattle and Walla Walla, Austin and Lubbock, or Newport News and Roanoke—exhibits fine-grained variations in planning structures, processes, and outcomes.

General Institutions

At first glance, the general institutions listed in box 3.1 are lofty abstractions far removed from everyday planning practice, but they can answer familiar questions about regional planning in the United States: Why doesn't this country conduct national spatial planning and regional redistribution as countries in Europe do? Why do U.S. citizen activists have such leeway to influence planning outcomes? Why is natural resource management in this

Box 3.1	General Institutions of U.S. Regional Planning Governance
democracy	civic engagement
equal opportunity, fairness	federalism and states' rights
liberty, independence	divided authority
private property rights	rule of law
dispersed authority localism, home rule	

country so different from that in China? Why don't state governments curb powers of local governments and follow Canada's lead by installing metropolitan governments?

Consider the imprint of U.S. institutions on regional planning.

- The nation's formation as a democracy, as opposed to a monarchy or theocracy, prioritizes government by the people, rule by majorities, equal status under the law, and respect for individual voices. Civic engagement is a widely respected democratic ideal. Planning efforts and resource allocation decisions typically require public hearings, direct election of policy makers, citizen participation, and sometimes a popular vote.

- Values of equal opportunity, fairness, freedom, and independence protect the rights of individuals to pursue life, liberty, and happiness. The fifth and fourteenth amendments to the Constitution guarantee equal protection under the laws and explicitly prohibit the taking of life, liberty, or property without due process. These private property rights and protections are considerable compared to those of other societies, but they are not absolute. The common good often trumps individual freedoms. Police powers, zoning laws, environmental regulations, the Americans with Disabilities Act, eminent domain provisions, and other rules limit what individuals can and cannot do.

- As a nation of "laws, not men," the United States uses legal documents such as national and state constitutions, charters, and bodies of law to express the rules of society and balance and safeguard order and liberty. Planning laws protect and regulate property, individual and group behaviors, and government exercise of power. Laws identify and protect certain species and habitats, grant easements, establish heritage areas, and provide for the declaration of disaster areas and ratification of treaties affecting global resources. Although debate over the substance and interpretation of laws endures, the premises of lawmaking and enforcement are paramount.

- Twin pillars of federalism and states' rights support experimentation in state-based laboratories of democracy. Hard-won compromise in drafting the U.S. Constitution ensured state sovereignty within a federal system. That the states were colonies with their own identities and traditions decades before the nation was formed provided a basis for 50 mini-republics, each with latitude to set goals and independently pursue alternative policies. Variations in regional planning across states highlight a range of interests and priorities.

- Federalism also implies divided authority. The hierarchical court system, enabling additional chances before justices at state and appeals courts, the federal bench, and ultimately the U.S. Supreme Court, reflects at once a national caution and a confidence about democracy. For regional planners, divided authority compels regional entities to aggregate authority from federal, state, and local entities and separates planning, implementation, and enforcement powers across planning agencies.

- Divided authority also inclines U.S. governance toward dispersed authority. Although values of localism and home rule, including protections from state and federal intervention in local affairs, are embedded in states' constitutions and local government charters, this does not imply vertical equity. Higher-level government may overrule local regulations, as happens in designated coastal zones and historic districts, and when national standards trump state and local preferences. Still, relative to other nations and systems, local governments in the United States have strong powers to shape their planning futures.

National institutions help account for why regional planning happens differently in the United States than it does elsewhere. The 27-nation European Union, for example, reflects its aim of unity in diversity in institutions that assay resource harmonization, economic integration, and common policies on sustainable development, security, and competitiveness. Regional planners pursue spatial planning as well as regional cohesion policies (redistribution to strengthen weaker parts of the union and narrow interregional disparities) and competitiveness. In contrast, the U.S. federal government has no spatial planning policy and resists overtly redistributive interregional aid.

Within North America, institutional variations differentiate regional planning in the United States from that of its neighbor Canada. Both nations are federal systems with divided authority and share a common foundation of democracy and civic engagement, yet important institutions differ. The Canadian Constitution imbues the provinces with considerable powers, including control over land, forests, water, and minerals (Hodge and Robinson 2001). Only a province may establish regional planning agencies within its territory, and the federal government must negotiate with provincial officials to create national entities. By one account, stronger provincial powers in Canada lead to "more robust metropolitan governmental and planning institutions in Canada than in the United States" (Rothblatt and Sancton 1998, 498). Among the differences are the more frequent mandatory reviews of local plans by regional authorities and the high prevalence of regional tax base sharing in Canada relative to the United States.

Studies contrasting the two neighboring nations also cite political and cultural institutions to explain bi-national differences. The higher levels of local political fragmentation in the United States (Goldberg and Mercer 1986; Rothblatt and Sancton 1998) and "sharply different organizing principles" (Lipset 1990, 225) that manifest as competitive individualism and egalitarianism in the United States and group rights and benefits in Canada also help to explain Canada's relatively stronger regional planning institutions. The merger of six jurisdictions in 1997 into an amalgamated City of Toronto, which was accomplished by provincial decree despite overwhelming opposition from Toronto voters, would simply not have happened in the United States.

Specific Institutions

Within the United States, subnational and substate differences abound. While some (e.g., Garreau 1981) note that state political borders are poor demarcations for cultural phenomena—media markets, dialects, and socioeconomic character routinely transcend state lines—state-level identifiers from drivers' licenses and tuition bills to tax codes and social service eligibility formally distinguish among New Yorkers, Arkansans, and New Mexicans.

State distinctions shape governance choices and processes (Elazar 1972; Fineman 2008). State laws enable and empower different types of local governments. Counties, for example, exist only as geographic, but not political, subdivisions in Connecticut and Rhode Island, where town governments assume traditional county roles. County governments dominate in southern states, however. State differences in incorporation, annexation, debt ceilings, taxes, and state aid to local governments similarly explain variations in local government operations (U.S. Advisory Commission on Intergovernmental Relations 1993). Local government arrangements vary according to state philosophies and practices. As of 2007, for example, the State of Nevada had a total of 19 municipalities, fewer than in Essex County, New Jersey, an area roughly one one-thousandth the size of Nevada and with one-third its population (U.S. Bureau of the Census 2008).

Region-scale identity is more elusive yet evident. Although regional flowers, flags, anthems, ID cards, and formal rights and responsibilities are rare, regional differences persist in building types, hometown sports allegiances, paces of life, dialects, cherished assets, foods, idioms, and attitudes. Regional culture and politics often shape regional planning operations within a small territory. For example, the Buffalo metropolitan area's history of tense intercounty relations and lukewarm enthusiasm for regionalism helps account for why that region lacks a regional planning council and multicounty planning efforts, unlike Rochester, its neighboring region just 65 miles east, which supports both.

ORGANIZING REGIONAL PLANNING GOVERNANCE

Regional planners achieve governance either by (1) creating regional organizations that encompass the territory of a planning problem; or (2) forging relationships and processes that mimic regional governance through informal means. Given institutions, history, and culture, not surprisingly U.S. regions make different choices, which yield varied outcomes for regional planning. Still, we can discern tendencies and trends.

Planning for a special regional resource or facility—say a dam, forest, canal, or environmentally sensitive area—typically occurs through resource-scaled, federal- or state-empowered special-purpose districts that enjoy ample independence and authority. When federal or state governments want even greater control over planning in a resource area, they may take over the territory themselves, as occurs in national parks and state forests. Powerful regional authorities are also common for big-ticket and high fixed-cost infrastructure systems, including those for airports, transit, water, sewer, and utilities in metropolitan or rural regions.

Multipurpose, multicounty governance entities are the exception in the United States. No metropolitan region has a single-tier, multifunction regional authority. Even Metro, the nation's most powerful regional government covering a mostly urbanized segment of the Portland, Oregon, metropolitan region, contains multiple local governments, including 25 cities, each of which wields independent planning powers. Besides Metro, the most prominent multipurpose regional entity is the Metropolitan Council in the Minneapolis–St. Paul, Minnesota, region. This governor-appointed regional service entity encompasses the Twin Cities and surrounding counties. City-county consolidations could align their planning, but such mergers are not only rare—roughly 35 have existed in the United States in the last two centuries—they are also noncomprehensive, thus leaving multiple jurisdictions holding independent planning powers within the consolidated territory.

Regional councils offer a more common model for planning. Numbering more than 500 in 47 states and covering roughly 90 percent of the nation's local governments, regional councils are advisory rather than authoritative and typically serve as cross-border planners and conflict resolvers (National Association of Regional Councils 2010). Nearly 180 of these regional councils also serve as a region's federally designated metropolitan planning organization (MPO), a designation that invests them with authority and gives them the responsibility for transportation planning and allocation of federal funds. For example, the Mid-America Regional Council serving the Kansas City metropolitan area is both a council of governments and the region's MPO for transportation planning. Roughly 200 other MPOs are independent transportation agencies that operate outside of regional councils.

Region-scale special districts, while narrow in function, may have significant influence over regional outcomes in realms as varied as soil conservation and housing. While pragmatic, this form of regional organization is often criticized for ultimately fragmenting its jurisdiction (Fahim 2009). Nevertheless, these single-purpose, region-scale special districts represent the United States' fastest-growing and most frequently found form of government (Foster 2001). It is also the most common type of planning entity at the county or larger scale. A prominent example is the Metropolitan Water District of Southern California, which operates the water infrastructure and programs for nearly 19 million residents in a six-county, 5,200-square-mile territory.

When formal structures are undesirable or impossible to achieve, regional planning occurs through voluntary local cooperation. Intermunicipal agreements exist for virtually any cross-border function from street cleaning to GIS. Although informal agreements seem simple, success at forging and sustaining them depends on often elusive levels of mutual interest and trust. Interviews of municipal officials in the Boston region revealed numerous stories of failed cooperation and defensive localism, even for emergency services, where mutual aid pacts are common. As one official noted in frustration, "every town has a $700,000 ladder truck because we can't share" (Barron, Frug, and Su 2004, 81). Local resistance to intermunicipal land use planning, education, or taxation is exponentially greater.

Hundreds of region-focused private or civic organizations also plan regionally. These entities range from nonprofit land trusts, such as the bluff lands of the Iowa Natural Heritage Foundation of the Upper Mississippi River, to prominent business and civic associations, such as Chicago Metropolis 2020. Although their planning powers are advisory, the impact of nonpublic entities can be significant, particularly if they have financial and political power and enjoy strong relationships with public planning authorities.

THREE QUESTIONS OF REGIONAL PLANNING GOVERNANCE

Whether developing a bike trail across multiple jurisdictions, protecting a multistate watershed, or sparking metropolitan prosperity, regardless of how a region organizes its regional governance, all regional planning efforts must attend to three key governance questions: By what authority? Exercised by whom? and In what territory?

To illuminate the range of alternative regional planning choices and practices, consider a governance audit of the six varied, familiar, and well-regarded multifunctional regional planning entities summarized in table 3.1. Each group takes its own approach to resolving these three questions, demonstrating that there is no single formula for regional planning governance. Instead, alternative governance pathways may be crafted along which regions can pursue their planning goals.

Table 3.1	Summary of Regional Planning Cases				
REGIONAL PLANNING ENTITY (YEAR ESTABLISHED)	TYPE	ANNUAL BUDGET (MID-2010)	AREA SERVED	TOPICAL SCOPE	FUNCTIONAL SCOPE
COLUMBIA RIVER GORGE COMMISSION (1986)	Federal regulatory entity	$871,000 from federal sources	Bi-state (OR, WA) resource and small town region alongside Columbia River	Resource protection, recreation, economic development	Develop, adopt and administer Scenic Area Management Plan, review plans for conformity, assist local and tribal governments, hear appeals, provide grants
BEAR LAKE REGIONAL COMMISSION (1973)	Bi-state COG created as legal entity	$100,000, with half from each state	Bi-state (UT, ID) resource region around Bear Lake in the high Rockies	Water, natural resource management, recreation	Coordination, cooperation, education, plan making, compliance review, advocacy, grants assistance
ADIRONDACK PARK AGENCY (1971)	State regulatory entity	$6.2 million, from state appropriation	Single-state (NY) resource and small town region in Adirondack Park	Forest preservation, wetlands protection, recreation	Set and enforce planning and zoning policy for public and private lands; implement park plan
METRO (1977; AS CHARTER REGIONAL GOVERNMENT, 1992)	Elected regional government	$457 million, from tax levy, user fees, and grants	Single-state (OR), three-county metropolitan (Portland) region	Water, zoo, convention center, parks, open space, land use and transportation planning, waste management	Full-service government with broad powers to make, implement, and enforce plans
SOUTHEAST MICHIGAN COUNCIL OF GOVERNMENTS (SEMCOG) (1968)	Voluntary association with federal and state designations	$11.1 million; roughly 20% from dues and rest from grants and contracts	Single-state (MI), seven-county metropolitan (Detroit) region	Transportation, environment, community and economic development, education	Technical assistance, data collection and analysis, coordination and facilitation, policy advocacy
REGIONAL PLAN ASSOCIATION (1922)	Nonprofit member-based organization	$5 million, half from members and half from grants, gifts, and contracts	Tri-state (NJ, NY, CT) metropolitan and resource region	Transportation, land use, open space, community development, housing, environment	Plan development, policy and plan advocacy, education, contract assistance

1. By What Authority?

Anyone, of course—a fourth grade class, online planning bloggers, multinational corporations, a graduate planning studio, newspaper editors, land developers, you—can plan a region. Yet the U.S. governmental system grants formal legal authority to adopt, implement, and enforce a regional plan, or empower another entity to do so, only to a federal, state, or local government. The anatomy of this authority varies across the six case study entities (table 3.2).

Table 3.2	**By What Authority?**								
REGIONAL PLANNING ENTITY	DELEGATED AUTHORITY								DEVELOPED AUTHORITY
	FROM FEDERAL	FROM STATE	FROM LOCAL	TYPE AND LEVEL					
				PLAN-NING	PROFES-SIONAL	REGULA-TORY	FINAN-CIAL	POLITI-CAL	
COLUMBIA RIVER GORGE COMMIS-SION	Planning and policy powers via scenic areas law	Bi-state compact		Low	High	Low	Medium	Medium	Funding from federal appropriation rather than local sources increases community tolerance for regional commission
BEAR LAKE REGIONAL COMMIS-SION		Advisory and policy powers via interstate agreement		Medium	Low	Low	Medium	Medium	Strong water management track record provides within-region credibility
ADIRON-DACK PARK AGENCY		Regulatory powers via law		High	High	High	High	Low	
METRO (PORT-LAND)	Program powers via MPO designation	Regulatory and policy powers via law and charter		High	High	High	High	High	Credibility established over time; home rule charter approved in 1992, extended in 2000
SOUTH-EAST MICHIGAN COUNCIL OF GOV-ERNMENTS (SEMCOG)	Program powers via designation as MPO and planning agency for water and air quality issues	Review powers via designation as point of contact	Coordination powers via voluntary agreement	Medium	High	Low	Low	Medium	Credibility enhanced by local elected officials as decision makers
REGIONAL PLAN ASSO-CIATION	None	None	None	None	None	None	None	None	Professional expertise, credibility, track record, political influence, financial resources

Sources of Authority With the exception of the independent Regional Plan Association (RPA), each of the six entities under discussion derives its regional planning authority from federal, state, and/or local delegations of power.

In some instances—SEMCOG, for example—multiple governments delegate authority. Member local governments acting in tandem as a council of governments authorize SEMCOG to carry out regional planning functions. With its designation as the Detroit region's MPO, the federal government authorizes SEMCOG to carry out water and air quality responsibilities as well as to adopt the region's transportation improvement plan (TIP) and allocate federal funds to implement it. Michigan's designation of SEMCOG as a "single point of contact" authorizes the council to review federal grant applications for consistency with regional plans and programs.

The audit obscures the degree of authority that is not delegated to the regional entities, however. Local governments under the Columbia River Gorge and Bear Lake Regional Commissions, for example, retain powers to zone, adopt development codes, and make final decisions on proposals brought before county or municipal planning boards or elected legislative bodies.

Types and Levels of Authority Delegated authority comes in different types, as specified when the regional body is established. The delegating government may limit or expand powers over time to reflect political context, culture, and will.

Gerald Hodge and Ira Robinson (2001, 120–132) identify five types of planning authority for plan making and implementation:

1. planning authority that develops determinative short- and long-term policies and agendas for the region;

2. professional authority that marshals and deploys talent, expertise, materials, and facilities to accomplish planning;

3. regulatory authority that makes and enforces the rules and laws governing public and private behaviors and activities of those under its purview;

4. financial authority that collects and allocates resources for regional planning, and that wields the power to tax, impose fees, and otherwise raise funds; and

5. political authority that legitimizes planning decisions and influences internal and external actors.[2]

---

2. This definition of political authority is broader than that offered by Hodge and Robinson, who limit political resources to the legitimacy stemming from decision makers' status as elected or appointed officials, thus making them directly or indirectly accountable to regional citizens and local authorities.

Assessing the six planning entities according to Hodge and Robinson's authority categories reveals several themes and patterns. First, planning authority and regulatory authority do not necessarily coexist. The Bear Lake Regional and Columbia River Gorge Commissions and SEMCOG may prepare regional plans, but they all lack authority to implement them. Second, as a consequence of divided authority, political authority is essential for effecting regional outcomes. Regional entities with strong political legitimacy, typically because elected officials or others with high credibility sit on their governing boards, have greater likelihood of implementing their regional plans.

Third, high regulatory powers are often accompanied by similar levels of other types of authority. Typically, agencies with ample authority to make and enforce policies also hold prominent professional, financial, and planning authority. As a directly elected regional government, for example, Metro also enjoys high political authority delegated from regional voters. The Adirondack Park Agency's comparatively low political authority, which stems from its appointed board, only modestly diminishes its otherwise potent combination of regulatory, professional, and financial powers.

Fourth, the presence of authority does not demand the exercise of that power. The Bear Lake Regional Commission, for example, has financial authority to assess fees on city and county governments, but shies away from doing so for political reasons as it strives to stay on good terms with host local governments (Patrick 2010).

Fifth, even when regional entities have formal planning authority, final say on and implementation powers for planning actions often rest in local governments.

Finally, not all regional planning entities have delegated authority. Land trusts, conservation leagues, property rights groups, and nonprofit planning organizations derive their powers from developed authority, which stems from internal and external capacity, such as a professional staff, ample expertise, strong relations with public entities, and sway resting in the persuasive powers of agency leaders and board members.

Regional planning entities with delegated authority also build developed authority, typically through a strong staff and board, sufficient expertise, and relationships. Such developed authority was instrumental in 1992, for example, in persuading voters in the Portland region to convert Metro from a metropolitan services district with limited powers to a charter regional government with expansive regional planning and implementation authority.

2. Exercised by Whom?

Regional planning entities may exhibit different approaches to determining who will exercise authority (table 3.3).

Table 3.3	Exercised by Whom, and How?				
REGIONAL PLANNING ENTITY	GOVERNING BOARD			STAFF SUPPORT	KEY GOVERNING PARTNERS AND RELATIONSHIPS
	VOTING MEMBERS	NONVOTING, EX OFFICIO	SELECTION		
COLUMBIA RIVER GORGE COMMISSION	12: 6 county reps, 6 state reps (3 per state)	1 ex officio USDA Forest Service	Appointed by relevant county commission, governor, Secy of Agriculture	9-member staff	Formal relations with the U.S. Forest Service; informal partnerships with civic groups, local resource-based actors and national interests, including Trust for Public Lands and Columbia Trust
BEAR LAKE REGIONAL COMMISSION	10: 8 elected city and county officials, 2 public members representing recreation and irrigation interests	2 state agency reps, one each appointed by governors; other ex officio at discretion of commission	Elected members appointed by relevant county legislature or mayor; public members nominated by interest groups and selected by commission	3-member staff	Close coordination with county planning and zoning commissions
ADIRONDACK PARK AGENCY	11: 8 public (5 in-park, 3 out-of-park residence); 3 ex officio state officers	None	Governor appointments	72-member staff, including at visitor centers	Public-private tensions common; ample citizen input invited
METRO (PORTLAND)	7: 1 president elected regionwide; 6 councillors elected by district	None	Elected by voters	Elected auditor plus 762 FTE across all operations and facilities	Charter requires 2 advisory committees with mandated citizen membership; nine other advisory committees currently operating
SOUTHEAST MICHIGAN COUNCIL OF GOVERNMENTS (SEMCOG)	51-member executive committee (policy body); General Assembly of 320 delegates and alternates from 160 members	None	Each member allowed delegates and alternates; executive committee determined per bylaws to ensure geographic representation	77-member staff	Most work completed through committees
REGIONAL PLAN ASSOCIATION	60 members, over half from business, with remainder including former elected officials	None, but separate committees for New Jersey, Long Island, and Connecticut interests	Selected by association	30-member staff and senior fellows	Significant partnerships with civic, educational, and business coalitions build clout and advance RPA goals

Who Decides? The size, composition, and selection rules for the regional planning entity's governing board is a fundamental dimension of regional planning governance.

Decision makers may be appointed or elected, and the former is the rule for entities that lack regulatory authority. Elected governing boards are accorded the highest political legitimacy, followed by indirectly representative governing boards for which elected officials are selected by legislative peers to serve on a commission. This occurs for both the Columbia River Gorge and Bear Lake Regional Commissions, for example. Appointed boards wield the least political authority and are often criticized for apparent favoritism for one interest or another. Such accusations are familiar to the Adirondack Park Agency, which has been accused of favoring environmental groups over those promoting development (North Country Public Radio 2010).[3] As a nonpublic entity, the nonprofit Regional Plan Association (RPA) has discretion to select governing board members using any formula it chooses. Its preference for well-connected and influential players riles certain interests, but is consistent with the association's fundraising and advocacy goals.

Staff Although professional staff members have little formal role in regional planning decisions, their credibility and productivity shape regional planning outcomes. The size and capacity of a regional planning staff—the Bear Lake Regional Commission has three staffers; Metro has 762—determines not only the scope of regional planning activity, but the nature, reach, and cost of operations as well. Staff credibility is essential for nonpublic entities. The RPA's success in championing its plans is dependent on the caliber of the staff, who produce excellent work and advocate successfully with public agencies to adopt and implement it.

Governing Partners and Key Relationships One byproduct of little delegated authority and shared regional interests is the need for strong partnerships to make and implement regional plans. Although regional actors may agree in general about a high regional quality of life for everyone, their ability to keep multiple groups aligned around specific policies, rules, investments, and actions is much more difficult. Determining which, if any, entity has the authority or legitimacy even to convene competing interests for a regional dialogue may be difficult. Not surprisingly, parties to voluntary regional arrangements may agree to disagree on topics for which neither consensus nor means to achieve goals exist. As a result, controversial but important topics from property rights to regional housing equity may go unaddressed.

---

3. Bearing in mind challenges presented by drawing insights from online comments, many of the story's respondents criticized the Adirondack Park Agency for lacking neutrality and acting like an environmental advocacy group.

Even with ample regulatory authority, tensions may infuse regional planning decisions. The Columbia River Gorge Commission contends with the "dueling visions" (Mason 2008, 116) of the urban-based Friends of the Columbia River Gorge, resource-based actors in the timber industry, a local property rights movement, and county officials whose plans the commission may review and approve. On the other hand, Metro draws upon elected government procedures and safeguards to legitimize its democratic process for decision making. SEMCOG can simply put aside a contentious issue for which there is neither consensus nor appetite.

3. In What Territory?

For regions of all types, particularly for natural territories—"nature has no need for walls, stone or otherwise" (Freyfogle 1998, 16–17)—setting boundaries is a challenge-filled dimension of regional planning governance. Different borders will change the defined scope of planning as well as the underlying dynamic of planning operations (table 3.4).

Boundary Type One boundary-setting filter is the degree of boundary flexibility. Flexible borders are logically desirable, but practically difficult. Public agencies typically have fixed, rarely redrawn boundaries. Portland Metro's complicated borders are based on the boundaries of its predecessor Metropolitan Service District. The boundary map held by the custodian of Metro records reveals hundreds of twists and turns that cut across political jurisdictions. Even borders for fixed, resource-based territories, as apply to the Columbia River Gorge Commission and the Adirondack Park Association, are adjusted only rarely. Only nonpublic, nontaxing regional planning entities (e.g., RPA) tend to operate with flexible, issue-based boundaries.

Boundary Scope A challenge for regional planners is setting borders that match the scope of the planning entity and problem (Meidinger 1998). Both overbounding and underbounding are common, particularly when borders reflect administrative jurisdictions, which bear little resemblance to a resource or service-based territory. Metropolitan planning entities are especially prone to underbounding, with boundary change lagging the pace and direction of growth.

Underbounding is most evident for Metro, which includes 25 jurisdictions in parts of three Oregon counties. Yet the Portland city-region, which encompasses the City of Vancouver and surrounding parts of Clark County in Washington State as well as the five-county Portland Metropolitan Area designated by the U.S. Office of Management and Budget, extends significantly beyond Metro's borders. Metro's origins as a services district accounts in part for the more circumscribed boundary.

Finally, regional boundaries—and policy applications—reflect political circumstances. Since its establishment in 1892, strong control over the use of pri-

Table 3.4	In What Territory?						
REGIONAL PLANNING ENTITY	REGION	BOUNDARY TYPE	BOUNDARIES				COMMENTS
			SIZE	POPULATION	UNDERLYING JURISDICTIONS		
COLUMBIA RIVER GORGE COMMISSION	Bi-state natural region	Fixed on resource region	292,630 acres along 85-mile stretch	55,000 residents, 2 million annual visitors	Two states, six counties, four Native American tribes; 70% in private hands		Urban areas exempt from plan
BEAR LAKE REGIONAL COMMISSION	Bi-state natural region	Fixed on county borders	2,000 square miles	8,000 residents	Two counties in two states, includes some national forest		Isolation from state capitals threatens annual funding
ADIRONDACK PARK AGENCY	Upstate New York natural region	Fixed on resource region	6 million acres	135,000 residents year-round; 200,000 seasonal residents	State lands (49%); all or parts of 12 counties (51%)		Park region designated in 1890s to encompass all of Adirondack Mountains
METRO (PORTLAND)	Portland (OR) Metro Area, political region	Fixed on borders of former Metropolitan Service District; may change by annexation	463 square miles	1.6 million residents	All or part of 25 municipalities in parts of three counties		400 square miles of Metro located within urban growth boundary
SOUTHEAST MICHIGAN COUNCIL OF GOVERNMENTS (SEMCOG)	Southeast Michigan political region	Fixed on county borders	4,600 square miles	4.8 million residents	Roughly 240 local governments plus school districts and higher education institutions		Voluntary dues-paying membership; numerous communities are not members
REGIONAL PLAN ASSOCIATION	Political and natural region centered on New York metropolitan area	Flexible by issue area	Varies from single site to entire Northeast	10 million or more residents	3 states, 31 counties, and more than 900 municipalities		To participate and benefit, state and local governments may be members

vate lands within the Adirondack Park has been controversial, making it matter whether one's property is inside or outside of park borders. To please urban constituents, the Columbia River Gorge Commission exempted more than 28,000 urban acres from rules that apply to other general management areas (Mason 2008, 115). Significant expansion of Metro's borders remains unlikely due to contentious battles over changes to the urban growth boundary and fallout from the 2004 passage of Measure 37, which mandates compensation for actions that diminish the value of private property (Dierwechter 2008).

BACK TO THE REGIONAL GOVERNANCE FUTURE

The governance audit reinforces the wide range of approaches to regional planning governance. By different means and structures, regional organizations and leaders seek to match the nature and strength of governance mechanisms to the scale and impact of their regional planning problems.

Such variation is neither new to nor necessarily problematic for regional planning practice. For more than 300 years, the governance pendulum in the United States has swung back and forth between the local entities that hold the strongest legal cards to address a regional problem voluntarily or not and higher-level governments that assert their power to compel action at the regional scale.

A general overview shows the pendulum hovering over central authorities during colonial times (Foster 2001). The Massachusetts Bay, Virginia, and Pennsylvania colonies operated under highly unified rule. As settlements proliferated far from government centers, colonial (and later state) governments readily ceded responsibility for governmental operations to burgeoning local settlements. The regional planning pendulum swung steadily toward local governments throughout the 1800s as state governments enabled local units to incorporate, annex, tax, plan, spend, borrow, and operate largely without direct state interference.

Amid intensive industrialization and metropolitanization in the late 1800s and the first three decades of the 1900s, local governments solidified their powers of self-determination. As states had a century earlier, local governments ceded regional planning and service delivery to three nonthreatening organizational release valves: region-scale, single-function services districts; newly empowered urban counties; and civic-led regional planning associations.

Starting with the Great Depression of the 1930s and continuing to the 1990s, the courts and the state and federal governments reassumed powers from local governments. This half-century "quiet revolution" in planning and public affairs saw both the reassertion of federal and state authority and imposition of centralized regulations over virtually every service realm, including education, housing, transportation, utilities, land use, infrastructure, social services, and the environment (Bosselman and Callies 1971; Derthick 1999).

Since 1990, the pendulum has hovered midway between local interests organizing as property rights, wise use, and taxpayer watchdog activists on one hand and regional coalitions advocating "common ground" priorities, such as regional equity and growth management on the other. Recognition of the nation's and many regions' sharply divided voter bases coupled with record-low trust in government has spawned a pragmatic "quieter revolution" in planning (Mason 2008). Quieter revolution planning is characterized by cross-sector, cross-function, cross-border partnerships; insistence on or inclination toward collaborative decision making; and recourse to citizen-initiated ballot measures and referenda as front-line planning tools.

REGIONAL PLANNING PRACTICE AHEAD

Looking out from 2011, in what direction might leaders and planners nudge the pendulum of regional governance control? Where is regional planning governance headed, normatively and practically?

Three basic pathways—greater central, local, or nongovernmental authority —mark the trail for regional planning governance. Each has precedents, pros, and cons, and each is likely to bear some traffic in coming decades as U.S. society pursues region-scale solutions to region-scale problems while balancing individual and collective interests.

Greater Central Authority

The advantages of centralized authority are well known. More centralized control can bring order, ease of coordination, more equitable outcomes, and increased efficiency from economies of scale and internalization of externalities. Its disadvantages are also clear. With centralization can come high degrees of conformity and bureaucratization, erosion of minority influence, greater potential for stifling innovation, diminished participation in governance, and the possibility of over-standardization.

The nature and scale of emerging regional issues, notably climate change, homeland security, and population migration, will shift regional planning governance toward higher-level entities. Only at these scales will societies achieve governance equivalence matching the territory of impact with the territory of costs and benefits as well as decision making. In practice, though, regional planners are likely to find themselves serving as international agents who are called upon to think globally and act regionally and to apply principles and policies forged in distant entities, such as the United Nations and climate change conventions, to more immediate regional concerns.

In the United States, a new era of greater centralization of regional planning authority is already under way, catalyzed by federal funding incentives. As Knaap and Lewis note in chapter 7, the Obama administration's Sustainable Communities Initiative signifies a major intervention and investment in collaborative, functionally integrated regional planning. From a governance perspective, the new federal program is notable for its leeway relative to previous federal interventions about specific organizational structures for regional planning.[4]

While the initiative requires multijurisdictional and multisector processes and outcomes, it is flexible about what specific structures might achieve these goals. The lead agency seeking its funding, for example, can be a city, town, or county government; a special district; or a private, nonprofit, or academic entity.

---

4. The rise of regional planning councils from the 1950s through the 1970s, for instance, resulted directly from the federal stipulation that federal funds flow only to such entities and not to individual municipal jurisdictions. Since the 1990s, formally designated metropolitan planning organizations have functioned similarly, serving as recipients and allocators of federal funds for transportation and related regional services.

This implies federal tolerance of, even encouragement for, regional planning by cross-sector, cross-functional networks rather than insistence upon formally constituted regional entities in the mode of an MPO or council of governments.

At the state level, calls for greater control over regional planning are likely to continue from local and regional interests unable to shape physical and economic outcomes adequately on their own. In addition, pressure may intensify for state control over regional affairs due to interest in greater state policy and planning intervention (Wolman et al. 2003), increased state scrutiny of local government arrangements (Indiana Commission on Local Government Reform 2007; Maine Office of Fiscal Program Review 2008; New York State Commission on Local Government Efficiency and Competitiveness 2008), and awareness that voluntary local collaboration remains a limited means to shape regional outcomes (Rosan 2007).

Nevertheless, other signs suggest that state activity in regional planning will remain modest and uneven and potentially even diminish. Most states enable but do not mandate regional planning; only a minority—Florida, Hawaii, Oregon, and Vermont among them—have histories of state control over local planning powers. New federal planning initiatives effectively bypass states in favor of working directly with region-level stakeholders. Even if the appetite for state-sponsored regional planning were high, severe fiscal challenges make expansion of state portfolios unlikely.

Relatively upbeat mid-2000s accounts of state activity in environmental planning were more tempered by the end of the decade (Rabe 2006; 2010). While Oregon voters approved Measure 49 in 2007 to scale back the strictest elements of Measure 37 (the strong property rights referendum passed in 2004), they divided along regional lines over the wisdom of state control of regional planning. Even in New Jersey, a state with strong regional plans protecting its Pinelands, Highlands, and Hackensack Meadowlands, survey respondents revealed ambivalence about strong state authority over regional growth management (Mason 2008).

All factors considered, a pendulum swing toward centralized planning at either the federal or state government level likely will rely on the funds carrot, albeit with strings attached, rather than the stick of mandates to effect regional planning.

Greater Local Authority

The pros and cons of strong local authority are well known. Decentralized authority supports individual freedom, protects special or minority interests, fosters efficiency through cost-braking competition, produces custom-driven local solutions to local problems, encourages buy-in and participation, and supports robust exchange of ideas. On the downside, dispersed power may privilege self-interest over public interest, sustain inequality, hinder clear communication and coordination, and facilitate defection from local agreements.

Precedent for voluntary local collaborative governance is ample. Recent years have seen the rise of mayors' caucuses, intergovernmental compacts, and other voluntary locally based approaches to regional problems that have had impressive outcomes and engagement in Chicago and Denver, among other regions (Foster 2001; McKinney and Johnson 2009).

Nonetheless, both theory and practice offer only modest hope that local-government leaders will voluntarily cede sufficient authority and power to set and realize regional planning goals. Despite notable longevity and activity by councils of government—not only SEMCOG, illustrated in this chapter, but equivalent councils in Boston, Atlanta, San Diego, and elsewhere—the prospects for comprehensive long-lasting regional planning via local collaboration remain dim. As Rosan (2007) found in a study of Boston, Denver, and Portland, three metropolitan areas with varying degrees and types of local planning authority, voluntary regionalism simply could not shape regions the way additional incentives and regulations could and did. Ultimately voluntary regional action "leaves communities in much the same position they are in if there is no regional coordination" (Rosan 2007, 292).

Although voluntary regional planning governance will likely escalate in a political environment of skepticism toward centralized planning, the difficult truth is that, as Dierwechter (2008, 238) colorfully put it, regions "are not 'things' that move in the same direction," but, rather, "knotty, stringy assemblages of diverse, contradictory, heterogeneous social processes operating at multiple spatial and temporal scales." When disagreements surface, or when the process of collaboration takes more time and energy than the benefits it yields warrant, subregional entities with independent powers and diverse interests are prone to go it alone in the face of region-scale challenges.

Efforts to enhance regional planning by granting local governments more, not less, authority present a wildcard possibility. In their analysis of local governments in Massachusetts, a nominally strong home rule state, Barron, Frug, and Su (2004) suggested that providing municipal governments with more authority could facilitate regional cooperation. Added control over budgets, land use, service delivery, and education, they argued, would free localities to work together and reduce pressures for competitive parochialism. Loosening the reins on local control might prompt local governments to cede willingly more authority to formal councils of government, thereby creating a more receptive landscape for regional cooperation.

Greater Nongovernmental Authority

Just as increasing state or local planning presents both favorable and unfavorable possibilities, so does civic planning, which entails broadening and deepening regional planning activities by nongovernmental organizations. The primary advantages of civic planning are an infusion of resources, expertise, and effort into planning processes; attracting passionate interest in planning matters; the potential to build and leverage citizen capacity; and ample citizen buy-in to facilitate plan visioning and action. The downsides are equally clear, however. Nonpublic processes are ultimately advisory and must rely on persuasion and public pressure to achieve action. If the civic effort is not perceived as being sufficiently representative, its outcomes may lack public legitimacy or credibility.

These challenges notwithstanding, such quieter revolution models have represented major energy centers for regional planning since the 1990s. In states such as California, where citizens have plenty of powers of initiative and referendum, nongovernmental planning can achieve regional planning via the ballot. In other states, private efforts shape regional outcomes in ways as varied as community purchase of treasured lands to contentious court battles over private property rights (Mason 2008).

Acceleration of these trends is likely and may take a number of forms, from formalized visioning exercises to major planning efforts spearheaded by private nonprofit planning organizations, such as the Regional Plan Association. Such expansion reflects not only technological advances that facilitate community building and the increasingly sophisticated knowledge base and organized networks of citizen planners, but also the reality that *not* including citizens in regional problem solving may invite stiff legal, social, and economic opposition to proposed plans. To the degree that minimizing surprises and maximizing consensus and transparency are aids to planning outcomes, civic planning becomes a viable and important pathway for regional planning.

In this light, one prospect is increased public support for civic planning processes and powers. Public entities may grant the necessary authority in several ways. Formal delegation of public powers to make or implement plans subsequently adopted by public bodies is an excellent example. An alternative approach is the public-civic partnership, which draws upon citizen groups for legwork and to gain the local knowledge needed in crafting, advocating, and approving regional plans. A third, more modest, channel of support is achieved through monetary grants to nongovernmental planning groups to assist in citizen-created plans.

Whether and how federal, state, or local officials cede power to nongovernmental planning efforts remains uncertain. Points awarded for civic engagement in the federal Sustainable Communities Initiative grant process signal its seriousness about citizen planning, which may carry over to other federal and state grant programs. More likely outcomes may be (1) taking advantage of citizen expertise and interest through major regional efforts in visioning and performance measurement; and (2) using citizen groups as watchdogs for progress and accountability in regional planning. Regardless of means, civic involvement, like other planning processes, warrants critical assessment. Robert Mason (2008, 268) notes that "it should not be taken as a given, as often seems to be the case, that civic engagement improves environmental and social outcomes." He continues, "even when we can demonstrate that a program has fostered meaningful civic engagement, we need to further inquire about the sustainability of that civic engagement. Has social capital been accumulated? Has civic culture been enhanced?" (Mason 2008, 268–269).

A REGIONAL GOVERNANCE ETHOS

Given varied historical and institutional environments in U.S. regions, there is not— nor will there be—a single, automatically correct way to govern and plan a region, either structurally or operationally. Nonetheless, regional planners committed to sustainable outcomes may well contemplate a regional ethos that will be consistent with fundamental values and goals for a governance system. Consider these six key values and goals, which would form the core of such a regional governance ethos.[5]

1. **Efficiency**, signifying a commitment to minimize waste and maximize output value in service provision and regional governance processes;

2. **Fairness**, signifying a commitment to regional governance decisions and outcomes that are impartial and just for an entire regional community and its subparts;

3. **Accountability**, signifying a commitment to transparent and answerable regional governance systems and processes;

4. **Participation**, signifying a commitment to engage meaningfully those affected by regional governance choices and outcomes;

5. **Economic Development**, signifying a commitment to provide opportunities to thrive, thereby realizing potential and strengthening the vitality of people and places; and

6. **Environmental Sustainability**, signifying a commitment to steward environments responsibly to ensure their health and vitality for future generations.

The governance ethos not only reflects values, but also offers guidance for daily regional planning practice. In considering any choice, regional planners would consider a number of questions: Will this action lead to greater efficiency? How accountable or participatory is this process? What will be the impacts of this choice on economic and environmental fortunes? Is this outcome fair? By embedding such considerations into the routines of planning, the governance ethos offers a framework for deliberate goal-oriented decision making.

Yet battle-tested regional planners and philosophers will recognize in this ethos both realistic tradeoffs and the practical difficulty of simultaneously maximizing performance on all six goals. Tradeoffs are inherent to planning

---

5. Notably, these goals are reflected in the four basic recommendations identified by the chief operating officer of Portland's Metro (2010, 11): (1) invest in safe, livable communities; (2) promote economic development and good jobs; (3) protect our natural areas; and (4) reduce inefficiency, foster innovation, and demand accountability.

choices, of course. An extensive public participation process may build in certain inefficiencies. A development proposal that increases economic vitality for some may jeopardize the livelihood of others or diminish an environmental asset. Decisions may not be fair for everyone affected. A regional governance ethos does not aim to eliminate or paper over such tradeoffs, which will necessarily persist in any diverse collective. Rather, its goal is to recognize these tradeoffs fully in deliberating regional planning choices, and to hold out the six governance goals as aspirations and guideposts for regional planning practice.

CODA: THE WELL-QUALIFIED REGIONAL PLANNER

Regional planning in the United States is not distinguished from companion forms of city, state, or national planning by its substance. At each scale, planners address issues of transportation, housing, land development, and the environment. Nor does its distinction from these other scales stem from technical or engineering requirements that make regional planning especially difficult. Rather, what distinguishes regional planning is governance. This multijurisdictional enterprise involves multiple actors who have independent authority to make, act on, and enforce decisions for some, but not all, aspects of the regional space.

Thus the well-qualified regional planner in the twenty-first century will require intelligence, skills, and capacities to perform successfully in this challenging governance environment. Core qualifications mirror those for successful room sharing: a broad view of problem solving, regard for alternative perspectives and needs, creative thinking about alternative pathways to attain joint ends, negotiation and bargaining skills, a commitment to collaboration and consensus building, and skills in integrative analysis.

Such abilities boil down to proficiency in crossing borders and working effectively in heterogeneous cultures and environments. The well-qualified regional planner, therefore, must be adept across *jurisdictional* borders in order to work with ease in and across national, state, county, city, town, and district lines and appreciate that each level and entity has its distinctive culture, history, rules, practices, and processes. She must also be a generalist, who applies knowledge and understanding of interdependencies across *functional* borders in housing, transportation, human services, growth management, environment, landscape design, and other realms. Finally, the best regional planner will have the strengths and intelligence needed to work effectively across *sectoral* borders so that she will appreciate and incorporate perspectives, interests, and distinct missions and rules from the public, private, nonprofit, and academic worlds.

Perhaps the greatest capacity needed by regional planners, one currently reinforced by reverberating economic and environmental shockwaves from Wall Street to the Gulf Coast, is a deep appreciation for interconnectedness in an interdependent world. In the end, the challenge of regional planning governance in the twenty-first century remains the classic one faced by siblings sharing a room: how to make one's way together.

ACKNOWLEDGMENTS

Parts of this chapter are adapted from my essay, "Challenges Ahead for Regional Planning Governance," published in 2010 in *Town Planning Review* 81(5), pages 485–503.

REFERENCES

Barron, David J., Gerald E. Frug, and Rick T. Su. 2004. *Dispelling the myth of home rule: Local power in Greater Boston.* Cambridge, MA: Rappaport Institute for Greater Boston.

Bosselman, Fred, and David Callies. 1971. *The quiet revolution in land use control.* Washington, DC: Council on Environmental Quality.

Callenbach, Ernest. 1975. *Ecotopia: The notebooks and reports of William Weston.* Berkeley, CA: Banyan Tree Books.

Calthorpe, Peter, and William Fulton. 2001. *The regional city: Planning for the end of sprawl.* Washington, DC: Island Press.

DeGrove, John M. 2005. *Planning policy and politics: Smart growth and the states.* Cambridge, MA: Lincoln Institute of Land Policy.

Derthick, Martha. 1999. How many communities? The evolution of American federalism. In *Dilemmas of scale in America's federal democracy,* ed. Martha Derthick. Washington, DC: Woodrow Wilson Center Press; Cambridge, UK: Cambridge University Press.

Dierwechter, Yonn. 2008. *Urban growth management and its discontents: Promises, practices, and geopolitics in U.S. city-regions.* New York: Palgrave Macmillan.

Elazar, Daniel J. 1972. *A view from the states* (2nd ed.). New York: Thomas H. Crowell.

Fahim, Mayraj. 2009. A review of the pros and cons of increased interlocal cooperation in local government. *City Mayors* (November 19). www.citymayors.com/government/interlocal.html

Fineman, Howard. 2008. *The thirteen American arguments: Enduring debates that define and inspire our country.* New York: Random House.

Foster, Kathryn A. 1997. The civilization of regionalism. *The Regionalist* 2(2):1–12.

———. 2001. *Regionalism on purpose.* Cambridge, MA: Lincoln Institute of Land Policy.

Freyfogle, Eric T. 1998. Bounded people, boundless land. In *Stewardship across boundaries,* eds. Richard L. Knight and Peter B. Landres. Washington, DC: Island Press.

Frug, Gerald. 2010. Empowering the city: London/New York. *Urban Omnibus* (February 17). http://urbanomnibus.net/empowering-the-city-london-new-york

Garreau, Joel. 1981. *The nine nations of North America.* Boston: Houghton Mifflin.

Goldberg, Michael, and John Mercer. 1986. *The myth of the North American city: Continentalism challenged.* Vancouver: University of British Columbia Press.

Greenblatt, Alan. 2008. The Stuttgart solution. *Governing* (October 31). www.governing.com/topics/mgmt/The-Stuttgart-Solution.html

Hodge, Gerald, and Ira M. Robinson. 2001. *Planning Canadian regions.* Vancouver: University of British Columbia Press.

Indiana Commission on Local Government Reform. 2007. *Streamlining local government.* Indianapolis: Indiana University Public Policy Institute.

Kotkin, Joel. 2010. Welcome to ecotopia. *Forbes* (22 February). www.joelkotkin.com/content/00176-welcome-ecotopia

Lipset, Seymour. 1990. *Continental divide: The values and institutions of the United States and Canada.* New York: Routledge.

Maine Office of Fiscal and Program Review. 2008. *Report on "the initiative" to streamline state government.* Augusta.

Mason, Robert J. 2008. *Collaborative land use management: The quieter revolution in place-based planning.* Lanham, MD: Rowman & Littlefield.

McKinney, Matthew J., and Shawn Johnson. 2009. *Working across boundaries: People, nature, and regions.* Cambridge, MA: Lincoln Institute of Land Policy.

Meidinger, Errol. E. 1998. Laws and institutions in cross-boundary stewardship. In *Stewardship across boundaries,* eds. Richard L. Knight and Peter B. Landres. Washington, DC: Island Press.

Metro. 2010. *Community investment strategy: Recommendations from Metro's chief operating officer.* www.oregonmetro.gov/index.cfm/go/by.web/id/33898

National Association of Regional Councils. 2010. NARC history. http://narc.org/about-narc/narc-history.html

New York State Commission on Local Government Efficiency and Competitiveness. 2008. *21st-century local government: Report of the New York State Commission on Local Government Efficiency and Competitiveness.* Albany.

North Country Public Radio. 2010. Critics, lawsuit claim Adirondack Council sways APA decisions unfairly (January 4). www.northcountrypublicradio.org/news/story/15010/critics-lawsuit-claim-adirondack-council-sways-apa-decisions-unfairly

Ostrom, Elinor. 1990. *Governing the commons: The evolution of institutions for collective action.* New York: Cambridge University Press.

———. 2005. *Understanding institutional diversity.* Princeton, NJ: Princeton University Press.

Patrick, Jay. 2010. Who's looking after Bear Lake? Funding loss could leave regional commission dead in the water. *Herald Journal* (February 14). http://news.hjnews.com/news/article_d722a8e6-0c9f-58be-b76e-c2b2f2880880.html

Peirce, Neal R. 1993. *Citistates: How urban America can prosper in a competitive world.* Washington, DC: Seven Locks Press.

Rabe, Barry G. 2006. Power to the states: The promise and pitfalls of decentralization. In *Environmental policy: New directions for the twenty-first century,* eds. Norman J. Vig and Michael E. Kraft (6th ed.). Washington, DC: CQ Press.

———. 2010. Racing to the top, the bottom, or the middle of the pack? The evolving state government role in environmental protection. In *Environmental policy: New directions for the twenty-first century,* eds. Norman J. Vig and Michael E. Kraft (7th ed.). Washington, DC: CQ Press.

Rosan, Christina D. 2007. Metropolitan governance and local land use planning in Boston, Denver, and Portland. Ph.D. diss., Massachusetts Institute of Technology.

Rothblatt, Donald N., and Andrew Sancton. 1998. *Metropolitan governance revisited: American/ Canadian intergovernmental perspectives.* Berkeley, CA: Institute of Governmental Studies.

Rusk, David. 1999. *Inside game/outside game: Winning strategies for saving urban America.* Washington, DC: Brookings Institution Press.

U.S. Advisory Commission on Intergovernmental Relations. 1993. *State laws governing local government structure and administration.* Washington, DC.

U.S. Bureau of the Census. 2008. *Census of governments 2007.* Washington, DC.

Whitfield, Martin and Douglas Hart. 2000. American perspectives on economic development and environmental management: Changing the Federal-Local Balance. In *Integrating environment and economy: Strategies for local and regional government.* London: Routledge.

Wolman, Harold, Todd Swanstrom, and Margaret Weir, with Nicholas Lyon. 2003. Cities and state legislatures: Changing coalitions and metropolitan agendas. George Washington Institute for Public Policy Working Paper Number 3. (November). http://www.gwu.edu/~gwipp/papers/wp003.pdf

4

PLANNING FOR EQUITY, FIGHTING FOR JUSTICE
PLANNERS, ORGANIZERS, AND THE STRUGGLE FOR METROPOLITAN INCLUSION

Manuel Pastor and Chris Benner

Planners often face a fundamental tension in their day-to-day work. Because planning is inherently a technical process that requires high levels of professional expertise related to land use planning, zoning provisions, regulations, government structures and powers, and the like, frequently it is a professionally driven, top-down process. Many planners also hold a fundamental commitment to "equity planning," however, which includes public participation and promotion of strategies that can benefit the least advantaged. Many in this camp are painfully aware that, while their technical models and approaches can inform policy change, such change is rooted more fundamentally in the balance of political forces and community pressures (Krumholz and Forester 1990). Community pressures emerge in part from what we call social movement organizations, which are groups that may be versed in one or another aspect of planning issues (e.g., transportation or land use), but are committed primarily to bringing about deep social change and their alternative vision of how to organize society.

The Los Angeles Alliance for a New Economy, for example, has pioneered the highly technical device of community benefits agreements for downtown and regional developments, but their fundamental, overriding goal is to improve the lot of their city's working people (Beach 2008; Marcello 2007). Detroit's interfaith organization MOSES has demonstrated considerable expertise in explaining why fix-it-first investment in older transit infrastructure is a more efficient use of tax dollars than spending on new suburban road and highway construction. Nevertheless, its underlying goal is creation of an alliance of inner-city dwellers with people living in older suburbs in order to challenge the metropolitan distribution of power in the Detroit area (Pastor, Benner, and Matsuoka 2009).

What happens, then, when planners committed to social equity run into social movement organizations and their activities? It can result in a messy process filled with the conflicts such groups are designed and destined to bring to the table. It is even more challenging at the metropolitan or regional level, since jurisdictional lines complicate the tasks not only of planners but also those of organizers who seek to bring together multiple communities. Yet this is exactly where a new cutting edge is emerging in terms of both planning and organizing—where new movements toward "regional equity" intersect with planners' increasing interest in the regional scale.

Regional equity is a relatively new phenomenon. Growing out of deep roots in the community development and community organizing fields as well as various strands in the literature on spatial mismatch and regional planning, its adherents argue that, at least in part, the challenges facing low-income urban communities result from larger forces that have driven jobs and housing to far-flung suburbs. It suggests that the remedies cannot be purely the inward-looking asset building of traditional neighborhood development, but rather require a broad attempt to change the rules of the game via regional tax sharing, fair-share housing requirements, and improved public transit systems.

This sharp and powerful analysis applies to the regional scale, for the organizing side of the equation emerges simply because organizers think this is a way to get communities to form new connections and visualize a different set of political possibilities. But the planning side of it is complicated, because it runs counter to the usual jurisdictional lines of authority and up against—and alongside—the political impulses and distressed communities that voice regional equity concerns. The politics of planning is further complicated by the fact that other drivers for regional planning are centered on economic competitiveness and environmental protection, which have more powerful constituencies and, often, clearer strategies than those supporting the equity interests. This makes it easy for equity to slip off the agenda of even the most committed planner.

In this chapter we argue that regional equity planners and social movement regionalists need to strike a new balance in which planners embrace the organizing aspect necessary to lift up the equity corner of the economy-environment-equity triangle. To do this, we examine two case studies from California that are related to transportation planning and its relationship to regional equity. The first is the Sacramento Region Blueprint planning process sponsored by the Sacramento Council of Governments. It is followed by an examination of the effort to break the logjam of economic and environmental conflicts at the ports of Los Angeles and Long Beach.

The Sacramento case, we suggest, can be characterized largely as a top-down process that was led by professional planning staff and their partners. In this process, community and labor groups had seats at the table but lacked substantial social movement organizing, which put pressure on the process. In Los Angeles, by contrast, the process was far more bottom-up: a professionally led economic planning vision of promoting greater efficiency in goods movement in the region languished until a labor union effort to organize the trucking industry turned into a broad labor-community campaign to clean the ports and improve the quality of employment.

Equity concerns in the Sacramento case were clearly a component of the final blueprint process, but they were also less important than environmental and economic aspects of the plan, causing social equity advocates in the region to struggle to find ways of enforcing its equity goals. In Los Angeles, however, the labor-supported Coalition for Clean and Safe Ports was successful in passing the Clean Trucks Program, a landmark effort that reduces pollution as well as promotes the logistics industry and facilitates labor organizing in the industry. Our simple conclusion: regional equity may need good planners, but more importantly it needs good organizers. Planning for equity, in short, will also require fighting for justice.

It is our position that planners will be more effective in engaging with these struggles for regional equity if they hold a set of "soft" skills and capacities that are not taught often enough in planning schools. They include: (1) humility about their own power to make effective change, along with a deep appreciation for the power of social movement knowledge and expertise; (2) comfort with "fuzziness," particularly in the mismatches between jurisdictional authority and the political, economic, and social processes that shape regional development; and (3) an ability to embrace conflict in a principled way while addressing the uncomfortable and difficult issues that emerge when inequality is confronted directly. At the same time, planners have a set of technical skills that could be deployed to good effect. Because regional equity remains poorly defined and social movement organizations often react to inequality rather than promote a comprehensive vision, planners could help develop metrics of and help design more proactive visions for metropolitan inclusion.

We begin by defining regional equity and explaining the relationship to social movements and social change, then move to a discussion of participation in the planning process and of some of the specific challenges that equity-oriented planners might face at a regional scale. Because one of these challenges is the relative lack of regional levers with which to shift distributional outcomes, we turn to transportation—one arena that both activists and planners have seen as relevant to achieving regional equitable development. The case studies follow, and we conclude by highlighting the general lessons for planners' capacities and pointing to specific ways planners could help advance the notion of an inclusive metropolis.

REGIONAL EQUITY, SOCIAL MOVEMENTS, AND PLANNING

What Is Regional Equity?
Around the United States, a growing movement has been spurred on by advocates of social justice, who see regional equity as a central component of their efforts (Pastor, Benner, and Matsuoka 2009). Regional equity remains somewhat vaguely defined, partly as the inevitable consequence of being a new, evolving field. One straightforward working definition is that regional equity seeks to create places of opportunity and to link places with opportunity. The create part refers to the stuff

of traditional community development—ensuring that urban areas with few grocery stores and important economic resources are replaced with vibrant, walkable, and economically diverse neighborhoods that have access to healthy, affordable food sources and other essential services. The newer link component suggests that it is not necessary to bring jobs to every neighborhood but rather to provide residents with opportunities to connect, through public transit and workforce training, to regional poles of employment. Regional equity also promotes the notion that residents should be able to move to opportunity as needed, something that means that suburbs as well as cities should include affordable housing and that cities as well as suburbs should provide decent educational systems.

This regional equity view operates at three levels: analytical, practical, and political. Analytically its bedrock principle holds that many of the most challenging urban problems in the United States are not self-generated, but rather created by our patterns of metropolitan development, particularly the spatial configuration of cities and suburbs. Practically it suggests that new metropolitan strategies on housing, transportation, and economic and workforce development are crucial to tackling these problems and may be more effective at generating equitable outcomes than either traditional community development efforts or broad national policy. Finally, the regional equity view suggests politically that the regional scale is a productive one in which to foster new progressive organizing, partly because it is the actual scale for many problems, but also because a confluence of interests at the regional scale make it possible to create new sustainable coalitions among unlikely partners.

The regional equity perspective also pays attention to issues of economic competition and sustainability in ways that appeal beyond the usual low-income constituencies, thus intersecting with the other recent driving forces behind the revitalization of regional planning. Indeed, it argues that inclusion of low-income groups is central to recovering regional economies and, hence, is in everyone's interest (Pastor and Benner 2008). As a result, regional equity proponents have been experimenting with policies that traditionally would not have been associated with antipoverty efforts or community development, fields concerned historically with building low-income housing, launching local job training programs, and reconstructing distressed neighborhoods. Likewise, these same proponents have sought to move beyond a traditional left-leaning politics that is sometimes characterized by oppositional protest against business, casting aspersions on suburbs, and arguing for localist, often inward-looking neighborhood development. Instead they support developing programs that can promote "just growth" strategies that simultaneously link economic expansion with social justice (Pastor et al. 2010).

Why Social Movements?

The regional equity perspective can be understood to consist of three main variants: (1) *community development regionalism*, in which the main interest is in using regional levers to promote a new form of community revitalization; (2) *policy reform regionalism*, the primary emphasis of which is on shifting government rules to distribute metropolitan resources better; and (3) *social movement regionalism*, where the principal goal is building on a sense of grievance in order to mobilize communities for mass collective action at a regional level (Pastor, Benner, and Matsuoka 2009). All three exist in a regional playing field that is already crowded with other initiatives, including business-sponsored, public-private collaborations and smart growth initiatives focused on the environment and urban form. The regional equity approaches have much in common—more than they share with the business-led and smart growth efforts. Nonetheless, the regional equity approaches also have significantly different constituencies, unequal access to resources, and sometimes differing strategies.

We think that it is possible to thread together the three variants under one regional equity tent: community developers work on projects that demonstrate what is possible; policy reform strategists focus on changing policy to make the possible the norm; and social movement regionalists build power to shift politics and thus policy. In our work, however, we have generally privileged the social movement element, thinking that the nitty-gritty of constituency mobilization and regional coalition building not merely offer a method to change tax rules and zoning regulations, but rather that the regional scale is a platform for building new, unexpected coalitions that can model the possibilities for new politics that can go on to be employed at the state and national levels.

While a movement organizer's broad ambition of social transformation may underlie his goal, the planner's focus is more often on moving policy and projects. This raises a very specific question: Does the participation of social movement organizers in regional planning processes help achieve equity in ways that planning alone does not? The answer to this question lies in understanding the ways that social movement engagement with regional planning processes can lead to new issues as well as new actors. To explore this, consider the community participation tradition in planning.

How Has Participation Intersected with Planning?

Genuine participation in the planning process requires both planners and the community to engage with each other. The relationship between them is usually unclear and sometimes contentious. Some argue that, because planners generally have more power than community members, they also have more responsibility to design a just process. While the planning profession has a strong tradition of taking care in designing effective participatory processes as well as a strand of promoting community empowerment, its reputation for effectively engaging with or supporting strong, independent social movement organizations is much weaker.

During the 1960s, when model cities programs included an element of community empowerment, Sherry Arnstein (1969) published her classic "Ladder of Citizen Participation," in which she situates community power—or the lack thereof—in the public decision-making process. Four years earlier, Paul Davidoff (1965) defined advocacy planning as how planners might include or represent the voices of the poor in a pluralist planning process. Although participation and advocacy planning literatures typically have been separated in the urban planning curriculum, we suggest that they are two sides of the same coin.

On one side, public agencies choose how to engage in public participation by approaching the mixed question of intent and ability. Nicholas Freudenberg, Barbara Israel, and Manuel Pastor (2010) offer a typology of participation strategies they label "Potemkin," "kabuki," and "authentic." Potemkin participation concerns facades, like those erected to dupe Russian monarchs into perceiving villages where there really were none. Potemkin planning is about including communities in formal hearings only after the actual decisions already have been made. Kabuki participation takes its name from classic Japanese theater that is characterized by highly stylized drama and elaborate makeup; it is the sort of participation where experts may spar with each other (e.g., using environmental impact reports). Another example is seen when opportunities are created for communities to rush formal hearings with protests rather than proposals. Often the intent behind both Potemkin and kabuki participation is simply to fulfill magisterial planning requirements or deflect criticism from a planning agency.

Authentic participation, on the other hand, seeks community voices and common ground. Although planners routinely are taught how to fill out environmental impact report (EIR) forms, analyze demographic data, or work with geographic information systems (GIS), they also require distinct skills and techniques that will enable participation (Freudenberg, Israel, and Pastor 2010). Community-based participatory research—wherein community residents participate in selecting issues, designing studies, interpreting findings, and presenting results to policy makers in order to reduce their burden and promote better public policies (Minkler et al. 2008)—is one of the most widely accepted ways of involving communities and building community capacity for effective participation (Ellis and Shepard 2004; Israel et al. 2005).

The literature also highlights that "participation without redistribution of power is an empty and frustrating process for the powerless" (Arnstein 1969, 359). As a result, Arnstein's top rung on the ladder of participation is "citizen control," while the top rung on Elizabeth Rocha's (1997) ladder of empowerment is "political empowerment," and Freudenberg (2004) refers to the highest level on his continuum of community as the "right to make decisions." At the risk of oversimplification, while each of these ladders adds its own perspective to political engagement and uses slightly different terms, at the top of all of them is a community that has the power to affect the decisions governing their lives.

Rocha (1997) suggests that as planners disburse funds for programs or institutions, they consider the empowerment ladder so that the neighborhood reflects a continuum of empowering institutions. This is certainly advocacy planning. Pierre Clavel (1994, 147), however, raises an important issue when he asks, "[Can] advocate planners serve neighborhood community interests when they [are] funded by a wider constituency?" The implicit notion here is that the neighborhood is pitted against the larger city or the region. This leads to the following question: What do advocacy planning and building community capacity mean when the playing field is the region?

Social Movements, Regional Scale, and Equity Planning

In general, regional planning is even more likely than local planning to be inauthentic—that is, to fall into the Potemkin or kabuki category. In part, this is because regional planning itself is often weak in jurisdictional strength and form and poorly designed in terms of reflecting community will. For example, consider the relatively low levels of power exercised by the typical council of governments (COG), which often amounts to little more than a discussion group with its principal influence being its capacity to control transportation dollars, but not economic incentives or land use decisions.

Moreover, the general political structure of a COG—one jurisdiction, one vote—is designed to be a sort of Potemkin facade. If Los Angeles (population 3.7 million) has the same vote as Lomita (population 20,000), the tiny city can offset the many-times-larger one in the general assembly of the local COG. Thus, the real decisions are more than likely going to be made elsewhere.[1] This is one of the reasons why so many new business-led regionalist groupings, such as Joint Venture: Silicon Valley Network or Chicago's Metro 2020, have taken over where voting rules fail and real politics begins.

Regional planning is also much less likely than traditional local planning to have planners themselves play a central role in advocating for social equity. While the early, classic statements of Edward Blakely (1989) and of Norman Krumholz and John Forester (1990) show that something of a tradition of equity planning exists at local or city levels, regional planners generally have not been in this camp and instead remain a bit more above the fray of localized political conflicts. To the extent that regional planning has been connected to some form of advocacy, this is more to businesses and environmentalists than to equity proponents. The resuscitation of regional planning, for example, has been driven primarily by concerns about economic competitiveness (Future-Works 2004; Henton, Melville, and Walesh 1997) or environmental and design issues including advocacy for smart growth or new urbanism. Frequently equity is mentioned as one of "the three *E*s" —environment, economics, and equity— but it is the weak corner of that triangle.

Even for those equity-oriented planners who might want to work at the regional level, it is hard to know where to start. Myron Orfield (1997), for

---

1. The Southern California Association of Governments (SCAG) also has a regional council in which smaller cities are grouped together into districts. Lomita, for example, is combined with Carson and Torrance, but even there the City of Los Angeles has only one vote despite having 15 times the population of the Lomita district.

example, has suggested that the key to regional equity is tax sharing between cities and suburbs. As much analytical sense as that makes, it has been virtually impossible to sell politically. David Rusk (1993) points to the power of annexation, which is also hard to "will" into existence. Not only are city-county consolidations rare, they can generate as much community resistance as support; even minority communities worried about their dilution of place-based political power may balk (Savitch and Vogel 2004).

In short, the structural features that trigger regional inequity may not be amenable to direct efforts to reverse them and may explain why so much of the organizing is in areas such as transportation. While these efforts may be less directly related to the causes of regional inequity, they at least afford levers with which to make change, and they can make the promise of regional equity more real to community groups representing distressed neighborhoods.

Finally, the challenge of community capacity is particularly important in the regional arena. Organizing to represent a neighborhood is difficult enough. Organizing to link poor neighborhoods together and secure their collective voice in regional planning exercises, however, requires groups to have a high level of research and technical capacity as well as an ability to make the approach relevant for community members and to engage them in processes that can seem abstract and far removed from their daily lives. Wedding the technical skills with the organizing and narrative elements also can be tough. It requires anchor organizations with sufficient scale to do the work, experience in a wide range of issues, and ability to select surgically the exact point at which they will intervene. As discussed below, at critical times in recent years Los Angeles happened to have such a group, while Sacramento did not, and this disparity was reflected in the outcomes.

TRANSPORTATION PLANNING AND REGIONAL EQUITY

The central animating concern of regional equity is how regional forces impact and could improve social equity. Regional equity is a broad concept that covers a wide range of issue areas that are as diverse as affordable housing, workforce training, tax policy, and the power of annexation. To offer a clearer view of the interplay of regional planners and regional equity proponents, we focus on a single issue area (transportation) in one state (California) because holding the issue area and overall state legislation constant can control for certain background elements and allow us to draw clearer lessons.

Transportation is a particularly instructive arena for examining dynamics between planners and social movements for a number of reasons. First, in the past, transportation policy and planning have comprised a key component of the processes that create regional inequality. For example, spending on federal highway systems and the way funding highway construction continues to be favored over creation and maintenance of public transit has fueled urban sprawl and the outward movement of resources. Tackling transportation, therefore, is crucial to creating more equitable regions.

Second, transportation is tremendously important for shaping economic opportunity for disadvantaged communities. To the degree that our metropolitan regions have sprawled, spatial mismatch between jobs and under- and unemployed residents has been the result. Transit systems are important but not sufficient to close the gap. (Social networks and job training also matter.) Equally important, transit systems can be key job creators both in the construction phase and in the industries that transit serves.

Finally, and perhaps most significantly, transportation has been a spark for many of the social movement efforts that have been at the forefront of the regional equity movement. It is where organizers have chosen to build capacity and intervene, allowing us to consider the impact on planning of well-developed organizing efforts.

In Los Angeles, for example, the Bus Riders Union (BRU) was formed in 1992 as a way of organizing that city's low-income and working-poor populations. In 1994, popular protests against a major fare hike were led by the union, which successfully obtained temporary restraining orders to stop the Metropolitan Transportation Authority from its fare hike implementation. By 1994, the BRU and others filed a lawsuit against the transit authority arguing that suburb-serving light rail was funded at the expense of the bus system, which was used by the region's working poor. That eventually led to a 1996 ruling that reversed a hike in bus fares and mandated the authority to make a $1 billion investment to increase bus service (Gottlieb et al. 2005). Since that time, the BRU has grown to include some 3,000 dues-paying members, of which 200 are active. Accomplishments since 1994 include redistribution of more than $2.5 billion to bus riders through federal civil rights consent decrees, substantial expansion of service hours, expansion in ridership, new infrastructure (including bus-only lanes) to reduce transit times, and maintenance of low fares.

In Detroit, MOSES, an affiliate of the Gamaliel Foundation, provides another example. Founded in 1997 with the explicit goal of becoming a social movement regionalist organization, it has grown to include more than 65 faith-based congregations and five institutions of higher learning. Perhaps its greatest success was related to the Fix-it First proposals, which required the State of Michigan to prioritize repairing and maintaining existing roads, sewers, water systems, and schools ahead of building any new infrastructure—an approach publicly embraced in September 2004 by Governor Jennifer Granholm at a mass meeting of 4,500 people.

Promoting transit was an integral part of this initiative. Detroit's extremely limited rail system circulates solely around the downtown, and its highly fragmented transit system has different authorities for Detroit and the suburbs. This patchwork creates significant problems for many people who need to commute from Detroit to suburban job locations, as it requires transferring among buses at the border of the city, and often city schedules are not coordinated with those in the suburbs. In 2003, MOSES was instrumental in pushing for creation of DARTA (Detroit Area Regional Transportation Authority) as part of an inter-

governmental agreement among three public agencies: the City of Detroit, which
runs city-based transit; SMART (Suburban Mobility Authority for Regional
Transportation); and RTCC, the Regional Transit Coordinating Council (Pastor,
Benner, and Matsuoka 2009).

Another example is the Northwest Indiana Interfaith Federation, which
came into being in Gary in 1996 and merged suburban organizations with
those in the distressed central area of the city. While Operation Holy Ground,
the federation's first campaign, was decidedly local and focused on getting
local city councils to take direct action in reducing the number of drug houses
operating in their neighborhoods, the federation realized that no matter how
many abandoned buildings and crack dealers were removed, the systemic
causes of concentrated poverty deeply rooted in regional patterns of development and investment remained (Cheryl Rivera personal communication, 22
February 2006).

The federation chose transit for its first regional campaign and built on
data indicating that less than 1 percent of the $880 million regional transpor-
tation budget then in effect for the Northwestern Indiana Regional Planning
Commission was proposed for bus service. The federation argued that an efficient regional transportation system was being hindered by the fragmentation
of local systems, which were often designed to make access to white suburban
areas more difficult for central city blacks. Following the lead of the BRU in Los
Angeles, the federation cited Title VI of the 1964 Civil Rights Act and charged
the metropolitan planning organization (MPO) with distributing funds in a
racially discriminatory manner. This resulted in the establishment of a regional,
community-based coalition with sufficient influence and power over elected
officials to direct the establishment of the Regional Transportation Authority,
which meets the needs of the region including, in particular, the urban core
(Pastor, Benner, and Matsuoka 2009).

The Transportation Equity Network (TEN), originally founded under the
aegis of the Center for Community Change, a longtime national community
development intermediary, links these efforts together. TEN includes regional
equity champions from around the United States, such as the Los Angeles–
based Alameda Corridor Coalition and BRU, MOSES, the Northwest Indiana
Interfaith Federation, Missouri's Metropolitan Congregations United, and
West Harlem Environmental Action from New York City. While the Gamaliel
Foundation's affiliates help anchor TEN, the network provides important and
specific national infrastructure for other equity advocates. It has scored important national successes that include the insertion of language that encourages
local hiring and secures employment for low-income communities into a federal transportation reauthorization bill enacted in 2005 (Swanstrom and Banks
2009; Swanstrom and Transportation Equity Network 2008).

In short, transportation is a clear interest of both equity organizers and
regional planners, many of whom have direct responsibility for helping to allo-

cate transportation dollars. We next explore the intersection between planners and organizers in two distinct processes—a more top-down effort undertaken in Sacramento and what eventually became a bottom-up approach in Los Angeles.

REGIONAL PLANNING AND COMMUNITY ENGAGEMENT IN SACRAMENTO

California has seen the emergence of "blueprint planning" as a way to engage civic leaders, citizens, and other stakeholders in a process of deliberation centered on desired growth patterns. Blueprint planning emerged in the 1990s in response to California's sprawling growth and worsening transportation problems. Starting in 2005 the state legislature funded the California Regional Blueprint Planning Program, a voluntary, competitive grant program that encouraged MPOs, COGs, and rural regional transportation planning agencies to conduct comprehensive scenario planning. This results in consensus among regional leaders, local governments, and stakeholders on a preferred growth scenario, or Blueprint, for a 20-year (or longer) planning horizon. Blueprint plans aim to align transportation, housing, environmental protection, economic development, and livability objectives. The Blueprint program also creates a Blueprint learning network by which it shares lessons and best practices across the state (Innes, Di Vittorio, and Booher 2009).

According to the California Department of Transportation, "regional blueprints are [designed to be] collaborative planning processes that engage residents of a region in articulating a vision for the long term future of the region. The vision is developed from residents' values and priorities, and informed by advanced GIS modeling and visualization tools that demonstrate the impacts of growth and planning decisions" (Caltrans, n.d.). Generally, the process centers on the presentation of alternative growth scenarios for regions that can include denser, transit-oriented development.

Blueprint Planning in Sacramento

The Sacramento region implemented blueprint planning early. The planning process, which ran between 2002 and December 2004, when the final plan was adopted, was led as a partnership of the Sacramento Area Council of Governments (SACOG) and Valley Vision (n.d.), an independent, regional collaborative leadership organization dedicated to "working to secure the social, environmental and economic health of the Sacramento Region." The two-year-long planning process involved thousands of citizens from throughout the region, who used modeling technology that provided real-time feedback on policy choices. SACOG has received multiple national awards, both for the content of the Blueprint and the process that produced it. California Senator Barbara Boxer described the leadership behind the Blueprint process as "a model for other cities across California and around the nation," and Darrell Steinberg, the state senate's president protem, said that "communities throughout California and throughout the country are beginning to recognize that the SACOG Blue-print is in fact the blueprint for the entire country" (SACOG 2010a).

The planning process began from estimates arrived at in a base case study: By 2050, the region would grow from 1.9 million to 3.6 million residents, and the number of homes would double from 713,000 to more than 1.5 million. If contemporary development trends continued unabated, 661 square miles of vacant land would be converted to urban development, residents would drive more miles annually (with the average household spending an additional 30 minutes per day in the car), and an estimated 43 percent of wetlands and 21 percent of oak woodlands would be damaged.

The Blueprint preferred scenario for 2025 that was adopted as the ultimate plan is based on smart growth principles, which include transportation choices with more nonautomobile options, mixed-use and compact developments, housing choice and diversity, greater use of existing assets such as redevelop-ment and infill projects, quality design to make compact development more attractive, and natural resource conservation (SACOG, n.d.).

If the Blueprint were developed in full, residential density would increase. In the preferred scenario, only 305 square miles of new urbanized land would be created, compared to 661 square miles in the base-case scenario, and only 102 square miles of agricultural land would be converted to urban uses, com-pared to the base-case's scenario of 166. Communities would become more pedestrian friendly, with 69 percent of the population living in areas with good or excellent pedestrian features, compared to 34 percent in the base-case sce-nario; and 53 percent, compared to the base case's 26 percent, would live in communities with a balanced mix of jobs and housing.

In terms of transportation, access to transit would be emphasized along with reduction in overall vehicle miles traveled. In the base case scenario, only 2 percent of new housing and 5 percent of new jobs would be located within walking distance of a 15-minute bus or train service, but in the Blueprint sce-nario these figures rise to 38 and 41 percent, respectively. Automobiles would still be the dominant means of transportation, but the percentage of trips taken by car would drop from 93.7 to 83.9, total vehicles miles traveled would drop from 47.2 miles per household per day to 34.9, and the daily minutes of vehicle travel would drop from 81 to 67. The Blueprint preferred scenario envisioned some $12.8 billion in new transportation investments designed to expand tran-sit options and improve pedestrian and bicycle access as well as urban road infra-structure.

From the perspective of smart growth principles at a regional scale, the Blueprint is truly impressive. The $3 million planning effort demonstrated that a coordinated investment in redirecting transportation investments and in changing land use decisions can have a substantial impact on development pat-terns at a regional scale, including reductions in air pollution and greenhouse gas emissions.

The public participation process involved in the Blueprint planning was also remarkable. In all parts of the region more than 30 neighborhood-scale workshops were held to discuss the implications of various development scenarios. More than 1,000 citizens had the opportunity to be involved directly in the planning process and express their preferences for various types of planning solutions. These neighborhood workshops were followed by countywide scenario discussions in five of the six counties in the region. El Dorado County did not participate due to legal issues surrounding its general plan. Finally, more than 1,400 people participated in a final regional forum held on 30 April 2004.

The full Metropolitan Transportation Plan 2035 (MTP2035) that emerged during the blueprint process also addresses significant transportation-equity goals. As part of the Federal Highway Administration–mandated analysis of environmental justice (EJ) concerns, SACOG identified EJ areas throughout the region by using census-block groups where, in 2000, the population was comprised of 60 percent or more people of color, 40 percent or more of all households earned less than one-half the metropolitan statistical area (MSA) median income, or both. These areas amounted to 21 percent of the region's total population.

If the MTP were to be implemented as planned, SACOG estimates that, by 2035, 49.9 percent of the population in these EJ areas would live within one-quarter mile of high-frequency transit lines (up from 18.9 percent in 2005) compared with 6 percent of the population living in non-EJ areas (up from only 0.8 percent). The MTP envisions a 21 percent increase in investment in transit services by 2035, with a 150 percent increase in bus and rail service hours, including an increase in midday transit frequency. The MTP also envisions an increase in jobs accessible within a 45-minute transit travel time in EJ areas from 200,000 in 2005 to nearly 350,000 in 2035 (SACOG 2008).

Whether the region is able to meet these smart growth and equity goals remains to be seen. Much of what will determine this is controlled by local jurisdictions, not SACOG itself. Land use control remains almost completely local in California, and most local authorities in the region have a poor record for supporting dense or transit-oriented development. Furthermore, the improvements in transit service and expenditures envisioned in MTP2035 were contingent on revenue assumptions, including increased state support for transportation, that now seem highly unrealistic in light of California's continuing fiscal challenges.

The MTP2035 also assumed that by 2012 voters in Sacramento County would approve an additional 0.25 percent sales tax to support transit. This seemed reasonable during the economic buoyancy in 2007, but appears to be unlikely in the post-crash 2010s. Perhaps most important, SACOG itself only controls decisions on about 15 percent of the funds in their plan, and the implementation of the plan would reflect a significant expansion of local funding sources (including developers' fees) in overall transportation investment (SACOG 2008).

Still, signs that development patterns in the region have shifted somewhat are evident. According to SACOG Executive Director Mike McKeever, in 2004 detached single-family properties on lots larger than 5,500 square feet represented 68 percent of existing housing stock, and 80 percent of new housing being constructed. By 2008, only 32 percent of new houses were single-family units on large lots, making it nearly equal to the Blueprint's goal of 30 percent, and a substantial increase was seen in new attached residential units. Substantial progress had also been made in new housing construction near the three main employment centers in the region, with 25,000 of the 40,000 new housing units near these job centers that had been projected by the Blueprint were built, under construction, approved for development, or in the application stage (McKeever 2010). At a five-year-anniversary event celebrating the Blueprint, clear evidence of new mixed-used, transit-oriented development projects had emerged in multiple communities throughout the region (SACOG 2010b).

Inequities in transportation and transportation spending remain, however. Overall, the Blueprint envisions spending $14.3 billion, or 34 percent of total funds, on transit between 2008 and 2035. Although by U.S. standards this amount is admirably high, the Blueprint target cannot be reached without passage of an envisioned 0.25 percent sales tax increase and expanded state support for transit. Our analysis of all funding for projects actively programmed in the region's current Metropolitan Transportation Improvement Program (MTIP) found that only 20 percent of regional funding was earmarked for transit, compared to 78 percent for roads and 2 percent specifically for bicycles and pedestrians.[2] While Sacramento County garners the majority of total funds—an estimated $6 billion for currently active projects, more than half of the total $11.5 billion allocated—when adjusted for population, the county actually has the lowest per capita total of all counties in the region and only slightly more than half of what is spent per capita in Placer County (table 4.1).

Despite the impressively broad public decision-making opportunities surrounding the Blueprint process, SACOG's formal decision-making structures remain skewed toward small, predominantly white, suburban and rural jurisdictions in the region. A Brookings Institution study of 50 large MPOs in the United States found that SACOG had among the highest of the discrepancies between representation on the board based simply on jurisdictions as opposed to a hypothetical weighted-representation system based on the size of the populations in those jurisdictions. The magnitude of this discrepancy is essentially a measure of over-representation of suburban rather than urban populations (Sanchez 2005). SACOG's formal voting structure requires all votes to be approved through a population-weighted process as well as those that are jurisdiction-

---

2. The MTIP covers fiscal years 2007/2008 to 2011/2012, but some of the funds allocated to these projects were actually spent prior to 2007 or are expected to be spent later than 2012. Thanks to Bryan Pon, University of California Davis, for processing these statistics.

Table 4.1	Funding Allocated in SACOG's Metropolitan Transportation Improvement Plan, 2009–2012 *Source: Authors' analysis of SACOG MTIP 2009–2012.*							
	TOTAL (IN MILLIONS)				PER CAPITA			
COUNTY	ROADS	TRANSIT	BIKE/PED	TOTAL	ROADS	TRANSIT	BIKE/PED	TOTAL
EL DORADO	$771.5	$6.7	$13.5	$791.7	$4,399	$38	$77	$4,514
PLACER	$2,547.2	$65.1	$20.6	$2,632.9	$7,658	$196	$62	$7,916
SACRAMENTO	$3,959.5	$1,856.9	$173.6	$5,990.0	$2,868	$1,345	$126	$4,338
SUTTER	$579.3	$1.8	$0.6	$581.7	$6,353	$20	$6	$6,379
YOLO	$627.2	$363.1	$24.9	$1,015.2	$3,234	$1,872	$128	$5,234
YUBA	$438.7	$2.3	$1.4	$442.4	$6,127	$32	$19	$6,178
MULTIPLE COUNTIES	$423.3	$54.4	$0.6	$478.3				
TOTAL	$9,346.7	$2,350.4	$235.2	$11,932.3	$4,162	$1,047	$105	$5,314

Figures for per capita expenditures in columns 6 through 9 are derived by dividing the corresponding total dollar amounts (columns 2 through 5) by U.S. Census estimates of the total population (in 2008) of each county and of the six-county region.

based, but this doesn't affect who is actually represented on the board itself. Similarly, while SACOG doesn't keep official records of the race of their board members, a review in 2010 of photos, surnames, and online biographies suggested that, of the 33 board members, as few as 5 had racial backgrounds other than non-Hispanic white. Non-Hispanic whites may therefore constitute as much as 85 percent of the SACOG board, compared to the population in the region, which is only 59 percent non-Hispanic white (see figure 4.1).

SACOG is clearly a highly effective MPO, and the open, participatory planning processes they have developed should be lauded. At the same time, inequality in transportation spending and ongoing suburban biases in formal decision-making structures remain substantial. Now we consider how social movement organizations have engaged SACOG's participation processes, which are essentially driven from the top down, and the ongoing inequalities in influence and power.

Social Movements and the Blueprint
Social movement organizations became engaged in the blueprint process, but the obstacles they encountered in trying to make a significant impact on its planning component are part of a more general problem. In some ways social movement organizing efforts in Sacramento face a context that seems quite promising, but so far it has provided a somewhat weak and fragmented base for organizing. For example, the Sacramento metropolitan region has one of the

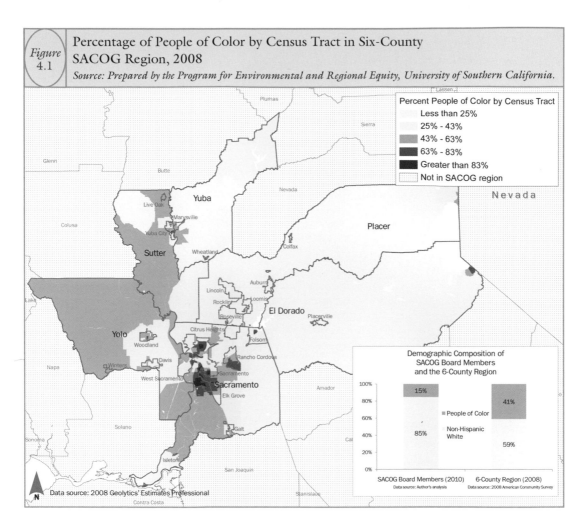

Figure 4.1

Percentage of People of Color by Census Tract in Six-County SACOG Region, 2008

Source: Prepared by the Program for Environmental and Regional Equity, University of Southern California.

highest unionization rates of all such regions in the United States.[3] Yet more than 60 percent of the region's union members are in public sector unions, which have had limited experience with social mobilization. The largest is the SEIU 1000, one of the strongest progressive political forces in California, but its focus principally has been on statewide policy and bargaining issues, rather than on building regional power. Much of the success of the Central Labor Council, the leader of which has a strong social movement orientation, has been in electoral politics, with few significant victories in private sector organizing or policy in recent years.

The Sacramento region also has another possible base for organizing in its large and diverse immigrant population. In fact in 2002, the Harvard Civil Rights Project determined that the city of Sacramento, based on its broad racial representation and relatively high levels of neighborhood integration, was the most diverse city in the country (Stodghill and Bower 2002). In contrast to

---

3. In 2009, the total union membership rate in the Sacramento-Arden-Arcade-Roseville Metropolitan Statistical Area was 23.5 percent (www.unionstats.com).

Los Angeles, where large-scale Latino immigration has provided a strong social movement base, throughout the Sacramento region immigration has been more diffuse and less politically visible.

Its role as the state capital makes Sacramento a frequent site of large-scale marches and demonstrations, but more often than not these are directed at influencing state-level policies. Many progressive organizations and activists who live in the region end up focusing more time on advocacy for state policy and neglecting building regional movements. Progressive elected officials, meanwhile, often use local office as a springboard to state-level office, which contributes further to the diffusion of attention to regional issues.[4]

In this context, during the first decade of the twenty-first century ACORN (Association of Community Organizations for Reform Now) was among the social movement groups that engaged most strongly with regional equity issues. For example, had it been enacted, California Assembly Bill 680, introduced by Darrell Steinberg in 2002, would have reallocated regional sales tax growth based on population share and smart growth policies designed to link affordable housing and job access. ACORN's mobilization of support was classic regional equity medicine stemming straight from the thought processes of Myron Orfield. It responded to the fiscalization of land use that has happened all over the United States but has been particularly prominent in California due to the limits on property taxes posed by that state's Proposition 13.[5] Classic regional equity organizing, with ACORN working in close collaboration with Legal Services of Northern California (LSNC), provided public support in the Sacramento region for the bill. While it passed the assembly, A.B. 680 lost in the senate, largely because of opposition from forces outside the Sacramento region that had concerns about the potential consequences elsewhere and the redistribution of local sales tax revenue that might result.

Thus, when the blueprint process was launched at the end of 2002, ACORN and its allies already understood the importance of regional planning and appreciated the challenges posed by passing major new legislation and policies. While Valley Vision and SACOG led the broad public-participation process, LSNC, in close collaboration with ACORN and other community organizations, began a process of educating and mobilizing community residents to participate actively in the blueprint process and ensure that equity principles were reflected in the Blueprint's neighborhood meetings. Starting in February 2003, and during the following year, LSNC coordinated neighborhood meetings that involved leaders

---

4. For example, Darrell Steinberg served on the Sacramento City Council from 1992 to 1998, before he moved to the California assembly and later senate.

5. "Fiscalization of land use" refers to the increasing importance of encouraging revenue production as the primary goal of land use decisions made by fiscally constrained local authorities. Promotion of retail sales and levying fees on new developments are methods that have been used particularly frequently. This trend emerged when the antitax environment of the 1970s and 1980s held sway. See Chapman 2008, and Schwartz 1997.

from more than 41 different community-based organizations to discuss the Blue-print and its consequences.[6]

On 20 September 2003, these organizations held a rally that brought more than 300 people to Trinity Cathedral in downtown Sacramento. Assembly-man Darrell Steinberg, Supervisor Roger Dickinson, and other local dignitaries were there, and they demanded equity and inclusion in local growth policies. The Blueprint findings to date and the importance of the countywide sessions were highlighted at the rally. Working in this manner, these organizations were able to prepare community leaders to participate in 18 of the 25 neighborhood sessions that took place between 18 March and 15 September 2003. Further-more, advocates were able to convince SACOG and Valley Vision of the need to include three specific diversity sessions in the blueprint planning process. These were specifically focused on trying to engage marginalized communities that frequently feel disconnected from traditional planning institutions and efforts. They were held in Del Paso Heights, South Sacramento, and the central city and focused on turning out those areas' representatives from the African Ameri-can, Asian, and Latino communities. Turnout exceeded expectations.

Despite this impressive mobilization, leaders of the initiative characterized much of their work as catching up to SACOG's schedule of Blueprint neigh-borhood meetings, which often amounted to two per week. In this process, at least early on, the original intent of conducting pretraining was abandoned in an effort just to turn out constituents to the sessions. Over time, the empha-sis of LSNC- and ACORN-led efforts moved beyond preparing for Blueprint meetings toward providing to community groups more general education on the impact of land use policies on families and neighborhoods.

Brian Augusta, LSNC's staff attorney who led this effort, also relied on leaders from community-based organizations to help spread the message of the importance of land use planning. Working with leaders from housing- and homeless-advocacy groups, social services providers, the faith community, and civil rights groups, Augusta created a land use leadership group, which met at least once a month from June through December 2003. Initially many of the

---

6. Organizations involved in this process included ACORN, Asian Resources, Building Unity, California Coalition for Rural Housing, Californians for Disability Rights, Chicano Consor-tium, Church Women United, Community Housing Opportunities Corporation, Environ-mental Council of Sacramento, Gray Panthers, Habitat for Humanity, Housing California, Housing Now, Interfaith Service Bureau, League of Women Voters, LSNC, Living Wage Campaign, Loaves & Fishes, Mercy Housing California, Mutual Assistance Network of Del Paso Heights, Older Women's League, Paratransit, Resources for Independent Living, Sac-ramento Area Emergency Housing, Sacramento Cottage Housing, Sacramento County Alli-ance of Neighborhoods, Sacramento Home Loan Counseling Center, Sacramento Homeless Organizing Committee, Sacramento Housing Alliance, Sacramento Self-Help Housing, Sacra-mento Valley Organizing Community, SEIU 1877, Serna Village Residents, Sierra Club, Spiri-tual Life Center, Strategies to Empower People, St. John's Shelter, St. Matthew's Episcopal Church, Surface Transportation Policy Project, Training Toward Self-Reliance, Transitional Living & Community Support, and Women's Empowerment Project.

leaders had little interest in the blueprint process, which they viewed either as irrelevant to their concerns or not inclusive. Nonetheless, all these groups were committed to regional equity and saw the value of land use planning in furthering that goal. The meetings resulted in agreement on a set of principles, which included stipulations that 15 percent of all new housing should be affordable to low-, very low–, and extremely low–income families and that a fair share of affordable housing should be built in every neighborhood.

Beyond the Blueprint

Participants also agreed broadly that a vehicle should be created to continue and expand their collaboration after expiration of the funding for this specific Blueprint effort. Leadership from the organizations crafted a set of principles to establish such a vehicle. The goal was not to create a single organization, but rather to develop a capacity-building approach that would help existing organizations in the region better articulate a common land use and equity perspective in their own work. Then, through this common message, they would bring greater focus and unity in the overlapping areas of their multiple agendas, as described below.

> When crafting its message, grass roots organizations consider their membership as the primary audience. They are successful within the cultural context of their organization. The message, however, may not resonate with elected officials or the public in general. The message may appear too strident or narrowly defined. Few groups have the capacity to craft a message for a larger audience and one that has the potential to unify the groups. We propose providing this capacity through staff who are constantly attentive to the internal agenda of the organizations, but free of the cultural imperatives which make collaboration so difficult. Staff would pick up on unifying themes, crafting messages that would resonate within each organization rather than restate its agenda. It is our experience that a well-crafted message can unify the groups in a campaign while they are each free to spin the message within the cultural context of their own organization. The message is not imposed, but offered as a unifying theme. (LSNC 2004)

LSNC also suggested creating a vehicle that could conduct research into and provide public education on these issues; support leadership development; and target advocacy, which required prioritizing efforts among the region's 28 jurisdictions—far too many for any grassroots organization to monitor effectively.

Ultimately, in 2007 the Coalition on Regional Equity (CORE) was created formally. It involves a broad coalition of affordable housing developers; environmentalists; advocates focused on transportation, the homeless, and poverty; social service providers; organized labor; the faith community; civil rights leaders; and health groups. Building on the organizational and social networks initiated during the blueprint process and subsequent affordable housing efforts, increasingly the coalition is visible in regional politics. Yet CORE decided specifically to focus on transportation equity as a priority area only in late 2009. To date, in part working closely with the Center for Regional Change at the University of California Davis, much of this work has focused on gaining an overview of regional patterns of transportation spending and decision making.

CORE also protested planned layoffs and service cuts at Sacramento Regional Transit, and it advocated for more transit spending overall. While the coalition has embraced promoting transportation equity as one of several key areas, few social movement organizations in the region have a history in advocating for transportation issues or knowledge of key transportation policies and decision-making processes. This has inhibited the coalition's ability to identify an issue quickly and mount a strategic campaign to win justice in this area.

Thus, the blueprint process itself and subsequent regional transportation decision processes remain driven by planning professionals and the region's wealthier residents, who feel more comfortable with these professionally driven planning processes. Involvement from marginalized communities and under-represented populations continues to take a back seat in relation to the economic growth, environmental concerns, and smart growth principles that drove the blueprint process. Indeed, in a recent celebration of the process's fifth anniversary, it was noted that while SACOG had made great progress on the environmental and design elements of the Blueprint, far too little attention had been paid to equity. Such attention will come from the goodwill and commitment of the planners who are involved, but it will also require an activist presence that can hold the Blueprint accountable to equity concerns.

TRANSPORTATION PLANNING AND MOVEMENT OF GOODS IN LOS ANGELES

The title of a chapter in Edward Soja's *Postmodern Geographies* (1989) has always struck us as having both an element of truth and more than an ounce of chutzpah: "It All Comes Together in Los Angeles." Soja meant that the city's polycentric nature, which represents a distinct break with the Chicago tradition, as well as the high levels of deindustrialization, racial inequality, and social tension that wracks Los Angeles reflect a series of intersecting trends that would mark the future for the whole country.

We continue to be impressed by this title, but would argue that, in fact, it all really comes together at the ports of Los Angeles and Long Beach, where nearly half of America's imports are off-loaded, even as the industrial landscape just to their north in South and Southeast L.A. has been devastated by globalization. Diesel traffic from trucks streaming in to pick up goods leaves a toxic soup that deeply impacts nearby communities of color and makes the area a hotbed for EJ activism. The transformation of the local trucking industry, from a system of large companies with predominantly white unionized

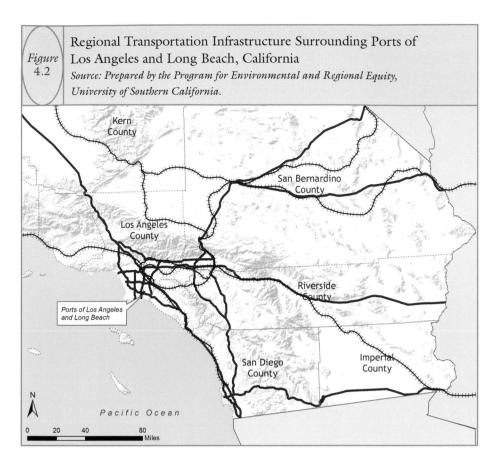

Figure 4.2
Regional Transportation Infrastructure Surrounding Ports of Los Angeles and Long Beach, California
Source: Prepared by the Program for Environmental and Regional Equity, University of Southern California.

employees to one comprised largely of Latino-immigrant independent owner-operators who barely make ends meet, is emblematic of the shaky labor systems and changing demographics in our country as a whole.

At the same time, however, these ports are forming a positive future for Los Angeles. They make up a linchpin in an overall effort to promote Southern California's logistics industry, a sector that posted significant job growth prior to the recession and involves middle-skill employment that would seem suited to the less-skilled and predominantly immigrant workforce in Los Angeles. It is little wonder that the ports and logistics attracted the attention and enthusiasm of regional planners at the Southern California Association of Governments (SCAG). As we argue, however, that attention bore little fruit until a group of social movement organizations—many of which were rooted in the regional equity perspective—took up the task of making the ports more sustainable, inclusive, and equitable.

Ports and Possibilities

An estimated 40 percent of U.S. imports move through either the port of Los Angeles or that of Long Beach (KERNCOG, SANDAG, and SCAG 2005), and Los Angeles has become the main conduit between the Asian market and consumers in the United States. Figure 4.2 shows the transportation infrastructure of the region. Through the economic downturn of the 1990s, the logistics industry was one of the only sectors to experience job growth (Husing 2004), although the fragmentation of its labor force, especially with the emergence of increasingly vulnerable and poorly remunerated owner-operators, has left clear winners and losers. The environmental side of the equation also accounted for some losers because the ports alone contribute an estimated 20 percent to Southern California's total diesel particulate emissions (Hricko 2008), which can cause asthma and are associated with cancer risk.[7] Logistics-generated truck traffic along the Interstate 710 freeway, the region's major transit corridor, increases the industry's overall contribution to health threats. The communities that border these ports and the I-710 are home largely to Latino, immigrant, and low-income families, and their excessive exposure to diesel particulates is now treated as an EJ issue. While the nation as a whole benefits from imported goods, and the region overall benefits from growth in the logistics business, some communities bear the environmental and health burdens directly.

Since regional leaders increasingly see the need to turn the benefits of the area's being a throughway for international commerce into local economic strength, improving the environmental sustainability of the ports and the logistics industry has become of strategic importance. Just after the turn of the twenty-first century, SCAG officials noted that, among 17 comparison regions, the Los Angeles metropolitan area ranked lowest in per capita income. SCAG argued forcefully that the logistics sector offered one means to pump up the economy and thereby increase per capita income and decrease the region's widening income divide. Regional economist John Husing (2004, iv) connected the dots in a report commissioned by SCAG.

> Investment in [logistics and distribution] would have the beneficial effect of allowing the region's logistics sector to accelerate by providing a growing base of good paying jobs which its marginally educated workers can learn via on-the-job experience and learning. This would appear to be the only route the region has available to helping those workers achieve growing standards of living while simultaneously correcting the recent deep slide in Southern California's relative prosperity vis-à-vis other major parts of the country. Importantly, this investment would do so while helping to mitigate the environmental difficulties caused by the inevitable increase in truck and rail traffic congestion and idling diesel engines.

Seeing this chance to tackle the economy, the environment, and equity simultaneously moved SCAG into action. In 2008, it published a goods-movement plan (SCAG 2008), and in 2010 it began reporting on the plan's implementation (SCAG 2010). At the same time, the port commissioners, looking at

7. The contribution figure includes only "on-port emissions," or those from ships, cargo-handling equipment, and in-port heavy duty trucks and locomotives (CARB 2006).

20-year projected increases in volume on the order of 300 percent, had drawn up plans for 84 development projects (LAANE 2007). But community opposition crystallized around serious environmental and EJ concerns, which stalled projects. Since the port area was plagued by air-related cancer and respiratory illness rates that are more than double those in the rest of the region, local community groups would not budge. For SCAG and the ports to get what they wanted, they needed to work with the community.

Ports and Politics

Equity planners' usual approach to this need to involve communities is to call for participatory planning. While this is good, it's also much harder to do in regional processes, which can seem distant to most would-be participants. Instead, a new social movement emerged to provide a sense of immediacy to community actors and a solution to the problem of balancing growth imperatives with the need to address both environmental and social equity issues affecting the corridor.

This movement came in the form of the Coalition for Clean and Safe Ports, an effort spearheaded by the labor-based Los Angeles Alliance for a New Economy (LAANE), which was able to secure passage of a Clean Trucks Program (CTP) for the port. Despite its labor focus, the real advantage LAANE brought to bear was as a coalition builder, something movement organizers often can do more effectively than planners.

LAANE is one of the pillars of regional equity in Southern California. The brainchild of Maria Elena Durazo, the current secretary of the highly influential AFL-CIO, LAANE started as a small think and action tank that promoted better conditions in the region's tourist industry.[8] It soon pivoted to embrace both public sector and development issues by working in coalition with unions, faith groups, and community organizations to secure a citywide Workers Retention Act in 1996, a citywide living wage ordinance in 1997, a community benefits agreement (CBA) for neighborhoods between the University of Southern California and the Staples Center in 2001, and another significant CBA at the Los Angeles airport in 2003. The latter also addressed EJ issues and the burden of noise and air pollution placed on low-income, minority neighborhoods. Subsequently, LAANE led an effort to stop Wal-Mart from building a store in the Southern California community of Inglewood in 2004 and is currently involved in a campaign to bring supermarkets—unionized, to be sure—to the "food deserts" of low-income South L.A.

As well as its actions, LAANE's framework marks the organization as a regional equity leader. It has utilized regional cluster analysis, identifying opportunities in industries such as tourism, the public sector, and now logistics that are rooted in Los Angeles and unable to move offshore to avoid worker pushback. The CBAs are also structured to take advantage of regional attractions

---

8. As of 2011, Madeline Janis, cofounder of what was then called the Tourism Industry Development Corporation, remains executive director of LAANE.

that are unlikely to move, and the regional framework has led them to build alliances with unlikely partners, including environmental leaders.

That history meant a great deal in the ports' work. Historically, unions and environmentalists have been in conflict, often with unions perceiving tighter environmental regulations to be potential job killers. EJ groups generally are smaller and can be wary of alliances with either mainstream environmentalists or strong labor groups. Putting these various interests together stymied SCAG, but not LAANE. Bringing its coalition-building experience to the table, LAANE worked hard to bring together the usual labor allies, such as the Teamsters, but also to welcome new allies, including mainstream environmental organizations such as the Natural Resources Defense Council, the Coalition for Clean Air, and community-based EJ groups such as East Yard Communities for Environmental Justice and the Coalition for a Safe Environment (Pastor, Benner, and Matsuoka 2009).[9]

Together, the Coalition for Clean & Safe Ports crafted its CTP to create better jobs for port drivers and cleaner neighborhoods in South L.A. and the region (LAANE 2007). The earlier deregulation of the trucking industry had led to a system of independent owner-operators in which drivers leased trucks and worked for hire. As a result, the rate of unionized truckers fell, and the trucking workforce shifted from being predominately white to principally Latino and immigrant; wages then fell to around $12 an hour after expenses (with no benefits). LAANE's (and the Teamsters') particular interest was in improving the lot of these workers, but they were also able to argue successfully that the then-current conditions of the drivers left little cash for truck upgrades. Transferring responsibility back to larger companies was thus key to meeting the environmental goals that would help the ports and the logistics industry realize their economic potential. The convenient side benefit was that workers would then be employed at those companies and open to unionization for purposes of improving working conditions.

The result of the organizing, which included attendance at formal hearings as well as a series of protests on the part of community members and truckers, was a clean air action plan adopted in 2006 by both ports. It required that 17,000 trucks be retrofitted or replaced to reduce emissions. This paved the way for the CTP, whose goal was to reduce port pollution from drayage (short-haul) trucks by 80 percent by 2012. The plan also included banning the most polluting trucks—those built before 1989—from entering port terminals by late 2008 and then in 2012 only allowing use of trucks meeting 2007 U.S. EPA emission standards.[10] To facilitate the transition, the ports agreed to implement a system of grants and subsidies for truck owners.

9. For more information on the coalition LAANE put together, see www.cleanandsafeports.org

10. The age of the fleet was indeed an issue. A saying in the industry holds that "ports are where old trucks go to die." Since this is short-haul work, breakdowns tend to be less problematic as they generally will occur close to home.

To implement the CTP, the coalition argued for a concessionaire system that would replace the independent owners with larger companies that have traditional employee relationships. The environmental argument for this system was that it would facilitate more rapid replacement of trucks because larger companies could bear the burden more easily and spread the risks across their larger fleets. This was perceived to be a very real issue because financially strapped small owner-operators were already cutting corners. They carved new treads in worn tires rather than replacing them, and used small, ad hoc shops, often on the side of the road, to do repairs rather than working with more sophisticated truck repair stations that could better maintain the sophisticated equipment in newer trucks. Therefore they would be hard pressed to take on either the debt to purchase a new truck or the ongoing costs of its maintenance. The labor angle suggested that replacing owner-operators with employers and employees would facilitate unionization.

The Port of Los Angeles decided to opt for the concessionaire approach, which incentivized then required licensed motor carriers to perform upgrades. Included in its plan was a requirement that, by 2013, independent owner-operators would no longer be allowed to serve the ports. In a federal suit based on the grounds that such regulation constituted an interference with interstate commerce, the American Trucking Association (ATA) won a temporary court order leaving the financial cost of clean-up on the owner-operators, who make about $10 to $11 per hour, yet their leased trucks require $60,000 of repairs over the span of a seven-year lease (Patel 2010).

Anti-union groups, which disagreed about or overlooked these high costs to drivers in the union-blocking independent-operator system, framed the concessionaire system as a strategy designed simply to boost union membership (PR Newswire 2010). In August 2010, however, a federal judge rejected the ATA's arguments and held that the port had the authority to require truck drivers and trucking companies to comply with its regulations. The judge ruled that air pollution from trucks had actually jeopardized the port's commercial future, with lawsuits over emissions stalling growth, and that the concessions agreement was a reasonable way for the port to manage its facilities (Dillon 2010).

The Port of Long Beach was dropped from the original lawsuit thanks to its negotiations with the ATA to drop the concessionaire requirement from its own clean trucks program. Patricia Castellanos, chair of the Coalition for Clean & Safe Ports (2008), publicly denounced this move. This meant that "drivers [at Long Beach] will also bear the responsibility for the proper maintenance of the trucks, fuel and all other associated operational costs, and their status will remain 'independent contractors'" (CFC et al. 2008, 2). A recent analysis, however, argued that the financing plan's structure puts drivers in a precarious situation. Daimler Truck Finance projects that 40 percent of the drivers will have difficulty making payments, which led the coalition to draw parallels between this strategy and the subprime mortgage crisis. Further, because drivers will be strapped for cash, they will be unlikely to perform routine maintenance, which keeps the trucks clean. The Long Beach version of the CTP, therefore, would be less likely to secure environmental or economic sustainability (Mongelluzzo 2010; White 2009).

Meanwhile, the Coalition for Clean & Safe Ports has been scaling up to the national level, making room for regionalist thinking in new places. Ports in New York–New Jersey, Oakland, and Seattle are forging ahead with their own variations on the CTP, encouraged by momentum from grassroots groups, which often represent those most affected by port pollution (Coalition for Clean & Safe Ports 2009). These coalitions are also pressuring Congress to "amend federal law to make it clear that local port officials can fully and legally implement the truck plan," avoiding lawsuits like those in California (Coalition for Clean & Safe Ports 2009). In late July 2010, Congressman Jerrold Nadler of New York introduced a Clean Ports Act modeled on the Los Angeles program and applicable to other ports. Such scaling-up from local and regional geographies to the national level is the stuff of social movements (Pastor and Ortiz 2009) and points to how regional equity efforts can be spread across the country, not simply by planners but by organizers.

During that period, the CTP won the EPA's 2009 Environmental Justice Achievement Award, and port pollution from the short-haul rigs already has been reduced by more than half. While port traffic itself has suffered from the Great Recession, the environmental roadblocks to logistics expansion have eased, and there is a reasonable chance that working conditions in that industry will improve as the economy eventually resumes growing.

Equity Advocates and Equity Planning

Simply stated, the backing of a social movement made it possible for regional and port planners to move forward. SCAG wanted to grow the logistics sector, with the ports at the heart of their plan for regional economic vitality. The port commissioners were all for growth, but community opposition prevented them from progressing. Plans, in short, were plentiful, but political support was lacking. Unlike Sacramento, Los Angeles enjoyed a standing infrastructure of community groups that had already gone regionalist (Pastor, Benner, and Matsuoka 2009). These groups also had a fairly sophisticated analysis of political and economic dynamics in the region and an ability to provide policy alternatives based on a coherent vision of governance and a strong scaffold of research (Pastor and Ortiz 2009). Rather than being invited by SCAG and port planners to participate and agreeing with preset efforts, however, these groups were able to push back with their own alternate, pragmatic policy package. While the process in Los Angeles and Long Beach was rather messy and included protests, lawsuits, and political conflict, the result is a model of how planners and social movements need each other for developing and implementing well-rounded, regionally equitable policy.

Next up on the agenda in Southern California is the other end of the logistics industry: warehousing operations in the so-called Inland Empire (San Bernardino and Riverside Counties). According to urban geographer Juan DeLara (2009, 7):

> Los Angeles and Long Beach pushed ahead of other ports by implementing regional policies that expanded their capacity to absorb larger shares of Asian imports. Part of this retooling involved a reterritorialization of the Ports' geographic scale. When local land constraints and social contests over development plans limited the ability of port interests to expand capacity near the docks, the urban hinterland—the Inland Empire—provided an alternative source of cheap land and labor that allowed for port volume expansion.

Indeed, the ports have been central to the development of the Inland Empire and vice versa. Just as there are environmental and labor struggles in neighborhoods bordering the ports, the megawarehouses and distribution centers in the Inland Empire have also brought pollution from the trucks moving the goods and low pay for the mostly Latino workforce. However, the civic infrastructure of the Inland Empire is much weaker, especially the partnerships between the labor and environmental communities (DeLara 2010). While it could be argued that this may ease SCAG's efforts to promote the logistics industry for the entire region, the ports' experience suggests that eventually communities will organize and respond, and in regional planning it is much better to make equity, sustainability, and authentic participation and voice coequal with economic growth as goals.

The lesson garnered from the ports' experience is that advocacy planning for regional equity requires advocates to lead the effort themselves. At the ports, community interests blocked expansion because the equity piece, which was mainly environmental but also economic, was missing. Once placed there through community organizing, however, the plans were freed to move forward.

The community in the Inland Empire is not as organized. The planners' response might be more meetings, while the organizers might respond by mobilizing interjection of the interests of the least advantaged into the planning process. When that happens, plans are more likely to be fair and to become realized. So environmental, economic, and equity planning really all come together when the community is not just incorporated into, but helps drive, the process.

REGIONAL PLANNING AND REGIONAL EQUITY

The wave of interest in regionalism and regional planning has been heartening to analysts who have long contended that the economic and environmental geography of the United States has shifted dramatically to metropolitan areas. Finally, planners and regional leaders are taking seriously the questions of industrial clusters and competitive advantage and considering the ways in which sprawl has chewed up our natural landscape, increased vehicle miles traveled and consequent air pollution, and led to an overconsumption of scarce water, power, and other resources.

Alongside this regionalist surge, a new movement for regional equity has developed. We use the word *movement* quite intentionally. While the regional equity perspective has some roots in academic literature and theorizing, it is also a reflection of the community and labor groups that have realized the ways in which racial segregation, spatial mismatch, and low incomes are connected to the sprawling and fragmented metropolitan landscape. More significantly, these groups have seen the metropolitan level as one in which they could make effective change through building new alliances with unusual partners and including those concerned about economic competitiveness and environmental sustainability.

Planners have the opportunity to catch up to this phenomenon and provide it with both support and opportunity in the years ahead. The traditions of equity and advocacy planning generally have been more focused on local economic development by helping poor minority communities receive city attention and boosting neighborhood prosperity. But as David Rusk (1999) contends, it is hard to do this while swimming upstream against the pressures of sprawl and the suburbanization of employment. Equity planning, in short, must go regional, matching the momentum that seems to be endemic to the organizing world.

To do this, planners will have to go beyond notions of simply encouraging participation in top-down planning processes. As important as these are, the Sacramento example shows that engagement can be difficult, particularly in planning for a distant future and about abstract issues. Instead, it will be critical to encourage these groups to foster the actual development of regional agendas and find ways to allow their efforts to bubble up into ongoing processes. The Los Angeles case, for example, illustrates the ways in which a community- and labor-led effort helped solve some difficult questions centered on how to clean up the ports, which had stymied planners' strategies to promote the development of the logistics industry. Moreover, these equity advocates did this by directly interjecting issues of equity into the process: environmental justice for the communities surrounding the ports and economic justice for truckers, who were hard pressed by the owner-operator system that had evolved in an era of deregulation.

To engage with social movements effectively, planners will need to augment their capacities in three broad areas. The first and perhaps foremost such area involves recognizing the limits of planning itself. Rather than emerging from planners' knowledge and skills or the formal and informal planning processes they help facilitate, many of the solutions to regional inequity and related planning problems will emerge from ideas possessed by community leaders and activists as well as from the processes that emerge in social movement organizing, which often conflict with planners' approaches.

In our Los Angeles example, few regional planners would have predicted that efforts to improve movement of goods in the region would come from labor-organizing efforts as they did. LAANE, an independent organization with strong roots in labor organizing as well as the flexibility to build broad social movement alliances, has been at the forefront of a range of innovative initiatives in the Los Angeles region. It has contributed to equitable planning and development by fostering living wage ordinances in a range of jurisdictions, community benefits agreements on multiple projects, and initiatives that limit the spread of big-box retail stores in Inglewood and Los Angeles. Humility is not a trait that tends to be taught in graduate programs, but a healthy dose is useful in order to see where the strength, power, and creativity to move policy actually may reside.

This is not an admonition against planning education itself. Indeed, LAANE's origins lie partly within UCLA's urban planning program. In 1991 to 1992, the very first project of that school's community scholars program was developed in cooperation with the Hotel Employees and Restaurant Employees Union and provided the basis for the creation of the Tourism Industry Development Corporation, the organization that later became LAANE. This program, however, was founded on a belief in the power of independent community and labor organizers and the importance of bringing planning scholars together with community organizers to study topical issues in depth. It has been an important way of building ties between planning students and social movement organizers and helping the students appreciate how much innovation and change in community and regional development efforts comes from outside the planning field itself.

A second broad set of capacities for planners in the regional equity arena includes the ability to engage with fuzzy boundaries and processes. Fuzziness is inherent in almost any regional planning process, given the weak basis of formal regional planning bodies in the United States and the multitude of local jurisdictions involved in regionalism. Regional planning can be more like the proverbial herding of cats than the highly regulated and proscribed processes that more often characterize local planning. In the absence of strong administrative powers, regional planners must engage with a wide variety of public and private sector entities in their search to find ways to promote a regional development vision and actually implement regional plans. Adding social movement organizations into this mix inevitably adds even more complexity and uncertainty.

Coping with uncertainty has long been recognized as a critical skill in planning (Christensen 1985), yet it remains difficult to realize in practice. Teaching students to be comfortable with operating at the intersections between issues and communities is, however, crucial for the future of the planning profession.

Finally, many times regional planning is seen as requiring skills for promoting collaboration across multiple constituencies. All too frequently, however, calls for collaborative planning seem irrelevant to the constituencies most marginalized and in need of greater equity. Typically, the ability to directly confront the difficult questions of racism, discrimination, and abuse of power that people in marginalized communities experience every day is called for in addressing equity effectively, but too often these issues are neglected in public discourse. Around the country, regional equity organizers are demonstrating the efficacy of the kind of collaboration we label "collaboration as principled conflict." It involves the ability to address directly real conflicts with opposing actors in goals, objectives, and even values in a way that recognizes the need to sustain long-term relationships, despite the parties' differences, while developing some sense of a common regional destiny.

The skills of humility, dealing with fuzziness, and embracing principled conflict are all inherent in analyzing and addressing power, which is at the core of what drives inequity. Inevitably, finding creative ways to blend the power analysis of community partners and the planning skills of professionals will be a messy process. But we remind readers that change always—and often *only*—looks good at the end. When the civil rights movement began, Martin Luther King Jr. was viewed as a villain by some, and his own government tapped his telephone. He now is widely recognized as an American hero. When the modern women's movement was launched, many viewed it as overturning tradition and threatening a dissolution of society. Today, strong and independent women on both the left and right are seen as holding a natural place in the political landscape, and while progress on closing the pay gap has been slow, few openly question the idea that men and women should receive equal pay for equal work.

As both a field of planning and a social movement, regional equity remains in that messy initial stage of development. Almost as many definitions of regional equity are extant as there are advocates for it, and regional equity strategies still often emerge primarily in a reactive mode. Activists frequently are better at protesting the inequities of current regional development processes, or challenging regional policies piecemeal, than they are at promoting comprehensive strategies for regional equity. Little consensus has been reached regarding what constitutes real success in promoting regional equity, despite promising and inspiring examples around the country.

Both developing a proactive regional equity agenda and measuring success in reaching such goals greatly need the traditional research and technical skills of planners. If coupled with the other capacity-building tasks we identify—acquiring humility, accepting fuzziness, and embracing (principled) conflict—planners will become able to bring traditional equity planning to a new level and, we hope, accomplish new achievements. The regional equity movement may be in its infancy, but its potential to reshape our metropolitan landscape and politics is promising. Planners can and should help realize these possibilities.

REFERENCES

Arnstein, Sherry. 1969. A ladder of citizen participation. *Journal of the American Planning Association* 35:216–224.

Beach, B. 2008. Strategies and lessons from the Los Angeles community benefits experience. *Journal of Affordable Housing. & Community Development Law* 17:77.

Blakely, Edward J. 1989. *Planning local economic development: Theory and practice.* Newbury Park, CA: Sage.

Caltrans. n.d. Regional blueprints. Sacramento, CA: Department of Transportation. http://calblueprint.dot.ca.gov

CARB (California Air Resources Board). 2006. Quantification of the health impacts and economic valuation of air pollution from ports and goods movement in California. Appendix A, Emission reduction plan for ports and goods movement. 21 March. Sacramento. www.arb.ca.gov/planning/gmerp/gmerp.htm

CFC (Consumer Federation of California), League of United Latin American Citizens, Los Angeles Alliance for a New Economy, and National Association for the Advancement of Colored People. 2008. Foreclosure on wheels: Long Beach's truck program puts drivers at high risk for default. Los Angeles.

Chapman, J. I. 2008. The fiscalization of land use. *Public Works Management & Policy* 12:551.

Christensen, K. S. 1985. Coping with uncertainty in planning. *Journal of the American Planning Association* 51:63–73.

Clavel, Pierre. 1994. The evolution of advocacy planning. *Journal of the American Planning Association* 60:146–149.

Coalition for Clean & Safe Ports. 2008. Polluted air here to stay with Long Beach port truck scheme: Public relations ploy won't change the deadly status quo. Press release. 15 February. Los Angeles. www.cleanandsafeports.org/fileadmin/files_editor/Polluted_Air_Here_to_Stay.pdf

———. 2009. Environmental, community and labor groups nationwide mark one-year success of Los Angeles Clean Truck Program. Press release. 1 October. Los Angeles. www.healthyports.org/fileadmin/files_nynj/10.01.09CCSPAnniversary.pdf

Davidoff, Paul. 1965. Advocacy and pluralism in planning. *Journal of the American Planning Association* 31:331–338.

DeLara, Juan. 2009. Remapping inland Southern California: Global commodity distribution, land speculation, and politics in the Inland Empire. Ph.D. Diss., University of California, Berkeley.

———. 2010. Presentation at Center for the Study of Immigrant Integration Faculty Seminar. (14 April). Los Angeles: CSII, University of Southern California.

Dietz, Thomas, and Paul Stern. 2009. *Public participation in environmental assessment and decision making.* Washington DC: National Academies Press.

Dillon, Raquel Maria. 2010. Judge: LA port's Clean Trucks Program can proceed. Associated Press (27 August). http://www.boston.com/business/articles/2010/08/27/judge_la_ports_clean_trucks_program_can_proceed/

Ellis, Juliet, and Peggy Shepard. 2004. Burden of proof: Using research for environmental justice. *Race, Poverty and the Environment* 11.

Freudenberg, Nicholas. 2004. Community capacity for environmental health promotion: Determinants and implications for practice. *Health Education & Behavior* 31:472–490.

Freudenberg, Nicholas, Barbara Israel, and Manuel Pastor. 2010. Community participation in environmental decision-making processes: Can it reduce disproportionate impact? Los Angeles: University of Southern California, Program on Environmental and Regional Equity.

FutureWorks. 2004. *Minding their civic business: A look at the new ways regional business-civic organizations are making a difference in metropolitan North America.* Arlington, MA: FutureWorks.

Gottlieb, Robert, Mark Vallianatos, Regina M. Freer, and Peter Dreier. 2005. *The next Los Angeles: The struggle for a livable city.* Berkeley: University of California Press.

Henton, Douglas C., John Melville, and Kimberly Walesh. 1997. *Grassroots leaders for a new economy: How civic entrepreneurs are building prosperous communities.* San Francisco: Jossey-Bass.

Hricko, Andrea. 2008. Global trade comes home. *Environmental Health Perspectives* 116:A78.

Husing, John. 2004. Logistics & distribution: An answer to regional upward social mobility. (9 June). Los Angeles: Southern California Association of Governments.

Innes, Judith, Sarah Di Vittorio, and David E. Booher. 2009. Governance for the megaregion of Northern California: A framework for action. Berkeley: University of California, Global Metropolitan Studies, Institute of Urban and Regional Development,.

Israel, Barbara, Eugenia Eng, Amy Schulz, and Edith Parker. 2005. Introduction to methods in community-based participatory research for health. In *Methods in community-based participatory research for health,* ed. Barbara Israel, Eugenia Eng, Amy Schulz, and Edith Parker. San Francisco: Jossey-Bass.

KERNCOG, SANDAG, and SCAG. 2005. *The Southern California megaregion. A case study of global gateway regions: America's third century strategy.* Washington, DC: Regional Plan Association.

Krumholz, Norman and John Forester. 1990. *Making equity planning work: Leadership in the public sector.* Philadelphia: Temple University Press.

LAANE (Los Angeles Alliance for a New Economy). 2007. The road to shared prosperity: The regional economic benefits of the San Pedro Bay ports' Clean Trucks Program. Los Angeles.

LSNC (Legal Service of Northern California). 2004. Annual report on activities in support of the Sacramento regional blueprint project. Sacramento.

Marcello, D. 2007. Community benefit agreements: New vehicle for investment in America's neighborhoods. *Urban Law* 39:657.

McKeever, Mike. 2010. Smart growth and climate change: California's SB 375 and Sacramento's Blueprint experience. In *Climate and transportation solutions: Findings from the 2009 Asilomar Conference on Transportation and Energy Policy,* ed. D. Sperling and J. Cannon. Davis: University of California, Institute for Transportation Studies.

Minkler, Meredith, Victoria Breckwich Vasquez, Mansoureh Tajik, and Dana Petersen. 2008. Promoting environmental justice through community-based participatory research: The role of community and partnership capacity. *Health Education & Behavior* 35:119–137.

Mongelluzzo, Bill. 2010. ILWU backs Long Beach Clean Trucks Program. 7 January. *Journal of Commerce Online.* www.joc.com/maritime/longshore-union-supports-long-beach-program

Orfield, Myron. 1997. *Metropolitics: A regional agenda for community and stability.* Washington, DC: Brookings Institution Press, and Cambridge, MA: Lincoln Institute of Land Policy.

Pastor, Manuel, and Chris Benner. 2008. Been down so long: Weak market cities and regional equity. In *Restoring prosperity in older industrial areas,* ed. R. McGahey and J. Vey. Washington, DC: Brookings Institution Press.

Pastor, Manuel, Chris Benner, and Martha Matsuoka. 2009. *This could be the start of something big: Social movements for regional equity and the future of metropolitan America.* Ithaca, NY: Cornell University Press.

Pastor, Manuel, Chris Benner, Rhonda Ortiz, Rosa Ramirez, Justin Scoggins, Jennifer Tran, and Mateusz Filipski. 2010. Just growth: Equity and prosperity for America's metropolitan regions. Los Angeles: Program on Environmental and Regional Equity.

Pastor, Manuel, and Rhonda Ortiz. 2009. *Making change: How social movements work and how to support them.* Los Angeles: University of Southern California, Program on Environmental and Regional Equity.

Patel, Sejal. 2010. *From clean to clunker: The economics of emissions control. Fresh perspectives from air quality regulators, licensed mechanics, port truck drivers, and freight carriers.* Los Angeles: Los Angeles Alliance for a New Economy.

PR Newswire. 2010. Teamsters mislead press on effects of Port of Los Angeles lawsuit, says ATA. (23 April). www.prnewswire.com/news-releases/teamsters-mislead-press-on-effects-of-port-of-los-angeles-lawsuit-says-ata-91922724.html

Rocha, Elizabeth. 1997. A ladder of empowerment. *Journal of Planning Education and Research* 17:31–44.

Rusk, David. 1993. *Cities without suburbs.* Washington, DC: Woodrow Wilson Center Press.

———. 1999. *Inside game outside game: Winning strategies for saving urban America.* Washington, DC: Brookings Institution Press.

SACOG (Sacramento Area Council of Governments). 2008. A creative new vision for transportation in the Sacramento Region: MTP2035. Sacramento.

———. 2010a. Recorded video messages from community leaders and state senate/congress. Sacramento. www.sacregionblueprint.org/implementation/anniversary5

———. 2010b. Local blueprint implementation highlight (video). Sacramento. www.sacregionblueprint.org/implementation/anniversary5/

———. n.d. Sacramento. www.sacregionblueprint.org/sacregionblueprint/the_project/principles.pdf

Sanchez, Thomas. 2005. *An inherent bias? Geography and racial-ethnic patterns of metropolitan planning organization boards.* Washington, DC: Brookings Institution. www.brookings.edu/metro/pubs/20060124_mpos.pdf

Savitch, H. V., and Ronald K. Vogel. 2004. Suburbs without a city: Power and city-county consolidation. *Urban Affairs Review* 396:758–790.

SCAG (Southern California Association of Governments). 2008. Multi-county goods movement action plan. Los Angeles.

———. 2010. Comprehensive regional goods movement plan and implementation strategy. Los Angeles.

Schwartz, J. 1997. Prisoners of Proposition 13: Sales taxes, property taxes, and the fiscalization of municipal land use decisions. *Southern California Law Review* 71:183.

Soja, Edward. 1989. *Postmodern geographies: The reassertion of space in critical social theory.* London: Verso Press.

Stodghill, Ron, and Amanda Bower. 2002. Welcome to America's most diverse city. *Time* (25 August).

Swanstrom, Todd, and Brian Banks. 2009. Going regional: Community-based regionalism, transportation, and local hiring agreements. *Journal of Planning Education and Research* 28:355–367.

Swanstrom, Todd, and Transportation Equity Network. 2008. The road to good jobs: Patterns of employment in the construction industry. St. Louis: Public Policy Research Center, University of Missouri.

Valley Vision. n.d. Civic leadership at a regional scale. Sacramento: Valley Vision. www.valleyvision.org/organization/index.html

White, Ronald D. 2009. Long Beach port settles truckers suit over clean air plan. *Los Angeles Times* (21 October). http://articles.latimes.com/2009/oct/21/business/fi-ports-settlement21

CHAPTER 5

REGIONAL PLANNING ON THE FRONTIER

Deborah E. Popper and Frank J. Popper

THE UNEXPECTED SURVIVAL OF THE FRONTIER

The U.S. frontier is by far the largest, longest lasting, and least recognized of its regions. To explore, assess, settle, exploit, regulate, and preserve it has long constituted one of the most important regional planning projects in the nation's history. The frontier has served as a major source—and often the central site—of planning's institutional forms, practices, and objectives in the United States. For much of the nation's history, and still today, popular or expert acknowledgement of frontier regional planning's extent has been weak. At different times and places the country ignored its frontier, its regionalism, or its planning, and often all three at once. Frontier regional planning has never been part of the planner's vocabulary, much less the nation's contemporary consciousness.

The frontier, both as idea and reality, obsessed the United States during the eighteenth and nineteenth centuries. The census tracked it zealously, driven by the nation's desire to develop itself, reach the Pacific, secure its expanding borders and settlements from Indian and European revanchist threats, become wealthy, and attain acceptance as one of the world's great powers—in short, to achieve what nineteenth-century leaders and pundits called Manifest Destiny. In the twentieth century, once that destiny seemed assured, the idea of the frontier gradually lost its hold on national thinking.

Yet the frontier persists, remaining sparsely settled by definition, remote from the vast majority of U.S. citizens, and demanding in topography and climate. Today the frontier occupies more than 55 percent of the nation's land. This striking figure is derived from calculations based on two metrics: the census's historical definition of census-block population densities as equal to six or fewer people per square mile (Boston has more than 13,000 people per square mile); and the New Mexico–based National Center for Frontier Communities (NCFC), which uses county population densities, distances, and travel times from major markets and public services in its calculations (figure 5.1).[1]

---

1. See the Rural Assistance Center (raconline.org) for more about definitions and calculations.

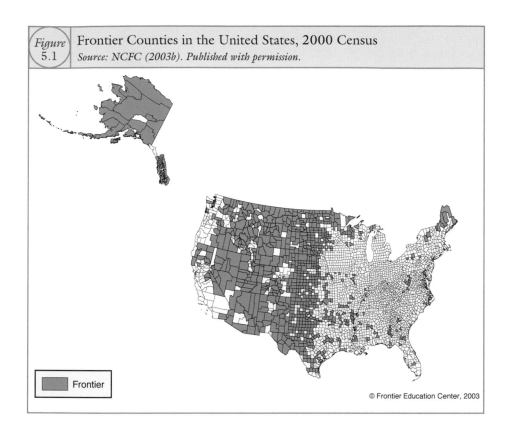

Figure 5.1 Frontier Counties in the United States, 2000 Census
Source: NCFC (2003b). Published with permission.

Frontier

© Frontier Education Center, 2003

Although initially it was contiguous, today's frontier lies mainly in the non-coastal West and in Alaska. The western frontier's eastern boundary falls roughly at the 98th meridian, the historic edge of the Great Plains. There are eastern pockets as well, in particular Appalachia, the lower Mississippi Delta, northern Maine, and the upper Midwest. Its definition as a region depends more on the on-the-ground conditions and relationships than location. The frontier constitutes its own region. It is not just a quaint-sounding term for the West. In fact most westerners do not live on the frontier but are in urban areas, places with much different conditions and needs from the frontier (Lang, Popper, and Popper 1995).

The western frontier has two main parts: (1) the mostly private lands of the Great Plains; and (2) those in or near federal public land holdings—primarily properties of the Interior Department's Bureau of Land Management (equal to one-fifth of U.S. land area all by itself), the National Park Service, Fish and Wildlife Service, and the Agriculture Department's Forest Service. The eastern frontier is primarily held privately (northern Maine, for example) or a mix of federal, state, and private lands, such as northern Minnesota. In 2007, by the census's definition, 0.9 percent of the U.S. population dwelled on the frontier, while the NCFC's figures put the percentage at 3.7.

As of the 2007 census estimates, the entire states of Alaska and Wyoming, with 1.0 and 5.4 people per square mile respectively, could qualify as frontier, and

From *Echo Burning*

Carmen came off the highway just short of Pecos and speared south on a small county road that led down into total emptiness. Within five miles, they could have been on the surface of the moon.

"Tell me about Echo," he said.

She shrugged. "What's to tell? It's nothing. When they were first mapping Texas a hundred years ago, the Census Bureau called a place settled if it had more than six people to the square mile, and we *still* don't qualify. We're still the frontier."

"But it's very beautiful," he said.

And it was. The road was snaking and diving through endless contours, with red rock canyons either side of it, tall and noble to the east, fractured and pierced to the west, where ancient streams had sought the banks of the Rio Grande. Tall dry mountains reared beyond, with an immense Technicolor sky above, and even in the speeding car he could sense the stunning silence of thousands of square miles of absolute emptiness.

"I hate it," she said.

—Lee Child (2001, 66)

Montana, with 6.5 people per square, barely missed the threshold. If using ground transportation, one cannot travel coast to coast across the country without entering the frontier. Almost every year new archaeological sites and natural wonders—those that are large, above ground, and easily visible had anyone seen (or reported) them earlier—appear on the frontier. Planes crash there, and no one finds them. Some counties have about the same populations they had when their states were territories. The United States, while no longer a new-frontier nation, still has one, but it has long been largely unaware of it and has not known how to plan for it.

Frontier regional planning departs from planning in the rest of the country in important ways. For nearly all of the urban and suburban United States, local governments do local planning. In these settings, metropolitan bodies often are responsible for most regional planning. Both local and metropolitan agencies tend to focus on property values and economic competitiveness, to which were added new emphases on environmental quality around 1970, and sustainability since 2000. This planning has its own traditions, techniques, and rules, as embodied, for example, in local zoning.

Frontier regional planning differs. It operates on a larger scale, focuses more on natural resources, and has more direct effects on smaller populations, which are always more rural and often poorer, more conservative, and more resistant to planning than their urban, suburban, or metropolitan counterparts. Frontier regional planning takes place more at the federal and state levels than locally. Its primary constituents are from deep-rural areas, but it often responds to urban interests beyond its borders. In the westernmost two-thirds of the country, including Alaska, frontier regional planning must deal with such noneastern factors as aridity, Native populations and their reservations, large federal landholdings and their checkerboard shapes, highly concentrated private landholdings, and large public universities as the only major ones in the state. Above all, it has to contend with the national illusion that the frontier disappeared generations ago and so requires no targeted national attention or regional planning.

As a result frontier regional planning has become deeply flawed. It lacks coherence or clarity in its purposes. It cannot set terms for acceptable future development or even show who, or what considerations, should determine it. On today's U.S. frontier, development and conservation; preservation and use; public and private responsibility; and local, state, regional, and national interests all contend with one another without any rationale for resolution. Conflicts are exemplified by Nevada's Yucca Mountain high-level nuclear-waste repository; Appalachia's mountaintop removal; Colorado's Animas–La Plata dam project; Alaska's Arctic National Wildlife Refuge; disputes over clear cutting and military bases across the country; proposed rights of way for returning long-haul railroads; the continuing controversy over the authors' proposed Buffalo Commons in the Great Plains; and most federal irrigation projects.

THE COURSE OF FRONTIER PLANNING

In the early years of the Republic, dealing with the frontier and its needs was unavoidable. Compromises struck to allow adoption of the Constitution in 1787 had the federal government acquire much of the nation's then-frontier land from the states. The government was deeply concerned that citizens settle the land quickly, so in the late eighteenth and early nineteenth centuries it offered a series of bills, known as Preemption Acts, that allowed pioneers and development companies to occupy federal land at progressively lower prices and under easier settlement terms. The frontier kept expanding through purchase (Louisiana and Alaska), conquest (most of the Southwest), or threats (most of the Pacific Northwest).

By 1862 the first of a string of Homestead Acts, which continued to be enacted into the early twentieth century, permitted settlers to take possession of the land at essentially no cost and with little or no federal supervision. By the late nineteenth century the overall process had succeeded brilliantly. The federal government had, in modern terms, divested most of its frontier holdings, privatized them, and spurred public-private partnerships for their use. Then the influential historian Frederick Jackson Turner declared the frontier closed, thereby beginning the generations-long obscuring of the frontier in the United States. The country's explosive urbanization, already well underway, pulled national attention and planning to the cities—their growth, industries, and new immigrants—and away from the putatively closed frontier.

The frontier's eclipse coincided with the rise of the federal bureaucracy. Frontier planning for public lands disappeared into a growing array of new programs that brought with them new responsibilities, while deep-rural private land remained largely unplanned. More federal public land became permanent rather than transitional and no longer awaited transfer to private ownership. In 1905, national forests, then parks (1916), and wildlife refuges (1939) became new bureaucratic designations based on conservation and recreation, which kept their populations low and ridded them of settlement rather than encouraging it. The extent of these lands, along with those held by the Bureau of Land Management, has remained largely stable or increased slightly with the creation of new national parks. Over time, however, government planning for the frontier largely has been weak and its constituencies unclear. Local government planning of frontier private land has been rudimentary.

As the federal bureaucracy acquired more muscle during the New Deal and later, the frontier became, if anything, a less obvious or distinct project. The 1934 Taylor Grazing Act abolished lower-48 homesteading (although it continued in Alaska, which had yet to become a state). In effect, this federally institutionalized a permanent public land frontier. The Federal Land Policy and Management Act (1976) explicitly declared that the bulk of the land, which now included Alaska, would remain in federal hands. The frontier's seeming emptiness made it the ideal place to locate large-scale activities that the federal government and large corporations—both headquartered well away from the frontier—preferred to remain unobserved. Weapons tests and production, military training, big mines, power plants, and national laboratories proliferated. The previous eras' inability to divest all the federal public lands became an accident that served post-1945 national purposes. The lands also met more

---

From *Disappearance: A Map*

I live in a place where people disappear. Alaska. Too large to comprehend.

People go out in planes, boats, on foot, and are never heard from again.

It is May, almost spring but still a time of potentially cruel weather, especially in the tumultuous arc of the Gulf of Alaska, the place where the North American and Pacific plates meet and violence is upheaved in tectonic battle. It is a place of earthquake, young mountains, and volatile glaciers, a place where the pressure of frozen millennia breaks in blue ice against a stormy sea, a place where exquisitely sharp peaks throw back the weather that tries to move inland from the sea.

Somewhere in this unvisited place a colleague has disappeared.

—Sheila Nickerson (1996, 3, 5)

individual, less public ends, such as off-the-grid ways of life, marijuana production, immigrant smuggling, vision quests, militia training, and the like.

TURNER'S INFLUENCE

The frontier's primary intellectual figure was Frederick Jackson Turner, the historian at the University of Wisconsin and Harvard, who returned repeatedly to one question: What influence has the frontier had on the nation? In 1893, early in his career, he presented his most influential paper at the American Historical Association.

It began with a sentence from an 1890 census report: "Up to and including 1880 the country had a frontier of settlement, but at present the unsettled area has been so broken into by isolated bodies of settlement that there can hardly be said to be a frontier line." He concluded, "And now, after four centuries from the discovery of America, at the end of a hundred years of life under the Constitution, the frontier has gone, and with its going has gone the first period of American history" (Turner 1962, 1 and 35). In this essay Turner argued that the United States remained a frontier nation, culturally and politically, with an enduring legacy of waves of pragmatic settlers improvising in order to adapt to challenging new lands. The paper struck academic gold, but what stuck most was the simple idea of a closed frontier.

Turner later focused again on the question of the frontier's impact. In a 1903 *Atlantic Monthly* essay he extolled the democratizing force of pioneering, but saw differences between early and later frontier experiences. The scale and challenges of settlement grew with every wave, and the "new West showed a growing tendency to call to its assistance the powerful arm of national authority" (Turner 1962, 257). Now he feared that later frontier needs might contribute to the consolidation of corporate power.

A generation later Turner (1925) wrote "The Significance of the Section in American History," his analysis of the relationship among the country's large-scale regions. The essay intentionally echoed his 1893 paper. Turner analyzed the link between section and frontier in creating a national political culture that, with the major exception of the Civil War, had worked. He told how the nation began as a small string of settlements scattered along the Eastern Seaboard, with the bulk of its population stretching westward barely to the Appalachians and dividing into two regions, North and South.

The frontier—a transitional area, malleable, full of still-to-be-exploited opportunities—served as a complicating and conciliating force between these two regions. Its possibilities raised, but also diffused, pressures between North and South as they negotiated national expansion. It was at once a safety valve and a national mission. Turner credited the political parties with reaching across and into regions and subregions to keep the country functioning. But now there were more regions and many new subregions, each differing from the others in resources and culture. To Turner the nation resembled a conglomeration of

European countries. What would result? Writing during the aftermath of World War I, he feared a hardened sectional politics that would lead to potentially devastating national effects.[2]

Turner looked to the nation's origins to understand the establishment of the frontier's critical role. As historian John Opie (1998, 95) writes, "Land—enormous unimaginable wilderness—was the silent partner in the negotiations in Philadelphia for a new government." The 1787 Constitutional Convention resolved the question of who owned the lands in the West (the federal government) and created a process to regularize them, then successively turn them into states as citizens moved into the territories, bought land from the government, and developed governance.

When the Louisiana Purchase acquired what is now the nation's midsection, it doubled the area of the United States and so made regularization more necessary and daunting. Dealing with the frontier became one of the young government's training grounds, continually demanding decisions that led to new government structures, devices, and responsibilities. Congress devoted much time to the frontier, trying to get its course right, falling short, and trying again. During its first hundred years, no decade passed without Congress revisiting its public land laws, and about half of its legislation dealt with the public land frontier.

In its vastness, the frontier was overwhelming, seemingly incomprehensible. To make it manageable and amenable to absorption, the fledgling government quickly imposed a new national geometry. At least in terms of property, the 1785 and 1787 Land Survey Acts turned the most unknown and mysterious part of the country into its most predictable, rational region. The Public Land Office divided federal acreage into regular, adjoining 640-acre squares (one square mile), as if each square and acre in it matched every other. Although not called planning, this action epitomizes a master plan and its execution, thus laying out the future and the means to get there. Each successive Preemption Act's terms reduced the fee, acreage minimums, or federal oversight for acquisition. Once enough squares were transferred and a sufficient number of people were in place, an area would become a territory, then with the addition of more people, a state, which denoted full settlement.

The frontier stimulated the federal government's information-gathering capability and established a baseline for doing national planning. Soon after acquiring the Louisiana Territory in 1803, President Thomas Jefferson charged Meriwether Lewis and William Clark to lead an expedition to scope out the newly acquired property, find out how to cross it, and determine its development potential. This would be the first of many frontier expeditions, such as those of Zebulon Pike, Stephen Long, John Wesley Powell, Ferdinand Hayden, Henry

---

2. Turner's successor as key thinker about the frontier was Walter Prescott Webb, whose books *The Great Plains* (1931), *Divided We Stand: The Crisis of a Frontierless Democracy* (1937), and *The Great Frontier* (1952) continued Turner's argument for regionalism's centrality in American history.

Gannett, and Clarence King, each of which was authorized to observe, evaluate, and report back. The missions were sometimes military, sometimes not.

The existing states could support these national exercises without feeling that the federal government was intruding on their own territory or possibly usurping states' rights. Such disputes only emerged as frontier land became settled. The expeditions created a federal repository of data, strengthened some agencies, and led to new ones, such as the Geological Survey, to retain and manage the data. The emerging information helped develop the region into settled land, thus making it no longer part of the frontier. Between 1800 and 1860 U.S. land east of the 98th-meridian frontier line grew from 226,085 to 1,087,379 square miles (Lang, Popper, and Popper 1995).

The assertiveness with which President Abraham Lincoln took up frontier planning seemingly was surprising for a leader with much else to do. In six weeks in 1862 alone, he signed into law four acts that together powerfully propelled the transition from frontier to settled land: the Organic Act, which created the Bureau (now Department) of Agriculture (May 15); the Homestead Act (May 20); the Pacific Railroad Act (July 1); and the Morrill or Land Grant Colleges Act (July 2). The legislation reflected both a logical wartime concern, which demonstrated that the nation would not tolerate separating the Pacific states and territories from the Union, and Lincoln's outlook, which had developed during his earlier career in Illinois. Having served as attorney for the Illinois Central Railway, he came to power as president with a sense of the opportunities offered for economic development by combining land, railroads, and new settlers. None of the four bills he signed into law in 1862 had immediate impact on the frontier, but each sought to speed turning the frontier into an area rich in thriving communities based on commercial agriculture. It was no accident that the Southern states, which were wary of the spread of slaveless Northern economies and values, had blocked such legislation before the Civil War.

After the war, frontier settlement resumed and quickened. Military planning efforts shifted to the West, where they established new forts for security along the frontier trails in order to overcome Native peoples. These forts and settlements required their own support, particularly for provisioning. Settlement first spread into the frontier territories along the rivers of the region's central axis, which offered the best and most convenient farmland. Settlers then pushed into less-desirable areas, moving west, north, south, and farther away from the water.

The initial building of the railroad drew huge resources into the frontier for construction and then even more for town building and real estate development. As the tracks crossed the country, planning became as much a corporate as a governmental function, and railroad companies decided the locations of towns and determined the distances between them. John Hudson's *Plains Country Towns* (1985, 70) details how each company had its own specifications for town siting and platting, but "in no instance was their involvement passive." The companies fixed on where the towns should be, laid them out, and chose whether the main street was to be crossroads or straight line, then set street and lot dimensions. "Only after the structure of the town was completely specified were any townlike activities allowed to locate there" (Hudson 1985, 71).

To draw buyers the planning had to make the towns seem like familiar, credible landscapes rather than wilderness. As new transcontinental routes came on line—five by 1890—they added regular stops that served as settlement outposts from which the frontier presumably would retreat (Reps 1979). The stops structured the region's commerce by enticing farmers and ranchers whose products could feed the nation and who would in turn buy the goods the rest of the nation wanted to sell. The frontier region held the promise of national plenitude. Walt Whitman's (1963, 220–221) often-quoted 1879 description of prairie and plains as "America's characteristic landscape" refers, if one reads on, not to their glorious openness and relative lack of people, but to their potential for economic development, which apparently was imminent, to support a large population of farmers producing crops to feed people all across the country.

It took at least the rest of the nineteenth century for the land-grant college system enacted in 1862 to contribute substantially to the region's agricultural transformation. The colleges' first task was to become established, and few, if any, of their early students or professors were ready to generate new knowledge (Johnson 1981). Instead, farming advances in production and technological initiatives derived from now-increased private acreage. For example, according to Walter Prescott Webb (1931), expanded Great Plains settlement depended on the Colt six-shooter, barbed wire, and the windmill that brought water up from the ground, none of which came from land-grant colleges. John Deere, the person and the company, produced the moldboard plows that could cut through the resistant Great Plains sod (Pudup 1987). The 1887 Hatch Act eventually fostered research by creating federal experiment stations partnered with the land-grant schools. In 1914, the Smith-Lever Act created state cooperative extension services that disseminated their findings, especially through the county agents the legislation also brought into being. Lincoln's 1862 acts shaped the rest of the nineteenth century's frontier planning, which was thoroughly modernist, optimistic, rationalist, and full-bore expansionist.

THE FRONTIER'S DOOR STANDS AJAR

Turner's triumphant claim of the frontier's end proclaimed not just that the settlement process had become embedded in the nation's psyche, but also that the program Lincoln began had become so well-established that it required little further attention—or perhaps intention. It would remain on track without the fanfare of Manifest Destiny. But the twentieth-century frontier proved more complicated, confused, and enigmatic. Instead of continuing to shrink, the frontier grew.

The historian Edwin Erle Sparks (1900, 9), who later became president of Pennsylvania State University, exultantly began his 1900 textbook *The Expansion of the American People, Social and Territorial* with this statement: "Expansion is a necessary law of human development and progress." He described the process in the United States, where it had already run its course: "The interior conquest being now complete, the frontier disappears" (Sparks 1900, 16). He now saw the country's expansion turning outward to the larger world. But only two years later he wrote in *The Chautauquan* that "man has retired before hostile nature" (quoted in Lang, Popper, and Popper 1995, 298), and the next year the census reported that, "it is a peculiar fact that, in spite of the great increase in population of [the] continental United States from 1890 to 1900, the unsettled area also increased, principally in the Western states" (Gannett 1903, 36). The frontier line barely budged thereafter. While its expansion occasioned no major jump, just small increases here and there, the frontier kept bearing surprises for the next decades (Otterstrom and Earle 2002).

The nineteenth century's exuberant expansionist and rationalizing planning model often proved unwise, especially when it overlooked local factors such as rainfall or soils. It also ignored other frontier planning models. Most notably, John Wesley Powell's 1878 report on the frontier's arid lands showed that the 1862 Homestead Act's allotment of 160 acres per settler would work only occasionally. He argued that the arid West should be divided into irrigation districts, with farmers in bottomlands working small plots while those in the uplands would need as much as 1,000 or even 6,000 acres apiece. The Spanish, Mexican, Mormon, and Texan settlers he mentioned used such arrangements. His recommendations, if implemented, would have fine-tuned frontier planning. But frontier planning began in an age and under circumstances incapable of such discrimination. Uniformity was the only administrative option.

From *The Big Burn: Teddy Roosevelt and the Fire That Saved America*

The Little G.P.s [foresters, Gifford Pinchot men] were horrified and perplexed by what they found in the people's land: instead of honest homesteaders they confronted land thieves, instead of Pinchot's vaunted Little Man Who Would Be King they found whiskey peddlers, instead of enlightened merchants they found six varieties of pimps—all operating in open defiance of the U.S. Forest Service. One man cut a swath in the woods just outside Taft, a half-acre or so, and opened a bar with a few whores. He did this under the eyes of several rangers. A flummoxed ranger sent a telegram to Missoula, no idea how to proceed.

"Two undesirable prostitutes established on government land," he wired. "What should I do?"

Another ranger wired back: "Get two desirable ones."

—Timothy Egan (2009, 75)

Turner's essays on the frontier and the section penetratingly addressed key issues of national destiny, and each is as revealing for its errors as for its truths. The frontier's role in the early negotiation between the North and South made it central in shaping government institutions and structures. Planning for the frontier had to reflect the interests of the regions as well as those of the West and the entire country. Once the frontier was declared closed, its planning fossilized. It was assumed to have been settled and represented by its states. But whether working with the narrow census density-based definition or Turner's broad cultural one, which considered the frontier a meeting ground and place of improvisation, it never really closed. Some new places reached the settled density, but increasingly the frontier contained places destined to remain unsettled, the planning of which was and would continue to be mostly the concern of the federal government. The frontier's status as a clear region was lost. Rather than actually closing, the frontier reached the end of *planning* for its closure, and no new regional planning structure emerged to address its needs.

Instead, planning focused on specific land uses—ranching, say, or logging or irrigation—rather than on the region as a whole. The hostile nature Sparks mentioned recurred repeatedly and either constrained agriculture's expansion in the desert and elsewhere or periodically forced its retreat in the grasslands. New programs—the Reclamation Act of 1902 and the Enlarged Homestead Act (1905), for example—sought to overcome these limitations, but their intent often was as much to stem out-migration as to promote in-migration. In the first half of the twentieth century, frontier planning's goals shrunk to simply retaining population, sometimes using relocation, but not seeking expansion. The efforts crested during the New Deal with the Agriculture Department's Resettlement Administration. Retention, however, meant a new, more deflationary view of the frontier's economic competitiveness. The earlier frontier was used to provide primary products: food, fiber, and minerals. If these did not

From *A Land of Little Rain*

East away from the Sierras, south from Panamint and Amargosa, east and south many an uncounted mile, is the Country of Lost Borders.

Ute, Paiute, Mojave, and Shoshone inhabit its frontiers, and as far into the heart of it as a man dare go. Not the law, but the land sets the limit. Desert is the name it wears upon the maps, but the Indian's is the better word. Desert is a loose term to indicate land that supports no man; whether the land can be bitted and broken to that purpose is not proven. Void of life it never is, however dry the air and villainous the soil.

—Mary Austin (1903, 96)

support the existing population, as experience now showed they frequently did not, how or why was one to stay?

Yet as the natural resource frontier foundered, the preservation frontier emerged, bringing with it serious cultural, perceptual, and programmatic shifts. Amid war and frenetic westward expansion, the federal government set aside Yosemite and Yellowstone National Parks in the 1860s and 1870s. In 1864 Congress removed Yosemite from development by giving it to California to preserve. Aptly, the ubiquitous Frederick Law Olmsted chaired the advisory committee that recommended this decision. Wilderness increasingly was accorded its own value. Just as the first transcontinental railroad reached completion in 1869, exploration of the Yellowstone region began, first by local Montanans and then, in 1871, under Ferdinand Hayden, the geologist heading the U.S. Geological and Geographical Survey of the Territories (later renamed the U.S. Geological Survey). The expeditions provoked in their members thoughts of preservation, a wish to keep Yellowstone from the usual path of subdivision and development.

By December 1871 both houses of Congress had before them a bill to preserve Yellowstone. As they took up the issue, Hayden wrote for *Scribner's* a description of its wonders, which he ended: "Why will not Congress at once pass a law setting it apart as a great public park for all time to come, as has been done with that not more remarkable wonder, the Yosemite Valley?" (quoted in Jackson 1957, 55). By March 1 the act passed. The legal and planning language establishing Yellowstone mimicked that used earlier for Yosemite, and it put in place a model for future programs. Both landscapes were presented as exceptional, and they were, but they signaled the establishment of a new goal that soon played as much a part on the frontier as development. Leaving things as they were and in the hands of government, usually federal, became the goal.

These initiatives linked to the then-new urban parks movement, but they differed in scale. Just as the creation of Central and Prospect Parks made major reductions in New York City's developable real estate market, Yosemite and Yellowstone removed substantial acreage from frontier development. Begun in the second half of the nineteenth century, this overall park creation project continues into the twenty-first. That nearby rural areas never filled out sufficiently to become the settlement equivalent of urban parks' city neighbors rarely drew attention. Instead, Yosemite, Yellowstone, and the many parks that followed were national in scale. These were parks in a settled nation rather than a neighborhood or city, and the bulk of their visitors came from far-off places. The set-aside lands have long proved to be economic anchors for their deep-rural surroundings (Power 2001), but that was not initially their purpose. Their regional planning is at best uncomfortable when it tries to achieve balance between preservation and growth.

The first national forest preserves, intended not so much for preservation as prudent use, also set a precedent, not just for a few set-asides but for a large, complex network. Marion Clawson (1983, 28) describes them as "the first *system* of permanent federal land reservation . . . created by the Federal Reserve Act of 1891" (emphasis in original). The Weeks Act in 1911 and the Clark-McNary Act in 1924 turned the preserves into national forests and also let previously private lands be so designated as well. In both cases, these were often holdings east of the Rockies. By then it was clear that the frontier had survived not only in the West, but also in Appalachia, northern New England, and the upper Midwest, and some of it was now designated national forest. New protected land categories, such as the fish and wildlife refuges and the Great Plains' national grasslands, later joined the national forests and national parks, and each further undercut the assumptions of the inevitably progressive, late-Victorian history that concluded with a closed frontier. But these changes in perception coexisted with older assumptions about the lands' role in their local economies, and such contradictions further weakened possibilities for frontier regional planning.

After the declarations of the 1890 census and Turner, a second, perhaps more official, end of the frontier came with passage in 1934 of the Taylor Grazing Act, the law that ended homesteading. The New Deal grappled with mixed objectives on the frontier. The Great Depression threatened most U.S. settlement arrangements, and the frontier was just as vulnerable as the cities. Rural areas initially drew people back, offering at least the possibility of a garden and shelter. The substantial workforce programs of the 1930s also kept then-current residents or brought new people to the frontier to build roads, trails, and other park facilities, drill new water holes, and construct dams. Some of the frontier population got moved. The Resettlement Administration, later renamed the Farm Security Administration, found the optimism of the earlier settle-everywhere approach misplaced, and so did the federal commission convened in 1936 to consider the future of the Great Plains. Instead, they determined, land needed assessment of its capability. Those living on land deemed submarginal should move elsewhere, preferably en masse. This required considerable planning to make the new places habitable. The old abandoned places also needed planning. Newly acquired federal holdings, such as the national grasslands, often were managed by local committees established for private benefit, with the Forest Service setting their fees in an odd new public-private combination (Wallach 1991).

All the New Deal's regional planning activity took place without a clear agenda for the frontier. Western writer Richard Manning (2009) faults New Deal policies in the Missouri Breaks region of eastern Montana for many of the area's later problems—its ever-declining population, stifled economy, and degraded habitat. In this hard setting, the population of the Missouri Breaks declined somewhat through the 1930s, and then kept falling.[3] That alone would not have incensed Manning, but New Deal policies working at cross-purposes

---

3. For example, the population of Garfield County, Montana, which lies at the center of the area, was 5,368 in 1920, 4,252 in 1930, 2,641 in 1950, and 1,244 in 2006, making it the nation's third least-populous county.

spent money on keeping people in place and then moving them out. Another policy built storage ponds almost every square mile for cattle, which reduced stream flow and grassland regeneration and made the cattle more dependent on the ponds, where water dried up more quickly and refilled more slowly. These inconsistent policies harmed wildlife, people, and the region's long-term economic and environmental health. The government was active, but not mindful. It utterly failed to make preservation, conservation, aridity, and low density work together, leaving a confused, angry legacy in the Missouri Breaks country that is echoed across the frontier.

The post-1945 frontier also saw ever more varied government, corporate, and individual activity in the forms of new recreational land uses for wider populations, the rise of contemporary environmentalism, the consequent appearance of antienvironmental and antigovernment groups, such as the Sagebrush Rebellion and the wise use movement, and the early stirring of ecological restoration. Planning, and the resistance to it, faced each other but, in a now-familiar pattern, neither undertook frontier regional planning.

TODAY'S FRONTIER

Frank J. Popper (1986) argues for the frontier's persistence. In early-1980s fashion, he marked a U.S. county map with colored pencils to show where the census's frontier population densities remained. The counties took up about as much of the country in 1980 as they had in 1880 and likewise became prevalent west of the 98th meridian, the eastern edge of the Great Plains. Similar results came from repeating the exercise in 1990 and 2000, and are likely to occur again for 2010 (Popper, Lang, and Popper 2000).

The frontier, however, had a new meaning in the United States late in the twentieth century. For Turner and the nineteenth-century censuses, the frontier was on its way to full settlement. It lacked the institutions typical of fully settled regions, but was expected to acquire them soon. The measure of population density conveyed more than a simple number, and its increase showed progress along a path of a kind held dear in this country and Europe by the generations that predated World War I: lock-step, inevitable, urbanizing, industrial, civilizing, national, rational, and above all led by themselves.

By the 1980s, however, the frontier had become an *f*-word to many, particularly historians, for whom it evoked an overly romanticized version of the country's past—white, male, racist, arrogant, jingoist, positivist, and antienvironmentalist. Other late twentieth-century critiques emphasized that no place really remained cut off from the baggage and benefits of urban civilization (Limerick 1987 and 1995). One could spend all day in frontier Kansas and still hear a live broadcast of the Berlin Symphony or attend a concert at the Topeka Symphony that night. If technology and infrastructure had penetrated all sorts of previously remote places, how could the frontier actually exist? Given modern-day conditions, what could its idea contribute? The intensity of the arguments added one more reason for the planning of the frontier to remain fragmented and unfocused. Avoiding the discussion was the easier course.

The modern frontier still faces many of its earlier difficulties. Journalist and filmmaker Dayton Duncan (1993, 1–2) captures its essence well.

> There is a part of America that exists miles from nowhere. People live there, but not many. So few, and sprinkled so thinly over such a vast territory, that even by standards of the covered wagon days this land would still be considered unsettled. It lies within the boundaries of the Lower 48, yet in many respects it is a different country. Counties the size of Eastern states have no doctor. A "town" that appears as a dot and a name on the map might turn out to be even less—an empty, abandoned building. Or it might consist of a post office, a gas station, a small grocery store, and a one-family residence—all under one roof. Out there, a minister might drive all Sunday to preach at four different services, and see a total of thirty parishioners. The neighborhood bar might be 75 miles away.

As a rule, the frontier's internal transportation and its links to the rest of the country and the world at large are poor. Modern telecommunication links have been slow to arrive, limited in coverage, and expensive. (In the lower Mississippi Delta, telephone service in Mink, Louisiana, arrived only in 2005.) Much of the frontier remains an extractor and exporter of natural resources. Many places lack enough people to support a vibrant local economy. Inconvenience, chosen or

---

From *Bead on an Anthill: A Lakota Childhood*

In my small community, before the [American Indian Movement] came, we were insulated from the world. The boys, including my youngest brother, rode Shetland ponies up and down an old wagon trail that ran next to the highway. It was called the Big Foot Trail. It was named after the chief whose people died at Wounded Knee. The boys raced their ponies along that trail. They could be seen in groups of seven or eight, riding everywhere together. We girls walked up the road on warm summer evenings to the white bluffs across from the community center. I still remember the smell of fresh hay in the evenings. Our families all knew one another. We all lived in houses set a mile or so apart. . . . The local policeman was a very large man with a big belly hanging over his belt. He had a family in our community. Although no one had a telephone, he always seemed to know when someone digressed and had too much alcohol to drink. We lived like that, isolated but serene in our innocence.
—Delphine Red Shirt (1998, 140–141)

imposed, means that some frontier people feel alienated from U.S. culture, the federal government, their state's government, or authority of any kind. In consequence, the frontier has some of the highest rates of poverty, disease, injury, crime, drug use, and inequality in income, wealth, and land ownership in the United States (NCFC 2007).

The frontier lacks political power. By definition it has a small part of its states' population and so cannot often influence their legislative agendas. The same is true for the U.S. House of Representatives. The frontier has more power in the Senate, where frontier states such as Alaska and Montana have as many votes as those with large populations including California and New York, but the senators tend to respond most to the more populous urban and suburban parts of their states. The frontier's lack of political power feeds back into its lack of economic power. It is unlikely to have large state or federal offices or a major branch of the state's university system, which today are important sources of economic growth and stability. Instead, it is more likely to receive (and seek) LULUs (locally unwanted land uses), such as prisons, hazardous waste facilities, power plants, and large mines.

In the nineteenth century the frontier's share of public goods grew. Its network of schools and post offices, for example, was once much more dense in response to a presumed rising demand for them. Churches, libraries, and banks increased. Now, frequently, such networks are thinning. Economic hardship increases pressure to cut them back further. Schools close due to both economics and an assumption that larger consolidated schools offer better education. Public libraries and churches struggle to stay open, and shared services and mobile provision hark back to circuit riders. Airline, railroad, and bus companies reduce coverage. Young people leave.

Public health, which was not a concept in nineteenth-century frontier planning, still suffers on the twenty-first-century frontier. Medical advances have often disadvantaged the frontier because they rely on costly, complex equipment, the financing for which then requires frequent use to recover upfront costs (Kraenzel 1980; NCFC). Frontier populations are too sparse to repay investment in this equipment. Typically, in fact, the frontier cannot support even low-tech medical facilities or attract medical staff, particularly doctors. Too often frontier medical, dental, and mental health services are available only on a rotating basis. A few states have programs to counter these problems, however. For example, Utah medical schools require students to do rotations that take them to sites throughout the state. The U.S. Health and Human Services Department's Office of Rural Health Policy also has grappled with the frontier's differences and needs, but these efforts are unusual rather than part of a widespread, cross-agency federal effort.

Sometimes the frontier encounters the irony of having too many people. Overpopulation tends to be an issue in high-amenity areas, places that outsiders perceive to offer exceptional recreation and aesthetics. Seasonal population spikes,

From *Refuge: An Unnatural History of Family and Place*

The Clan of One-Breasted Women

Over dessert, I shared a recurring dream of mine. I told my father that for years, as long as I could remember, I saw a flash of light in the night in the desert. . . .

"You did see it," he said.

"Saw what?"

"The bomb. The cloud. . . . In fact I remember the date, September 7, 1957. . . . It was an hour or so before dawn, when this explosion went off. We not only heard it, but felt it. . . . We pulled over and suddenly, rising from the desert floor, we saw it clearly, this golden-stemmed cloud, the mushroom. The sky seemed to vibrate with an eerie pink glow. Within a few minutes, a light ash was raining on the car."

I stared at my father.

"I thought you knew that," he said. "It was a common occurrence in the fifties."

It was at that moment that I realized the deceit I had been living under. Children growing up in the American Southwest, drinking contaminated milk from contaminated cows, even from the contaminated breasts of their mothers, my mother—members, years later, of the Clan of One-Breasted Women.

—Terry Tempest Williams (1991, 282–283)

whether of tourists or second-home owners, squeeze already limited services (NCFC 2003a). Large mines, oil and gas drilling, or construction projects also create boomtowns that quickly strain the supply of everything from housing to schools to health care. When the project ends, the bust sets in, and the oversupply creates a new burden that often fosters local sentiment that Washington, DC, large corporations, and/or the rest of U.S. society consider the frontier nothing more than a highly disposable resource colony, a terrestrial Outland.

Indeed, the people living in the frontier have remarkably little control over their own development, economy, environment, or tax revenue. Federal land agencies do not pay property taxes, but instead choose to offer their own compensation formulas—payments in lieu of taxes. The agencies set their rate, and Congress appropriates the money. States and localities neither determine the amount, nor can they confiscate the land for lack of partial, late, or what they consider inadequate payment. The resulting complaints have continued to fuel antigovernment forces that have succeeded the Sagebrush Rebellion.

Agencies in charge of public lands frequently find themselves in conflict with each other or internally. The Bureau of Land Management (BLM) controls

> ## From *Who Owns the West?*
>
> We like to claim the West is a place where you can have a shot at being what you want to be. You can come to terms with yourself. Freedom, in a livable community, is supposed to be the point of things. It's our prime mythology, and it sort of works out, more so if you're white and have some money.
>
> Men like my father, and the women who shared their ambitions, were our aristocracy. They are mostly dead. The West they left us is partway ruined, many of our enterprises are a considerable distance out on the rocks, and many of us are somewhat bewildered and heartbroke.
>
> We learned to name ourselves in what we took to be the nobility of their story. But they left us a society that's semifunctional at best. Up the Clark Fork River from the place where I live in Missoula, the Milltown Dam holds six and a half tons of sediment thick with toxic metals from the good old days in Butte. Our mountains erode under clear-cut logging, our farm towns are dying, we suffer the whims of a boom-or-bust economy, a history of semigenocidal racism, and a good-old-boys class system (we love to imagine we are enormously egalitarian, yet so many of us are powerless in any operative sense). And we're always broke.
>
> But we still listen to old promises in the wind. This time, we think, we'll get it right. And we'd better. We've about used up our chances. Like a house cat, the West has only got so many lives.
> —William Kittredge (1996, 37–38)

the largest acreage, but other large areas belong to the Forest, National Park, and Fish and Wildlife Services. The Department of Energy has large sites with nuclear facilities. The Environmental Protection Agency has oversight, but not prime responsibility, for many activities on public lands. Each agency has its own objectives and works within a specific management strategy. Some conflicts are obvious: The Fish and Wildlife Service must preserve species, which may limit mining on nearby BLM holdings or logging on Forest Service land. The Southwestern desert has seen much weapons testing (especially nuclear), which can conflict with other public trust obligations for public health or environmental management. Even within one category—wilderness as defined by the Wilderness Act (1964)—little consensus pertains, and much debate continues about what is wild and how to manage it (Rudzitis 1996).

Public lands often contain sites sacred to Native Americans. The National Park Service, for example, is responsible for Wyoming's Devils Tower, the first national monument Theodore Roosevelt created, but to Plains Indians it is the sacred Bear Lodge. Only a lawsuit forced the agency to create a management plan that recognizes obligations to Native Americans, mainly by restricting climbing during the month of June. Indian Pass in Imperial County, California, holds many Quechan pilgrimage sites, but is also a potential gold mine, and in 2001 Glamis Gold, Ltd., a Canadian mining company, sought BLM permission to extract gold. The Interior Department during the Clinton administration already had denied the request on cultural grounds, but Gale Norton, George W. Bush's interior secretary, reversed the decision and restarted the permitting process on the grounds that religious considerations were inappropriate (Yablon 2004).

Energy development creates endless conflict. A Utah start-up energy company, Blue Castle Holdings, is seeking approval from the Nuclear Regulatory Commission to build a nuclear power plant and has gotten leasing rights for land from San Juan and Kane Counties in eastern Utah. But Blue Castle's water demands will require diversion from other frontier places, which has generated opposition from the Fish and Wildlife Service and the Interior Department's Bureau of Reclamation. The company also needs a plan to dispose of spent fuel rods, most likely on the frontier (Waldholz 2010).

The many federal leases for natural gas, oil, and coal mining awarded in such states as Colorado and Wyoming have provoked enormous resistance. In 2002, for instance, as the BLM prepared to offer permits on 51,000 coal bed wells, environmental groups convinced the Interior Department's Land Appeals Board to ask for more study. Although the Bush administration issued a large number of permits, conservation groups kept fighting them (Burke 2002). Energy development, which is always risky, saw striking increases in job-related injuries and deaths (Ring 2008), and the Obama administration's Interior Department has been somewhat more cautious in leasing. For example, after review of 77 leases readied by the Bush administration, Interior Secretary and Coloradan Ken Salazar went ahead with only 17, canceling 8 and leaving the remaining 52 for indefinite deferral (Ring 2009). As of late 2010, the energy companies were appealing the decisions.

Preservation and recreational land uses that sometimes are promoted as having both positive economic and low environmental effects, although that is not always true, also can foster conflict. Development of new ski resorts, golf courses, and condos may run into issues involving water rights, sight lines, job development, and affordable housing. Local planning cannot fully resolve them, especially in communities in the midst of public lands (Power 2001; Rudzitis 2010). These projects, like those involving natural resources, need frontier regional planning and suffer in its absence.

FRONTIER FUTURES

The argument for planning that recognizes the frontier as a distinct region of the United States can appear anachronistic, but it fits well with contemporary regionalism. Douglas Reichert Powell (2007, 21) is clear: Regions spring not from their contiguity, but from their "set of relationships." Frontier communities share many such relationships, and frontier regional planning's first task is to revive the region's self-awareness and identity, show the relationships publicly, and thus create a frontier voice and vision. The core vision for frontier planning has always come from outside the region. In the nineteenth century, supporting the interests of the local Native American population, let alone their property values, economies, or cultures was anathema to frontier planning. External demand for the region's resources was given precedence, even after non–Native Americans comprised most of the population. Today, frontier regional planning must use and work with the local voice, which never has had a chance to speak for regional planning. And the frontier region lacks a visible governance structure to do the planning or an identity to support the structure. To move forward, voice and vision must develop simultaneously and do so at both the regional and subregional scales.

Possible subregional models already exist. Daniel Kemmis, former Missoula mayor, speaker of the Montana House, and now senior fellow at the Center for the Rocky Mountain West at the University of Montana, points to collaborative land management efforts as the most promising, especially under current conditions of diminished federal capacity and heightened global pressures. Collaborative planning differs from more traditional planning by using wider networks and a greater range of jurisdictions. It is also more open-ended in its definition of issues and solutions (McKinney and Johnson 2009). Groups such as the Henry's Fork Watershed Council (in Idaho), Quincy Library Group (California), Willapa Alliance (Washington), Malpai Borderlands Group (Arizona and New Mexico), and Applegate Partnership (Oregon) demonstrate how planning can bridge the differences between groups whose outlooks vary but who share commitment to a region (Kemmis 2001).

Scaled up or joined together, they could provide devices for the frontier region's voice and its policy development. The Quincy Library Group, for example, formed in 1993 to address northeastern California forest conflicts that sprang from potential logging declines and watershed deterioration. It put seemingly hostile loggers and environmentalists in one room and formed a framework for them to cooperate. They eventually began to work with federal agencies to arrive at solutions that none could have reached on their own. The comparable Quivira Coalition in New Mexico was established in 1997, when tensions ran high over grazing issues in the desert Southwest. The coalition successfully managed negotiations between environmental and ranching groups in order to find practices, research, and policies that would meet the objectives of both.

Such groups continue to emerge, and they often form around a watershed, development proposal, or threat to shut down a use of the land that provides local jobs and income. In a city, they would be neighborhood groups, with all the passion they bring to their issues. Though a single concern usually has been the impetus for each group's formation, the group and planning itself can only thrive by expanding to encompass a broader tangle of issues and less parochial interests. Frontier scale gives the groups much greater geographical heft, but the present condition of frontier regionalism often means their issues never get much attention nationally or even from other frontier places. As Patsy Healey (2006) has argued, however, collaborative planning works especially well with constituencies that are fragmented by place, class, or interest by building on what group members have in common. The device could be particularly useful for developing the noncontiguous frontier's identity and regional planning.

The Great Plains, a pivotal part of the frontier, offers another model for how frontier regional planning could work. Beginning just west of metropolises including Fargo, Oklahoma City, Omaha, and San Antonio and running to the base of the Rockies, the Plains area presents the clearest example of the settlement reversal Turner never expected. Much of the area seemed to reach settled status, but then population contracted in many places, with densities rolling back, often to frontier levels. The reversals left the Plains ambivalent about the frontier and many of the people and groups unwilling to plan for the conditions that persisted (Popper and Popper 2006). Yet twentieth-century censuses and the one in 2010 repeatedly show rural areas of the Great Plains dominating maps of national population loss.

The end of the twentieth century saw many attempts to revitalize regional visions for the Plains: the Land Institute's perennial polyculture experiments in Kansas, for example, or Northern Great Plains Inc.'s Meadowlark Project in North Dakota, which brings groups together to create future scenarios. The New Homestead Act, proposed to Congress in 2007 and 2008, was intended to offer incentives to people who were moving or returning to places that were losing population and to the multistate Buffalo Commons (Popper and Popper 1987). Each, with its own steps, plans, and actions, represents a possible route forward for the Great Plains.

Our experience with the Buffalo Commons offers useful lessons for regional planners across the frontier. The Plains forms the largest land area that population growth seemed to destine for settlement, which then reversed. Substantial population in-migration gave way at least twice—in the 1890s and during the "Dirty Thirties" Dust Bowl—to larger out-migration, and decline continues to this day. The Great Plains were promoted as an ideal destination for farmers, and early expectations fit the Jeffersonian agrarian vision, despite an inaccurate anticipation of a reliable water supply. Subsequent development led to high production, but only because of rising federal subsidies, heavy use of inputs, drawdowns on the biological and water base, and low-cost sales to other areas. Plains agriculture was shaped by the nineteenth century's frontier regional planning, which was nationally homogenizing and conceived and directed outside the region, and usually offered disappointing benefits. When this approach proved untenable, out-migration and decline resulted, and no new frontier planning took its place.

We have suggested that the ongoing Plains demographic, economic, and environmental problems would persist until another vision emerged, and we offered one that we based on ecological restoration (Popper and Popper 1987). If out-migration continued and intensified, in another generation the major tasks for much of the rural Plains frontier would be tearing down the fences, restoring the native plant and animal species, and supporting land use systems that relied on much more mobility across property lines. The short article, which was written for a general public and well-illustrated, set off widespread and enduring discussion of the future of the Great Plains.

The term *Buffalo Commons* entered the Plains vocabulary. Linked together, the words worked as metaphor, triggering images and ideas of what could happen there (Popper and Popper 1999). Civic, professional, academic, environmental, and government groups used the term and the authors to promote discussions of other Plains development paths. These groups included many individuals who indignantly rejected the Buffalo Commons, seeing it as Manifest Destiny perversely running in reverse. Editorials addressed its meaning and desirability and opened their newspapers' pages and Websites to reader response. Over time the term has become a Great Plains identifier. Among the many possible examples are a Buffalo Commons storytelling festival, string quartet, rural electric cooperative, furniture-design and software firms, and housing developments. Most recently Kansas's two largest newspapers editorially proposed a Buffalo Commons National Park on the state's Colorado border (*Kansas City Star* 2009).

Support for the idea strengthened, and its possibilities grew with the advent of actual Buffalo Commons land uses. The number of ranchers raising bison increased, and riparian areas improved as a result. Land preservation organizations, which were mostly absent from the Plains in 1987, began to acquire, restore, and educate people about the region. The InterTribal Bison Cooperative, a consortium of more than 50 tribes that was formed to promote bison restoration, provides education and training in bison management, advocates for bison, promotes buffalo culture (including art), and has helped tribes build their own herds. In South Dakota the Rosebud and Pine Ridge reservations

---

From *Coyote Nowhere: In Search of America's Last Frontier*

High Plains from Livingston, Montana
The land holds forth out here alone beneath skies filled with so many stars, planets, moons, and fizzling meteors that to look up at all of it is to knock out your head. The brain can't take in all of the information, all the truth that shines away up in the eternal dark. One look at this sky slams the message home. We aren't much of anything in the scheme of things. Eyes roll back into the head and thought processes short-circuit. That's what the northern high plains are. What they do to a person.
—John Holt (2000, 1)

of Lakota Sioux have adopted the Buffalo Commons as part of their land use plans. The Great Plains Restoration Council based in Texas formed in 1999 with the explicit aim of creating the Buffalo Commons.

For the Plains, the Buffalo Commons has become a unifying image that suggests new—and in some ways old—regional paths. It encourages ecology in economic development. Banks now lend for bison. Buffalo count in the allocation of federal public land grazing permits. New mobile slaughterhouses are available or in development. The numbers and types of initiatives keep growing, emerging from the ground up, and spreading out. The Buffalo Commons works as soft-edged planning rather than through the more usual rules and regulations. It suggests a planning approach, principles to pursue it, and a succinct framework to guide future actions (Popper and Popper 1996; 1999). We did not specify today's Buffalo Commons land use reality. In fact, the impressive results are more varied and far-reaching than we, or planning, generally could have imagined. A comparable coherent frontier metaphor could spark similar soft-edged regional planning by stirring individuals and groups to discuss, wrestle with, and create their own projections, projects, and meanings.

Even before a metaphor is established, however, the frontier could unite to oppose obstacles to development. Whatever their economic base, areas that are remote, sparsely settled, and low in population have already recognized that they have special needs in terms of transportation, communication, health, education, and social services. Yet public and private decisions about new routes, programs, and investments are made mostly in response to larger numbers or the interests that represent them—that is, to people and groups not on or of the frontier. Even an organization like the Western Governors' Association must put its larger urban, suburban, and exurban constituencies first.

A permanent or term-limited federal commission on recognizing and rectifying barriers for frontier places could bring the entire region together. The body might explore such bread-and-butter topics as setting appropriate application requirements for federal and state grants, staffing expectations for servicing these grants, and statistical calculations for compliance with requirements when the frontier numbers are too small or variable to mean much. Such a commission's recommendations could, for the first time ever, create a national frontier policy based on the frontier's needs rather than others' needs of it.

Because the frontier has so much public land, the commission could also assess impacts of federal and state public land policy on low-density areas. An obvious place to start would be the payment in lieu of taxes, its terms, and its reliability. Another may be exploring ways to strengthen and broaden organizations such as the Quincy Library Group as a way to improve governance. The commission also could try to resolve the continual conflicts between federal agencies of all kinds and their state counterparts as they affect the frontier. Recognizing that ever since the Lewis and Clark expedition, a large, unacknowledged share of the nation's scientific research has occurred on the frontier, the commission could examine whether enough of it is actually helping the region and how it might help more.

If the commission was truly effective, it could move on to address larger issues and serve as a forum for competing development ideas. As a body, it may be charged with assessing outcomes of traditional and alternative patterns. The commission could be particularly well-suited for this task because the frontier's large public land holdings offer the chance for government influence not easily available elsewhere. The commission might even examine the significance of the federal government's triple role for the frontier as its zoning board, funding source, and landlord—something, no doubt, that would have intrigued Turner.

By embracing its own regional planning, the frontier could recover its true promise and original place in the nation. Federal planning first appeared on the frontier. Planning as a modern professional field, however, emerged later in cities, which seemed easier to grasp and control. Today, local planning falls short because few modern land use issues—and certainly not the most compelling ones—are merely local. The problem is determining how to move beyond the local level. The surviving frontier offers opportunities for new methods that will challenge old ways. As a region it is sometimes contiguous, sometimes not, and linked by distinctive conditions rather than governments. New planning inspired or empowered by the frontier will offer innovative approaches to regional planning: a second chance for both the frontier and planning in the United States.

REFERENCES

Austin, Mary. 1903. A land of little rain. *Atlantic Monthly* 91 (January):96–99.

Burke, Adam. 2002. Energy boom's forward guard stalls out in Utah . . . for now. *High Country News* (13 May).

Child, Lee. 2001. *Echo burning*. New York: G. P. Putnam's Sons.

Clawson, Marion. 1983. *The federal lands revisited*. Baltimore, MD: Johns Hopkins Press.

Egan, Timothy. 2009. *The big burn: Teddy Roosevelt and the fire that saved America*. New York: Houghton Mifflin Harcourt.

Gannett, Henry. 1903. *Statistical atlas of the United States*. Washington, DC: U.S. Census Office.

Healey, Patsy. 2006. *Collaborative planning: Shaping places in fragmented societies*. 2nd ed. New York: Palgrave.

Holt, John. 2000. *Coyote nowhere: In search of America's last frontier*. New York: St. Martin's Press.

Hudson, John C. 1985. *Plains country towns*. Minneapolis: University of Minnesota Press.

Jackson, W. Turrentine. 1957. The creation of Yellowstone National Park. *Montana: The Magazine of Western History* 7 (summer):52–65.

Johnson, Eldon L. 1981. Misconceptions about the early land-grant colleges. *Journal of Higher Education* 52(4):333–351.

Kansas City Star. 2009. New park to save the Plains (14 November).

Kemmis, Daniel. 2001. *This sovereign land: A new vision for governing the West*. Washington, DC: Island Press.

Kittredge, William. 1996. *Who owns the West?* San Francisco: Mercury House.

Kraenzel, Carl F. 1980. *The social cost of space in the Yonland*. Bozeman, MT: Big Sky Books.

Lang, Robert E., Deborah Epstein Popper, and Frank J. Popper. 1995. Progress of the nation: The settlement history of the enduring American frontier. *Western Historical Quarterly* 26(3):289–307.

Limerick, Patricia. 1987. *Legacy of conquest: The unbroken past of the American West*. New York: Norton.

———. 1995. Turnerians all: The dream of a helpful history in an intelligible world. *American Historical Review* 100(3):697–716.

Manning, Richard. 2009. *Rewilding the West: Restoration in a prairie landscape*. Berkeley: University of California Press.

McKinney, Matthew J., and Shawn Johnson. 2009. *Working across boundaries: People, nature, and region*. Cambridge, MA: Lincoln Institute of Land Policy.

NCFC (National Center for Frontier Communities). 2003a. Seasonal population fluctuations in rural and frontier areas. Ojo Sarco, NM. www.frontierus.org/seasonal.htm

———. 2003b. Frontier counties in the United States, 2000 concensus. Ojo Sarco, NM. www .frontierus.org/documents/map7.htm

———. 2007. Poverty in frontier America: Higher rates of poverty document the critical need for policy changes. Research brief. Ojo Sarco, NM. http://frontierus.org/documents/Frontier%20 Poverty.pdf

Nickerson, Sheila. 1996. *Disappearance: A map*. New York: Harcourt Brace.

Opie, John. 1998. *Nature's nation: An environmental history of the United States*. Belmont, CA: Wadsworth Publishing.

Otterstrom, Samuel M., and Carville Earle. 2002. The settlement of the United States from 1790 to 1990: Divergent rates of growth and the end of the frontier. *Journal of Interdisciplinary History*. 33(1):59–85.

Popper, Deborah E., and Frank J. Popper. 1987. The Great Plains: From dust to dust. *Planning* (December):12–18.

———. 1996. The storytellers. *Planning* (October):18–19.

———. 1999. The Buffalo Commons: Metaphor as method. *Geographical Review* 89(4):491–510.

———. 2006. The Buffalo Commons: Its antecedents and their implications. *Online Journal of Rural Research and Policy* 1(6). http://ojrrp.org/journals/ojrrp/article/view/34

Popper, Deborah E., Robert Lang, and Frank J. Popper. 2000. From maps to myth: The census, Turner, and the idea of the frontier. *American Journal of Comparative Cultures* 23(1):91–102.

Popper, Frank J. 1986. The strange case of the contemporary frontier. *Yale Review* 76(1):101–121.

Powell, Douglas Reichert. 2007. *Critical regionalism: Connecting politics and culture in the American landscape*. Chapel Hill: University of North Carolina Press.

Powell, John Wesley. 1878. *Report on the lands of the arid region of the United States*. Cambridge, MA: Harvard University Press.

Power, Thomas R. 2001. *Post-cowboy economics: Pay and prosperity in the new American West*. Washington, DC: Island Press.

Pudup, Mary Beth. 1987. From farm to factory: Structuring and location of the U.S. farm machinery industry. *Economics Geography* 63(3):203–222.

Red Shirt, Delphine. 1998. *Bead on an anthill: A Lakota childhood*. Lincoln: University of Nebraska.

Reps, John W. 1979. *Cities of the American West: A history of frontier urban planning*. Princeton, NJ: Princeton University Press.

Ring, Ray. 2007. Disposable workers of the oil and gas fields. *High Country News* (2 April). www.hcn .org/issues/343/16915

———. 2009. The federal energy two-step. *High Country News* (21 December). www.hcn.org/ issues/41.22/the-federal-energy-two-step

Rudzitis, Gundars. 1996. *Wilderness and the changing American West*. Hoboken, NJ: John Wiley & Sons.

———. 2010. *The ongoing transformation of the American West*. Chicago: University of Chicago.

Sparks, Edwin Erle. 1900. *The expansion of the American people, social and territorial.* Chicago: Scott, Foresman.

Turner, Frederick Jackson. 1925. The significance of the section in American history. *Wisconsin Magazine of History* 8(3):255–280.

———. 1962. *The frontier in American history.* New York: Holt, Rinehart, and Winston.

Waldholz, Rachel. 2010. Water fallout: Utah's first nuclear plant won't float without water rights. *High Country News* (1 March):7.

Wallach, Bret. 1991. *At odds with progress: Americans and conservation.* Tucson, AZ: University of Arizona Press.

Webb, Walter Prescott. 1931. *The Great Plains.* Boston: Ginn.

———. 1937. *Divided we stand: The crisis of a frontierless democracy.* New York: Farrar and Rinehart.

———. 1952. *The great frontier.* Boston: Houghton Mifflin.

Whitman, Walt. 1963. *Prose works 1892.* Vol. 1: *Specimen days.* New York: New York University Press.

Williams, Terry Tempest. 1991. *Refuge: An unnatural history of family and place.* New York: Random House.

Yablon, Marcia. 2004. Property rights and sacred sites: Federal regulatory responses to Native American religious claims on public land. *Yale Law Journal* 113:1623–1662.

CHAPTER **6** GREEN REGIONS,
GREEN REGIONALISM

Timothy Beatley

A VISION OF GREEN REGIONS

The central argument of this chapter holds that a true shift toward sustainability ultimately will require what I call *green regions:* spatial units that mix urban settlements with surrounding hinterlands and ecosystems and that together yield compact, sustainable cities and settlement patterns. Additionally, such regions can be the source of much of the renewable energy, sustainably sourced water and food, and other goods and materials that will be needed to nurture and sustain growing American populations in the future.

I refer to the practice and perspective that arise from this kind of region as *green regionalism,* where green is meant to bear a double meaning. First, it suggests ecological or sustainable approaches, such as reduction of energy and resource consumption and limitation of pollutants. But I also use green in the chlorophyllic and biophilic senses, which indicate that a region is respectful of and conserves nature and integrates it into planning and design.

The region is the appropriate spatial focus because it offers the possibility of taking into account and planning for ecosystems and natural systems, from forests and habitats, to larger watersheds and aquatic systems, to the working landscapes of woodlands and farmlands that can serve to sustain urban populations. Regional landscapes and natural systems provide important, though sometimes forgotten, ecological benefits and services. For instance, forests sequester carbon, moderate air pollution, retain stormwater, and provide other benefits, and wetlands provide natural flood retention and water quality benefits (e.g., American Forests, n.d.; Windhager et al. 2010).

What constitutes or defines the boundaries of a region remains an open question. Within the long history of multistate, regional, and ecosystem-defined planning and management efforts—from the New Jersey Pinelands to the Florida Everglades and San Francisco Bay—arose a variety of jurisdictional, policy, and management structures and arrangements that correspond to them (Layzer 2008; Steiner 1983). A number of jurisdictional and legal bases for green regional planning also exist, including habitat conservation plans (HCPs) under the federal Endangered Species Act (ESA) and a series of bioregional councils established in California. The scale of the vision for green regions offered here, however, encompasses the region that is centered on one or more cities or urban areas, which more essentially may be considered to be green metropolitan areas.

This chapter attempts to describe emerging green regions and elucidate current trends and methods in green regionalism, to review good practice in this area, and discuss current challenges and future directions. Metropolitan and regional planning efforts in several key cities—Vancouver (Canada), Brisbane (Australia), Tucson (United States), London and Cardiff (United Kingdom), and Barcelona (Spain), among others—serve as examples. They show both what is possible with a vision based in green regionalism and provide interesting and sometimes inspiring examples of leading-edge regional sustainability efforts. These green regions are included because they are perhaps most like or applicable to the political and institutional context of regions in the United States.

As described here, green regionalism includes understanding that sustainability plans and actions can, indeed must, occur at every scale. Sustainability is best understood as a nested framework, which includes actions from the level of a building or rooftop to that of a region or bioregion. We know that cities and built environments, along with the urban populations living in them, are responsible for much of the consumption of energy and resources today. At the same time, they also represent perhaps the best single hope for reaching a condition of sustainability in the future.

As Herbert Girardet (2006, 10) has presciently written: "There will be no sustainable world without sustainable cities" and, by extension, sustainable regions. Declining global oil supplies and the need to transition beyond fossil fuels present especially difficult and profound challenges to reimagining future cities and metropolitan regions. Compact and dense regional urban form provides the possibility of dramatically reducing our resource and land consumption, at the same time as they can enhance quality of life and livability.

While sustainability planning at the neighborhood, city, or regional level is sometimes described as a distinct endeavor with a discrete set of topics, it is and must also be highly integrative. A vision of a sustainable region must include and address a wide range of issues and policy realms, from housing and development location to energy production and efficiency, green building, parks and landscape conservation, transport planning, and economic development, among many others. Successful regional sustainability efforts consider and incorporate these different planning realms, but they also understand the special emotional and perceptual roles that regions can play in providing the overarching framework for binding a unified ecological vision and practice together.

THE ECOLOGICAL AND EMOTIONAL VALUE OF GREEN REGIONS

While everyone lives in a neighborhood, on a street, or in some smaller-scale spatial unit, humans also relate to—and *need,* I argue—larger landscapes to define their lives. These larger regional landscapes and environments are also important definers of "home," and they provide significant emotional succor and become important sources of stability, constancy, and rootedness in a place. A key premise of green regionalism is the value and importance of the natural and ecological qualities of place.

Kirkpatrick Sale (1991, 43) defines a bioregion as "a life-territory, a place defined by its life forms, its topography and its biota, rather than by human dictates; a region governed by nature, not legislature." Green regions represent opportunities to develop connections with and closeness to natural environments and suggest the chance to learn about and develop important competencies for caring for flora, fauna, and natural systems. In green regions citizens recognize common species of plants and trees, are able to name the major watershed in which they live, and can recognize the signs of seasonal change.

Two significant and important insights from bioregional thinking are that scale matters and that, with local and regional reorientation, adapting to new behaviors and practices becomes possible. Regional awareness permits, indeed requires, more cautious and responsible consumption and lifestyles. Sale (1991, 54) eloquently argues:

> For if there is any scale at which ecological consciousness can be developed, at which citizens can see themselves as being the *cause* for the environmental *effect*, it is at the regional level; there all ecological questions are taken out of the realm of the philosophical and the moral and are dealt with as immediate and personal. People do not, other things being equal, pollute and damage those natural systems on which they depend for life and livelihood if they see directly what is happening; nor voluntarily use up a resource under their feet and before their eyes if they perceive that it is precious, needed, vital; nor kill off species they can see are important for the smooth functioning of the ecosystem.

Effective strategies to advance sustainability will require regional scale and perspective, and regional planning must provide a necessary and essential spatial lens for imagining more sustainable forms of future growth and development. Biodiversity conservation, a shift toward renewable and low-carbon energy sources, local and regional food production, and waste management, are among the issues that will require being tackled at regional levels.

Local sustainability projects and initiatives can accomplish much, to be sure, but they often suffer from scalability limitations, remaining pilot initiatives and demonstration projects. Additionally, they sometimes work at cross-purposes with each other, failing to take advantage of synergies and opportunities for coordination and cooperation. A framework of green regions can provide an important unifying context and lens that help to integrate and coordinate local efforts. Green regionalism is especially well suited to the current times and challenges, such as landscape adaptation response to climate change impacts.

It is also important to understand the role of regions and places in shaping broader sustainability values and attitudes, citizens' emotional and psychological health, and planetary or ecological health in the narrow sense. One of the clear insights from bioregionalism is the potentially important role that localized and regional production of food and energy can play in reconnecting individuals to other individuals and the larger communities and environments in which they live. The local food movement, for instance, is as concerned with reestablishing personal, meaningful connections between farmers and land stewards and the more urban residents who consume the food grown as it is with nutrition and physical health.

Especially at the regional level, moreover, important social and emotional ties arise that can at once enhance enjoyment, ensure that lives and living are meaningful, and strengthen and support more sustainable practices and policies.

In contemplating effective regional sustainability plans and planning, several planning and policy considerations are important, including the region's scale, boundary definitions, and jurisdictional powers. The long history of thinking about and practicing in bioregionalism is helpful here and entails several regions where bioregional ideas and policies have been applied and considered in experiments. At the core are ideas of organizing management and planning around ecological boundaries, nurturing greater awareness of environmental processes and impacts, developing a deeper sense of place and commitment to landscape, and a relocalizing and regionalizing of food, energy, and economy (Sale 1991; Thayer 2003).

One of the interesting questions in bioregionalism is how to define the bioregion. What logical biological, ecological, or landscape unit, or other criterion is appropriate? To a large degree this is emotional—in what sense do residents of a region or place identify with that allocation and its particular set of boundaries. The Shasta bioregion in Northern California, for instance, can be said to hang together and serve as a psychologically meaningful region because of Shasta Mountain's essential visual and ecological defining quality.

Sometimes bioregional units, such as the bioregional planning councils formed in California, have official or formal functions that can be useful as devices for planning and raising awareness. In some cases, as with the Cuyahoga Bioregion in Cleveland, a bioregion may also encapsulate and correspond roughly with a metropolitan region. Metropolitan-area planning and governance with serious and important ecological and sustainability goals are emerging in a number of places.

The concept of regional sustainability holds that attachment to landscape and place are important and ought to be encouraged. Some of the most interesting contemporary work in social psychology suggests that emotional health is or will be linked to landscape and environmental health.

Glenn Albrecht at Murdoch University in Western Australia has coined the term *solastalgia* to describe the sense of emotional distress he has encountered in residents of regions where significant and serious landscape destruction occurs. He first encountered this in the Upper Hunter Region of New South Wales, an area ravaged by open-pit coal mining. Working with *nostalgia*, Albrecht (2005, 17; 2007) defines solastalgia as "the pain or sickness caused by the loss or lack of solace and the sense of isolation connected to the present state of one's home and territory."

While solastalgia is a kind of regional or place-based pathology, perhaps even more interesting is work by Albrecht and others toward identifying the healthy or healthful emotional qualities of a region that bode well for reaching many of the sustainable outcomes described above. Albrecht (2010) offers the concept of *soliphilia* to describe regions where a shared sense of connection and solidarity seems to exist, and he defines it as "the love of and responsibility for a place, bioregion, planet and the unity of interrelated interests within it." Love of region, place, and environment is intrinsically of value, but it is also very helpful in bringing about the behavioral changes and political commitments needed to move toward sustainability.

GREEN REGIONS WITH A HOLISTIC VIEW

Regional efforts at sustainability have the potential advantage of providing the perspective to see the larger picture spatially and temporally and thus to set a broader vision and direction. A map that shows what a region or metropolitan area might look like in 50 or 100 years can shape awareness and attitudes and become an important force in influencing behavior and identity. A region's physical and ecological boundaries are also important, as are the powers and administrative organization of the entity or entities that have charge of regional sustainability planning. Some of the examples of regional entities and agencies described in this chapter have extensive regulatory and planning powers (e.g., those in Brisbane and London), while others are involved mostly in planning, coordinating, and educational functions.

The process and structure of regional sustainability planning are critical as well. Few urban regions have embarked on regional sustainability planning programs that are as impressive and comprehensive as that in Vancouver, British Columbia. The region's concerns about sustainability have resulted in an unusual fusing of green goals with the somewhat more traditional regional planning goals related to land use, housing, and infrastructure. Metro Vancouver, the organization in charge, is a regional government that holds considerable powers and operational responsibilities.

Metro Vancouver has developed an impressively broad sustainability frame-work for guiding its efforts. Together, its statements of regional vision, role and mission, and values, along with a series of sustainability principles, guide and give context to its suite of plans, policies, and regulations. A set of measures and targets has been identified and is monitored, and progress is reported annually in a sustainability report. To its credit, Metro Vancouver (2010, 8) has "for-mally put the concept of sustainability at the center of its operating and plan-ning philosophy." Its brief and concise vision statement sums up well these priorities and the region's "unshakeable commitment to the well-being of cur-rent and future generations and the health of the planet" (Metro Vancouver 2010, 10).

Metro Vancouver's set of regional plans reflects its understanding that achieving regional sustainability and advancing a regional vision require a com-prehensive approach. The plans include those for management of solid waste, air quality, and drinking water as well as one for parks and greenways and even a regional homelessness plan. Its regional growth strategy is among the more important plans in this suite, and a new draft was released in fall 2009.

The value of having an agency with regional service responsibilities and powers is incalculable. Metro Vancouver specifically has responsibilities for regional growth management, waste management, and air quality. Many of its service responsibilities (water, wastewater, solid waste, parks, and affordable housing) directly influence sustainability and provide potent levers for changes in practices and policy. Metro Vancouver has a strong service-provision role in the region as well as a regulatory role.

It is important to recognize, however, that regional bodies of this kind are presented with other opportunities to influence regional sustainability, such as through education, partnering, studies and analysis, and pilot and demonstra-tion project funding. Metro Vancouver, for instance, understands that its role extends well beyond regulatory and service provision: "Metro Vancouver serves as the main political forum for discussion of significant community issues at the regional level. It acts as a facilitator, convener, partner, advocate and a signifi-cant instrument for providing information and education to the community" (Metro Vancouver 2009a, 7).

To this end, a number of new and creative initiatives are being undertaken by Metro Vancouver to raise public and professional awareness about sustainability. They include convening an annual series of dialogues on the future of the region's sustainability. In 2010, some 16 dialogues were organized in various areas around the Vancouver region (Metro Vancouver, n.d.). To its credit, Metro Vancouver's role has evolved in positive ways to encompass sustainability more fully, including giving support for and doing work in green building promotion.

Similarly, in the United Kingdom the Greater London Authority (GLA), created in 2000, is described as a "strategic authority . . . [that] works closely with the [33] boroughs to deliver the Mayor's long-term strategy for London, ensuring that the big picture of the capital is taken into account at the local level" (GLA, n.d.). Much of the GLA's work deals with developing regional strategy plans and documents, including major ones that address biodiversity conservation, climate change and energy, and spatial planning, among others. The GLA has the power to ensure that local plans are consistent with the larger ones, but much of its function appears to be aimed at motivation, guidance, and inspiration. Accomplishments in sustainability planning and policy in the London region to date primarily have come about due to the commitment and strong advocacy of former mayor Ken Livingstone.

As does Metro Vancouver, the GLA recognizes the importance of educating and leading by example. Part of the important role of such regional agencies is seeing that new sustainability initiatives are launched and then providing financial underwriting. One recent London example is Capital Growth's new program, which is run by London Food Link. It was created with £150,000 of GLA funding and benefited from the strong support of the current mayor, Boris Johnson. Its goal is to create 2,012 new food-growing spaces by the year 2012 (Capital Growth 2009).

In Australia, regional plans reflect a strong emphasis on and concern with sustainability and sustainable development. In part this reflects an emphasis at the national level, and most of the regional plans reference and embrace the goals set out in the National Strategy for Ecologically Sustainable Development adopted by the national government in 2002 (Government of Australia 2002). Regional plans for each of the country's major urban regions contain clear and explicit commitment to sustainability along with land use, transportation, and energy elements, all of which give tangible meaning to such commitment. Australian metropolitan areas are contained within the relatively extensive boundaries of single states, and because state governments prepare Australia's regional plans they carry much weight. These plans serve as bases for approval of local council plans and guide significant transportation and infrastructural investments by state governments (Beatley and Newman 2009).

Best efforts at green regionalism also understand that progress must be gauged and monitored over time and that, too often, sustainability is criticized as being rhetorical rather than real. Metro Vancouver, for instance, has developed a set of regional indicators and publishes yearly sustainability reports that inform constituents about progress made. These indicators include such things as per capita water use (declining), amount of solid waste generated per capita (rising), recycling rates by sector, percentage of work trips made by means other than by car (transit and walking are going up, while car usage is lessening), regional greenhouse gas emissions (lowering), hectares of regional parklands per capita (showing slight decline), and urbanized land area in the region (remaining steady).[1] They provide important snapshots of how well an area is doing in terms of sustainability and whether each trend is moving in the preferred direction. A comprehensive set

---

1. One hectare is equal to 2.47 acres.

of regional sustainability indicators is essential, as is a formal process and schedule for making available to the public and decision makers progress reports concerning the achievement of the adopted vision and goals.

The holistic approach to green regionalism advocated here also raises important questions about these efforts' temporal timeframes. A perennial criticism of planning holds that most plans are decidedly short-term, despite their orientation toward the future. Ideally, green regions of the sort suggested here should strive for a longer timeframe in their planning efforts. Many of our most pressing environmental and sustainability problems and challenges will require a much longer temporal perspective. Climate change, biodiversity protection, and ecosystem restoration all require a timeframe comprising hundreds of years.

Moreover, for regions to achieve their conservation goals effectively, projecting forward to comprehend impacts over periods of 100, 200, 500, even 1,000 years is not unreasonable, and in fact would serve to alter significantly the sense of what is acceptable or permissible in the short term. Advocacy of such longer timeframes is unusual, but not unprecedented: Bruce Tonn's (1996; 1998) important articles argue for 500-year plans, for example. The planning reality is quite different, of course, with few regional efforts embracing even a 50-year timeframe (e.g., Portland 2040), and most are much shorter in scope. Regional plans even fail to extend to the average length of a human life, let alone the life spans of such long-lived creatures as sea turtles that often live 100 years, and bowhead whales, which can reach 200 years of age.

Those limited instances that do exist show the power of working with longer temporal frames for green regionalism. For instance, for the Greater Puget Sound region the Cascade Land Conservancy has prepared a 100-year vision and plan, which it calls the Cascade Agenda. While its vision and targets are bold, extending 100 years is understood to be a necessary step toward reaching them: "The 2105 conservation goal is to have 4.1 million acres, or 77% of the region protected" (Cascade Land Conservancy 2005, 31). Longer planning timeframes are possible, and they will be essential to laying out and bringing about bold visions for green regions.

GREEN REGIONS AS ECOLOGICAL REGIONS

Natural systems and features of varying magnitudes represent the essential building blocks of regional plans. Beginning with the largest natural systems—rivers and large-scale hydrology, topography and regional climate, for example—they reduce in size to the neighborhood scale as it concerns ecology and hydrology. A green region acknowledges these ecological conditions as assets, understands their values and benefits, and works hard to protect them and to fit the more urban and built elements of place into this biological and ecological matrix. Ecological principles and goals should drive a regional plan in theory, and it must set the framework in which a variety of actions and activities, from transport and infrastructure planning to designation of new growth areas, might be sustainable.

The ecological goals and methods employed in green regionalism have a well-established heritage, and they draw notably from the thinking of regional luminary Benton MacKaye and, more recently, Ian McHarg. At a relatively early date, MacKaye (1940, 351) authored an essay entitled "Regional Planning and Ecology," in which he stated presciently that "regional planning is ecology . . . . Its object is the application or putting into practice of the optimum relation between the human and the region." Achieving a balance, a harmony, a fitting into the carrying capacities and capabilities of the region's environment, are still central to any notion of a green region today.

At present, many good examples of green regions exemplify and illustrate the importance given to ecological conditions and assets. In Brisbane, the South East Queensland (SEQ) Regional Plan has undertaken an impressive effort at mapping in order to take stock of ecosystem elements and ecological assets (figure 6.1). The SEQ plan required extensive mapping of natural areas, including regional landscape and rural production areas, such as forests, agricultural lands, and water and groundwater resources. Also mapped are sensitive coastal lands, world heritage sites, nature conservation areas, and some 29 biological wildlife corridors. Special habitat areas—important sites of Koala habitat, for instance— are also mapped.

Many of the best regional plans place water concerns, both for its supply and its quality, at their core. In South Australia, the Adelaide Regional Plan attempts to accomplish an impressive "whole of water cycle approach," and a single metro-wide map shows "current sources, use and disposal of Adelaide's water" (Government of South Australia 2007, 31). Such mapping exercises effectively convey the magnitude of regional water demands, spatial and environmental implications, and opportunities for regional use and policy changes. Detailed regional water management standards are derived from this analysis, including the need to use water more efficiently and to shift to water-sensitive urban design, a version of the low-impact development discussed in the United States.

The regional policy plan for Cape Cod in Massachusetts also focuses on water and water quality. It identifies and seeks to protect the region's groundwater, which is the sole source of drinking water for the Cape. This regional plan extensively maps the locations of the six groundwater "lenses" from which water is extracted as well as the areas of wellhead protection and groundwater recharge that are essential to using and sustainably managing this limited regional resource (Cape Cod Commission 2006).

In a number of U.S. metropolitan areas, a comprehensive ecological and environmental inventory has served as an important planning step. In Washington, DC, for instance, as early as 1968 the Metropolitan Washington Council of Governments (MWCOG 1968) prepared an "ecological reconnaissance" of the region. The layers include geology, elevation and slope, soils, streams and hydrology, floodplains, groundwater, and woodlands, among others. In Washington and elsewhere these natural elements shape everything that follows.

Along with the extent of impervious surface, trees, forests, and native vegetation are important regional ecological assets that should be taken into account in any regional planning effort. The amount and extent of canopy coverage is often extensive and provides tremendous ecological and environmental benefits, from cooling and climate moderation to air quality, stormwater retention, and wildlife habitat and biodiversity conservation. Impressively, Vancouver's regional canopy coverage is equal to a little less than one-half of the regional land area (about 46 percent in 2002). The organization American Forests has established urban and regional targets, and many cities and metropolitan regions have now

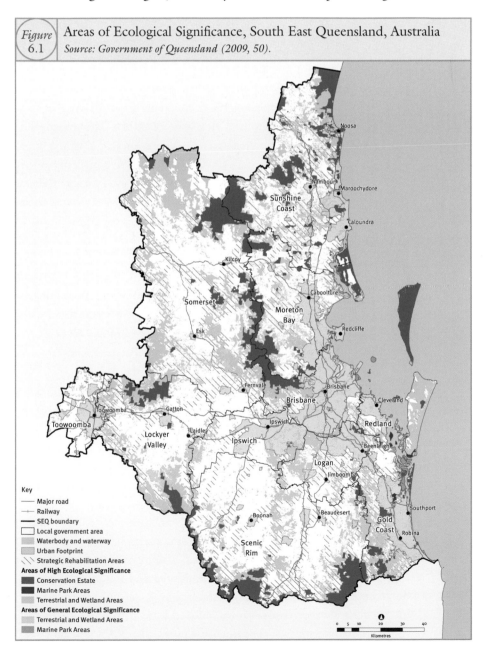

Figure 6.1	Areas of Ecological Significance, South East Queensland, Australia
	Source: Government of Queensland (2009, 50).

established ambitious tree planting goals and targets. Cities such as New York, Los Angeles, and Houston have each set the goal of planting a million new trees, usually over a period of five to ten years.

Regional climate is another important factor to take into account and map. German cities and urban regions commonly incorporate an extensive climatologic element in their planning. Mapping prevailing regional wind direction has led to development of important sustainability policies and projects, such as the one in Freiburg, where building location, height, and design must all consider these flows in order to address the particular goal of not impeding the recuperative winds that flow into the city from the nearby Black Forest.

GREEN REGIONS AND BIODIVERSITY

Often extensive biodiversity and habitat require protection and management, both of which are important bioregional goals. Bolder visions for regional land and biodiversity conservation are needed. The Tucson and Pima County, Arizona, region is an excellent example of this scale of effort. The award-winning Sonoran Desert Conservation Plan (SDCP) represents one of the most extensive regional habitat conservation efforts anywhere. A concerted effort to plan and protect biodiversity in this fast-growing region was brought about in 1997 with the federal listing of the cactus ferruginous pygmy-owl (*Glaucidium brasilianum cactorum*) as an endangered species. A broad coalition of organizations joined with Pima County to prepare the SDCP, an ambitious ecosystem- or bioregion-based conservation plan.

In light of the extent of local population growth and the prevailing patterns of urban sprawl in the Tucson metropolitan area, habitat protection presents a challenge. The region's population has more than doubled since the 1970s, resulting in significant loss of desert habitat (Huckelberry 2002). Most of the growth has occurred through low-density urban sprawl. Tucson's central core, moreover, lost much of its vitality and population at the same time.

Development of the SDCP was overseen by an 84-member steering committee. The initial draft was prepared under the guidance of a scientific technical team known as the Sonoran Desert Conservation Plan Science Technical Advisory Team, or STAT, headed by Professor William Shaw of the University of Arizona. The plan is based on extensive biological data and habitat mapping. Out of an estimated 12,000 species, some 55 designated as vulnerable were selected as the focus of conservation efforts.

The SDCP consists of several main elements: ranch conservation; riparian restoration; mountain parks; historical and cultural preservation; and critical habitat and biological corridors. The geographical scale of the plan is unusually large, covering an area of nearly 6 million acres. A map and vision of a regional conservation reserve are at the heart of the plan. A careful, science-based approach was used to identify conservation lands. Those with habitat supporting five or more vulnerable species were included in the plan's "biological core."

Described as "the most ambitious of its kind," the plan's proposed reserve system would dwarf others that have been planned or implemented in other western cities (Davis 2002).

The plan has already garnered praise from many quarters, and it has won some 14 national awards, including the American Planning Association's national Outstanding Planning for a Plan award in 2002. Important conservation results included the creation of the Ironwood Forest National Monument and support for the designation of Las Cienegas National Conservation Area. The plan's map of biological resources and conservation lands has been folded into Pima County's comprehensive plan, which serves as the county's main template for guiding future growth and development. A set of development guidelines has been adopted, and it establishes a minimum of conservation set-asides for proposed rezoning within the so-called conservation lands system. The plan's maps and vision have been widely circulated within the Tucson–Pima County region and already have shaped effective expectations about future land development and growth.

Among the important positive lessons offered by the Pima County experience are the importance of taking a broader, ecosystemwide approach (e.g., moving beyond a single, or even just a few species); the tremendous technical and informational value of tools like geographic information systems; the importance of being able to answer questions that come up along the way, and to rebut criticisms and empirical critiques; the great value of partnerships; and that good, solid scientific and technical analysis is done in an open, transparent way. A number of things make the Pima County plan especially unique and exemplary, including its comprehensive nature, the boldness of its vision, and its science-based methods. A decision was made early on that the conservation plan would not be driven simply by the immediate needs of satisfying Section 10 of the ESA. The plan broadly addresses biodiversity in the county, considering what it will take to protect and preserve all of its biodiversity, not simply ESA-protected species. Extensive environmental education about the desert environment directed especially at children and schools, including a program called Sonoran Desert Kids, has worked hand in hand with the SDCP. Especially when cultivated among young people, knowledge about and concern for desert ecosystems may be laying an essential foundation for an informed and committed citizenry at the same time it profoundly enhances their lives.

Another important and unusual element of the Pima County approach is the effort to join concerns about biodiversity protection with those for cultural and historical resources. Indeed, a team formed and staffed to consider these resources met alongside the STAT. The resulting implementation actions and program will address conservation in its broadest sense—that of history, culture, and archeological resources, along with biologically based criteria. This is very sensible in that considerable overlap often occurs between these various resources, but perhaps more importantly because the approach expands the constituency of and support for the plan.

While the U.S. Fish and Wildlife Service has yet to approve the plan formally, the prospects for successful implementation are good. For example, a multiple species–habitat conservation plan, seen as an implementation tool under the broader SDCP, was submitted in late 2010, and many important conservation actions have already been undertaken. Citizens of Pima County have approved several relatively large bond measures, including one in 2004 for $174 million, for habitat acquisition. Many other initiatives are encouraging as well, such as efforts by the City of Tucson to redevelop and encourage infill development, thus addressing urban sprawl, at least partially. More than 230,000 acres already have been protected through a combination of deeded lands and grazing leases (Fonseca and Jones 2009). The power of the broad vision can also be seen in the fact that developers' and landowners' expectations have already shifted significantly in response to the widespread dissemination of the plan.

GREEN REGIONS AS BIOPHILIC

A green region's ecological assets hold the potential for residents to visit, see, interact with, and otherwise enjoy the nature around them. From the increasingly compelling evidence, we recognize that healthy and productive lives require ready access to nature. Through his book *Last Child in the Woods*, journalist Rich Louv (2005) has ignited a national and international debate by arguing that contemporary people suffer from what he terms *nature deficit disorder*, which results from living lives deficient in access and exposure to nature. This idea relies heavily on the concept of *biophilia*, which was popularized by Harvard biologist E. O. Wilson, who holds that the species *Homo sapiens* has coevolved with nature and natural environments, and that we want and need contact with nature (Kellert, Heerwagen, and Mador 2008; Wilson 1984). The extent to which its citizens have access to nature becomes an additional measure of a successful green region.

Many of our best, most-lauded examples of green regionalism do in fact emphasize access to nature. Regional plans for Scandinavian cities, for example, emphasize the importance of setting aside large blocks of greenspace in close proximity to urban neighborhoods. Copenhagen's famous regional plan of 1947, known popularly as the Fingers Plan, steers regional growth along the fingers of its rail system, while preserving large wedges of green land in between. That, in combination with investments in bicycle infrastructure and transit, makes it relatively easy for residents to enjoy outdoor nature close to home. The City of Copenhagen continues to work to increase the extent of parks and recreational areas within the city, including creating new areas to make swimming safe in formerly polluted harbor waters.

Similarly, in Helsinki an extensive network of urban greenspaces allows residents to move from the city center to large outlying blocks of old-growth forest. In Oslo, a combination of efforts at containing urban growth and protecting natural lands has resulted in provision of large forested stretches near the areas where most people live in this urban region. Residents frequently visit these beloved forests, which are known affectionately as the *marka*. The city also has endeavored to expand its footpaths and cycle paths, and its current plan states its intention to "develop a continuous green structure from the forest to the fjord and along the coastline" (City of Oslo 2008, 53). Plans to "daylight" the streams and rivers that flow into the city essentially will bring them back to the surface, restore their natural functioning, and reinstate their importance as ecological and recreational elements in the city.

The network of open space and natural spaces in the Greater London region includes the Green Belt, Metropolitan Open Land, and Blue Ribbon Network. The latter is an important component of a regional network of greenspaces, and this one includes the Thames River as well as smaller streams and canals (GLA 2009a). Smaller green elements tailored more on a neighborhood scale then fit within this larger regional framework. In London this includes the innovative concept of the East London Green Grid. The goals in London include expansion of the green network and the extent of nature within and around the city while devoting special concern to areas with greenspace and nature deficiencies.

The East London Green Grid is envisioned to be a "network of interlinked, multi-purpose open spaces with good connections to the areas where people live and work, public transport, the Green Belt and the Thames" (GLA 2006, 6). The purpose of this partnership of the London Development Agency, East London boroughs, and other regional agencies and central government is to tie together functionally and psychologically the fractured and fragmented pieces of the existing urban landscape—its marshes, riverbanks, canals, paths, and trails. In the words of the visionary Ken Livingstone, a former mayor: "It will grow to become the living thread that weaves together the communities of East London—new and old" (GLA 2006, 44). Interestingly, the Green Grid is being framed as a green network that is important not only for recreation but also for resilience in the face of increased flooding and the impacts of climate change.

GREEN REGIONS AND SUSTAINABLE URBAN FORM

In Brisbane, the South East Queensland (SEQ) Regional Plan demonstrates just how essential it is to combine a regional conservation vision with an effort to steer urban growth in ways that will bring that vision into being. The SEQ plan calls for growth to be accommodated largely within the metropolitan region's delineated "urban footprint," and indeed a significant portion of the region's growth will occur through infill (Government of Queensland 2009). The target for 2016 is 40 percent of the region's growth, which will increase to 50 percent by 2031. The plan presents a compelling vision of what the region will look like and where its growth will and will not be accommodated. It also sets up a clear spatial template in which each individual local government council must develop its own local growth management strategy (LGMS) that will be consistent with the overall regional plan.

The SEQ regional plan sets minimums both for density targets and the number of dwelling units each local council must accommodate within its plan's timeframe. A review of local LGMSs suggests that the localities are allowed considerable flexibility and creativity in planning. Brisbane's plan, for instance, calls for accommodating three-quarters of its future growth through infill and redevelopment and at the same time preserving and expanding green areas in designated activity centers and growth corridors. It sets the impressive goal of 40 percent of the city being devoted to native, natural habitat.

The best regional sustainability plans understand these two essential prongs—conservation and protection; growth containment and management—and they work to build up both. It is hard to identify an area or sector that is presently more critical or has greater implications for environment and sustainability than that of land use and growth patterns. While in the United States examples of successful regional land use planning and growth containment are few, extensive experience from cities outside this country demonstrate its value, importance, and feasibility.

Vancouver's new regional growth strategy was released in November 2009, and was still under deliberation as of this writing. It reflects, nonetheless, many of the key elements in a regional sustainability initiative. This plan is a natural extension of, and builds upon, the earlier Livable Regions Plan and reflects a continuing commitment to the same vision and many of the regional goals of the earlier plan. Metro Vancouver is the lead agency and it prepared the draft plan, known as *Metro Vancouver 2040: Shaping Our Future,* which presents a regional vision and identifies strategies and actions in some detail (box 6.1). Like its predecessor, the Metro Vancouver plan seeks to maintain a compact regional urban form and steer most future growth into higher-density corridors and centers.

At the same time, and largely as a consequence of this compact form, the plan seeks to continue to protect large green areas outside the urbanized towns and centers. Historically, these green areas have been referred to as the Green Zone, and it includes an extensive agricultural reserve of some 60,000 hectares. Protected green areas also include significant watersheds, wetlands, forests, and natural habitats of various kinds. To achieve this regional growth vision, some notable challenges must be faced and identified in the plan. These include significant population growth (the region is expected to grow by about 35,000 persons per year), protecting the region's natural resource base, responding to climate change through both mitigation and adaptation, and protecting farmland and food-production potential.

Increasingly, many planners argue that sustainability ultimately requires a commitment to cities and that compact urban form is the best single antidote to environmental degradation, resource consumption, and global warming. In *Green*

Metropolis, David Owen (2009) refers to Manhattan to make a strong case for this. He assembles and presents some compelling evidence of the "greenness" of compact and dense Manhattan, such as its relatively high density, at least by American standards, of 67,000 people per square mile and its being an urban environment in which most residents can and do get around without automobiles. Of all New Yorkers, 82 percent travel to work by public transit, walking, or bicycling. As a result, per capita greenhouse gas emissions are very low, and the city's residents tend to live richly. Owen sums up this idea in the book's subtitle: "Why Living Smaller, Living Closer, and Driving Less are the Keys to Sustainability."

Advocates of green or ecological urbanism argue that dense cities hold the most promise for arriving at future sustainability and resilience. Barcelona is an outstanding example of sustainability's virtues and the values inherent in compactness, which, along with density, is an important tool for biophilic cities. This Spanish city also is heralded frequently for its many efforts to enhance and improve urban livability. Overall, Barcelona is home to nearly 15,000 inhabitants per square kilometer, and in parts of the city—such as the Gràcia district, where residents have access to extensive green areas—the density approaches 30,000 persons per square kilometer. Despite this level of density, it is an urban region that boasts an impressive amount of nature and greenspace, including the 8,000-hectare Collserola Park.

Even land conservation organizations recognize that much of the solution to conservation relies on cities. In its 100-year vision for Greater Puget Sound, the Cascade Land Conservancy (2005, 2) declares the importance of cities and regional urban growth patterns: "We must make our cities vibrant and vital, providing a magnet for many of the people coming this way."

Vancouver's efforts put regional spatial planning at their center, and efforts at both regional and local levels have led to impressive results. Between

---

| Box 6.1 | Vision Statement from Metro Vancouver Regional Plan, 2009 |
| | *Source: Metro Vancouver (2009b, 10).* |

Vision: Our Guide for the Future

Metro Vancouver has a vision to achieve what humanity aspires to on a global basis— the highest quality of life embracing cultural vitality, economic prosperity, social justice and compassion, all nurtured in and by a beautiful and healthy natural environment.

We will achieve this vision by embracing and applying the principles of sustainability, not least of which is an unshakeable commitment to the well-being of current and future generations and the health of the planet, in everything we do.

As we share our efforts in achieving this vision, we are confident that the inspiration and mutual learning we gain will become vital ingredients in our hopes for a sustainable common future.

2001 and 2006, the extent of the urbanized area in the region did not expand. As growth continues and the population of the region's urbanized land remains constant, densities will necessarily increase, which will permit more efficient, sustainable living conditions. Improvement in the sustainability of various forms of mobility, such as transit, walking, and bicycling, will become even more possible.

The city of Vancouver, which is already an exemplar of successful dense, compact urban form and its environmental benefits, has sought to accommodate even more growth within its borders. Mayor Gregor Robertson famously declared that Vancouver will be the greenest city in the world by 2020, and he has embraced and advanced the concept of EcoDensity, which makes the connection between environmental sustainability and urban density even more explicit as well as an object of official municipal policy. The tenets of EcoDensity hold that a green and sustainable city will find more ways to accommodate people and dwelling units.

To this end, Vancouver adopted its EcoDensity Charter in 2008 and has undertaken a number of actions that facilitate further densification, among them changing codes to permit laneway housing; suites-in-suites housing, which allows secondary units to be created from existing flats; and other forms of what has been called "gentle density" (City of Vancouver 2008a; 2008b). Commendably, Vancouver's EcoDensity initiative is an idea that joins concerns about sustainability with those about livability and housing affordability, thus providing an important insight for other emerging green regions.

GREEN REGIONS AS RESILIENT

Global shocks such as long-term decline in global oil supplies and climate change will both elevate the importance of a regional focus for sustainability planning and challenge it severely (Newman, Beatley, and Boyer 2008). While debate continues about when—and if—peak oil production will be reached, indications are ominous as production in existing oil fields continues to decline and global demand keeps rising sharply (McKibben 2010a).

This will mean many things for cities and regions, such as further support for relocalizing and reregionalizing production of everything from energy to food to building materials. Climate change adds further complications by projecting major new pressures: rising seas, increased flooding and severe weather events, and heat waves and drought in many places. Changing climate may make producing sufficient global—and local—food supplies even more difficult, for instance, which suggests a serious need for regional adaptation plans.

On a regional scale, some of these climate adaptations will include steering development and infrastructure away from coastal edges and high-hazard flood zones; instituting new residential building standards—in coastal regions "passive survivability" has received new emphasis, for example; protecting and restoring natural systems and ecological infrastructure (e.g., wetlands, with their ability to mitigate and adapt to changing sea levels; or trees and urban forests for their capacity to cool cities); and a host of actions and strategies for building and fostering social capital and social resilience.

Resilience-planning strategies are already under way in a number of regions in the United States (Beatley 2009), even though, generally speaking, few regions or metropolitan areas have fully accepted the need to do this (Pilkey and Young 2009). The word *resilience* captures much of this agenda, and it has been argued that, while perhaps not replacing *sustainability,* as a term and concept it ought to be given equal importance as an overarching goal and vision.

Regional plans can be developed on an effective and appropriate scale to plan for and address climate change, both mitigation for it (i.e., emissions reduction and sequestration) and adaptation to it (e.g., responses to specific changes). To varying degrees and in various ways, all the metropolitan areas discussed in this chapter are addressing the climate change challenge. On the mitigation side, regions have set emission-reduction targets, some of which are rather ambitious. Metro Vancouver's goal is a 33 percent reduction in greenhouse gas emissions by 2020 (compared to 2007 levels), and the Greater London Authority strives for a 60 percent reduction by 2025 (from 1990 levels). Further, more detailed climate plans and strategies are frequently prepared at the regional level. The GLA, for instance, has actually prepared two specific and detailed climate change strategies—one for mitigation and another that specifically addresses adaptation.

London's draft strategy for climate change adaptation identifies a number of serious impacts that will be felt by the region and offers recommendations to enhance regional resilience. Metropolitan London will experience hotter, dryer summer months and warmer, wetter winters as well as an increase in flooding and extreme weather events. The region will face serious adaptation challenges, among them drought, overheating on top of already serious urban heat island effects, flooding, and vector-borne diseases (e.g., tick-borne Lyme disease).

The GLA climate adaptation strategy identifies a number of specific steps and actions, including increasing forest canopy cover from 20 to 25 percent by 2025 and adding some 100,000 square meters of new green rooftops by 2012 (GLA 2010a). At a more regional level, opportunities exist to understand ecosystem protection and conservation as ways of adapting to climate change. The London Rivers Action Plan, for instance, explores the idea of more effectively utilizing the region's river system as an approach to retaining seasonal floodwaters and, at the same time, creating or enhancing new ecologically important habitat and providing new prospects for connecting urban populations with nature. The plan explicitly embraces the strategy of restoring and naturalizing the region's streams and rivers as being the best way to adapt to changing climate (GLA 2009b).

Regions can become more climate resilient by reducing their use of energy and investing in renewables. In London, ten low-carbon zones have been targeted, and the London Development Agency is investing £3 million in projects to help leverage private capital and demonstrate innovative techniques and measures (GLA, n.d.). Selected through a competitive process, the proposed strategies and projects differ from borough to borough. Projects and measures range from the distribution of free grow-your-own starter packs (in Barking and Dagenham), to installation of photovoltaic panels at local schools (Haringey), to home energy efficiency improvements and heating system upgrading (Lewisham and Southwark, respectively).

Additional examples of regional resilience planning include entities that serve either to encourage new renewable energy production or to mandate it. The Cape Cod Commission's new renewable energy standard is one example. For any proposed development or redevelopment project subject to the Developments of Regional Impact review, at least 10 percent of the electrical needs of the development must be produced onsite, although the commission can waive this requirement in exchange for other energy-related project features, such as passive solar design. While it is a modest standard, it makes a significant step forward and should help to advance a better-distributed energy system there.

Some climate change impacts will be borne by a region's biodiversity. As habitats shift due to changing temperature and climate, many species are predicted to face severe impacts and have difficulty adapting in response. Fragmented land use and obstacles created by roads and development are likely to commit a large number of species to extinction in the face of long-term climate change. One recent study of extinction risks estimates that midrange climate scenarios suggest that, by 2050, some 15 to 37 percent of species will be unable to migrate or shift with changing habitat (Thomas et al. 2004).

The Brisbane metropolitan region represents another exemplary effort to contain growth and conserve large areas of nature at a regional level. It starts with a strong analysis of ecological context and states its overarching goal to be protecting the region's unique biological diversity. Within the SEQ region, the City of Brisbane has the largest single local council and is relatively large in area compared with other Australian cities. Consequently, the city has been an especially important leader in regional conservation, and a number of its efforts and the planning currently underway fit within the larger SEQ regional vision.

Specifically, Brisbane has identified a core biodiversity network, which emphasizes biological corridors and gives priority to projects that facilitate wildlife movement and connectivity throughout the city. One of the most impressive early efforts is the construction of multispecies "fauna-friendly crossing structures." One built in 2004, for example, includes a double-arched land bridge with native trees and vegetation that facilitates animal movements. Other innovative features include a series of eight-meter-high glider poles on which species such as the squirrel glider may rest or from which they may launch; rope ladders or so-called canopy bridges; fauna underpasses and culverts for amphibians; and exclusion fencing that steers animals

to crossing points. Griffith University's Centre for Innovative Conservation Strategies did a study of the effectiveness of the crossing structures and found that they
do work, resulting in significant reduction in roadkill (Veage and Jones 2007).

Recent concerns about potential, very serious, long-range impacts of climate
change have provided even more support for Brisbane's strategy of constructing
corridors and connections, such as Brisbane Forest Park, which includes a significant
altitudinal range that will permit some species to adapt to changing climate. A special report was commissioned to identify actions that the city should undertake to
safeguard and permit adaptation to these likely changes in temperature and climate
by the unique flora and fauna in the city and region (Low 2007).

Movement corridors are key, as is protection of areas in the city that have
higher elevations, which allow species to adapt to shifting habitat zones, but
many other things could be done to facilitate successful long-term adaptation.
These include preserving "cool sites" in parks and landscapes, such as south-
facing slopes, rock outcrops, and deep gullies that offer relief to some animals
and plants; enhancing habitats (e.g., designing permanent deep pools in rivers and aquatic systems); and conserving long-range pollinators that facilitate
genetic adaptation, in particular flying foxes (bats), honeyeaters, and lorikeets.

Captive breeding of some regional species of plants and amphibians is also
suggested, and steps may be taken to replace important species of trees and vegetation (e.g., the paperbark, a nectar tree important for long-range pollinators) that
have been lost or are at risk of being lost to sea level rise and "coastal squeeze."
Tim Low (2007) includes the following among the policies and actions needed to
ensure long-range ecological, biodiversity, and landscape resilience in the face of
climate change, about which the Brisbane region and city offer guidance:

- conserve corridors and increase connectivity;

- plant trees (perhaps shift to species from more northerly areas);

- conserve "cool sites" within bushland ("south-facing slopes, rock outcrops,
  and deep gullies offer relief to some animals and plants");

- enhance habitats by increasing climate refuges (e.g., shady riparian vegetation);

- restore waterway habitats (e.g., permanent deep pools);

- reduce other stresses to increase resilience to climate change (control excessive burnings);

- reduce weed threat and invasion of nonnative plants into bushland;

- identify significant species at risk from climate change;

- conserve long-range pollinators (flying foxes, honeyeaters, lorikeets);

- monitor habitats and species to record climate-related declines;

- translocate species (a last resort);

- practice conservation in captivity;

- cultivate, store genetic material; and

- promote research.

Green regionalism also offers significant hope and promise for the miti-gation side of the climate change agenda—that is, the many ways in which regional strategies can help reduce consumption and create new opportunities for energy production from renewable sources, thus significantly reducing car-bon emissions. Regional landscape assessments offer the possibility of identify-ing places and opportunities for wind energy, for instance, and a spatial scale and geography that can permit the development of a diverse and multifaceted renewable energy portfolio.

GREEN REGIONS AND SUSTAINABLE METABOLISM

Modern urban regions require immense material inputs, produce prodigious amounts of waste, and have a complex and interconnected metabolism, not unlike a living organism. Yet our city planning and urban management poli-cies and systems often fail to acknowledge its existence, let alone opportu-nities to shape and guide it in sustainable ways. We treat these urban inputs and outputs, resources and material streams, discretely and individually rather than holistically. The move toward sustainable cities will require an important shift in our view of them, no longer seeing them as linear, resource-extracting machines, but as multifaceted and interactive metabolic systems, each with its own peculiar flows and cycles. In addition, things traditionally viewed as nega-tive outputs (e.g., solid waste and wastewater), ideally will be re-envisioned as productive inputs that will satisfy other urban needs including food, energy, and clean water.

A sustainable regional metabolism entails working toward several key goals at once. They include reducing the extent of the required material and resource flows, converting linear flows to circular ones (i.e., closing loops), and sourcing and deriving national inputs in the most equitable and least ecologically destruc-tive ways possible.

Understanding the nature and magnitude of the resource flows a city requires is a first step. London is among the few cities and regions to have done this, and the GLA commissioned the report *City Limits: A Resource Flow and Ecological Footprint Analysis of Greater London*. Completed in 2002, it provides a comprehensive picture of the flows and resource demands of this metropolitan region with a population of about 8 million, and it set the stage for a number of sustainability plans and initiatives.

A key conceptual outcome of the study was an examination of London's urban resource flows (figure 6.2). Among others, the study's key findings show

Figure 6.2	Resource Flow and Ecological Footprint Analysis of Greater London, 2002
	Source: Best Foot Forward (2002, 7).

The main findings of the project were:

- The population of Greater London in 2000 was 7.4 million.

- Londoners consumed 154,400 GigaWatt hours (GWh) of energy (or 13,276,000 tonnes of oil equivalent), which produced 41 million tonnes of CO_2.

- Londoners consumed 49 million tonnes of materials. On a per capita basis, this represents 6.7 tonnes.

- 27.8 million tonnes of materials were used by the construction sector.

- 26 million tonnes of waste was generated, of which 15 million tonnes was generated by the construction and demolition sector, 7.9 million tonnes by the commercial and industrial sector and 3.4 million tonnes by households.

- 6.9 million tonnes of food was consumed, of which 81% was imported from outside the UK.

- Londoners travelled 64 billion passengerkilometres (pass-km), of which 69% was by car.

- Water consumption reached 876,000,000,000 litres, of which 28% was leakage.

- The ecological footprint of Londoners was 49 million global hectares (gha), which was 42 times its biocapacity and 293 times its geographical area. This is twice the size of the UK, and roughly the same size as Spain.

- The ecological footprint per London resident was 6.63 gha. This compares with the UK average ecological footprint of 6.3 gha, and exceeds the global "earthshare" of 2.18 gha.

- The ecological footprint of London tourists was estimated at 2.4 million gha, which equates to an additional 0.32 gha per Londoner.

- The predicted "earthshare" in 2050 is estimated at 1.44 gha per capita. For Londoners to be ecologically sustainable by 2050, a 35% reduction by 2020 and an 80% reduction by 2050, of their ecological footprint will be needed.

- Ranges of "business as usual" and "evolutionary" scenarios were prepared to reflect current practice and existing improvement targets. "Revolutionary" scenarios were prepared to demonstrate that a combination of technological and behavioural changes could achieve interim sustainability targets for 2020.

Ecological footprint of Londoners (*48,868,000 gha or 6.63 gha per capita*), by component, showing actual size and the UK.

Food 41%
Energy 10%
Transport 5%
Materials and waste 44%
Degraded land 0.7%
Water 0.3%

that Londoners annually consume 154,400 gigawatts of energy and in the process produce 41 million tons of CO_2. They require almost 50 million tons of materials (including building materials and food) and generate 26 million tons of waste. Overall, the ecological footprint associated with these resource demands is almost 300 times the land area of Greater London. Most of the region's critical inputs, such as food and energy, are imported and derived from unsustainable sources.

This material flow analysis has shaped planning and policy in the region to a considerable degree, and the GLA, in turn, has produced a series of impressive regional strategic plans that seek to address these unsustainable material flows. The so-called London Plan contains a section concerning policies entitled "London's Metabolism: Using and Managing Natural Resources." Household waste recycling and composting targets are set in this crosscutting document, as are targets for reuse of construction and demolition waste. Most construction aggregate needed for London comes in from outside the city, making reuse opportunities especially promising. This document also addresses means for improving air quality as well as water supply and reuse, among other topics.

The London Energy Strategy sets the goal of reaching a 60 percent reduction in the city's carbon emissions by 2050 and proposes a variety of other metabolism-related targets. Among other proposals, the strategy envisions each of London's 34 boroughs becoming home to at least one zero-energy development and identifying appropriate new sites for renewable energy production. Similarly, a new regional food strategy calls for more local production and processing that will shorten the supply lines and be achieved through more sustainable means. A number of particular actions are identified, including ways to come by new mechanisms for linking local farmers with consumers along with efforts to develop producer collaboration schemes to strengthen local and regional farming, to establish local food distribution and wholesaling hubs and to extend and expand programs for collecting and utilizing household kitchen waste (London Development Authority 2006).

London has promoted and encouraged a focus on progressive green building projects, especially zero-energy and carbon-neutral concepts, in a trend it proposes to continue and promote further. One of the best on-the-ground examples of a housing project with a sustainable material flow orientation is BedZED—Beddington Zero Energy Development in the London borough of Sutton—which has incorporated explicit utilities for local materials, for instance. This innovative green project reflects an effort to tackle unsustainable resource flows and achieve a more sustainable, circular urban metabolism. The goal of providing a minimum of one-half of all the building materials needed for this neighborhood by sourcing them from within a 35-mile radius was achieved. Local materials included wood siding from municipal forests and bricks from a nearby manufacturer. Such practices build the local economy, help to increase residents' knowledge about and care for their home places, and reduce the ultimate ecological footprint of buildings.

London's regional planning effort has spawned the development of a number of other plans and planning strategies designed to address one or more of the metabolic flows and components of its regional ecological footprint. The interest in healthier local and sustainable food sources that has taken on a new importance throughout North America and western Europe is reflected in London as is the rather large size of the food component of the city's ecological footprint.

Green Regions, Food, and Energy

One increasingly important measure of a green region is the extent to which it protects and nurtures its food-production abilities. Interest in local and regional food production has been renewed for a variety of reasons that include nutrition, taste, and sustainability. Among the many obstacles to producing and processing food locally and regionally is the fact that much of the infrastructure that once existed for growing and processing food in metropolitan regions is no longer available.

For instance, most beef processing takes place in a few large slaughterhouses, which usually are located at significant distances from urban populations. The classic 1929 study, *How Great Cities Are Fed*, noted that at that time some 30 "sizable meat-packing establishments" existed in New York City, 11 of which were located in Manhattan (Hedden 1929, 64). A green region understands the importance of restitching its food system and rebuilding its food production, processing, and distribution capabilities in order to ensure a healthier, more sustainable, and more resilient regional food system. Interestingly, Hedden's early study employs much of the terminology now used by the local and regional food movement. Chapter 2, for example, is entitled "Watersheds, Milksheds and Foodsheds." Understanding a region's foodshed is an especially important task in regional planning, one that bolsters efforts to protect prime agricultural land in the region and to nurture a resilient regional agricultural economy and sector.

Few metropolitan regions have done more than London to think about and plan for food, and in 2006 the Mayor's Food Strategy was released. This thorough, comprehensive assessment of London's current and future food needs lays out the vision "of a world-class, sustainable food system" (London Development Agency 2006, 11). The plan sets targets and identifies actions, then organizes them according to the stages of the food chain (i.e., primary production, food preparation, and food disposal).

In 2010, the GLA released a comprehensive assessment of whether—and in what ways—growing food was considered in London's planning system, and it offered a number of specific actions that could be taken. The report, *Cultivating the Capital*, concludes that, in fact, substantial food is being produced in the metropolitan area, in which nearly 500 farms are operating and producing more than 8,400 tons of vegetables and fruits (GLA 2010b), but this amounts to a very small fraction of the food consumed annually by residents.

Whether a goal of producing all or a significant percentage of the metropolitan region's food needs is practical and realistic, more could be produced closer to where people live. The report also recommends encouraging more commercial agricultural production in the city's Green Belt, providing incentives to form new farmers markets and other community food distribution points, and finding ways to fit food production into urban neighborhoods.

The extent of regional food and agricultural production is an important measure of sustainability and underlies a set of principal indicators to be studied over time. In Metro Vancouver, agriculture is tracked in several ways, including the number of hectares encompassed by the Agricultural Land Reserve and the changes in agricultural land over time. Several other novel measures are used as well, such as the number of different agricultural products grown in the region; gross receipts for small farms; and the total number of farm operators in the region by age, because aging of farmers and the paucity of younger farmers entering the field are significant concerns (Metro Vancouver 2009a).

The vision of a "bountiful" region—one that may be able to produce much if not all of its own food needs—is increasingly relevant and compelling. It requires a combination of protecting the land base needed to ensure the goods' production as well as the capability and capacity to store, process, and distribute them to a regional population.

Part of the goal in regional sustainability planning will thus be to ensure that a region is able to satisfy a significant amount of its own biophysical needs, namely water, energy, and food. Protecting and nurturing the working landscapes in green regions will be essential and should entail efforts to support new and viable harvesting operations for farms and forests, means for serving nearby urban markets, and, one hopes, emphasis on sustainable and restorative techniques and management principles. In the Seattle/Puget Sound region, for instance, organizations such as the Cascade Land Conservancy play an important role. It has created a Working Lands Revolving Fund to help establish farms and ranches in the region, for instance.

Bill McKibben (2010a) and other adherents to the peak oil concept argue that long distance, fossil fuel–drenched food production simply will not be possible in the years ahead.[2] Bolstering local and regional food production capabilities, he believes, will be essential. Especially since 2005, many cities and urban regions have seen the emergence of elements of a more resilient food system: new efforts to connect with and support local and regional farmers, development of new food processing and other food and agricultural infrastructure, and new and creative approaches to growing food in urban environments—from rooftops and balconies to suburban lawns and building facades. Increasingly, food and its production are understood to be essential elements of community infrastructure that are as important as roads, sewer systems, and water.

---

2. "Peak oil" refers to the notion that, if it has not been reached already, peak production of oil globally will be attained soon.

These positive trends suggest that, especially as far as food is concerned, a more sustainable metabolism is possible. Emerging practice suggests that in most regions of the world, even in high-latitude colder climates, cities and urban regions will be able to grow much more of the food they need than is commonly considered possible. For instance, the creative use of movable greenhouses is exemplary, as demonstrated by the experiences of Eliot Coleman, who grows plant-based food in Maine year round, and Pete Johnson, who operates a year-round community-supported agriculture (CSA) program in Vermont (McKibben 2010b).

Food waste is a commonly underappreciated regional waste flow. In Oregon's Portland region, estimates suggest that some 180,000 tons of food waste are thrown away each year, and Portland Metro has created a regional program to capture a portion of this waste and redirect it to food banks and use it to address food insecurity in the region. Metro's Fork It Over! program makes it very easy to recover this waste. Restaurants and retail food stores have access to information and phone numbers online, and a state Good Samaritan law—in combination with a similar federal provision—protects these businesses from liability. Food waste in Portland represents about 15 percent of the waste sent to landfill, and it has an estimated value of some $300 million. Capturing and diverting this edible waste stream clearly has benefits (Portland Metro, n.d.).

Similar initiatives are under way in London, and recently that city's Waste and Recycling Board funded an effort to recover 300 tons of food annually by means of the FareShare Community Food Network. As a result the equivalent of 800,000 meals will be diverted from regional landfills each year, but this is just the tip of the iceberg for the city, where it is estimated that 8.3 million tons of edible food are discarded. Work on finding ways to capture and redistribute this surplus food helps address food insecurity, creates jobs, and reduces London's carbon and greenhouse gas emissions (GLA 2010c).

While London has made great progress in incorporating eco-cycles and material flows into its planning, few cities have done as much to put the idea into practice as some in Sweden, with Stockholm being the most impressive. Its city leaders even went so far as to reorganize the structure of municipal departments and agencies to coordinate their work better and to take a comprehensive approach to material and resource flows.

Although few examples are presently under way, planning for material flows in the design of new neighborhoods or urban districts makes considerable sense. Hammarby Sjöstad, a new urban ecological district in Stockholm, is an important project in this regard. It remains one of the best demonstrations of the merits and value of designing holistically, with metabolism in mind from the beginning. Here, eco-flows and cycles have been analyzed and studied, and the goal of closing loops was borne in mind from the outset. These efforts and their felicitous outcomes, now commonly described as the "Hammarby model," provide a powerful example of how this metabolic flow–based view can manifest in new approaches to urban

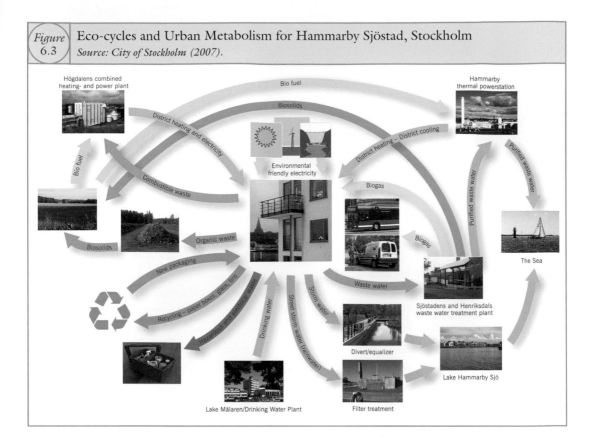

Figure
6.3 Eco-cycles and Urban Metabolism for Hammarby Sjöstad, Stockholm
Source: City of Stockholm (2007).

design and planning. Figure 6.3 depicts these flows and shows how the efforts made to connect them led to substantial energy and conservation benefits.

For instance, many apartments at Hammarby Sjöstad are equipped with stoves that utilize biogas extracted from wastewater generated in the community. Biogas also provides fuel for buses that serve the area. Neighborhood solid waste collection is accomplished through an innovative vacuum-based underground collection system that allows efficient separation of organic, recyclable, and other kinds of waste. Once burned, combustible waste is returned to the community as electricity and hot water, and the latter is delivered via a district heating grid. Stormwater from streets is directed into a special filtration and purification system, while that from buildings and other living areas is guided to the neighborhood's green features—green roofs and wetlands, for example—and both streams are kept separate from wastewater treatment. Many other green features have been used in this neighborhood, including access to the Tvärbanan, a high-frequency light-rail system running through it and an extensive pedestrian and bicycle network that makes it possible to live here without owning a car. Other Swedish cities have pursued a similar eco-cycles course, including Malmö, which has redeveloped its Västra Hamnen (western harbor). Here, 100 percent of the district's energy needs are provided locally from a mix of renewable technologies including a wind turbine, roof- and facade-mounted solar hot water–heating panels, and use of seawater and deep-aquifer water for heating and cooling. As in Hammarby Sjöstad, an extensive waste recycling system has been incorporated. All surfacing materials, such as tile and stone, used in the district were chosen with their ability to be reused later borne in mind. Some homes are equipped with special food-waste collectors (for instance, tanks below the sink). In Uppsala, a fleet of buses is powered from biogas extracted from organic household waste, and a similar initiative is under way in Oslo.

Sustainable energy production can be added to the other goods and services that can be provided more locally and regionally. An increasingly common regional goal is provision of all or most of a community's energy from local renewable sources, ideally through a distributed, decentralized network, and many new and emerging models of how this might work are under consideration. Another Swedish city, Växjö, has declared its intention to be fossil fuel free, and is pursuing this objective via a similar conversion of waste streams into productive urban inputs. Sandvik II, its principal municipal power plant, has been converted from burning oil to being fueled entirely by local wood waste, a by-product of the vital local timber and wood products industry. The wood—mostly in the form of bark and the top portions of felled trees—is collected from within a 100-mile radius. In the United States, a similar example is the Joseph C. McNeil Generating Station in Burlington, Vermont, where city power is generated entirely from wood waste. Plans are now under way to connect the plant to a series of greenhouses, in essence using the waste heat to grow food for the city.

The view of cities as complex sets of metabolic flows may also help guide us in dealing with those situations that mandate some degree of reliance, especially in the shorter term, on resources and energy from other regions and parts of the world. By understanding that, despite great efforts to promote local and regional production, food will still need to be transported to large U.S. cities, efforts can be made to mitigate or compensate for the energy consumed and the carbon emitted in the process.

Perhaps that will mean contributing to a fund that supports solar and renewable energy projects, or those aimed at carbon sequestration. This view of cities may suggest the need to forge new sustainable and equitable relationships among various world regions. Likewise, possibly it will prompt cities to strive for new, sustainable relationships with international hinterlands through mechanisms that include sustainable sourcing agreements, region-to-region trade agreements, and urban procurement systems based on green certification standards. Embracing a metabolic view of cities and metropolitan areas takes us in some interesting, potentially very useful directions.

This new paradigm of sustainable urban metabolism will require profound changes in the ways we conceptualize cities and metropolitan regions as well as how we plan and manage them. New forms of cooperation and collaboration among municipal agencies and various urban actors and stakeholder groups will be required. For instance, municipal departments will need to formulate and implement strategies to integrate resource flows. New organizational and governance structures are likely to become necessary—perhaps cities will need their own foreign policy ministers, for example—as will new planning tools and methods for such things as mapping resource flows that will become standard requirements for preparing comprehensive plans.

Thus, analysis of regional flows, their inputs and outputs, helps to identify opportunities to make a shift toward sustainability. Understanding waste flows in a region as being as much positive as negative can create opportunities for initiatives and programs to redirect or reuse these wastes, creating jobs and economic value while reducing regional pollution and waste.

GREEN REGIONS AND ECOLOGICAL FOOTPRINTS

William Rees's pioneering work with ecological footprints, and that of his student and colleague Mathis Wackernagel, have forever changed planners' understanding of cities and human settlements (Wackernagel and Rees 1998). We now commonly recognize that the lives and lifestyles of urbanites—and even more, suburbanites—rely on resources and ecological services that often originate many thousands of miles away. The land and sea area needed to provide food and energy and to sequester carbon adds up to an increasingly large footprint, at least for northern, industrialized nations. As the Worldwide Fund for Nature (WWF 2007, 4) notes, ecological footprint analysis "gives the fullest picture possible of the human impact on the Earth's resources." The WWF (2010) has been most active in using the footprint concept, and its *Living Planet Report* tracks the rise in our global ecological footprint as well as the biocapacity we have to support it.

Although not yet commonly utilized at regional or metropolitan levels, several efforts have been made to calculate a city's ecological footprint. Among the more impressive regional/bioregional ecological footprint studies and plans is one concerning Wales, which was a joint effort of the WWF (2007) and the Welsh government. The One Planet Wales challenge argues for a systematic reduction in the country's citizens' footprint that will become more consistent with it utilizing a fair share of the world's resources.

In 2001, the study found the ecological footprint of Wales to be 5.25 global hectares per person, which would require the country to occupy a total land area about seven times its actual size. This is more than three times the 1.3 global hectares of biocapacity calculated to be the Welsh fair share of land area available on the planet. As the challenge report states, "If everyone in the world lived like we do in Wales, humanity would need three planets to support itself" (WWF 2007, 3). The Wales study breaks down in considerable detail the portion of the footprint accounted for by different sectors. For instance, food comprises about one-quarter of Wales's footprint, and another quarter is devoted to home and energy. Travel and tourism, consumables, services, and capital are also significant sectors making up the footprint.

To meet the footprint goal, the One Planet Wales challenge lays out targets and footprint reductions by sector, endorsing the goal of proposing both short-term steps and longer-term strategies, which will extend from 2020 to 2050. The plan also calculated what would result from applying the business-as-usual scenario and found that, if no actions were taken, by 2050 the Welsh footprint would actually grow by 30 percent. The goal is a challenging 75 percent reduction of the footprint by that target year, but considering predicted incremental yearly progress makes it seem more realistic.

The plan identifies a number of ways to reconceptualize the sectors and impacts that account for the present large footprint. One Planet Food is envisioned, for instance. This program imagines a "transformation of the food system at each stage of the supply chain, with an agricultural-environmental agenda on the producer side, and a healthy diet agenda on the consumer side" (WWF 2007, 7). Low-impact imports and farming and demand-side management are other recommended policies. One Planet Buildings are envisioned as well. They would involve shifting toward sourcing building materials locally, more sustainable practices, and the design and building of zero-energy new housing.

Few other regional plans have explicitly incorporated analysis of their ecological footprints, or even a passing reference to them. The metropolitan regional plan for Perth, Western Australia, is another example. It actually includes a table displaying relative footprints of nations, although no real targets or goals are expressed in terms of the footprint. Some regional visions and visioning exercises have included footprint measures. Notably, in Alberta, Canada, imagineCALGARY identifies an explicit goal: reducing the city's current footprint, which is rather large by Canadian standards, to less than the country's present average of 7.25 hectares per capita by the year 2036 (City of Calgary 2006).

Clearly, more could be done to apply ecological footprint analysis along with eco-cycles and metabolic analyses to regional plans and planning. As shown by the WWF studies, it also will be important to calculate regional biocapacity as a measure of the extent of regional "overshoot" and as another measure of how ecologically responsible a region or metropolitan area might be considered.

The ecological footprint idea has met with resistance from some urban design and city advocates, who see it as antiurban. While this is certainly a tension, it should be clear that, given similar overall levels of affluence, the ecological footprints of residents of compact, walkable, transit-rich cities will be much smaller than those who live in more suburban or exurban communities.

GREEN REGIONS AS GLOCAL REGIONS

Some versions of bioregionalism set the goal of attaining complete or nearly complete resource self-sufficiency. This goal seems unrealistic and, to a certain degree, undesirable. Necessarily, green regions of the future will be connected to other regions and the rest of the world. A more realistic goal for green regions is what some have called self-reliance (Shuman 2000)—understanding that even with significant, positive shifts toward local and regional production of food, materials, etc., and advances in import substitution—urban regions will still need to draw resources and goods from other regions and parts of the world. The concept of "glocalism" holds that regions have a duty both to shift to the local and regional and to recognize and accept their global duties and responsibilities that reflect the inherent interconnectedness of the planet.

Exactly what is required to attain regional glocalism remains a subject for debate, and how local consumption and policy can help support sustainability globally also needs much further exploration. Yet important opportunities already exist today. The policy levers for effecting change will certainly include traditional land use planning and management, but other measures, programs, and initiatives will be included as well. Through their material flows and consumption patterns, large cities and urban regions exert tremendous pressure on global biodiversity, and one measure of a sustainable city is the extent to which it seeks to moderate or reduce those impacts.

The emergence of third-party-verified eco-labeling systems for forests and fisheries (e.g., the stewardship councils for forests and marine life) suggest that reasonably effective means now assist local consumers in making less globally damaging choices when selecting products. Nascent market mechanisms promoting fair trade globally remain underdeveloped, but there is hope for the future. (For instance, the Netherlands hosts more than 300 fair trade shops [*wereldwinkels*], and cities and green regions could do more to help grow such retail opportunities.) Re-envisioning the role of cities and urban regions as responsible consumers in a globalized economy that values a flow of largely anonymous goods and materials is a major challenge.

Local and regional governmental units in green regions have the opportunity to shift their own purchasing decisions. New York City, for instance, currently purchases an estimated $1 million worth of tropical hardwoods each year. South American species such as ipe and garapa are used for such things as benches, boardwalks, and ferry landings. Even the ten-mile-long Brooklyn Bridge Promenade is constructed of greenheart, another South American hardwood.

Recognizing the environmentally destructive impact of such purchases, New York City is now looking for ways to reduce its use of this wood. In 2008 Mayor Michael Bloomberg announced a plan to reduce significantly the city's purchasing of tropical hardwoods, calling for an immediate 20 percent reduction followed by even greater ones once the city has researched and piloted sourcing for alternative kinds of wood and other materials (City of New York 2008).

In his speech at the United Nations, Bloomberg described tropical deforestation as an "ecological calamity," and observed that it may be responsible for as much as 20 percent of greenhouse gas emissions. Cities like New York need to become better stewards of the global environment, he believes: "New Yorkers don't live in the rain forest. But we do live in a world that we all share. And we're committed to doing everything we can to protect it for all of our children" (City of New York 2008). Other cities have adopted similar policies. Closer to the Amazonian source of these kinds of wood, for instance, the Brazilian city of Sao Paulo has also adopted a policy that, for city projects, bans the use of illegally harvested timber, and many other cities have adopted some form of green procurement, despite the legal obstacles they may encounter.

Cities and regions could take many additional steps and actions on the global scene that will add meaning to their global sustainability commitments. Several years ago Sister Cities International started a program to encourage cities to work together around sustainable development. While it has not blossomed into the effort for which this author had hoped, the concept of ecological sister cities remains a potent one. City-to-city and region-to-region exchanges, partnerships, and efforts at sharing technical and financial resources hold much promise.

Taking advantage of the expertise and experiences they developed in London, for example, a team of designers helped a poor neighborhood in Johannesburg, South Africa, design and build a zero-carbon community center. Ivory Park is a large informal settlement with few resources and terrible living conditions, and through this partnership one city helped in a small way to improve the quality of life and promise of sustainability in another city and region. This kind of collaboration offers another way that cities and regions can comprehend the emerging practice of sustainability. They can utilize a new, *glocal* point of view, which applies to cities and regions that are doing work to protect their regional environments and resources and striving to live and source more locally, while still understanding the importance of their global commitments and connections.

PROSPECTS AND PROMISE OF GREEN REGIONALISM

I have argued here that the region is an essential scale and level for planning sustainability, reducing ecological footprints, and conserving ecological systems and biodiversity. Green regions are critically important to set the stage for, and will likely determine the success of, many sustainability initiatives and projects at the level of the city or community. Many of the toughest problems we face today, from climate change to managing in the face of diminishing oil supplies, will require regional strategies to ensure effectiveness. I call this broad concept *green regionalism,* which is at once a point of view, set of values, and vision, but it is also a set of practices and policies for advancing all three. Green regions offer the best hope to motivate and inspire us, imagine and chart different future paths, and connect us emotionally and psychologically to place and each other.

Green regionalism challenges us to tackle local and regional problems as well as to acknowledge the larger global impacts of our practices and lifestyles. While conserving and living within the bounds of regional resources and ecological systems remain essential goals, the green regionalism proposed here must increasingly be understood as something that takes into account the status and condition of the larger world. Green regions are interconnected and globally embedded; they acknowledge a responsibility to a larger planetary commons. They can be understood as a positive force for protecting the environment and addressing poverty at a global level.

As discussed here, there are now many new tools and analytic frameworks that will help advance these regional goals. The emergence of the concepts of urban metabolism and ecological flows and of methodologies that work with ecological footprints and their assessment at once offers new ways to analyze a region and to shift or move it toward greater sustainability. In turn, these new tools and frames of reference are helping us identify opportunities at the regional and local levels to generate power from distributed regional sources and reduce our high-carbon, fossil fuel–intensive footprint by growing and processing more on local and regional bases.

At the same time, we face significant challenges in applying these ideas and methods, and much work will be needed in applying them in specific regions. The majority of the urban regions or metropolitan areas in the United States, for instance, lack the jurisdictional authority and power that places such as Vancouver, London, and other exemplary cities presently hold. Institutional structures to support regional sustainability planning and management often are lacking as is sustaining political support. Such support will be even harder to muster for efforts at more extraregional or global levels. Nevertheless, considerable insights may be gleaned and creative strategies learned from the many stories of current programs.

Exactly what constitutes the appropriate geographical definition or scale of a green region remains an open question and presents a practical challenge in moving forward. Is a green region defined by the few counties surrounding a major city, or by larger ecological, geographical, or natural features? How much area comprises a green region, and might it be more productive to plan for and manage green megaregions that encompass even larger expanses and multiple urban centers?

Whether it is possible to organize boundaries of green regions so that, in some general sense, they correspond to landscapes and urbanscapes that are important to people also remains unclear. The very defining, even the naming, of a green region actually could serve to create the conditions to which residents will relate and that they will embrace and accept as their "home." Nurturing citizens and leaders who will connect emotionally with and care about the regions in which they live remains a major goal.

It is interesting to consider the gradual shift in environmental planning, especially in coastal areas, toward marine bioregions—offshore boundaries and marine ecosystem entities that make sense as planning and management units. Yet they may be largely beyond visual, visceral, or direct experience for most nearby land-based residents. How do we instill a sense of reverence or love for environments and life that are largely outside urbanites' sensorial reach? I would argue that, on our "blue planet," we need to make special efforts to foster emotional connections—as well as those having to do with policy and planning—with marine environments. Perhaps we will call it *blue regionalism*. Here, sustainability of marine life and habitats will be taken more squarely into account, and the undersea life so seemingly remote will become integral to our planning community.

Extending our reach temporally may be similarly difficult. Longer-term visions, perhaps on the order of hundreds of years, will be needed to guide our shorter-term decisions, but fostering a sense of longer, deeper time is not easy. Arriving at regional policy and planning aimed at reducing the impacts of our rather large ecological footprint and metabolism as they affect regions many hundreds or thousands of miles away is not simple, either. Despite these many challenges—or perhaps because of them—however, green regionalism holds much potential as a framework and vehicle through which to understand our commitments, both global and local, to integrate across the many sectors in which we work and to advance the broader agenda of sustainability.

REFERENCES

Albrecht, Glenn. 2005. "Solastalgia": A new concept in health and identity. *PAN* 3:41–55.

———. 2007. Solastalgia: The distress caused by environmental change. *Australasian Psychiatry* 15 (September):S95–S98.

———. 2010. Soliphilia and citizen power. *RSA Comment* (8 March). http://comment.rsablogs .org.uk/2010/03/08/soliphilia-citizen-power/

American Forests. n.d. Trees and ecosystem services. www.amfor.org/resources/urbanforests/ naturevalue.php

Beatley, Timothy. 2000. *Green urbanism*. Washington, DC: Island Press.

———. 2009. *Planning for coastal resilience: Best practices for calamitous times*. Washington, DC: Island Press.

Beatley, Timothy, and Peter Newman. 2009. *Green urbanism Down Under: Learning from Australia's sustainable communities*. Washington, DC: Island Press.

Best Foot Forward. 2002. *City limits: A resource flow and ecological footprint analysis of Greater London*. London: Chartered Institution of Wastes Management Environmental Body. www .citylimitslondon.com/download.htm

Cape Cod Commission. 2006. *Cape Cod regional policy plan*. Barnstable, MA.

Capital Growth. 2009. Capital Growth launches £150,000 fund to help Londoners boost food growing. Press release (4 December).

Cascade Land Conservancy. 2005. The Cascade agenda: 100 years forward. (May). http:// cascadeagenda.com

City of Calgary. 2007. *imagineCALGARY long-range plan for urban sustainability*. Calgary, AB. www.imaginecalgary.ca/imagineCALGARY_long_range_plan.pdf

City of New York. 2008. Mayor announces plan to reduce the use of tropical hardwoods. (11 February). www.nyc.gov/html/om/html/2008a/pr045-08.html

City of Oslo. 2008. *Oslo toward 2025: The 2008 municipal master plan*. Oslo, NO.

City of Stockholm. 2007. *Hammarby Sjöstad: The best environmental solutions in Stockholm*. Stockholm: GlashusEtt.

City of Vancouver. 2008a. *Vancouver EcoDensity charter*. (10 June). Vancouver, BC.

————. 2008b. *EcoDensity: An introduction to building communities that are green, livable and affordable in Vancouver.* Vancouver, BC.

Davis, Tony. 2002. Pima County, Arizona, hopes to save desert with new conservation plan. *Arizona Daily Star* (15 December).

Fonseca, Julia, and Cory Jones. 2009. Progress report: Measuring effectiveness of open space land acquisitions in Pima County, Arizona, in relation to the Sonoran Desert Conservation Plan. Tucson, AZ: Pima County Administrator's Office. www.pima.gov/cmo/sdcp/reports/d52/Acquisition_Analysis.pdf

Girardet, Herbert. 2006. *Creating sustainable cities.* Devon, UK: Green Books.

Government of Australia. 2002. National strategy for ecologically sustainable development. Canberra. http://environment.gov.au/about/esd/publications/strategy/intro.html

Government of Queensland. 2006. *South East Queensland regional plan.* Brisbane, AU.

————. 2009. *South East Queensland (SEQ) Regional Plan 2009–2031.* Administrative draft. Brisbane, AU.

Government of South Australia. 2007. *Planning strategy for metropolitan Adelaide.* (December). Adelaide, AU.

GLA (Greater London Authority). 2006. *East London green grid primer.* (November). London.

————. 2009a. *A new plan for London: Proposals for the mayor's London plan.* (April). London.

————. 2009b, *London rivers action plan.* (January). London.

————. 2010a. *The draft climate change adaptation strategy for London.* Public consultation draft (February). London.

————. 2010b. *Cultivating the capital: Food growing and the planning system in London.* (January). London: GLA Planning and Housing Committee.

————. 2010c. £362,000 boost for charity to stop surplus food being dumped in landfill. Press release (22 March). London. www.london.gov.uk/media/press_releases_mayoral/%C2%A3362000-boost-charity-stop-surplus-food-being-dumped-landfill

————. n.d. Working in partnership. London. www.london.gov.uk/who-runs-london/london-boroughs

Hedden, W. P., 1929. *How great cities are fed.* Boston: D. C. Heath.

Huckelberry, Chuck. 2002. The Sonoran Desert conservation plan. *Endangered Species Bulletin* 27(2):12–15.

Kellert, Stephen, Judith Heerwagen, and Marty Mador, eds. 2008. *Biophilic design: The theory, science and practice of bringing buildings to life.* Hoboken, NJ: John Wiley.

Layzer, Judith A. 2008. *Natural experiments: Ecosystem-based management and the environment.* Cambridge, MA: MIT Press.

London Development Authority. 2006. Healthy and sustainable food for London: The mayor's food strategy. (May). London.

Louv, Rich. 2005. *Last child in the woods: Saving our children from nature deficit disorder.* Chapel Hill, NC: Algonquin Books.

Low, Tim, 2007. Climate change and Brisbane biodiversity: A critique of the climate change and energy taskforce final report, with recommendations for biodiversity added. (August). Brisbane, AU: Brisbane City Council.

MacKaye, Benton. 1940. Regional planning and ecology. *Ecological Monographs* 10(3):349–353.

McKibben, Bill. 2010a. *Eaarth: Making a life on a tough new planet.* New York: Times Books.

————. 2010b. Breaking the growth habit. *Scientific American* (April):61–65.

Metro Vancouver. 2009a. *Metro Vancouver sustainability report.* (January). Vancouver, BC.

————. 2009b. *Metro Vancouver 2040: Shaping our future.* Regional growth strategy draft (November). Vancouver, BC.

Metro Vancouver. n.d. Future of the region sustainability dialogues. www.metrovancouver.org/region/dialogues/Pages/default.aspx

MWCOG (Metropolitan Washington Council of Governments). 1968. *Natural features of the Washington metropolitan area: An ecological reconnaissance.* (January). Washington, DC.

National Research Council. 2000. *Watershed management for potable water supply.* Washington, DC: National Academy Press.

Newman, Peter, Timothy Beatley, and Heather Boyer. 2009. *Resilient cities: Responding to climate change and peak oil.* Washington, DC: Island Press.

Owen, David. 2009. *Green metropolis: Why living smaller, living closer and driving less are the keys to sustainability.* New York: Riverhead Books.

Pilkey, Orrin, and Rob Young. 2009. *The rising sea.* Washington, DC: Island Press.

Portland Metro. n.d. Why donate surplus food? www.metro-region.org/index.cfm/go/by.web/id=749

Sale, Kirkpatrick. 1991. *Dwellers in the land: The bioregional vision.* Gabriola Island, BC: New Society Publishers.

Shuman, Michael H. 2000. *Going local: Creating self-reliant communities in a global age.* New York: Routledge.

Steiner, Frederick. 1983. Regional planning in the United States: Historic and contemporary examples. *Landscape Planning* 10:297–315.

Thayer, Robert. 2003. *LifePlace: Biregional thought and practice.* Berkeley: University of California Press.

Thomas, Chris D., Alison Cameron, Rhys E. Green, Michel Bakkenes, Linda J. Beaumont, Yvonne C. Collingham, Barend F. N. Erasmus, Marinez Ferreira de Siqueira, Alan Grainger, Lee Hannah, Lesley Hughes, Brian Huntley, Albert S. van Jaarsveld, Guy F. Midgley, Lera Miles, Miguel A. Ortega-Huerta, A. Townsend Peterson, Oliver L. Phillips, and Stephen E. Williams. 2004. Extinction risk from climate change. *Nature* 427 (8 January):145–147.

Tonn, Bruce E. 1996. 500-year planning: A speculative provocation. *Journal of the American Planning Association* (Spring):185–193.

———. 1998. Philosphical aspects of 500-year planning. *Environment and Planning A* 20:1507–1522.

Veage, Lee-Anne, and Darryl N. Jones. 2007. Breaking the barrier: Assessing the value of fauna-friendly crossing structures at Compton Toad. Nathan, Queensland: Centre for Innovative Conservation Strategies, Griffith University.

Wackernagel, Mathis, and William Rees. 1998. *Our ecological footprint: Reducing human impact on the earth.* Gabriola Island, BC: New Society Publishers.

Wilson, E. O. 1984. *Biophilia.* Cambridge, MA: Harvard University Press.

Windhager, Steven, Frederick Steiner, Mark T. Simmons, and David Heymann. 2010. Emerging landscapes: Ecosystem services as a basis for design goals. *Landscape Journal* 29:2–10.

WWF (Worldwide Fund for Nature). 2007. One planet Wales: Transforming Wales for a prosperous future within our fair share of the Earth's resources. Report summary (October). Cardiff, UK.

———. 2010. Living Planet Report, 2010. Gland, Switzerland: WWF International.

CHAPTER 7

REGIONAL PLANNING FOR SUSTAINABILITY AND HEGEMONY OF METRO-POLITAN REGIONALISM

Gerrit-Jan Knaap and Rebecca Lewis

In the United States, the notion that metropolitan growth should be planned at the metropolitan scale is not new. Frequently, the birth of metropolitan planning is traced to the plan for Chicago that Daniel Burnham developed at the turn of the twentieth century or to the origination of the Regional Planning Association in the 1920s (Mitchell-Weaver, Miller, and Deal 2000), while others associate it with London in the mid-1800s (Wheeler 2000). In the post–World War II era, support for planning at the metropolitan scale has largely, if not perfectly, waxed and waned with the federal government's political cycles. With some exceptions, the country's Democratic administrations have tended to favor regional approaches to metropolitan planning, and Republican ones generally opposed it.

The 2008 election of President Barack Obama, a Democrat, fostered a renewed interest in metropolitan planning. Many of these ideas were floated during the election campaign and promoted most strongly by the Brookings Institution (2007) through its Blueprint for American Prosperity initiative. Although not new, the institution's arguments for metropolitan planning did include the debatably newer concepts of smart growth and sustainability. These principles were salient in the widely praised regional planning exercises of Portland Metro, Envision Utah, and several California-based metropolitan planning organizations, all of which were novel both in their metropolitan approach to growth management and their use of advanced geographic information systems (GIS) and other planning support systems.

To date, metropolitan planning has also gained a foothold through the Obama administration's singular urban policy program known as the Sustainable Communities Initiative. Under this banner, the secretaries of the Departments of Housing and Urban Development (HUD) and Transportation (DOT) as well as the Environmental Protection Agency (EPA) have signed a memorandum of understanding stating that they will "work together to ensure that these housing and transportation goals are met while simultaneously protecting the environment, promoting equitable development, and helping to address the challenges of climate change" (DOT 2009). Further, in the 2010 budget, Congress appropriated $150 million to HUD for a Sustainable Communities Initiative to improve regional planning efforts. Approximately $100 million of this funding was given to integrated regional planning initiatives through HUD's Sustainable Communities Planning Grant Program. Without question, this is the most substantial federal support for metropolitan planning to be instituted in more than a decade.[1]

In this chapter we explore the practice and prospects of metropolitan planning today. Beginning with an examination of metropolitan institutions and their role in regional planning, we then review the planning experience of several metropolitan areas around the United States, which brings us to conclude that the prospects for metropolitan planning are better than at any time in recent history. This expectation stems largely from growth in the capacity to analyze transportation, land use, housing, and environmental issues at the metropolitan scale due to increases in governments' ability to engage the public in metropolitan-wide growth issues and in support from the federal government. We also conclude, however, that implementation issues remain formidable and neither new planning technologies nor memoranda of understanding signed by federal cabinet secretaries are likely to overcome this vexing problem.

METROPOLITAN INSTITUTIONS

A wide variety of institutions have been engaged in metropolitan planning over the years. Some trace the practice of metropolitan planning to park and boulevard planning and the City Beautiful movement of the early twentieth century. Specifically, Burnham's plan, which was commissioned by the Merchants Club (later merged with the Commercial Club of Chicago) and published in 1909, is often viewed as the first metropolitan plan. Another monumental event in metropolitan planning was the *Plan for New York and Its Environs* prepared by the

---

1. "The goal of the Program is to support multi-jurisdictional regional planning efforts that integrate housing, economic development, and transportation decision-making in a manner that empowers jurisdictions to consider the interdependent challenges of economic growth, social equity and environmental impact simultaneously. Three funding categories are being considered:

1. Funding to support the preparation of Regional Plans for Sustainable Development that address housing, economic development, transportation, and environmental quality in an integrated fashion where such plans do not currently exist;

2. Funding to support the preparation of more detailed execution plans and programs to implement existing regional sustainable development plans (that address housing, economic development, transportation, and environmental quality in an integrated fashion); and

3. Implementation funding to support regions that have regional sustainable development plans and implementation strategies in place and need support for a catalytic project or program that demonstrates commitment to and implementation of the broader plan." (HUD 2010)

Regional Plan Association in 1929. During the 1930s and 1940s, additional experiments in regional planning and government were attempted, but many of them, such as the Tennessee Valley Authority, were not metropolitan in scope and tended to focus more on conservation and economic development.

Metropolitan institutions expanded in number and scope in the postwar era. During the years between 1945 and 1980, the growth of councils of government (COGs), metropolitan planning organizations (MPOs), and countless special-purpose districts, councils, boards, authorities, and commissions was fueled largely by federal funding requirements. The logic of metropolitan planning is straightforward. Because transportation and wastewater networks, natural ecosystems, and social and economic interdependencies extend beyond the boundaries of most local governments, they require regional-scale planning and management. Further, the spatial extent of many of these systems (perhaps excepting ecosystems) generally is defined by the boundaries of metropolitan areas.

Indeed, this dichotomy between natural and man-made systems perhaps defines the distinction made by Robert Fishman (2000) between "metropolitanists" and "regionalists." Metropolitan regionalism—as espoused by the metropolitanists like Thomas Adams, director of the New York Regional Plan, and implemented by highway engineers—was designed to create the transportation links that would support metropolitan growth and prosperity, especially in the central city. Organic regionalism, on the other hand, was envisioned by regionalists like George Perkins Marsh, when he posited that the city is only one element in the larger framework of the region and that it poses a major threat to the balance of nature. Fishman (2000) claims that we have the materials for a new synthesis of these two traditions, but practice has moved much more in the direction of metropolitanism than regionalism or some synthesis of the two views.

Given the interdependencies of both natural and man-made systems, planning at the metropolitan scale is not easy, and plan implementation is even more difficult. Authority to plan and manage land use is vigorously protected by local governments, and the ability to manage land use is central to metropolitan planning. In every metropolitan area, except perhaps that of Portland ceding any degree of land use authority to metropolitan governments is anathema. As a result, the success of metropolitan planning depends less on an area's government than its governance. That is, it hinges on a governance structure that is not dependent upon the authority of a general-purpose metropolitan government but on the ability of multiple and disparate governments to coordinate their efforts.

Institutions and governance structures in metropolitan areas vary widely. They include associations of general-purpose local and special-purpose metropolitan governments, private and quasi-public groups, and nonprofit organizations. Perhaps the institutions with the most prominence at the metropolitan scale, however, are COGs and MPOs, which now dominate the practice of metropolitan planning. These are the institutions with which its greatest prospects reside.

Councils of Government

COGs are critically important players in metropolitan planning. Sometimes called regional councils, regional commissions, regional planning commissions, planning district commissions, or development districts, COGs are essentially voluntary associations of local governments. According to the National Association of Regional Councils (2006a):

> A regional council is a multi-service entity with state and locally-defined boundaries that delivers a variety of federal, state and local programs while continuing its function as a planning organization, technical assistance provider and "visionary" to its member local governments. As such, they are accountable to local units of government and effective partners for state and federal governments.

It is important to note that the terms *council of government, regional council,* and *regional planning commission* do not always refer to the same type of body. Not all councils of government are regional; some serve only one or two counties. Most COGs are established by state statutes while others are nonprofit organizations (Illinois Association of Regional Councils, n.d.).

Although most COGs are creatures of their states, the federal government has always played a major role in growing and sustaining COGs. Four federal laws, all enacted in 1965, were responsible for the rapid growth in the number of COGs: the Housing and Community Development Act; Public Works and Economic Development Act; Appalachian Regional Development Act; and Water Resources Planning Act (Meck 2002). The federal Office of Management and Budget's Circular A-95 specifically required that a regional planning agency be created to review local applications for approximately 39 federal grant programs, but by 1980 the government was continuing funding for only one—metropolitan transportation planning. After the dramatic reduction in federal aid, several states increased their levels of support. In part to replace lost federal revenues, COGs also became engaged in purchasing programs, training, forecasting, data collection, and some forms of service provision (Meck 2002).

While COGs derive legitimacy by fulfilling federally mandated functions, they are fundamentally voluntary organizations that have only the authority ceded by their members, which, in most cases, is extremely limited. As voluntary organizations, COGs tend to avoid controversial or redistributive tasks. According to Victor Jones (1962, 304), "metropolitan associations of local governments are so afraid of assuming responsibility for making decisions about a metropolitan problem—of appearing in the slightest to act as a 'government'— that special districts will inevitably be proposed." Nelson Wikstrom (1977) suggests that this makes them particularly reticent to address social issues, and Urlan Wannop (1995) notes that COGs often lack clear statutory direction and operate on small fluctuating budgets. For all these reasons, COGs have been, and remain, severely limited in their ability to develop and implement metropolitan plans.

Perhaps most fundamentally, COGs' structures limit how representative and accountable they can be. Because their general assemblies and executive boards typically are made up of local government officials, they have no direct accountability to the citizens of the region. Royce Hanson (1966, 34) said it this way: "A basic problem of the councils in meeting this challenge is reflected in the limited interests, power, and time of its participants, all or most of whom are elected officials with primary political loyalties to and duties in their own jurisdictions."

Also, COGs are widely viewed as having a suburban bias. Because vote apportionment typically is based on member jurisdictions rather than population, the votes cast by multiple suburban jurisdictions easily outnumber the single vote of a central city.

Metropolitan Planning Organizations

In metropolitan planning, the dominant player is now the MPO, which was established by the Federal-Aid Highway Act of 1962 to provide local input for urban transportation planning and to allocate federal transportation funds for metropolitan areas with populations of more than 50,000 people. Then, as now, states had considerable flexibility in designating an MPO. It may be part of state government, a regional COG, a planning district, or an independent entity (Wolf and Farquhar 2005). Currently, nearly one-half of extant MPOs fall within COGs and serve the same general geography (National Association of Regional Councils 2006b). In some large metropolitan areas, such as Boston and San Francisco, however, regional planning agencies and MPOs are separate entities. In Washington, DC, and other metropolitan areas, the MPO functions almost as though it were an autonomous agency within a COG (Meck 2002).

MPOs' prescribed functions are five-fold:

- set the stage for regional decision making in the metropolitan area;

- determine and evaluate alternative transportation improvement options;

- prepare and maintain the region's long-range transportation plan, or MTP (metropolitan transportation plan);

- develop four-year transportation improvement programs (TIPs); and

- engage the public in developing the TIP. (DOT 2007)

Like the support for COGs, backing for MPOs diminished during the 1980s, under President Ronald Reagan's administration. Although MPOs were still required to prepare TIPs, new regulations left it to the states to define the organizations' specific roles. As a result, according to Bruce

McDowell (1984, 132), MPO capital planning came "basically [to] confirm what is going on in the fragmented region, rather than providing any area wide leadership." Mark Solof (1998) relates that, in compiling their annual TIP capital plans, many MPOs were reduced to rubber-stamping the decisions of state agencies.

Federal support for MPOs resumed first under the Intermodal Surface Transportation Efficiency Act (ISTEA) of 1991, then later with passage of the Transportation Equity Act for the 21st Century (TEA-21) in 1998. ISTEA required the federal government to certify transportation planning activities in metropolitan areas that have populations of more than 200,000. Certification required MPOs to work with transportation organizations, local and state governments, and citizens to meet the requirements of the planning process. To receive federal highway and transit funding, the MPO's certification had to be renewed every three years.

ISTEA also required MPOs to consider multiple modes of travel. Rather than focus solely on transit and highways, they also had to consider freight, bicycle, pedestrian, and air travel. Planning requirements expanded to include those previously reserved for state transportation agencies as well. These included leadership roles in constrained, long-range plans and transportation improvement plans. Large MPOs were given the responsibility of allocating some categorical funds in consultation with state DOTs. Further, although they retained control over most types of funding, state DOT projects had to be selected in cooperation with MPOs (Goetz, Dempsey, and Larson 2002). Under TEA-21, long-range plans were required to be constrained fiscally (i.e., revenue sources needed to be identified). This effectively revised how TIPs were approached, and they changed from serving as wish lists to being more realistic guides for transportation investment decision making (McDowell 1999). ISTEA and TEA-21 also expanded the purview of MPOs beyond transportation into land use and environmental concerns (Wolf and Farquhar 2005).

Sheldon Edner and Bruce McDowell (2002), however, assert that intergovernmental institutional arrangements were largely unchanged by ISTEA because MPOs continued to lack the strength of individual member jurisdictions. Given the continuing decision-making power of states, MPOs often end up as observers rather than decision makers in the project identification process. Todd Goldman and Elizabeth Deakin (2000) note that the institutional structure of MPOs reflects the legacy of COGs, which tend to confer and inform, not plan or govern. Like COGs, and generally for the same reasons, MPOs often are criticized for having a suburban bias. The one-vote-per-local-government system, many argue, creates a bias toward highway spending in the suburbs instead of transit spending in central cities (Lowry and Balling 2009; Nelson et al. 2004). Additionally, highly populated central cities are outnumbered by suburban jurisdictions, which leads to an inequitable distribution of limited resources. More fundamentally—even after ISTEA—MPOs have been relatively powerless in the face of powerful local and state governments (Solof 1998).

Despite their limitations, MPOs play a critical role in metropolitan planning, which is required to receive federal transportation funding. While few regions have gone above and beyond the federal funding requirements, without them and without MPOs it is likely that many metropolitan regions would not engage in any metropolitan planning at all.

Special-Purpose Governments

Like MPOs, many other metropolitan institutions have specific functions, such as economic development, public transportation, housing, or wastewater treatment. These can encompass many transit districts, port authorities, economic development commissions, and park districts. According to Kathryn Foster (1997, 2), special districts are "autonomous local governments that provide a single or limited service." Special-purpose governments or districts provide critically important functions and are the fastest growing class of government institutions in most metropolitan areas.

Transit districts are especially important. Transit networks provide the backbones of many large U.S. cities, and they are destined to play a growing role in sustainability planning. But many transit agencies are not connected strongly to planning processes led by MPOs, and thus they may play a disproportionately small role in metropolitan planning (Bay 2009).

Port authorities, utilities, and some economic development organizations are quasi-public or public-private partnerships that often cover areawide jurisdictions. States charter and fund some, while others are handled by local referenda and tax revenues. The degree to which these organizations become involved in regional planning, however, varies extensively. Many, perhaps most, focus primarily on their own missions and pay little attention to larger metropolitan planning issues.

The implications of the growth in number of special-purpose metropolitan governments, their degree of autonomy and the extent of their influence on the practice of metropolitan planning cannot be over-emphasized. Not only does the fragmentation of service delivery increase the difficulty of service planning and coordination, but the growing financial and political independence of special purpose organizations makes it increasingly difficult for top-down planning at the metropolitan scale. These features essentially assure that metropolitan planning and governance are accomplished through voluntary coordination rather than command and control. Further, as sustainability issues come to the fore, it becomes increasingly critical for energy and wastewater utilities to be metropolitan in scope and that they engage in metropolitan-wide planning and decision making.

Private Organizations

On the private nonprofit side, perhaps the most common and familiar organizations are chambers of commerce, although they do not always serve entire metropolitan areas and they primarily engage in business promotion. According to Marc Weiss (n.d.), however, some chambers of commerce have been effective in designing and implementing strategic economic development plans for their respective regions. The Commercial Club of Chicago is probably best known for its involvement in metropolitan planning. Utility companies in most metropolitan areas are also privately held, but they typically have not engaged in metropolitan planning.

Nonprofit organizations have become increasingly influential as advocates for many social issues, among them affordable housing, education, and employment opportunities; equity in the distribution of public investment and services; environmental quality; and racial and social justice. Advocacy organizations, which often are funded by local and national foundations and philanthropies, focus specifically on smart growth, sustainable development, or regional planning, and they can be quite effective at shaping state and local policies.

National organizations such as the Citistates Group and the Alliance for Regional Stewardship assist metropolitan civic movements by providing encouragement and advice concerning growing larger and improving organizing methods. In particular the Urban Land Institute has organized its Reality Check exercises in metropolitan areas nationwide. In these exercises, large groups of people use chips or LEGO® blocks to indicate where they prefer to have anticipated growth to take place. They have effectively raised public awareness and mobilized political interest in metropolitan growth issues (Urban Land Institute 2008).

This short overview reveals the difficulty of and institutional challenges facing metropolitan planning and plan implementation. COGs facilitate dialogue among local governments, collect data, conduct studies, and provide certain public services, but they have little inclination and no authority to influence the decisions of their member governments. Federal statutes require planning by MPOs, some of which have developed extensive technical capacities to model and analyze transportation and land use alternatives. But most MPOs have weak connections to the public at large and primarily remain deferential to state departments of transportation. While large in number, special-purpose governments that provide critical urban services dealing with potable water, wastewater, and transit, among many other metropolitan needs, tend to be highly fragmented. Finally, business, environmental, and civic organizations are active and influential in multiple policy arenas, but their interests vary extensively, and few have the legitimacy to lead metropolitan planning efforts. Of course, there are exceptions.

THE PRACTICE OF METROPOLITAN PLANNING

Despite the institutional complexity of metropolitan governance, several such areas across the country have conducted visioning exercises and created impressive plans. In the six case studies included here, the types of actors involved, scope of issues addressed, tools used for analysis, and plans' degree of success all vary, but they offer interesting models for ways in which the practice of metropolitan planning may expand.

Portland, Oregon

The Portland metropolitan area lies at the northern tip of the Willamette Valley and includes Clackamas, Multnomah, and Washington Counties in Oregon, and Clark County in Washington State. Oregon's part of the metropolitan area has long served as the flagship of the state's heralded land use program, which is widely recognized as the most progressive and influential in the country (Knaap and Lewis 2009). The entire metropolitan planning process, in fact, can be traced to requirements set up under Oregon law, which explains both why metropolitan planning in Portland is so significant and why its influence does not extend into Washington.

Portland's Metropolitan Service District (Metro) was created by the state legislature in 1977 and merged with the Columbia Region Association of Governments in 1979. A voter initiative in 1992 established Metro as the only directly elected regional government in the United States. Metro serves as both MPO and COG, and by state statute it is responsible expressly for both transportation and land use planning for the three-county region in Oregon.

Metropolitan Planning As John Landis (2008, 2) states, Portland 2040 "heralded a new and ongoing period in American metropolitan planning: the era of the regional vision plan." The Portland plan was the first of its kind in the United States, although inspiration was drawn from metropolitan Toronto. The Region 2040 planning process began in 1992 and included the 25 cities and three counties within the Metro boundaries. In 1995, Metro adopted the 2040 Growth Concept, a 50-year vision for urban growth in the region. As required by law, the plan was reviewed and updated in 2005.

The metropolitan planning process in Portland began with Metro's enabling legislation, which called for the development and adoption of regional goals and objectives. To fulfill this responsibility, Metro incorporated into the periodic urban growth boundary (UGB) review process the task of creating regional urban growth goals and objectives (RUGGOs), as state law required. Beginning in 1989, well before Portland 2040 was launched, Metro started developing the RUGGOs, which were adopted in 1991.

Metro's charter called for the creation of a long-term future vision and a framework plan that would include a collection of regional functional plans, echo the RUGGOs, and ultimately replace them.[2] This plan was required to address the UGB, transportation system, rural land protection, and housing, among other topics. The Regional Framework Plan, adopted in 1997, incorporated the Regional Transportation Plan, 2040 Growth Concept, Regional Urban Growth Goals and Objectives, and the Urban Growth Management Functional Plan that was adopted in 1996 to implement the 2040 Growth Concept.

Extensive public participation and technical analysis were devoted to developing the 2040 Growth Concept. Metro made unprecedented use of GIS data and analysis in preparing the plan. Rich parcel data, fine-grained environmental data, and advanced land use–transportation models were all used extensively. Central to the development and implementation of the 2040 Growth Concept were the GIS data and tools of the Regional Land Information System, and Metroscope, a sophisticated GIS-based spatial allocation, visualization, and data accounting system that connects an econometric model with a transportation model and two real estate models.

Using these tools, Metro developed three alternative land use scenarios, which featured (1) continued spatial expansion; (2) increases in density with little spatial expansion; and (3) satellite cities. Developed in-house with some help from consultants, they were not the products of public participation exercises. After examining each of these alternatives using quantitative indicators, a preferred scenario was developed that contained the best features of each of the scenarios. The Metro board adopted this preferred version only after soliciting the extensive involvement of the public and stakeholders, and it then became the basis of the 2040 Growth Concept plan.

The 2040 Plan Rather than being a comprehensive regional plan, the 2040 Plan deals with urban structure by identifying key places in the region and then providing a transportation plan to link them. It also provides guidance for maintenance of the UGB over time, and it integrates a system of greenspaces into the urban area.

The 2040 Growth Concept emphasizes 10 design types that serve as the building blocks of the regional strategy: central city, main streets, regional centers, town centers, station communities, neighborhoods, corridors, industrial areas and freight terminals, rural reserves/open spaces, and neighboring cities/ green corridors, all of which are illustrated in the 2040 Growth Concept map (figure 7.1). In addition to the UGB, current and future light-rail lines and rail stations are displayed as well. The plan emphasizes both the revitalization of existing areas and the preservation of the rural landscape.

The 2040 Plan includes an integrated set of policies for growth management and specific tools to assist local governments in meeting those goals. Working closely with local governments, Metro crafted polices addressing the

---

2. Throughout this case study, we rely on Metro (2010a).

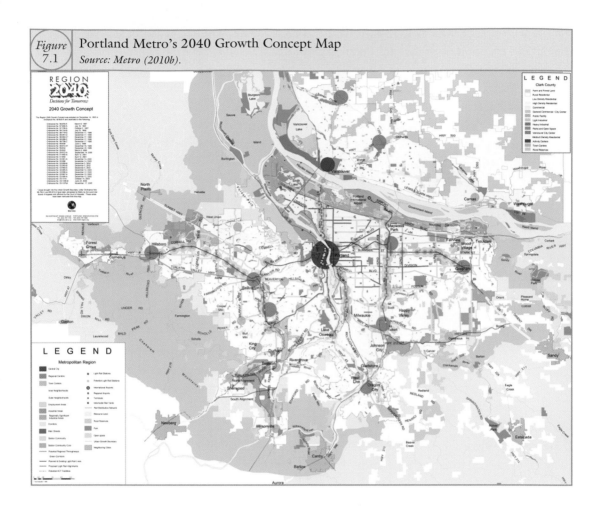

Figure 7.1 Portland Metro's 2040 Growth Concept Map
Source: Metro (2010b).

accommodation of projected growth, a regional parking policy, water quality and floodplain management, regulation for large-scale retail development,
affordable housing, and coordination both among neighboring cities and
between land use and transportation. Beyond establishing growth management
goals and policies, the 2040 Plan also deals with environmental needs by means
of policies for conservation, parks, greenways, water quality and supply, and
habitat.

Implementation Because of the legal framework set in place by Oregon's
planning law and the Metro charter, the 2040 Plan's connections to land
use decision making are strong and direct. State statutes require that Metro
establish and manage a regional UGB, and they give Metro the authority to
make binding decisions regarding development within the boundary (Oregon
State Legislature 2010). Through its charter, Metro also has the authority to
review local plans for consistency with regional plans and the legal authority to require local governments to alter their plans to make them consistent
with the regional plan. The regional transportation plan (RTP) in Portland

is also integral to implementation. In it, the goals of the 2040 Growth Concept guide its strategies, and the RTP has strong land use–transportation connections. Oregon's Department of Transportation asserts influence through Metro rather than outside of it.

As required by its charter, Metro updated the Regional Framework Plan in 2005. Chapter 8 of that revision—"Implementation"—lists the various statutes, codes, and ordinances that serve to put the plan in action (Appendix 1).[3] The charter also requires Metro to monitor progress toward the plan's implementation. The 2004 performance measure report includes 122 pages devoted to data and information on implementation progress. The report, however, contains neither a progress assessment nor policy recommendations based on advancement to date. Nevertheless, several academic papers have reported on Portland's planning success (Hanley and Knaap 1998; Knaap and Lewis 2009; Song and Knaap 2004).

Central Utah

Surrounded by the Wasatch Mountains, the Great Salt Lake, Utah Lake, deserts, and federally owned land, the greater Wasatch region is home to nearly 80 percent of Utah's population. It is politically conservative, and its governance is fragmented. The region spans ten counties and includes 88 cities, more than 150 special districts, and two MPOs: the Mountainland Association of Governments (MAG) and the Wasatch Front Regional Council (WFRC). MAG's jurisdiction centers on the Provo area while WFRC focuses on the Salt Lake City region, and each of the five counties also has its own council of governments.

Unlike the approach taken in Oregon, regional planning in central Utah is decidedly a bottom-up, voluntary effort. Envision Utah, a private nonprofit entity originally known as the Coalition for Utah's Future from its founding in 1988 until 2008, has played the dominant leadership role. The coalition began as a small nonprofit organization with strong leadership and close ties to state government. Although Utah's state planning laws are relatively weak, its government has supported regional planning in important, often subtle ways.

Regional Planning   The Envision Utah project was launched in 1996 in order to analyze long-term growth, create a vision for the future, and pursue strategies to realize that vision. Today it is a public-private partnership that includes more than 100 representatives of cities, state agencies, businesses, industries, civic and environmental organizations, and the public at large. Initially, the MPOs' leaders resisted engaging in the process, but later leadership changes at the WFRC made them integral to the analysis and implementation of the regional vision. Envision Utah receives funding from local and national foundations; grants and in-kind support from state, local, and federal government agencies; and private sector funding. Early on, then-governor Mike Leavitt supported the project, which was

---

3. Appendices are found at the end of this chapter.

also served well by the strong leadership provided by businessman Robert Grow, Utah Jazz owner Larry Miller, and several other individuals who would later go on to serve in the state government.

Public participation, including such techniques as surveys, community meetings, and interactive Web sites, has been part of the project from its inception. The focus then was on collecting information on community values, which Envision Utah used to frame the language employed throughout the process. Much of the public outreach material was built upon extensive data, modeling, and analysis developed with technical support from the state. WFRC and MAG conducted transportation modeling to feed into the exercise. In public engagement events, citizens created maps that were aggregated and used to develop four alternative growth scenarios based on common themes: (1) baseline, or trend; (2) municipal plans; (3) walkable communities; and (4) clustered growth. State assistance again helped Envision Utah evaluate scenarios and construct the Quality Growth Efficiency Tools used to assess the performance of each scenario. Quality-of-life benchmarks were observed in the evaluation of the consequences of each scenario over a 30-year period.

After technical committees tested scenarios, members of the public were engaged again to evaluate them at community meetings and with online surveys based on reported benchmarks. The preferred scenario was walkable communities, while clustered growth was a close second. Based on public input and technical analysis, the Quality Growth Strategy was presented to the steering committee for review and refinement in order for it to be adopted as the long-term strategy for the future of the greater Wasatch region. The visioning exercise culminated in development of a set of goals for the future and strategies to assist in achieving them.

The Quality Growth Strategy Rather than a regional plan, the Envision Utah project produced a set of seven primary goals, 31 strategies, a Quality Growth Strategy map, and toolboxes for local governments. Compared with the trend scenario, the Quality Growth Strategy includes slightly smaller lot sizes, a wider variety of housing types, lower land consumption, new development along major roads and rail lines as well as clustered in urban areas, an expanded transit system, lower transportation costs and water consumption, and better air quality. Initially, centers and corridors were not components of the Quality Growth Strategy map, but they have been added in later iterations.

Since 1999, the Quality Growth Strategy has been updated, and Envision Utah has led several similar exercises in the region, one of which was called Wasatch Choices 2040. In 2006, Envision Utah led Wasatch Choices with the MPOs and transportation agencies in the region. This visioning workshop focused primarily on land use and transportation, and the scenario analysis and public involvement informed the regional transportation plan. The report on Wasatch Choices 2040 includes nine growth principles and ten implementation strategies for local governments. The MPOs and Envision Utah also identified activity centers, which are and will continue to be coordinated with the transportation system (figure 7.2).

Implementation In sharp contrast with Portland Metro, Envision Utah has no statutory foundation for implementation. As a private, nonprofit organization it must rely on its ability to influence the actions of others. Toward that end, the Quality Growth Strategy along with 31 specific strategies was presented to the Envision Utah board in 1999 in a structured table. The table presented the logic underlying each strategy, an example of each, and the organizations suggested for putting them into action (Appendix 2). In addition, Envision Utah reached out to 89 local governments, launched several smaller-scale visioning exercises, developed toolboxes to assist others with implementation, all of which led to its receiving several awards. Envision Utah also extended its outreach and technical support beyond urban counties to rural areas. As of 2003, working through various codes and ordinances, 60 percent of local governments in the Greater Wasatch area had adopted their own Envision Utah–supported strategy.

In 1999, the State of Utah passed legislation that created the Quality Growth Commission. Introduced by former governor Leavitt, this legislation directed the Governor's Office of Planning and Budget to provide support to the Quality Growth Commission. Although the commission holds no regulatory authority, it does have responsibilities in three broad areas: technical assistance, administration of a land conservation program, and as an advisory entity to the governor and legislature on

Figure 7.2 Wasatch Choices 2040 Poster
Source: Envision Utah.

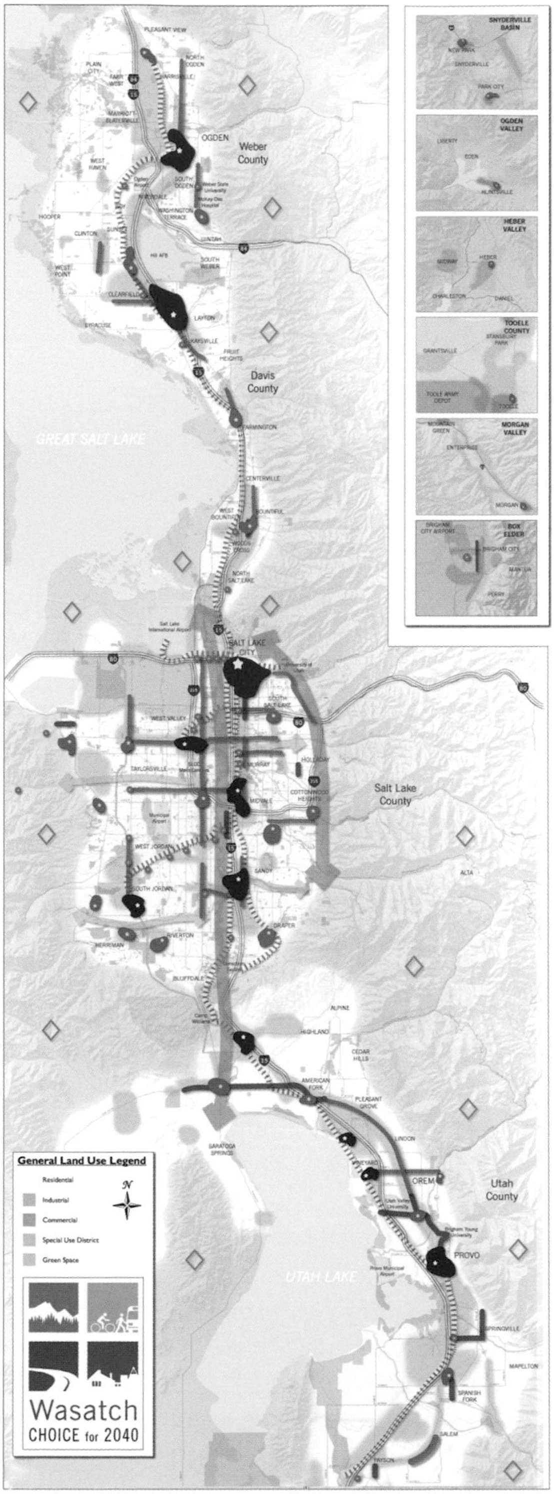

growth management legislation including Quality Growth principles and areas. Staffed by the Governor's Office of Planning and Budget, the commission also certifies local governments and service providers as Quality Growth Communities and Quality Growth Service Providers. State funding, however, is not tied to certification in any formal way.

On the ground, new transit lines, smaller lot sizes, and a shift in development types illustrate the success of the project. Moreover, Envision Utah officials note a sea change in local perceptions of the Quality Growth Strategy. While many local people resisted the strategy at first, now they largely embrace the principles of Envision Utah. Additionally, nonprofit groups and state, local, and regional agencies collaborate in a way that would have seemed impossible prior to Envision Utah.

Sacramento, California

The capital city of Sacramento lies in the state's fertile Central Valley. Unlike the San Francisco Bay area just a short distance to the west, the Sacramento region is more rural, less densely populated, and politically more conservative. The metropolitan statistical area (MSA) includes four counties: El Dorado, Placer, Sacramento, and Yolo. The adjacent Yuba City MSA includes Yuba and Sutter Counties. Both MSAs lie within the service area of the Sacramento Area Council of Governments (SACOG).

SACOG serves as the regional council and MPO for the six-county region, which includes 22 cities. Under California law, SACOG also serves as the regional transportation planning agency (RTPA) for Sacramento, Sutter, Yolo, and Yuba Counties. In California, RTPAs are required to adopt the regional transportation plan and regional transportation improvement program. El Dorado and Placer Counties each have their own RPTA. Beyond transportation planning functions, SACOG also approves the distribution of affordable housing in the region.

While California's land use laws are considered progressive, they also are highly deferential to local government, and although Sacramento is the seat of the state government, to date state agencies have not played a major role in metropolitan planning. Instead, much of the work on the Sacramento Region Blueprint was performed with the assistance of Valley Vision, a civic nonprofit organization.

Metropolitan Planning   Shortly after the regional council component of SACOG launched its Blueprint project in 2002, it made the important decisions to plan using a 2050 horizon, thus thinking beyond traditional planning horizons, and to employ an advanced planning support system (SACOG 2010a; 2010b). This system, I-PLACE³S, is a GIS platform developed by the California Energy Commission, and it served as the primary technical component of the plan. The I-PLACE³S tool uses parcel-level data to integrate community participation and urban planning and design with quantitative analysis.

Throughout the planning process it was able to provide real-time feedback during public workshops.

As in Portland and central Utah, public engagement was a critical element in the development of the Blueprint plan, but the engagement process in Sacramento differed from those of its predecessors. Rather than going straight to citizens as Portland and central Utah had, SACOG partnered with local governments to organize and conduct workshops at varying scales. They were held first at the neighborhood level, then the county and finally the region levels. First SACOG and Valley Vision crafted an exercise that allowed participants to compare alternative planning scenarios at the neighborhood level. Next they were developed for the region by SACOG, which used input from local planning and public works directors and reduced them to county scale for use in those workshops. Participants in public engagement workshops made alterations to these scenarios. The base case represented what would happen if current land use policies did not change at all. Based on public input from the county-level workshops, four scenarios were refined and presented at a summit of region-level elected officials, following which SACOG developed the preferred scenario.

Most of the process was conducted in-house, but it also included work from some outside consultants. SACOG's current director, Mike McKeever, was instrumental in building the technical analysis framework. Valley Vision, which had not been involved with SACOG previously, played a large part in bringing stakeholders to the table. Interestingly, state agencies were not deeply engaged, and rather than working with a top-down process led by state and regional agencies, Sacramento sought to set up a bottom-up process led by local governments and citizens.

The Preferred Blueprint Scenario   In December 2004 SACOG's board of directors adopted the Preferred Blueprint Scenario, which calls for development based on seven smart growth principles: (1) a variety of transportation options; (2) a variety of housing types; (3) compact development; (4) use of existing assets; (5) mixed land use; (6) open space and farmland preservation; and (7) encouragement of attractive communities. Unlike Portland and Denver, for example, Sacramento works with a regional vision rather than a regional plan, and it is implemented through the local governments and the regional transportation plan. The vision is composed of goals and objectives, development types, and a map.

The Blueprint's map (figure 7.3) shows how the region can grow according to the principles at a concept level. Though the map was developed using parcel-level data and analysis, it is not meant to be applied in a parcel-level manner. The map includes different types of land uses and a variety of classifications for centers and corridors.

Implementation The Blueprint plan leaves implementation largely to local governments. Small grants are made available in order to encourage these local governments to adopt the vision and principles of the Blueprint scenario.

Additionally, SACOG identifies and disseminates best practices, and in 2005 SACOG led several seminars on the plan for local government officials.

These governments were asked to develop individual strategies for promoting the Blueprint scenario's planning principles. Each jurisdiction was asked to

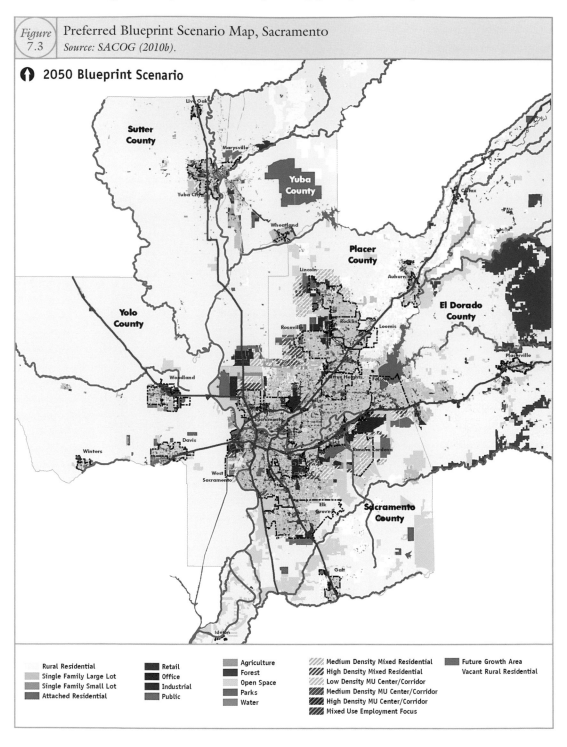

Figure 7.3 Preferred Blueprint Scenario Map, Sacramento
Source: SACOG (2010b).

pass both a resolution in support of their growth allocation and the 2035 map as well as a statement of what actions they will pursue to implement the growth allocation. Local governments have used a variety of strategies that range from general plan updates to integrating principles into development review processes to initiating area-specific plans for implementing the principles.

In addition, the Preferred Blueprint Scenario is implemented by means of MTP2035, which includes several performance metrics (Appendix 3). This was the first time the regional transportation plan had been guided by a long-term vision for the region. In the past, SACOG's MPO arm had worked independently of its COG, which resulted in the implementation of transportation plans without consideration for land use or long-term growth patterns. In MTP2035, performance-based planning is an important part of implementation in Sacramento, and it is used to distribute $42 billion transportation funding over 28 years.

Denver, Colorado

The Greater Denver region, which includes nine counties and the cities of Denver, Aurora, and Boulder, is located in the Front Range Urban Corridor between the Rocky Mountains to the west and High Plains to the east. The Denver Regional Council of Governments (DRCOG) serves as the region's COG and MPO. Similar to others, DRCOG's functions include transportation planning, technical assistance, and data distribution, but it also serves as the area's agency on aging and its clean water authority.

The State of Colorado is not considered a leader on land use issues, but the Denver region has become recognized as a successful pioneer in management of bottom-up growth. The Metro Mayors Caucus, a voluntary collaboration of 37 mayors in the Denver metropolitan region, has assisted DRCOG. This unusual organization, formed in 1993 to provide a nonpartisan means to ensure regional cooperation on issues that affect the entire metropolitan area, has been instrumental in crafting an equally unusual approach to metropolitan planning.

Metropolitan Planning   Metro Vision 2020 was approved by DRCOG's board of directors in 1997 and then updated ten years later to extend its planning horizon to 2035. Stressing regional cooperation as the key to providing a quality environment, the Metro Vision Guiding Vision established the framework for the original Metro Vision plan. During the plan's creation, DRCOG held two Metro Growth Forums with more than 500 attendees. A 40-member taskforce comprised of stakeholders was convened by DRCOG to analyze growth scenarios for the region that had been produced in-house using GIS. The taskforce considered 11 alternatives that offered a broad range of policy and investment strategies, then selected four scenarios for further study: (1) dispersed; (2) compact; (3) corridor; and (4) satellite development. Once evaluated and analyzed against the 1992 Guiding Vision, a preferred scenario was crafted from the best features of all four alternatives.

To update the plan in 2007, DRCOG held four regional public workshops
and based revisions on the original plan. Scenarios and the UGB were revised as
part of this process. During scenario workshops, DRCOG used MetroQuest, an
interactive tool that allowed participants to explore alternative scenarios, which
focused on two main areas of influence: the extent of the transportation system
and that of urban development. Specifically, the four scenarios varied in the degrees
of UGB expansion, density, capacity on both the fiscally constrained highway and
transit networks, and pricing changes on the transportation network. To evaluate
the scenarios as part of this update, 12 outcome measures were considered, all of
which relate broadly to environment, land use, and transportation.

Metro Vision Plan   Metro Vision 2020 included six core elements: (1) the
extent of development; (2) open space; (3) the freestanding communities of
Boulder, Brighton, Castle Rock, and Longmont; (4) a balanced multimodal
transportation system; (5) urban centers; and (6) environmental quality. This
included constraining development to 747 square miles. The DRCOG board
of directors approved the preferred development scenario in 1995, and after its
creation, urban center candidates, growth boundaries, and a fiscally constrained
transportation network were identified. A clean water plan was also adopted.
While the Metro Vision plan is accompanied by a UGB, local governments des-
ignate their own growth boundaries rather than having DRCOG construct a

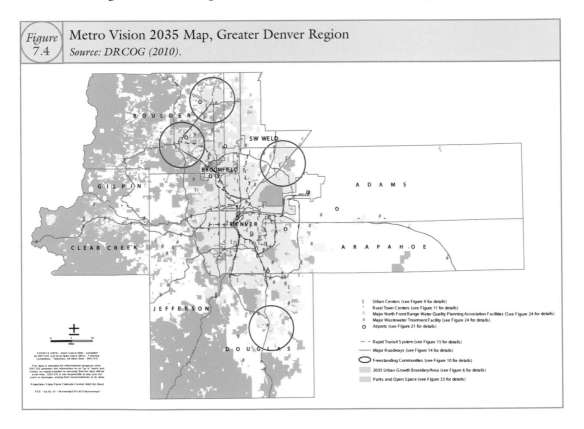

Figure 7.4   Metro Vision 2035 Map, Greater Denver Region
Source: DRCOG (2010).

boundary at the region scale—that is, its board votes on the amount of land to include in the growth boundary, the location of which is established by the plans and policies of local government. When the DRCOG board of directors adopted the plan by resolution in 1997, it included implementation strategies and instruments.

The update to Metro Vision 2035 was based on scenario analysis conducted by the DRCOG board of directors, who decided to expand the UGB for the first time by adding approximately 22 square miles and make modest updates to the 2030 transportation network (Locantore et al. 2009). The Metro Vision plan's map (figure 7.4) is simplistic because it displays only urban centers, rural centers, the UGB, freestanding communities, major transit lines, and major roadways. Although it addresses environmental issues to some extent, it focuses primarily on land use and transportation.

Implementation In 1996 the DRCOG board of directors formed a steering committee that recommended implementation strategies and created a standing Metro Vision Policy Committee. When developing the implementation strategies, four tenets were observed: These strategies all had to be voluntary, flexible, collaborative, and effective. They were crafted to address growth from a regional perspective and maintain control over growth at the local level without requiring new legislation. Plan consistency was a key strategy offered by the steering committee. Explicit implementation strategies address integration of transportation and land use plans at the regional level; air quality integration with growth and development decisions; water quality integration with development and transportation plans, water and sewer service areas planning; and tax policy and revenue sharing.

The Metro Mayors Caucus and DRCOG collaborated to prepare the Mile High Compact (Appendix 4), a voluntary agreement among the region's cities and counties to manage growth by adhering to Metro Vision 2020. As of 2008, 44 communities, which together constitute nearly 90 percent of the region's population, had signed on to the compact. Ultimately, the plan is implemented locally, but DRCOG notes that local governments recognize the value of considering growth from a regional perspective, even while maintaining local control. Because it is voluntary, the Mile High Compact illustrates how cities and counties can become committed to managing growth with the region in mind.

Chicago, Illinois

The Greater Chicago metropolitan area is large and fragmented. It encompasses three states, 17 counties, more than 1,500 governments, nearly 8,000 square miles, and almost 10 million people. The region is bounded by Lake Michigan to the east, but is not bound by geographic features in other directions. Illinois and Indiana have never been active in land use policy at the state level and Wisconsin was only slightly more involved.

The Chicago-area MPO and COG were separate organizations until very recently. In 2007, state legislation merged the Chicago Area Transportation Study (CATS) with the Northeastern Illinois Planning Commission (NIPC) to form the Chicago Metropolitan Agency for Planning (CMAP). This new agency now serves as both MPO and COG for seven Illinois counties: Cook, DuPage, Kane, Kendall, Lake, McHenry, and Will (CMAP, n.d.; NIPC 2007a). The adjacent urbanized areas are served by two other MPOs: The Gary region to the east has the Northwestern Indiana Regional Planning Commission, and the Southeastern Wisconsin Regional Planning Commission serves the Milwaukee region to the north.

Private and nonprofit organizations have long played an important role in planning for metropolitan Chicago. The Commercial Club of Chicago was founded in 1877 by a small group of businessmen, who felt that their city would benefit from "a cohesive civic force to shape the development of the city" (Commercial Club of Chicago, n.d.). In the traditions of the 1909 Burnham Plan of Chicago, the Metropolitan Planning Council was established in 1934 and continued its work generally as an advocate for good government in support of Chicago's planning practices. Toward the end of the 1990s it extended its mission to develop, promote, and implement solutions for regional growth. More recently, the Openlands Project and the Center for Neighborhood Technology became important and influential advocacy organizations, not just in Chicago but around the nation.

Metropolitan Planning   Chicago has a storied planning history. Although perhaps best known for Daniel Burnham's plan from 1909, recently private and public organizations alike have also published regional plans. While the City of Chicago itself has never formally adopted any of these plans, a number of them have exerted influence.

In 1997, the Commercial Club of Chicago commissioned Elmer Johnson (1999) to write the plan called *Chicago Metropolis 2020*. A partner in a Chicago law firm and a former executive vice president and director of General Motors, Johnson relied on support from the Metropolitan Planning Council, the Federal Reserve Bank of Chicago, and several other nonprofit organizations and universities. No public body ever endorsed the plan, and public involvement with it was limited to invited high-level officials. It is primarily textual, and no scenario analysis or formal consideration of alternative futures was conducted. The plan addresses six issues: education, economic development, taxation, governance, transportation, and land use and housing. Perhaps its unstated purpose was to stimulate regional planning in the public sector. One of the principal recommendations and accomplishments of Chicago Metropolis 2020 was the merging of CATS and NIPC.

Prior to the merger, NIPC developed several regional plans, the most recent being an exercise launched in 2001 called Common Ground: A Blueprint for Regional Action, which resulted in the award-winning 2040 Regional Framework Plan. To develop it, NIPC organized subregional workshops that were clustered by demographic and development types rather than geographical boundaries. NIPC held a major regional forum and 14 subregional workshops in which working groups arrived at 52 goals divided among five themes to define the region's future. The major regional forum and the subregional workshops covered topics such as education, water supply, transportation, and economic development. NIPC stitched together subregional outputs to create a regional scenario. Based on the results of these workshops, regional goals were endorsed by NIPC in 2003. Subsequently, calling together stakeholders in 13 municipality clusters, it conducted additional workshops in which participants considered multiple layers of data using a tool called Paint the Region, which allowed them to paint maps to include centers, corridors, and green areas. NIPC analyzed the results of these workshops and through several cluster synthesis meetings and one dealing with regional synthesis, created a regional map.

The 2040 Regional Framework Plan   The plan NIPC adopted in 2005 features centers, corridors, and green areas, and it establishes a regional framework for regional and local planning (figure 7.5). Its intention is to use centers and corridors to promote development in centers and decrease travel between them. The corridors provide more efficient connections among centers and particularly improve connections among centers in rural areas. The inclusion of green areas was a new concept in such regional planning, though other metropolitan areas had used centers and corridors in the past. Five core themes also emerged: livable communities, diversity of people, healthy natural environment, global competitiveness, and collaborative governance.

Implementation   NIPC collaborated with local government officials, civic leaders, and key interest groups to implement the 2040 Regional Framework Plan. The strategy also relied on horizontal coordination of the metropolitan clusters the plan identified, and encouraged working with neighboring clusters on plan implementation.

Institutional relationships established through the creation of the plan and the iterative planning cycle mandated by the federal transportation planning program formed the primary vehicle for implementation. NIPC continued to work with clusters of local governments to facilitate coordination between local plans and the 2040 plan as well as among the local governments making up a single cluster. The plan also was linked to the regional transportation plan via an interagency agreement signed in 2001 by NIPC, CATS, the Illinois Department of Transportation, and the regional transit authority (Appendix 5).

Implementation of this plan did not progress far, however, before CMAP was created in 2007. At that time, NIPC was working on identifying implementation strategies and actions. The legislature had charged CMAP with creating a new comprehensive plan, which it did as one of its first tasks, calling it GO TO 2040. Its vision was built on NIPC's goal-setting work using its Common Ground process. The plan was published in October 2010, and its implementation has begun.

Implementation is centered around five principles: support for transit, walking, and bicycling; a range of housing options; environmental protection; access to green space; and design, aesthetics, and local historic character.

Figure 7.5	2040 Regional Framework Plan Map, Greater Chicago
	Source: NIPC (2007).

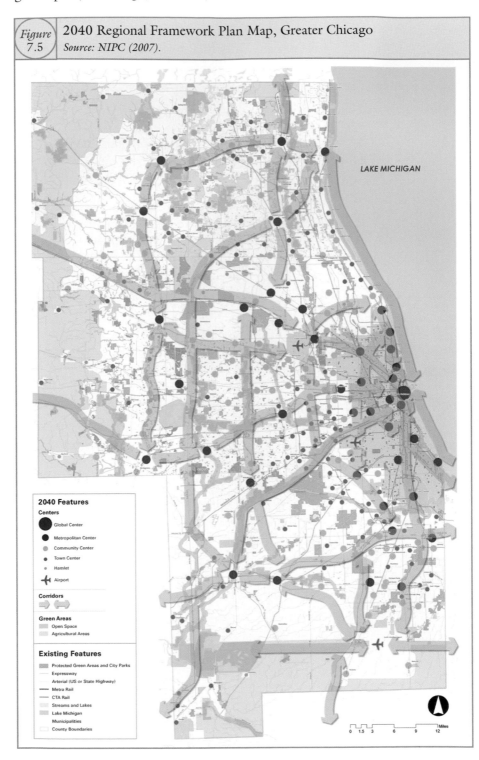

Washington, DC

The Washington, DC, metropolitan area is, perhaps, the most institutionally complex in the nation. The MSA includes the seat of the federal government (the District of Columbia), two states, 23 counties, several municipalities, and the National Capital Planning Commission, the Maryland-National Capital Park and Planning Commission, and the Northern Virginia Regional Commission. Planning for the District of Columbia is done by the district's Office of Planning, with oversight by the U.S. Congress. Baltimore, Maryland, only 35 miles to the north, has its own constellation of planning institutions. But it is less the large number of government institutions involved than the complexity of their interrelationships and the lack of a clear hierarchical structure that makes planning and governance of the metropolitan area so difficult.

For more than 50 years the Metropolitan Washington Council of Governments (MWCOG) has served as the COG for the entire region. Though MWCOG began as an informal association of local governments, it gradually became the region's predominant planning organization during the mid-1960s. The Transportation Planning Board (TPB), the area's MPO, became associated with the MWCOG in 1966 and, with its separate board of directors and staff, the TPB still continues to function like an autonomous agency within MWCOG.

Because Washington, DC, is the home of the federal government, it is also the site for the headquarters of many national interest groups, including the National Resources Defense Council, Smart Growth America, Sierra Club, National Association of Home Builders, and American Planning Association. Many of these groups and several local business, civic, and environmental groups are all active in metropolitan planning debates. This depth and breadth of interest group talent in Washington contributes to the intensity and veracity of the debate, but also to the institutional complexity.

Metropolitan Planning In the national's capital region, metropolitan planning has a rich and tumultuous history. In 1962, MWCOG worked with the National Capital Regional Planning Council to prepare *A Policy Plan for the Year 2000,* which featured the concepts of wedges and corridors, where open space would be preserved in wedges and development would occur along radial spokes that trace transportation corridors. In 1972, MWCOG revised the plan, reaffirming the wedges and corridor approach.

In the early 1990s MWCOG began the Partnership for Regional Excellence, which included more than 200 stakeholders from the private, public, and civic sectors. Its report, published in 1994, highlighted the need for integrated transportation, land use, and environmental planning. The partnership also endorsed seven goals related to achieving a regional vision.

Following the 1989 Regional Conference on Growth and Transportation, the TPB began a visioning exercise, for which it convened three citizen taskforces that focused on transportation in the region. In 1998, capping a nine-year effort, the TPB adopted the vision.

In 2006 the TPB conducted a Regional Mobility and Accessibility Scenario Study to consider alternative configurations of land use and transportation patterns for the year 2030. It considered five scenarios in the study and examined the impact of each on transit, vehicle miles traveled (VMT), and congestion. This "What If" study looked solely at how the region might respond to different growth scenarios and did not consider the challenges of implementation, politics, or funding.

In 2005 MWCOG, with the Washington chapter of the Urban Land Institute and the Washington Smart Growth Alliance, cosponsored an exercise it called Reality Check. The exercise prompted MWCOG, the Greater Washington Board of Trade, and the Community Foundation for the National Capital Region to launch an effort called Envision Greater Washington. Following a 90-day exploration period, a group of 50 stakeholders recommended a metropolitan-wide visioning effort that followed the example of Envision Utah. The MWCOG executive committee, citing a desire to avoid duplicative efforts, declined to endorse the initiative.

In 2007 its fiftieth-anniversary year, MWCOG launched a new initiative called Greater Washington 2050, and a coalition was established by MWCOG to "create a new, comprehensive, regional approach to solving these challenges—not business as usual" (MWCOG 2010, 1). Because it recently had engaged in several visioning endeavors, and in the wake of the aborted Envision Greater Washington effort, the Greater Washington 2050 Coalition chose not to launch a major new initiative, but rather to tie together earlier work, such as the TPB vision from 1998, its work on regional activity centers (2002), and the National Capital Region Climate Change Report (2008).

As part of Greater Washington 2050, two new initiatives were undertaken: a scenario thinking workshop and a public survey called Priorities for a Growing Region. The four scenarios dealt with (1) an extended economic recession and massive government debt; (2) low oil prices derailing strong climate change policies; (3) federal government dispersal from the region; and (4) a green industrial revolution. Rather than creating a detailed spatial plan, MWCOG created a framework called Region Forward.

Region Forward Approved by the MWCOG board of directors in January 2010, this policy framework for regional growth is intended to adopt clear, measurable goals, measure progress toward them, and execute a regional compact. The Greater Washington 2050 Compact (Appendix 6) contains goals that relate to physical development—such as those dealing with land use, transportation, environment, climate, and energy—and others categorized as social and economic—e.g., economic, housing, health and human services, education, and public safety. The compact also commits MWCOG to measuring a long list of performance measures in order to monitor progress toward meeting those function goals.

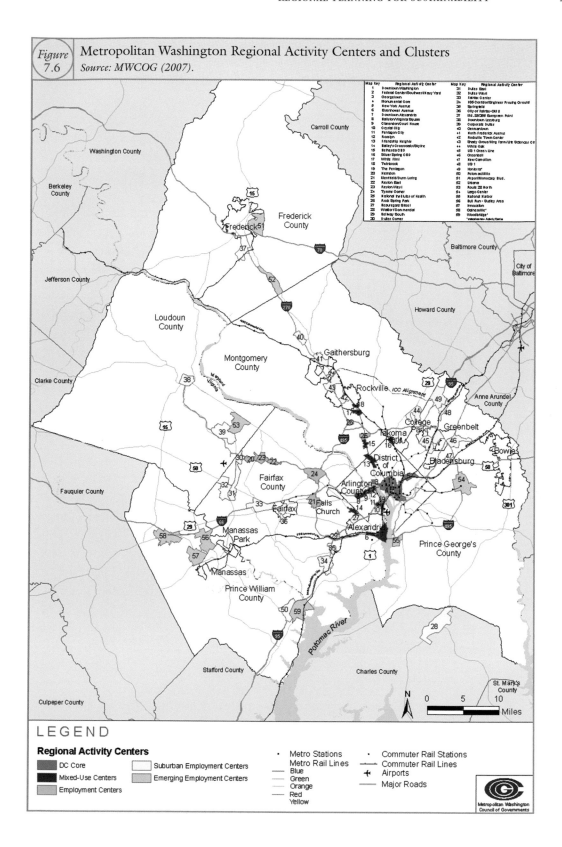

Figure 7.6 Metropolitan Washington Regional Activity Centers and Clusters
Source: MWCOG (2007).

Region Forward does not include a spatial vision for future growth, but instead is tied to previous MWCOG-supported initiatives including Reality Check, a regional activities centers map, TPB visions, and the climate change reports. The statements of goals and objectives are also general, however. The only spatially explicit goal and its corresponding measure deal with the percent of growth in activity centers. The regional activity centers map serves as the spatial expression of the 2050 effort (figure 7.6). The centers are classified into different categories: DC core, mixed use, employment, suburban employment, and emerging employment.

Implementation   The MWCOG board of directors approved Region Forward in January 2010, making it too recent to assess progress toward implementation. MWCOG intends to integrate Region Forward into its work, "changing the way it does business with a new, more comprehensive approach to regional planning" (MWCOG 2010, 13). Specifically, MWCOG plans to:

- communicate Region Forward and build support by reaching out to every corner of the region;

- seek approval of the compact by all of its member counties and cities—to date, 16 jurisdictions have signed on to the compact (Appendix 6); and

- seek endorsement of this effort by businesses, civic groups, individuals, and neighboring regions through their regional councils and MPOs.

In addition, following a series of scenario workshops, MWCOG will update the regional activity centers maps by 2012. It intends to incorporate regional progress reports in order to begin regular monitoring of progress toward the goals, with the intent of creating comprehensive progress reports every three to four years. These will be used to inform regional leadership and influence policy stances and decisions. MWCOG will commission surveys of area residents similar to the one conducted by the Greater Washington 2050 Coalition. They will provide public feedback and track opinions that relate to regional issues and future priorities. MWCOG will also prepare a strategy toolbox that will outline a comprehensive approach to implementing the vision. This toolbox will include best practices and recommendations that apply to both the local and regional levels.

REVIEW OF CASE STUDIES

There is no doubt that the practice of metropolitan planning changed significantly following Portland's pioneering 2040 planning exercise. While no two planning exercises are identical, in many respects they share more similarities than differences, and many of them include the following innovative features (Landis 2008).

- A vision, not a program: Rather than a particular zoning map or capital improvement list, most regional planning exercises are intended to yield visions for how the future may look. This helps the broader community understand what the future may hold compared to what existing trends might be delivered.

- The choice of future growth, not necessarily the accommodation of growth: All of the regional plans we have discussed were guided by external forecasts of employment and population growth, but none were strictly bound to achieve such growth. This created greater opportunities to shape the future rather than succumb to one that was projected.

- A broad metropolitan agenda: Unlike traditional comprehensive plans, the metropolitan planning processes we have described explicitly addressed concepts such as regional equity, urban design, historic preservation, resource conservation, and environmental protection. As a result, the process attracted the interest of a more inclusive range of constituencies than had been common in previous, more narrowly focused exercises.

- A bottom-up, collaborative process: Although almost all of these planning processes involved some degree of public participation, each metropolitan scenario exercise went to great lengths to engage the public in all aspects of the process. This not only increased the legitimacy of the process, but it also enhanced the prospects for successful implementation.

The leadership and sets of participating organizations were also relatively similar. In four cases, the process was led by a combination of MPO and COG. The two exceptions are Envision Utah and the early efforts in Chicago. Although the state and two MPOs were deeply involved in Utah, that program's leadership was provided by a nonprofit organization. In Chicago, the impetus for the process originated in the private sector, but eventually the process came to be led by the newly formed CMAP.

The reasons for COG and MPO leadership are relatively clear: COGs are the only organizations with direct connections to local governments and metropolitan-wide legitimacy concerning land use issues; and federal regulations make MPOs responsible for metropolitan transportation planning. Largely for these reasons, most of the analyses and elements of the preferred plans focus on transportation and land use issues. Few plans consider environmental issues or other types of infrastructure in any significant depth. In that regard, all of these plans fall short of being what might now be described as sustainability plans (Wheeler 2000).

All of the efforts involved nongovernment advocacy organizations, which offered obvious advantages. Metropolitan planning's scope may be wide, but the depth of its political support is shallow. As the plans' scope grew to include environmental concerns, housing, transportation, and other issues, attraction to the process expanded to include advocacy groups that represented corresponding interests. Further, the expertise and technical capacity many of these groups brought to the table were substantial and often became incorporated into the analysis. Perhaps more important, such advocates are politically influential. Since neither COGs nor MPOs have express authority over land use, advocacy groups can serve as catalysts for changing policies of the government offices that do hold such authority. Nonetheless, inclusion has disadvantages. For example, the disparate groups involved in Washington's 2030 process were unable to reach consensus on how to move forward, which was essentially what prevented that effort from continuing on to more productive levels.

The steps taken in the six planning processes examined here were also quite similar. All involved extensive public participation activities in order to identify goals, objectives, and principles first, then to explore alternative development options, and finally to choose a preferred plan. All focused on end states with 30- to 50-year horizons, and each of them gave explicit consideration to the interplay between land use and transportation. Each one included a set of performance indicators with which to monitor progress so that alternative scenarios could be compared, and in the end the preferred scenarios in all cases featured some combination of centers and corridors.

The technical tools used in the processes varied in construct but not in kind. The critical role of GIS cannot be overstated. While plan maps for metropolitan areas have been produced since the 1930s, the ability of GIS to conduct analyses at the metropolitan scale and to illustrate the results of such analyses substantially increased the planners' ability to engage the public. The best examples of this were in Sacramento and Chicago, where GIS tools were used to elicit real-time feedback concerning subarea scenarios. GIS models are also central to land use models that, in several exercises, were able to explore the impacts of alternative investments in transportation infrastructure. GIS data also made it possible to compute most performance indicators, such as total acres of land developed, amount of farmland lost, acres of open space, impervious surface, and much more.

The transportation models used in every case study required four steps, and until very recently they represented the state of the art. While these models are very useful for estimating vehicle miles traveled, identifying congested links, and in some cases estimating effects on land use, they continue to have significant limitations. In most cases the ability to analyze land use impacts was crude at best, and estimating transportation mode choice was highly speculative. As a result, estimates of air quality impacts were highly imprecise as well. Further, the four-step transportation models used by MPOs are not well-suited for addressing the small-scale urban design issues that can potentially increase walking and bicycling.

Other models were quite limited in use or sophistication as well. Estimates of air pollutants were generated using crude, now outdated models. Early exercises did not address greenhouse gas emissions. None considered residential energy consumption or were connected to water quality models. In short, the focus on wedges and transportation corridors, the dominance of transportation and land use models, and the emphasis on metropolitan growth provide compelling evidence that metropolitan regionalism retains its hegemony over organic regionalism, even in this new age of sustainability.

Finally, and unfortunately, in almost every case the evidence of successful influence on development patterns is weak. Only in Portland is it clear that the process has had influence on the ground. This is no surprise, however. The Portland example is the oldest, employed some of the best data and planning support tools, and had the political backing of Metro's charter and Oregon's state law. Even then, the evidence of successful growth containment and infill is greater than that of accelerated growth in centers and corridors. Further, the exclusion of Vancouver, Washington, just across the river from Portland, remains a significant caveat on Metro's success and speaks to the importance of state government. States did not play a dominant role in any of the case studies, but there is no doubt that state laws and agencies were highly influential in framing the planning efforts in Chicago, Portland, and Utah.

In other cases, success is measured more in terms of process. In all of our case study regions, some form of metropolitan plan now serves to guide decision making concerned with transportation investment, and many people participated in its development. Every example arrived at some degree of consensus on its preferred scenario, and in many of them we see evidence that some local government responded with changes in its own plans. Finally, and perhaps most importantly, the officially sanctioned preferred scenarios or plans provided MPOs with a vision for the future that goes beyond simply extrapolating from past trends.

CONCLUSIONS

In the United States, planning and growth management at the metropolitan scale has advanced considerably since 1990. Based in part on recent advancements, the Obama administration is poised to provide considerable financial support for new regional planning efforts. Specifically, the Sustainable Communities Initiative provided $150 million of financial support. How much impact such federal funding will have will depend on a number of the factors addressed in this chapter. Success depends specifically on the physical, cultural, and political context of a given metropolitan area, its sources and strength of leadership, the breadth of organizational participation, the technical capacity of the combined organizational team, and the institutional governance structure.

While the technical capacity to develop metropolitan plans has grown considerably, one cannot assume that every metropolitan area possesses it. Some have indeed developed highly advanced GIS databases and transportation planning support systems, but many others have few GIS layers available. Data on land use and zoning are notably absent for most metropolitan areas (Nedović-Budić et al. 2009). Many MPOs lack credible transportation models, even the simple, four-step models that most of them use presently. If it must be devoted to data and model development, $150 million will not go far, as the funds required to develop data and transportation models for just one metropolitan area can run into the millions of dollars. If that funding is widely distributed across multiple governments, agencies, and interest groups, there is danger that it will be spread so thin as to be inconsequential.

Perhaps most important, our review provides little evidence that metropolitan plans can be implemented successfully without extensive institutional reform. Although special-purpose metropolitan governments and advocacy groups have proliferated in recent years, the structure of governance of these regions has not changed significantly since the turn of the twentieth century. COGs have formed and in many places joined forces with MPOs, but these collaborations remain largely voluntary and have no power to compel local government to pursue anything other than its own parochial interests. It is probably not a coincidence that Portland, which mustered the political will to convert a COG into the nation's only directly elected regional government, has achieved the most measureable implementation success. If the $150 million HUD intends to distribute can motivate metropolitan areas to adopt similar regional government institutions, it will have spent its funds well.

ACKNOWLEDGMENTS

We would like to thank Gordon Garry, Alan Matheson, John Mataya, Simon Montagu, Ethan Seltzer, and Ron Thomas for comments on an earlier version of this draft. Any remaining errors or omissions are our own.

REFERENCES

Bay, Paul N. 2009. Role of transit agencies in the regional transportation planning process. TCRP Project J-11/Task 6. www.apta.com/resources/reportsandpublications/Documents/TCRP_J11_Agencies_Role_in_Regional_Planning_Process.pdf

Brookings Institution. 2007. *MetroNation: How U.S. metropolitan areas fuel American prosperity.* Metropolitan Policy Program at Brookings. Washington, DC. www.brookings.edu/reports/2007/1106_metronation_berube.aspx

CMAP (Chicago Metropolitan Agency for Planning). n.d. GO TO 2040: Metropolitan Chicago's official comprehensive regional plan. Chicago. www.cmap.illinois.gov/2040/main

Commercial Club of Chicago. n.d. The Commercial Club of Chicago. Chicago. http://www.commercialclubchicago.org/index.html

DOT (U.S. Department of Transportation). 2007. *The transportation planning process: Key issues. A briefing book for transportation decisionmakers, officials, and staff.* (September). Washington, DC: Transportation Planning Capacity Building Program; Federal Highway Administration; and Federal Transit Administration. www.planning.dot.gov/documents/BriefingBook/BBook.htm

——. 2009. DOT Secretary Ray LaHood, HUD Secretary Shaun Donovan and EPA Administrator Lisa Jackson announce interagency Partnership for Sustainable Communities. Press release (16 June). Washington, DC. www.dot.gov/affairs/2009/dot8009.htm

DRCOG (Denver Region Council of Governments). 2010. Map gallery: Metro Vision 2035 Summary. Denver, CO. www.drcog.org/index.cfm?page=Maps

Edner, Sheldon, and Bruce D. McDowell. 2002. Surface-transportation funding in a new century: Assessing one slice of the federal marble cake. *Publius* 32(1):7–24.

Envision Utah. n.d. *The history of Envision Utah.* Salt Lake City. http://envisionutah.org/historyenvisionutahv5p1.pdf

Fishman, Robert. 2000. *The American planning tradition: Culture and policy.* Washington, DC: The Woodrow Wilson Press Center.

Foster, Kathryn A. 1997. *The political economy of special purpose governments.* Washington, DC: Georgetown University Press.

Goetz, Andrew R., Paul Stephen Dempsey, and Carl Larson. 2002. Metropolitan planning organizations: Findings and recommendations for improving transportation planning. *Publius* 32(1):87–105.

Goldman, Todd, and Elizabeth Deakin. 2000. Regionalism through partnerships? Metropolitan planning since ISTEA. *Berkeley Planning Journal* 14(2000):46–75.

Hanley, Paul F., and Gerrit-Jan Knaap. 1998. The spatial reconfiguration of the Portland metropolitan area: A preliminary assessment and baseline analysis. In eds. Said Easa and Donald Samdahl, *Transportation, land use and air quality: Proceedings of the American Society of Civil Engineers.* Reston, VA: American Society of Civil Engineers.

Hanson, Royce. 1966. *Metropolitan councils of government.* Washington, DC: U.S. Advisory Commission on Intergovernmental Relations.

HUD (U.S. Department of Housing and Urban Development). 2010. Sustainable communities planning grant program advance notice and request for comment. Docket no. FR-5396-N-01. 75 Fed. Reg. 6690 (10 February 2010). www.hud.gov/sustainability/scpgpnofa.pdf

Illinois Association of Regional Councils, n.d. History of Illinois regional councils. Springfield. www.ilarconline.org/news/3-1.php

Johnson, Elmer W. 1999. Chicago Metropolis 2020: Preparing metropolitan Chicago for the 21st century. Chicago: Commercial Club of Chicago.

Jones, Victor. 1962. Cooperation pattern. *National Civic Review* 51(6):302–308.

Knaap, Gerrit-Jan, and Rebecca Lewis. 2009. Growth patterns and trends. In eds. Gregory K. Ingram, Armando Carbonell, Yu-Hong Hong, and Anthony Flint, *Smart growth policies: An evaluation of programs and outcomes.* Cambridge, MA: Lincoln Institute of Land Policy.

Landis, John. 2008. To be or not to be Los Angles: Regional vision planning in the West, 1995–2007. ACSP-AESOP Joint Congress, Chicago.

Locantore, Jill. K., A. Simon Montagu, Steven D. Rudy, and Erik E. Sabina. 2009. Scenario analysis helps identify sustainable land use and transportation policies. *Projections: MIT Journal of Planning* 9:106–118.

Lowry, Michael B., and Richard J. Balling. 2009. An approach to land-use and transportation planning that facilitates city and region cooperation. *Environment and Planning B: Planning and Design* 36(3):487–504.

McDowell, Bruce D. 1984. The metropolitan planning organization role in the 1980s. *Journal of Advanced Transportation* 18(2):125–133.

———. 1999. *Improving regional transportation decisions: MPOs and certification.* Washington, DC: Brookings Institution.

Meck, Stuart, ed. 2002. *Growing smart legislative guidebook.* Chicago: American Planning Association.

Metro. 2010a. Regional framework plan. Portland, OR: Metro Regional Government. www.oregonmetro.gov/index.cfm/go/by.web/id=432/level=3

———. 2010b. 2040 Growth Concept map. Portland, OR: Metro Regional Government. http://library.oregonmetro.gov/files/2040_growth_concept_reduced.pdf

MWCOG (Metropolitan Washington Council of Governments). 2007. Metropolitan Washington regional centers and clusters. Washington, DC. www.mwcog.org/store/item.asp?PUBLICATION_ID=299

———. 2010. Region forward: A comprehensive guide for regional planning and measuring progress in the 21st century. Washington, DC. www.mwcog.org/store/item.asp?PUBLICATION_ID=368

Mitchell-Weaver, Clyde, David Miller, and Ronald Deal. 2000. Multilevel governance and metropolitan regionalism in the USA. *Urban Studies* 37(5–6):851–876.

National Association of Regional Councils. 2006a. What is a regional council? Washington, DC. http://narc.org/regional-councils-mpos/what-is-a-regional-council.html

————. 2006b. What is a metropolitan planning organization? Washington, DC. http://narc.org/regional-councils-mpos/what-is-a-metropolitan-planning-organization.html

Nedović-Budić, Zorica, Gerrit-Jan Knaap, Nama Raj Budhathoki, and Branko Cavrić. 2009. NSDI building blocks: Regional GIS in the United States. *URISA Journal* 21(2):5–24.

Nelson, Arthur C., Thomas W. Sanchez, James F. Wolf, and Mary Beth Farquhar. 2004. Metropolitan planning organization voting structure and transit investment bias: Preliminary analysis with social equity implications. *Transportation Research Record: Journal of the Transportation Research Board* 1895:1–7.

NIPC (Northern Illinois Planning Commission). 2007a. Realizing the vision: 2040 Regional framework plan. Chicago. www.nipc.org/2040/

————. 2007b. Download the 2040 Plan: 2040 regional framework map. Chicago. www.nipc.org/2040/download.htm

Oregon State Legislature. 2010. Oregon revised statutes, chapter 268: Metropolitan service districts. Salem, OR. www.leg.state.or.us/ors/268.html

SACOG (Sacramento Area Council of Governments). 2010a. Metropolitan transportation plan 2035: FAQ. Sacramento, CA. www.sacog.org/mtp/2035/theplan/faq/

————. 2010b. The Blueprint vision. Sacramento, CA. www.sacregionblueprint.org/adopted/

Solof, Marc. 1998. *The history of metropolitan planning organizations.* Newark: North Jersey Transportation Planning Authority.

Song, Yan, and Gerrit-Jan Knaap. 2004. Measuring urban form: Is Portland winning the battle against urban sprawl? *Journal of the American Planning Association* 70(2):210–225.

Urban Land Institute. 2008. Reality check guide: A tool for ULI district councils and their partners. Washington, DC. http://commerce.uli.org/Content/NavigationMenu/MyCommunity/RegionalVisioningandCooperation/RealityCheckGuide/Reality_Check_Guide1.htm

Wannop, Urlan. 1995. The regional imperative: Regional planning and governance in Britain, Europe, and the United States. London: Jessica Kingsley.

Weiss, Marc A., n.d. Metropolitan governance and strategic planning in the United States: A report to the metropolitan strategic plan association of Barcelona. Washington, DC: Global Urban Development. www.globalurban.org/metro_governance.htm

Wheeler, Stephen M. 2000. Planning for metropolitan sustainability. *Journal of Planning Education and Research* 20(2):133–145.

Wikstrom, Nelson. 1977. *Councils of government: A study of political incrementalism.* Chicago: Nelson-Hall.

Wolf, James F., and Mary Beth Farquhar. 2005. Assessing progress: The state of metropolitan planning organizations under ISTEA and TEA-21. *International Journal of Public Administration* 28:1057–1079.

APPENDICES: IMPLEMENTATION STRATEGIES

Appendix 1
Portland, Oregon: Implementation Method for the Regional Framework Plan

REGIONAL FRAMEWORK POLICY	IMPLEMENTATION RECOMMENDATION(S) OR REQUIREMENTS
LAND USE	
1.1 Urban Form	● Metro Code 3.07, Urban Growth Management Functional Plan (UGMFP), Titles 1, 2, 6, 11, and 13 ● MTIP program ● TOD program
1.2 Built Environment	● Metro Code 3.07, UGMFP, Titles 1 through 7, 11, and 12 ● Regional Transportation Plan
1.3 Housing and Affordable Housing	● Metro Code 3.01, Urban Growth Boundary and Urban Reserve Procedures ● Metro Code 3.07, UGMFP, Titles 1, 7, and 11
1.4 Economic Opportunity	● Metro Code 3.07, UGMFP, Titles 1 and 4
1.5 Economic Vitality	● Metro Code 3.07, UGMFP, Title 1
1.6 Growth Management	● Metro Code 3.01, UGB Amendment Procedures ● 3.01.005, UGB Amendment Procedures ● 3.01.020, Legislative Amendment Criteria ● Metro Code 3.06, Policy & Purpose: Designating Functional Planning Areas ● Metro Code 3.07, UGMFP, Titles 1 to 7, 11, and 12
1.7 Urban/Rural Transition	● Metro Code Chapter 3.01, UGB Amendment Procedures ● 3.01.005, UGB Amendment Procedures ● 3.01.020, Legislative Amendment Criteria ● Metro Code 3.06, Policy & Purpose: Designating Functional Planning Areas ● Metro Code 3.07, UGMFP, Title 5

Source: http://library.oregonmetro.gov/files/rfp_chapter_8_implementation.pdf

Appendix 2
Envision Utah: Implementation Strategies—Goal 1: Enhance Air Quality

	STRATEGY	WHY	WHO	HOW
A1	Foster and promote walkable development where feasible	• Provides more transportation choices • Provides greater mixture of housing type and cost • Promotes and maximizes benefits of mixed-used areas • Promotes small business • Provides pedestrian access to the services of daily living • Reduces cost of infrastructure and services • Improves air quality • Increases sense of community, safe lively streets, gathering places • Reduces crime due to more active community centers • Reduces water usage due to smaller yards • Reduces land consumption, eases development pressure on open lands • Defines community edges, provides better access to open space/parks	Envision Utah will work with local governments, developers, realtors, Quality Growth Efficiency Tools Committee (QGET), Quality Growth Commission, State (Governor and Legislature)	• Envision Utah will identify and disseminate information on advantages of walkable communities. • Envision Utah will communicate with Councils of Government and local governments (mayors, city councils, planning commissions) regarding benefits. Provide "tool box" to local governments on how to create walkable communities. • Envision Utah will communicate with developers and realtors regarding the advantages of walkable products. • QGET will help localities run infrastructure cost model for their community and plan for infrastructure needs as development patterns change. • Envision Utah will work with Quality Growth Commission and Legislature to identify possible state financial incentives for development of walkable communities.
A2	Promote the building of a regionwide transit system to make transit more convenient and reliable	See: GOAL II: PROMOTE MOBILITY & TRANSPORTATION CHOICES		
A3	Foster transit-oriented development (TOD)	See: GOAL II: PROMOTE MOBILITY & TRANSPORTATION CHOICES		
A4	Encourage polluters to use best available technology to meet standards and, where possible, further reduce emissions	• Improves air quality • Provides capacity for further economic growth	Division of Air Quality, Envision Utah work with industrial corporations, point and area sources	• Work with large and small emitters to encourage compliance • Gather and disseminate information regarding regional environmental and economic benefits of compliance • Create air quality awards to acknowledge progress in reducing industrial emissions • Encourage regional market for trading emission reduction credits

Appendix 2 *(continued)*
Envision Utah: Implementation Strategies—Goal 1: Enhance Air Quality

	STRATEGY	WHY	WHO	HOW
A5	Encourage energy efficiency ordinances	● Improves air quality ● Increases affordability of living	local governments, Utah Office of Energy and Resource Planning, Office of Energy Services	● Work with local governments to adopt market-driven approaches to encourage energy efficiency options for new construction. Examples include: mortgage incentives, awards programs ● Look for guidance to models such as the State of Utah's guidelines for state buildings, State of Washington's "Super Good Cents" program ● Encourage state (Public Service Commission) to incentivize energy efficient improvements to homes and offices (e.g., utility rebates for expenditures on insulation, windows, solar panels, efficient lighting, etc.)
A6	Promote creation of a network of bikeways and trails, especially commuter trails linking daytime destinations	See: GOAL II: PROMOTE MOBILITY & TRANSPORTATION CHOICES		
A7	Support strategies to reduce ozone and save energy	● Improves air quality; reduces production of ground-layer ozone, a major contributor to summertime air pollution ● Reduces energy consumption in the summer ● Improves general comfort and quality of life; would help to revitalize outdoor aspects of community in the summer	Utah Office of Energy and Resource Planning, Utah Office of Energy Services, Utah Division of Air Quality	● Support the NASA/Utah Office of Energy Services "Cool Communities" program ● Inform builders, architects, designers, planners, and road builders about the benefits of strategic vegetation and highly reflective building and paving materials ● Encourage state to provide tax incentives for use of "cool" building materials
A8	Support strategies to reduce particulate emissions	● Improves air quality, reduced wintertime pollution ● Improves health, particularly for children, elderly, and chronically ill ● Improves visibility and scenic values	Utah Division of Air Quality, Wasatch Front Regional Council, Mountainland Association of Governments, Utah Department of Transportation	See: GOAL II: PROMOTE MOBILITY & TRANSPORTATION CHOICES
A9	Promote Telework	See: GOAL II: PROMOTE MOBILITY & TRANSPORTATION CHOICES		

Source: www.epa.gov/smartgrowth/pdf/envision_utah.pdf

Appendix 3
Sacramento, California: Realizing the Blueprint

SACOG helps cities and counties across the Sacramento region implement the Blueprint in small and large ways. From helping staff in the early stages of planning, to funding projects, SACOG has many tools and services available to communities.

Video & PowerPoint Libraries

SACOG continues to develop videos and PowerPoint presentations to educate community members about core principles behind the Blueprint project and transportation alternatives with visual examples.

Computer Visual Simulations

SACOG developed a web-based 3D simulation model for 56 square miles of regional study areas to help visualize a range of potential activities on infill development sites. SACOG also developed software that allows planners and designers to remove existing buildings from the simulation and add in "new" building types that displayed potential development.

I-PLACE³S

I-PLACE³S enables users to create and evaluate multiple development scenarios against a set of basecase conditions. It demonstrates how planning and design choices, made by a community, have impacts on development patterns, modal choices, redevelopment potential, and livability to name a few.

Development Review

At the request of a local government SACOG will evaluate a proposed development project for its consistency with the Blueprint Principles and Vision Map. SACOG also provides technical planning assistance in the development or update of general plans, community plans, and specific plans.

Training Workshops for Staff & Elected Officials

SACOG provides free educational opportunities for anyone interested in planning related issues. The SACOG Planners Committee has workshops at its monthly meetings on technical and policy topics that local government planners are addressing. Workshops are also held for elected officials and planning commissioners on policy related topics.

Photo Simulations & Image Library

Photo Simulation PowerPoints are very effective tools to show the public how public investment can attract infill development and build attractive, vibrant neighborhoods. Also available for viewing, SACOG created a series of photo simulations for a variety of projects around the region. SACOG has developed a library of photographic images for local governments, community groups and businesses to use in promoting good land uses, alternative transportation modes, and the connections between the region's urban and rural communities.

Community Workshop Facilitation

Local jurisdictions and public and non-profit organizations occasionally hold community planning workshops. SACOG staff and resources can be made available to workshops that address community growth and revitalization issues. Services provided include facilitation, smallgroup leadership, educational resources and technical expertise.

Funding Programs

SACOG provides direct grants to support project specific efforts in cities and counties that implement the Blueprint principles. The support comes in the way of competitive financial assistance. There are four programs that award grants on a two-year cycle: air quality, bicycle/pedestrian, transportation demand management, and community design.

Form-Based Code Handbook

SACOG's Form-Based Code Handbook provides background information on form-based codes, when to use it, and, most importantly, a practical step-by-step guide on how to create one. Although the case studies are not actual form-based codes, they illustrate the steps and considerations needed to create a form-base.

Source: www.sacregionblueprint.org/implementation/pdf/blueprint-book.pdf

Appendix 4
Denver, Colorado: Mile High Compact

THIS AGREEMENT is made and entered into this 10th day of August 2000, pursuant to Article XIV, Section 18(2)(a) of the Constitution of Colorado and Section 29-1-203 of the Colorado Revised Statutes, by and among the cities and towns of the State of Colorado, and the counties of Colorado, bodies politic organized under and existing by virtue of the laws of the State of Colorado.

I. WHEREAS, the Cities and Counties recognize that growth and development decisions can impact neighboring jurisdictions and the region; and II. WHEREAS, Metro Vision 2020, collaboratively created by DRCOG members, business, environmental and neighborhood leaders; provides a regional framework for local decisions on growth and development within the Denver Regional Council of Governments' (DRCOG) region; and III. WHEREAS, the Cities and Counties are willing to make a commitment to the accommodation and encouragement of planned growth and development, to the orderly extension of urban services, to the enhancement of the quality of life, to the protection of the environment, and to the promotion of the economic viability of their respective communities and the region; and IV. WHEREAS, the Cities and Counties support planned growth and development to maximize efficiency through coordination among jurisdictions, provide for the orderly extension and integration of urban services, promote the economic vitality of the Cities and Counties and enhance the quality of life of its residents; and V. WHEREAS, the Cities and Counties have Comprehensive/Master Plans that provide for the development within their respective jurisdictions; and they recognize the need to have consistent and coordinated comprehensive plans and master plans in order to provide for the orderly growth and development of the region; and VI. WHEREAS, the Cities and Counties desire to voluntarily and collaboratively set forth the principles defined herein that illustrate their commitment to address the nature and location of growth within their individual and overlapping jurisdictions and the region as a whole.

NOW, THEREFORE, in consideration of the mutual promises and covenants contained herein, the undersigned Cities and Counties (hereinafter referred to as we) agree as follows:

1. **Metro Vision 2020.** We acknowledge that Metro Vision 2020 is the comprehensive guide for the development of the region. Moreover, we agree that Metro Vision 2020 is a dynamic document that reflects changes in the region.

2. **Comprehensive/Master Plan.** We acknowledge that comprehensive/master plans are critical tools in translating the community's vision into more specific goals, policies and programs to manage their long-range growth consistent with the communities' and the region's vision. We agree to develop and approve comprehensive master Plans for each of our respective communities and to update these plans on a regular basis, as determined by each jurisdiction.

3. **Comprehensive/Master Plan Principles.** We recognize that there are certain fundamental principles that guide the development of a comprehensive/master plan. We agree to rely on the following principles in developing or amending our comprehensive/master Plans:

   - *Metro Vision 2020.* Local comprehensive/master plans will be consistent with the regional vision provided by Metro Vision 2020 and will incorporate its core elements:

     - Designating the extent of urban development within a specified area;

     - Creating a balanced multi-modal transportation system;

     - Establishing a hierarchy of mixed-use, pedestrian and transit-oriented urban centers;

     - Preserving four free-standing communities of Boulder, Brighton, Castle Rock and Longmont;

     - Development of a regional open space system;

     - reserving the region's natural environment, especially air and water quality.

   - *Public participation.* The comprehensive plan/master plan will be developed through a public participation process with the specifics determined by each jurisdiction, but which will include a public hearing prior to the adoption of the comprehensive plan/master plan.

   - *Reflection of community values.* The comprehensive/master plan will be a reflection of the community's values and the region's vision.

   - *Translate the vision into specific goals, policies and programs.* The comprehensive/master plan will translate the vision for the community into specific goals, policies and programs and/or provide implementation strategies.

   - *Provide for the broad needs of the community.* The comprehensive/master plan will provide for the diverse life-style, and life-cycle needs of the community (residential and business).

- *Long-range view.* Local comprehensive/master plans will address the development and re-development of the community for a fifteen-to-twenty-year period.

- *Dynamic.* The comprehensive/master plan will be a dynamic document and be able to reflect changes in the community.

- *Long-range plan for major infrastructure.* The comprehensive/master plan will address the major infrastructure that will be needed to support the development of the community. The incremental, implementing elements of the long-range plan will be identified in the capital improvements/project plan.

- *Coordinated.* The comprehensive/master plan will coordinate the various elements, such as transportation, land use, community facilities, that must come together in order to provide for the desired quality of life.

- *Intergovernmental collaboration.* Issues that overlap or affect neighboring jurisdictions or districts will be addressed in a collaborative process.

4. **Elements of a Comprehensive/Master Plan.** We agree to include and/or address the following elements within our comprehensive/master plans.

   - *Land use and growth coordination.* This element includes identification of the desired land use patterns, where growth is anticipated or desired to occur over the time period of the plan, and the anticipated amount of development at the end of twenty years or buildout. An urban growth boundary/area will be based on these decisions.

   - *Provision of services and community facilities.* This element provides a description of the essential services and community facilities (for example, schools, fire, police recreation, libraries, etc.) to be provided or available to the community, the level of such services, and what services and/or community facilities are necessary in the future to address future growth for the plan period.

   - *Utilities.* This element provides a description of how utilities with sufficient capacity will be provided to serve planned development and redevelopment. Such utilities should include, but not be limited to water, wastewater and drain age.

   - *Transportation and transit.* This element addresses how the community plans to accommodate the transportation demand for the timeframe of the comprehensive/master plan, including alternative modes of transportation such as trails and bikeways, and transportation demand reduction strategies. This element also reflects Metro Vision 2020 regional multimodal transportation plans.

- *Parks and recreation.* This element addresses how the community provides future parks and recreation facilities and opportunities to serve the community. Plans for trail corridors, bike paths, etc. will be coordinated with overlapping and neighboring jurisdictions.

- *Open space.* This element addresses the community's future open space preservation which will be coordinated with, but not limited by, the plans of overlapping and neighboring jurisdictions and the Metro Vision 2020 Open Space Plan.

- *Economic viability.* This element includes a review and projection of the economic viability of the community based on existing and projected commercial/ industrial activities and employment included in the comprehensive/master plan and their impacts on the other elements of the plan.

- *Housing.* This element addresses how projected population changes, and development and redevelopment are anticipated to affect the mix, affordability, availability and redevelopment needs of the community's housing stock. The relationship between housing and jobs may be addressed in the context of the subregion or to the individual community.

- *Urban design/Community image/Identity.* This element addresses how the community will shape its boundaries and urban landscape to further its identity and image.

- *Environmental resources and hazards.* This element identifies key environmental resources, such as wildlife corridors and habitat areas, which are important for the community to preserve and to identify hazard areas that should not be considered for development. This could also be included as part of the land uses element since it provides the basis for future land use. This element addresses the effects that the location and type of growth and land development have on air and water quality.

5. **Urban Growth Areas or Urban Growth Boundaries.** We agree to adopt Urban Growth Areas or Urban Growth Boundaries, as established by Metro Vision 2020, within our comprehensive/master plans, or in the case of counties by resolution of the Board of Commissioners, and to allow urban development only within those areas. We will encourage and support the efficient development within our Urban Growth Areas or Urban Growth Boundaries consistent with the goals of Metro Vision 2020. Modifications to Urban Growth Areas or Urban Growth Boundaries will be addressed through Metro Vision 2020's flexibility process. We agree to address nonurban growth outside of the Urban Growth Area or Urban Growth Boundary through subregional planning, intergovernmental agreements, comprehensive/master plans or revised Metro Vision policies.

6. **Comprehensive/Master Plan Approval.** We will develop our comprehensive plan/master plan through an inclusive public participation process including, but not limited to, a public hearing.

7. **Comprehensive/Master Plan Implementation.** We will use our comprehensive/master plan for updating local zoning and development regulations. Moreover, we will develop and adopt policies, procedures, and/or ordinances to implement and enforce our comprehensive/master plans that are consistent with the provisions of our comprehensive/master plan.

8. **Coordination with Other Plans.** We will work to coordinate our plans with neighboring and overlapping governmental entities and work to integrate our plans at a sub-regional level.

9. **Intergovernmental Agreements.** We will enter into additional intergovernmental agreements, when necessary, to address discrepancies and/or inconsistencies at the jurisdictional boundaries or any other planning and coordination matters.

10. **Dispute Resolution.** Individual communities will pursue dispute resolution processes.

11. **Term.** We will annually jointly evaluate the effectiveness of the processes set forth herein and to propose any necessary amendments. If any parties consider withdrawing from the agreement, they must notify DRCOG by April 1st with the action to be effective by the following January 1st.

12. **Intent of Agreement.** This Agreement is intended to describe rights and responsibilities only as between the named parties hereto. It is not intended to and shall not be deemed to confer rights to any persons or entities not named as parties hereto. We, by signing this Agreement, intend to implement its provisions in good faith.

13. **Execution in Counterparts.**

Source: http://www.drcog.org/index.cfm?page=MileHighCompact

> **Appendix 5**
> Chicago, Illinois: 2040 Implementation Strategies

Realizing the Vision

If current development trends continue, inefficient land consumption, the degradation of natural resources and overloading of the transportation system will affect our quality of life. To successfully manage these changes, officials at the regional and local levels must actively work together to make planning decisions for the benefit of the region as a whole. Rather than set forth prescriptive solutions, the *2040 Regional Framework Plan* is a guiding structure to integrate regional and local plans, policies and goals. Our diverse region requires differing approaches to realizing the vision, but with local/regional coordination and the involvement of all segments of the population in community planning and design, the vision can be achieved.

Regional Role

NIPC will continue to be an active resource to help with *2040 Plan* implementation, including facilitating meetings, providing technology tools and conducting statistical forecasts and other research, while coordinating agencies and local governments. NIPC also will develop a Report Card of performance indicators aligned with the plan's five core themes. Published annually, this will help establish accountability for implementation progress, growth, development and redevelopment.

Local Role

Land use is primarily in the hands of local governments. Every decision at the local level is important to building a better regional community. The *2040 Plan* will unfold one step at a time through careful, deliberate and coordinated action. By using the resources NIPC offers, proactively updating local comprehensive plans and regulations, and using a collaborative process, local action can lead to a healthy and vibrant Chicago region in 2040.

Source: www.nipc.org/2040/2040popularsummary.pdf

> ### Appendix 6
> Washington, DC: Metropolitan Washington Council of Governments
> Model Resolution

PROPOSED [JURISDICTION] RESOLUTION ADOPTING
GREATER WASHINGTON 2050 COMPACT

WHEREAS, [Jurisdiction] recognizes and values its status as part of the economically vibrant and socially diverse National Capital Region; and

WHEREAS, [Jurisdiction] takes part in regional planning and activities through its participation in the Metropolitan Washington Council of Governments; and

WHEREAS, in January 2008, COG established the Greater Washington 2050 Coalition, a public-private advisory panel, consisting of local government officials, representatives of the Region's business and environmental sectors, and members of the public representing numerous and diverse civic interests, to help shape the Region; and

WHEREAS, the Coalition sought to leverage existing regional and local vision plans and reach regional agreement on local actions that can help achieve common regional goals; and

WHEREAS, the Coalition examined how other regions have approached similar efforts, sponsored a workshop on future economic, environmental, and demographic trends and changes that could affect the National Capital Region, and commissioned and published a survey of public opinion on regional matters in 2008 and 2009; and

WHEREAS, after almost two years of work, the Coalition unanimously approved its final report, Region Forward – A Comprehensive Guide for Regional Planning and Measuring Progress in the 21st Century, which includes nine regional goals in four themes of accessibility, sustainability, prosperity, and livability; and establishes regional performance targets and indicators to measure required progress toward goals; and

WHEREAS, the COG Board approved the Region Forward report in January 2010, and recommended that local governments execute a voluntary regional compact incorporating these regional goals, and commit to consider regional implications in their local decisions and actions; and

WHEREAS, the [Jurisdiction's policy body], after review and consideration of these goals and their potential benefit to the Region and to the residents and businesses of [Jurisdiction], believes that adoption of the voluntary Greater Washington 2050 Compact to be in the public interest of [Jurisdiction].

NOW, THEREFORE, BE IT RESOLVED, BY THE [JURISDICTION'S POLICY BODY] THAT

1. [Jurisdiction] hereby endorses the voluntary Greater Washington 2050 Compact and, within {Jurisdiction's] legal, financial, and political limitations, commits to follow the principles and goals therein in its decisions and actions.

2. [Appropriate official] is hereby authorized to sign the voluntary Greater Washington 2050 Compact on behalf of [the Jurisdiction].

3. Staff of [Jurisdiction] is hereby directed to familiarize itself with the voluntary Greater Washington 2050 Compact and to alert [executive and policy officials of Jurisdiction] on significant regional implications of proposed decisions or actions.

Source: www.mwcog.org/uploads/committee-documents/Yl5ZW1ZX20100407110701.pdf

CHAPTER 8

ENGAGING THE PUBLIC AND COMMUNICATING SUCCESSFULLY IN REGIONAL PLANNING

John Fregonese and C. J. Gabbe

It is tempting to think of a successful regional plan solely in terms of the nuts and bolts of urban planning—focusing on streetscapes, land use and transportation policy changes, transit-oriented development, zoning codes, governance issues, and the host of other important elements. But the human element of creating and shaping a successful regional plan is just as important. The increasingly diverse and mobile regional public, with its high expectations for transparency, has banished the days when public involvement in a planning process simply meant holding a public hearing or two and hoping more than ten people would show up.

Today's enduring and successful regional plan must include an active, two-way approach to communicating with the public. When we describe communication in regional planning, we define it as a broad, double-sided style of engagement— true give and take between planners and the public that begins at the outset of the regional planning process and continues throughout the plan's adoption and implementation phases. Mutual communication signifies that as much effort is expended listening as speaking. Outreach programs that simply broadcast a point of view do little to gather information from the public. It is crucial that citizens feel confident that their opinions are truly sought and seriously considered.

From Daniel Burnham's *Plan of Chicago* and Portland Metro's Region 2040 Plan to Envision Utah and Louisiana Speaks, plans that have led to long-term impacts engaged their target audiences by using a wide range of effective communication techniques. While all were technically strong, each of these plans resonated with the public because it communicated effectively and reflected a new, shared vision of its city's or region's future.

We are practicing planners, not researchers, and this chapter is based on our experiences and successes plus the lessons about engaging the public in regional planning that we have learned along the way. We have chosen the approach described here because it generates public excitement about regional planning. Our findings stem from our experiences rather than comparative analysis.

We have found that successful engagement strategies go beyond simply giving the public the illusion of choice. They truly provide a range of choices, and public input is used to help shape regional planning decisions. In four of the five case studies in this chapter, the public was asked to choose a preferred scenario, and the region's final scenario largely reflected the tradeoffs with which the public grappled. Then, each plan was designed to address specific problems, and we were able to demonstrate to the public, as well as to the stakeholders and decision makers, how certain solutions would improve day-to-day life in the region.

Our examples demonstrate that no one size fits all when attempting to engage the public in a regional plan. In fact, the best plans are products of their time. They push the envelope to help create new ways of thinking about regional planning while the planning is underway. We believe that today's best practices will lead to new advances tomorrow and, if also technically sound, the plans that successfully capture the imagination of the public will be the ones most likely to be implemented.

By today's standards, for example, the outreach in the 1909 plan of Chicago looks more like a full public relations campaign than meaningful public engagement, but it actually was the first major planning outreach at the regional scale in the United States. In the past 100 years, community and professional expectations for regional engagement have evolved to include full-fledged participation and complete transparency. This is exemplified in the PLANiTULSA process, which has engaged the public in an iterative conversation about the biggest challenges facing the city and region of Tulsa, Oklahoma, by using a mix of fun, map-based planning workshops, surveys, values research, traditional media, and the latest social media technology.

TEN PRINCIPLES FOR ENGAGING REGIONAL COMMUNITIES

Our work throughout the United States has enabled us to identify ten key principles needed to develop effective region-scale engagement and communication strategies.

1. Think Strategically About Whom You Are Trying to Reach

Every major planning process should begin with development of its communications strategy. We have found it useful to think in terms of a pyramid that segments audiences into four primary categories: motivated citizens, fans of planning, the interested public, and the uninterested public. A successful engagement strategy enumerates the best ways of interacting and communicating with each of these groups (figure 8.1).

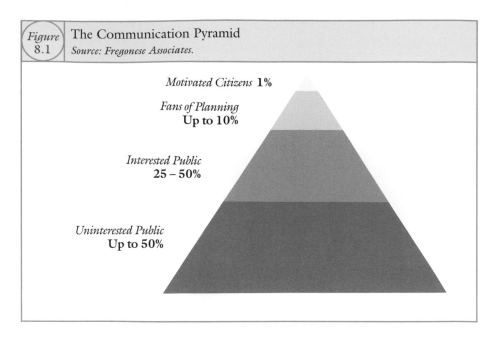

Figure 8.1   The Communication Pyramid
Source: Fregonese Associates.

Motivated citizens include the involved stakeholders as well as other people who are personally interested and willing to attend a meeting. These people have the highest level of involvement in a plan and usually represent less than 1 percent of the population. Fans of planning will read documents that require a few minutes or less, watch videos, keep up with the project's Web site, and follow the plan's progress by means of social media. This group can be quite large—as much as 10 percent of the population. While members of the interested public may not attend a workshop or planning event, they may read about the plan in the newspaper, hear about it via word of mouth, and follow the story passively. This group may comprise between 25 and 50 percent of the population.

Finally, those people in the fourth segment, the uninterested public, will be difficult to reach and engage. Traditionally, planning and politics have marginalized some members of this group, who may become interested in the planning process if invited or encouraged by someone within their community whom they trust and respect. While other members of this group may not be directly engaged, however, this does not mean that they have no role in the plan. Such seemingly marginal engagement can feel frustrating to planners, especially since the uninterested public may constitute up to 50 percent of a region's population. At a minimum, however, it is critical to include in the planning process strategies such as scientific surveys and values research that can assess the values and opinions of the less-than-interested public.

2. Start Every Planning Process by Researching and Understanding Community Values

It may seem like a given, but every plan should begin with an accurate representation of community values. Gaining an understanding of what they are through values research is critical to ensuring that plans reflect local and regional culture. Planners cannot simply assume they know what local standards are. Comprehending the shared ideals of a region is a first step toward defining big ideas and creating specific messages for targeted audiences. Values research has evolved over the years to become a quantifiable science. Interestingly, while each region's values are different, some nationally shared principles appear in many regions.

Values research and analysis provides a means to ensure that a plan reflects the core values of a diverse regional community. It also allows planners to design a plan that benefits the broadest segment of the community, not just motivated citizens involved directly with the planning process. In addition, values research becomes a means for helping all citizens, whether motivated or not, to understand their own community better and to challenge or confirm long-held assumptions. Envision Utah (n.d.) conducted research in 1997 specifically targeted at planning and at identifying Utahans' overarching values. The following key values, among others, guided the public-driven planning process and ultimately led to the preferred scenario.

- Utahans are personally satisfied with the current quality of life and very optimistic about the near-term possibilities.

- Wasatch Front residents recognize that growth brings a number of problems and challenges. Most believe, however, that future growth will make things better.

- New residents have a more positive view of growth than do longer-term residents.

In 2008 planners in the Grand Traverse, Michigan, area enlisted values research to guide the development of that region's vision. They found that most people shared the perception of the "timeless," high quality of life in the region; a feeling that it was not experiencing the same economic pain as the rest of the country; a recognition that protecting the environment is very important; and the perception that the region's attitudes toward growth are generally progressive. The research also revealed that the residents place a high value on peace of mind, which they associate with scenic beauty and nature, friendly neighbors, and a sense of safety and security.

3. Create Engagement That Is Fun as Well as Relevant

In many areas of the country, the public meeting has earned a reputation for allowing only one-way input, which makes it difficult for citizens to see how their ideas are affecting the process. The painful reality is that this traditional mode of public involvement is boring. The public wants and deserves better. By creating interactive workshops, planners can harness the "wisdom of crowds." Such workshops are created on the premises that involving many people is a good thing and that recognizing the multitude of perspectives that many people add to the meeting and the process is critical. Bringing many different people into the crowd—whether they are from different neighborhoods, have had different life experiences, or hold a variety of outlooks—must be viewed as and trusted to be central to making a good plan.

If the workshops are set up to be fun, creative, and socially stimulating, the process will enable communities to gather and share their best ideas. The role of the public in workshops is not to redraw the zoning map or sketch pictures that make their city look like an idyllic utopia. A workshop should feel like a gathering of friends and neighbors. The best regional planning workshops have lively atmospheres, with groups of six to ten residents gathering around large, table-sized maps and experimenting with different visions for the future of their neighborhood, city, and region. The large geographic area represented by a region may bring people from different parts of the same area to a table, where they are able to share their insights with their fellow participants.

Fun, hands-on, map-based exercises are useful for giving members of the public and stakeholders a canvas for exploring a variety of options. It is crucial that the exercises not seem too technical or design-oriented, however. Ultimately, planners must publicly take responsibility for analyzing the results of these workshops, then synthesizing them with technical information in a transparent and accessible way. This huge responsibility must be identified and acknowledged at the outset.

4. From the Beginning, Involve Citizens and Stakeholders Who Have Many Different Perspectives

Not everyone from any given region shares the same values, of course. Regional communities are diverse, and they will encompass views, values, and experiences that span the entire spectrum. It is thus critical to involve as many people from as many different backgrounds as possible. Understandably, many planners focus their community involvement on the individuals and groups least likely to be critical of planning or the planning process. Human nature causes us to crave feeling safe and supported in our way of thinking. Despite that, it is crucial to engage groups that either have not been involved in past planning efforts or were opposed to those efforts and plans. A place at the table needs to be made for everyone, and the process must anticipate providing ample opportunity for airing and discussing contrary views.

It is also important to identify the geographic scope and interests of stakeholder groups within a region. For example, the PLANiTULSA process included a concerted effort to meet regularly with neighborhood, citywide, and regional stakeholder groups to address any ideas, questions, or concerns quickly and directly. Although it is often impossible to reach complete consensus in a planning process, everyone involved needs and deserves the opportunity to share ideas. When considering the direction a region could take, the best plans are likely to be those that arise from a clash of ideas and passions. We have found that, even when all groups cannot get exactly what they want, their constituents must recognize that they have been part of an inclusive conversation and had an evident impact on the final product.

5. *Make Plans Easy to Understand and Highly Visual*

Plans that get implemented are user friendly and easy to understand. Keep in mind that most of the people who become essential to implementing a plan are not the planners. Daily decisions by investors, citizens, elected officials, and agency staff will either make or break a plan.

First, planning documents must be jargon-free, avoid the alphabet soup of planner acronyms, and utilize plain, compelling language. Often it is helpful to convene a focus group of laypeople to read sections, share impressions, and point out areas that are unclear or laden with jargon. Next, plans need to show clearly the impacts that have resulted from citizen and stakeholder engagement in the planning process. Third, a plan's length must assist in its comprehension— it should not be short on details, but each of its levels should include digestible chunks of information into which people can delve, depending on their interest. Finally, presentations should be simple and visually stunning. For example, prepare PowerPoint presentations that incorporate text sparingly and communicate key concepts via easily understandable charts, images, and visualizations.

6. *Leverage the Internet, Social Media, and New Technologies*

Since the mid-1990s, planning's use of the Internet and new communication technologies has exploded, as it has in every facet of our society. Technology itself does not provide a community with a more effective voice in the planning process, but when it is used as a tool to build stronger neighborhood and local social networks, it can catalyze the public's role. It presents planners with an incredible opportunity to use tools that can bring more people into the conversation, increase transparency, and ultimately create stronger plans.

Every project needs a Web site, but more specifically it needs one that is easy to navigate and acts as a portal to a variety of multimedia content related to the planning process, its purposes, and products. The Web site should be developed on a platform that can be revised easily, since a beautifully designed site does no good if it is too complicated to update frequently. It is important to remember that not everyone has online access or is using social media, so this strategy must be used in conjunction with others and as a complement to them. Early in the planning process, technology access and skill or capacity needs to be assessed systematically for different groups.

Beyond the project's Web site, a full social media strategy should be employed. Although this realm is evolving rapidly, as of this writing the primary tools are Facebook, Twitter, LinkedIn, and YouTube. Each one attracts its own particular audience and provides a different medium for communicating ideas, updates, and plan discussions.

Increasingly, members of an area's public look online for their information when they want it and for the purposes each individual determines. Beyond simply providing information, however, the power of the Internet is best leveraged when it enables sharing ideas, opinions, and likes and dislikes with family, friends, and peers. Using social media appropriately can make planning fun, interactive, interesting, and accessible to a wide range of people. It can be empowering, but its use carries with it a requirement for understanding, to the extent possible, who is online and who is not.

We have found that clear communication without a corporate or overly "official" demeanor works well. Short, informal updates are usually best. The ability to contribute uncensored feedback and to spread the word easily is also critical. For example, on a plan's Facebook page, we may post real-time workshop images or behind-the-scenes photos of staff working on the community's input. With such pictures, a short explanation of how the public's contribution is being used would be included. Still, the real added value comes from helping members of the community engage with each other and bringing in other people through social media tools.

7. Integrate Print and Web Content

Although digital media is a crucial element in the twenty-first century, we believe that printed materials, such as newsletters or newspaper inserts, will continue to play a role in planning for the foreseeable future. Successful newsletters are targeted to specific audiences, easy to understand and digest, visually compelling, and include strong calls to action or vehicles for participation, such as surveys. Combining media by using the printed element to provide a quick overview, then directing readers to the details and more in-depth material posted on the Internet, has also proven to be very effective. In general, it is wise to create synergies consciously between media and events by seeing that every strategy has a role in maximizing the overall effort.

8. Create Video Content

Preparing thought provoking, visually stimulating video content is an increasingly critical aspect of effective communication in regional planning. Some time ago, traditional television and its few network broadcast channels dominated, then cable arrived and offered many more viewing options. In the last decade, use of online video has exploded, although only recently has it gone beyond supplying just low-resolution clips, movie trailers, and music videos. Now Web ads and other video content form a critical part of many marketing and political campaigns.

We see the future of video trending toward personalized, high-resolution content, all of which will utilize high-definition technology, and it will be the users, rather than the broadcaster, who select the content. Planners must be prepared for this major shift, and make sure that their content is sure to be selected by users. Generally it is best to create clips that can be viewed in less than five minutes and range in style and content from short "documentary" videos to expanded versions of 3D fly-through visualizations. The key is to post new video content regularly and use it as a springboard for discussion about the topics it broaches.

This short-form video content offered online can be supplemented with professionally produced, full-length documentary films that explain major issues in fair and engaging ways. As part of the Louisiana Speaks regional plan, Louisiana Public Broadcasting aired "Louisiana Speaks: Our Voice, Our Plan, Our Future," which was also made available online. In addition to summarizing the key issues presented by Louisiana's recovery, this video directly tied into a citizen survey, to which about 27,000 people responded.

9. Use 2D and 3D Visualizations

Although planners may be tempted to think they can capture the hearts and minds of the public with facts, data, maps, and sound arguments, the most powerful way to share ideas is by visual communication. Visualizations offer much more than just a method of sharing the final plan. As tools, they can be almost lifelike and illustrate for the public and decision makers the differences and tradeoffs between alternatives.

Two highly successful techniques are 2D photomorphs and 3D fly-through visualizations (figure 8.2). The 2D photomorph employs a before-and-after technique: A specific place is photographed, then the plan elements being envisioned

Figure 8.2	Visualizations of a New Mixed-Use Center in Tulsa, Oklahoma
	Source: PLANiTULSA.

BEFORE

AFTER

This *2D photomorph* shows how an existing intersection could be transformed in the future.

3D modeling helps illustrate a variety of perspectives.

PLANiTULSA

are added. For example, a worn, auto-oriented commercial strip could be shown, then supplemented with new streetscapes, pedestrian amenities, and mixed-use buildings. The key is to make the changes realistic; they should neither over- nor understate what the plan and its policies may become.

Fly-through visualizations are more complicated to put together, although they can be developed from start to finish with low-cost software on any home or office computer. The best 3D fly-through videos begin at a high-placement, large-area aerial scale, fly down to a superimposed plan map, then zoom in to a smaller demonstration area that represents how the region could look in the future. The fly-through can even fade into a photomorph of a specific corner or intersection. This technique allows viewers to envision how the area fits into the larger picture. It also demonstrates the relationship between the plan and what actually happens on the ground, thus providing an accurate sense of how a place could change going forward. It is ideal for soliciting feedback about alternative futures.

10. Create More Than Just a Plan

The savvy planner knows that traditional planning processes and products cannot fully meet the needs or expectations of twenty-first-century regions and their citizens. Instead, successful regions make use of results from a public engagement process in order to create a series of interrelated products that replace the traditional 100-page written plan directed at a relatively small audience. Each of these products should be written succinctly, made visually interesting, and designed to address specifically the principal issues that emerged from the public engagement campaign.

A vision—an overarching, general, and inspirational document about a city's or region's future—is typically short, descriptive, and imaginative. For example, when Dallas adopted its first comprehensive plan in 2006, the planning process started with a vision of a "city filled with many neighborhoods with unique character, safe parks, bustling transit centers, a thriving urban downtown, and excellent employment opportunities" (City of Dallas 2006, 3). This vision, which was arrived at through an extensive outreach and communications campaign, serves as the basis for what Dallas has set out to achieve. Such a vision should be followed up with three distinct elements.

- A policy plan: The plan itself provides a series of policies for a city or region to incorporate in order to move forward toward achieving its vision. Its development should be approached the way an operating manual is prepared, because it will rarely be read from beginning to end, but instead will be referred to as needed. Ensuring ease of access to its information and policies should be the paramount consideration in preparing its design.

- A strategy: The strategic plan identifies the most critical near- and mid-term actions, which will move the city or region toward implementing its plan and realizing its vision. This document focuses on achieving specific outcomes.

● A monitoring process: It is important to include a means by which to keep track of the community's progress in implementing the plan and to note where changes may need to be made. The results arising from the monitoring component should be communicated to decision makers and the public on a regular basis.

IN PRACTICE: A SAMPLE REGIONAL PLANNING PROCESS

To illustrate how these ten principles are put into practice, the general steps used to engage and communicate with the public in a state-of-the-art regional planning process are outlined below. We have also suggested several key engagement strategies to employ at each step in the process. Although the schedule for each regional plan will vary, we have found that a period of about 18 months allows for carrying out a detailed analysis and action-oriented process.

1. **Establish a baseline understanding of the region's values.** We conduct both in-depth interviews with community leaders and stakeholders and quantitative public values research. Statistically valid surveys provide important confirmation of attitudes and values shared across a community. In the planning process, such up-front understanding also helps with responding to overarching issues by implementing strategies consistent with community attitudes and beliefs. Releasing key findings helps build a base of shared public understanding.
   Key engagement strategies: interviews; public surveys; Web and social media presence

2. **Hold a kickoff event at which you present interesting content, such as an analysis of regional challenges and a synopsis of the results of the values survey research.** This event should feel something like a regional celebration, at which the baseline analysis of the region's opportunities and challenges is presented.
   Key engagement strategies: major event; seek in-person and Web-based feedback

3. **Conduct public, map-based workshops focused at the regional scale at several key locations around the region.** These workshops typically work best if they include a game exercise using a map of the study area as its game board and icons representing possible development options for pieces. The regional workshop focuses on regionwide issues, such as land use, transportation, housing, the environment, and economic development. It considers urban and natural systems that cut across neighborhood boundaries, such as major roadways, transit systems, and riparian corridors. Each workshop should challenge its participants with the task of deciding where new growth should and should not occur, the general form that new growth should take, and the nature of the transportation elements that will serve it

best. Opportunity areas for change should be highlighted as well. Participants grapple with the issues and tradeoffs related to placing growth in different locations given environmental, institutional, and infrastructure constraints. *Key engagement strategies: public workshops; seek in-person and Web-based feedback*

4. **Digitize, analyze, and share the combined workshop results.** Employ both online communication and face-to-face meetings to show the public what generally shared ideas and assumptions have emerged from all of the workshops. *Key engagement strategies: host interactive open houses; generate buzz through social media; solicit feedback in-person at open houses using keypad polling as well as via the Web*

5. **Lead neighborhood-level public workshops that address urban design and other specific issues.** Smaller workshops allow the public to work at the neighborhood level, a scale with which most people are familiar. Working at this level in specific areas of the region provides the opportunity to focus on relevant and specific issues that may not affect all parts of the region or may affect different parts in different ways. *Key engagement strategies: public workshops; seek in-person and Web-based feedback; stakeholder and formal neighborhood group work sessions*

6. **Simulate and evaluate multiple futures.** Rather than focus on a single future for the region, we use scenario planning to explore a range of possible futures. Developing a series of land use and transportation scenarios using geographic information system (GIS)–based tools, such as the Envision Tomorrow Suite, makes alternative futures more readily understood. Detailed alternative scenarios consider opportunities for infill development, redevelopment, and new growth, for example. Next they are evaluated to predict what impact they may have on a variety of quality-of-life indicators. *Key engagement strategies: scenario designs based on themes that emerge from regional and neighborhood workshops*

7. **Present these future scenarios to the public via visualizations and video, and provide the audience with multiple means of providing feedback.** Breaking the scenario into its specific elements, such as carbon footprint, housing mix, open space, and the like, allows a citizen to prefer the open space component of one scenario but favor the transportation elements of another. Once ideas emerge that generate excitement and receive significant public support, the next step entails determining the appropriate strategies needed to make them happen. *Key engagement strategies: major events; videos and visualizations; online and printed surveys*

8. **Use the public's scenario feedback to develop a vision for the region.**
   The vision is a way to explain what the region strives to be. It arises from broad-based citizen input and reflects a consensus about participants' values, goals, and desires for the future. The vision forms a foundation for the comprehensive plan.
   Key engagement strategies: open houses; seek in-person and Web-based feedback

9. **Develop a policy plan, a strategic plan, and a monitoring plan all based on public feedback and best practices.** The components of the policy, strategic and monitoring plans are developed iteratively, and stakeholders and the public are given ample opportunity to comment. We have found that an online log that includes every comment, and all changes that are made as a result, maximizes transparency in the planning process.
   Key engagement strategies: seek Web and print feedback; public work sessions and hearings

FIVE REGIONAL PLANS

To further illustrate our principles and expectations, we turn to five regional plans that have developed notable strategies for engaging the public and/or communicating broadly during the planning process and afterward. The plans span a timeframe of slightly more than one century, and they represent a wide variety of geographies and of strategies for engagement and communication. The element they all have in common is that each one adopted an action-oriented, campaign-style approach to communicating with their audiences, thus eliciting input and ultimately generating support (table 8.1).

Burnham's Plan of Chicago

Daniel Burnham's 1909 *Plan of Chicago* continues to be held up as the gold standard for envisioning the future of a city and a region. While "the Plan itself was forward-looking, . . . in some respects the publicity techniques the planners used to generate support, especially after its release, were even more innovative and modern" (Chicago Historical Society, n.d.).

The plan's sponsor, the Commercial Club of Chicago, engaged in what was a major public relations campaign for its time, because it recognized that, in addition to elected decision makers, voters would be crucial to realizing the plan's funding and implementation elements. Walter L. Moody, the first managing director of the 328-member Chicago Planning Commission, led the publicity effort, which included 500 lantern-slide shows (an early twentieth-century version of a PowerPoint presentation) seen by more than 150,000 people in total and a document called "Chicago's Greatest Issue: An Official Plan," written for and mailed to the region's citizens. A simpler version of the plan entitled *Wacker's Manual of the Plan of Chicago: Municipal Economy*

Table 8.1	Comparison of Five Regional and Comprehensive Plans				
PLAN (DATE)	REGION. TYPE OF PLAN	LEADERS' ROLE(S)	TOOLS AND TECHNIQUES	CITIZEN-ENGAGEMENT HIGHLIGHTS	MAJOR RESULTS OF IMPLEMENTATION
BURNHAM'S PLAN OF CHICAGO (1909)	Chicago region. Comprehensive plan	Disseminate information; generate support; participate through using a large committee; integrate political strategy with plan	500 lantern-slide show presentations; screenings of a two-reel film; mailers; eighth-grade civics curriculum	Support provided basis for getting funding and approval of implementation	Many elements of present lakefront, highway system, rail system, parks, street layout, and civic center attributed to plan
PORTLAND METRO'S REGION 2040 PLAN (1997)	24 cities and the urban portion of 3 counties within the Portland metropolitan region. Regional plan	Generate support; utilize stakeholder networks; implement strategic actions through policy decisions	Values survey; video; workshops; regionally distributed brochure and survey about scenarios; group meetings; slideshows	Regional growth concept based on public participation; significant increase in support for compact development in the region	Guidance for growth and development through 2040; identification of region's future centers and corridors
ENVISION UTAH (2002)	Wasatch Front Region around Salt Lake City. Regional plan	Bring together public, private, and nonprofit stakeholders; work with decision makers to implement strategic actions	Values analysis; workshops throughout the state; newspaper/Web survey; Web site; group meetings and slideshows	Implemented through continued outreach and influence	Created first planning toolkit for Utah; supported significant rail expansion; led to follow-up Envision projects around the state
LOUISIANA SPEAKS (2006)	Southern Louisiana, including New Orleans, Baton Rouge, Lake Charles, and surrounding coastal areas. Regional plan	Act as champions; generate support; utilize stakeholder networks; implement strategic actions	Initial priorities survey; Web site; stakeholder workshops; public television documentary; regionwide survey with multiple feedback channels	Significant interaction with citizens created a broadly supported and recognized plan	A plan that led to a coastal-protection master plan; numerous comprehensive plans for parishes; development of statewide planning resources
PLANiTULSA (2010)	City of Tulsa, Oklahoma. Comprehensive plan	Generate support; utilize stakeholder networks; implement strategic actions	Values poll; interviews; group outreach; 3 citywide workshops; small area workshops; social media including YouTube, Twitter, and Facebook; printed and online surveys	Significant impact on scenarios and action items; social media campaign led to high levels of youth participation	Unanimously adopted by the Tulsa City Council in July 2010; first implementation steps in progress

was incorporated into the eighth-grade civics curriculum for Chicago students (Burnham Plan Centennial 2009).

The successful outreach process even included a two-reel silent film called *A Tale of One City*. This innovative, multifaceted public relations approach was ahead of its time, and in many ways it still serves as the inspiration for all regional planning communications campaigns today. The plan has had a major impact on the present form of Chicago, including its lakefront, highway system, parks, and growth patterns.

Portland Metro's Region 2040 Plan

Region 2040 is the regional plan that has been put in place in Greater Portland to map out a growth management strategy for the metropolitan region. In 1992 what became the Region 2040 Growth Concept was inaugurated with an extensive survey of citizen values that was followed by a modeling process and analysis of four alternative concepts. Based on input from policy makers, planning professionals, businesses, and citizens throughout the region, a preferred growth concept was developed. It focused higher-density development along transit corridors and in centers while preserving natural areas and the character of existing neighborhoods.

When looking for a model to emulate, Portland Metro closely followed Walter Moody's concepts pioneered 85 years earlier in Chicago. It then translated them into contemporary 1990s media. In place of the pamphlet, a brochure was mailed to all of the 550,000 residents of the region. Metro received a strong showing of more than 17,500 mailed responses to the survey questions it had included in the brochure.

Chicago's silent movie was replaced in Portland with a ten-minute video that Metro developed and distributed through video store franchises and local libraries, which resulted in some 50,000 viewings. Throughout the process leading to adoption of the plan, a slideshow was shown hundreds of times to citizens and stakeholder groups. Over about five years, the process raised public awareness of the Metro 2040 project from a mere 5 percent of the region to a respectable 25 percent. Regional attitudes about and recognition for the connections and tradeoffs between density and sprawl changed significantly as well.

The strong public engagement campaign segued into the plan's successful implementation. After the Metro Council and a key local government advisory committee unanimously adopted the Region 2040 Growth Concept, Metro developed tools that included functional plans requiring conformance by local jurisdictions, urban reserve designations, and the urban growth

Portland Metro used creative video outreach that resulted in some 50,000 viewings.

Source: Photograph © Fregonese Associates.

boundary revisions required by state law. Each implementation tool included continuing public involvement. These efforts were consolidated into the Regional Framework Plan, which was adopted by the Metro Council in December 1997. The implementation of the Region 2040 Growth Concept has been attributed to many benefits in the Portland region, ranging from a decrease in average per capita vehicle miles traveled to the region's regular spot at or near the top of "most livable city" rankings.

Envision Utah

In 1998, Envision Utah was formed to develop a regional growth management strategy for Salt Lake City and environs, an area encompassing 1,200 square miles of the Wasatch Front region. The intent behind Envision Utah was to create a neutral, statewide facilitator that could bring together a diverse range of stakeholders to make informed decisions about how Utah should grow. The planning process included governments, local businesses, and the public.

This unique, values-driven process blended extensive public involvement with scientific analyses that employed GIS techniques. Among the key issues addressed

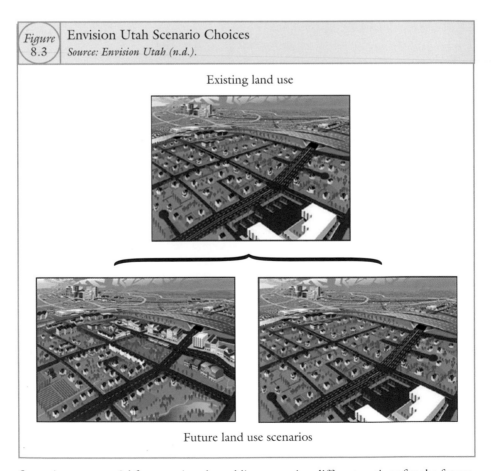

| *Figure* 8.3 | Envision Utah Scenario Choices *Source: Envision Utah (n.d.).* |

Existing land use

Future land use scenarios

Scenarios are essential for engaging the public concerning different options for the future.

were approaches to controlling urban sprawl, protecting environmental quality, strengthening the regional economy, and providing affordable housing. The process included three alternative growth scenarios in addition to the state-generated "base case" (figure 8.3). In 1998 and 1999, input from three rounds of workshops and a widely circulated newspaper and Web survey led to selection of a preferred scenario.

Envision Utah used a sophisticated values analysis to ensure that the topics and language used in communicating with the public focused on what mattered to Utahans. For example, the term *smart growth* was rejected in favor of *quality growth*. New ideas, such as light-rail transit, mixed-use development, and higher density, were communicated as choices of which some but not all people may approve. Throughout the process, freedom of choice was emphasized. Like Metro in Portland, Envision Utah included an extensive outreach campaign with video, billboards, newspaper inserts, and widespread group meetings and PowerPoint slideshows. During the outreach campaign, the Internet was becoming more widely available, which enabled Envision Utah to receive 60 percent of more than 17,000 responses via its Web site. The high Web response was notable, and Envision Utah helped lead the first wave of Web-based community engagement.

Development of Envision Utah's quality growth scenario was based on the public's preferred scenario and then refined using land use and transportation models as well as regional population and employment projections. This quality growth scenario would lead to less land consumption than the base case, and it would also use considerably less farmland, increase transit ridership, and accommodate a wider range of housing choices. Significant savings will be realized as well on infrastructure costs for roads, sewers, and other services that the expanded urban area will require.

Unlike a government-sponsored project such as Metro Portland, Envision Utah was stakeholder driven and therefore implemented through continued outreach and influence. Envision Utah has partnered with more than 100 Utah communities to promote better planning tools, supported the expanding development of a major rail transit system, and convened various regional planning projects that continue to implement many of its goals.

Louisiana Speaks

Louisiana Speaks began in 2006 as part of a long-term recovery plan for the Louisiana Recovery Authority, the planning and coordinating body that oversaw the rebuilding of southern Louisiana in the aftermath of Hurricanes Katrina and Rita in 2005.

This planning process engaged a range of stakeholders that included the Coastal Protection and Restoration Authority, Louisiana State University, parishes, cities, nonprofit organizations, elected leaders, and local citizens. Workshops throughout the region were employed for initial public engagement to solicit local knowledge and advice for the region's recovery and growth. They

Louisiana Speaks workshops included a map-based exercise that focused on land use, transportation, environmental, and economic tradeoffs for the state.

Source: Photograph © Fregonese Associates.

focused on planning for coastal protection and restoration, land use and transportation, and economic development.

The plan was a huge success, and the innovative public engagement process even included many of the Louisianans who had left the state after the storms. The process began with a survey of 2,500 residents and evacuees, who provided valuable guidance on regional priorities and preferences. It was followed by a series of in-depth stakeholder interviews and workshops. Once regional scenarios were developed, Louisiana Speaks employed a range of public involvement strategies, including a multimedia campaign and a regional Emmy Award–winning television program aired by Louisiana Public Broadcasting. More than 27,000 Louisianans participated in the planning process in a number of different ways, among them reading newspaper inserts, calling a toll-free number, taking part in the Internet-based polling, and answering a telephone survey (Noah 2009).

The input received helped create a vision for southern Louisiana that focused on three main goals: (1) recover sustainably; (2) grow smarter; and (3) think regionally. This vision was followed with a series of important implementation actions and plans, and as of this writing the implementation of Louisiana Speaks continues. It is presently led by the Center for Planning Excellence (CPEX) based in Baton Rouge. CPEX secured grant funding from the Environmental Protection Agency's Smart Growth Program and has allocated resources to parishes across Louisiana that are working to develop their own comprehensive plans. These plans now form a growing web of smart growth planning in Louisiana that is implemented by ready-to-use zoning tools produced by CPEX.

PLANiTULSA

PLANiTULSA is the first major update in more than 30 years of the comprehensive plan for Tulsa and from the beginning it was designed to engage and energize the public concerning the city's future. The plan started with a statistically valid poll of 1,000 Tulsans augmented by a series of stakeholder interviews. In collaboration with city staff, a highly involved advisory committee, and stakeholders, the project team then designed and conducted three citywide visioning workshops, later adding an additional overflow event due to popular demand. A transportation workshop and a series of neighborhood-scale planning workshops were also presented.

The public response was tremendous. About 2,000 workshop participants created nearly 200 maps to envision potential futures for the city. Input from these workshops helped the team develop four 30-year scenarios for land use and transportation, and they were unveiled in May 2009 to a standing-room-only crowd in downtown Tulsa.

PLANiTULSA is a prime example of a modern public involvement process that put to use both Web-based social media components and more traditional techniques. The project's Web site served as a single-stop source for information, news, and updates throughout the project. In addition to offering a library of project-related information, the site also acted as a portal to the plan's Facebook, LinkedIn, Twitter, and YouTube components. Each of these elements attracted loyal and distinct followings. The Facebook group included nearly 1,000 members, predominately younger Tulsans. With more than 100 members, the LinkedIn group included many local professionals and has featured lively plan-related discussions. The city's Twitter feed, which was used to share short updates about the project, represented a wide cross-section of the community among its nearly 2,200 followers. Lastly, the four short 3D scenario videos hosted on YouTube received on average about 1,500 views each (PLANiTULSA, n.d.).

This social media strategy was complemented by a full strategy using traditional media, which ranged from newspaper and television news to the popular local hip-hop station. The PLANiTULSA buzz became so intense during the 2008 to 2010 period that the planning process generated between 375 and 400 stories in local traditional media alone. The excitement instilled by the planning process and the trust built within communities by volunteer champions of PLANiTULSA were pivotal to the resulting engagement of large numbers of people who traditionally had been marginalized in planning projects. For the first time, they had an opportunity to get involved, share their opinions, and, most importantly, see the impact on the larger planning process that came from their feedback.

In June 2009 nearly 6,000 Tulsans weighed in on which scenario they preferred by answering either printed or online surveys, and the planning team used the results to create the city's vision and its policy and strategic plans. PLANiTULSA was adopted in July 2010 and the City of Tulsa is beginning to implement the first recommendations of the strategic plan, including revising zoning and subdivision codes, planning for neighborhoods and small areas, instituting a new multimodal transportation approach, and constructing several prototype buildings as demonstration projects.

BIG IDEAS, KEY MESSAGES, AND DIVERSE AUDIENCES

Planning communication at the city and regional scales relies on identifying and understanding audiences and explaining planning in ways that are relevant to people's lives. This requires seeking the involvement of local citizens and leaders at every step of the process and constantly asking for feedback in order to ensure that the engagement process is truly local. This process begins at the plan's kickoff and continues beyond its adoption into the years of implementation.

Several lessons emerge from the five case studies we have presented. While there is no such thing as a formula in planning, the best plans have been created by taking large concepts and highlighting specific messages that are then targeted toward different audiences.

Big planning ideas will not resonate unless they are boiled down into specific, easy-to-understand messages. One of the best examples of this sort of effective messaging occurred during Louisiana Speaks' recovery process. The key message that emerged was that Louisianans had an opportunity to guide their destiny: "Our Voice. Our Plan. Our Future." This, along with direction about the future of the region, came about because a full-fledged engagement campaign had been mounted that offered a range of opportunities for local people to shape the plan's direction. One of the most successful ways the program disseminated the plan's messages was with a documentary film written and developed especially for Louisiana Speaks, based on the stories and views of people from across the region, and outlining many of the tradeoffs that coastal Louisiana faced.

In PLANiTULSA, the project team created a series of targeted messages. Some of the most effective ones were those that resonated with young adults, and Retaining Youth, a focused workshop theme, was even introduced. Approximately 19 percent of survey respondents were under the age of 30, and another 38 percent were in the 30 to 49 age group. Such a high percentage of participation by relatively youthful residents can be attributed to specific messages and the social media strategy that targeted them. By developing key messages geared toward a younger demographic, the team was able to draw that particular audience into the process and fine-tune specific implementation strategies.

The best plans are those that catch the interest of diverse audiences—from business leaders and PTA presidents to schoolchildren and retirees. The first step in attracting more than "the usual suspects" is to brainstorm with a group of local people about which specific communities should be included in the planning process. The definition of community can be broad, ranging from a city neighborhood to a group of active seniors. After the list is created, it should be shared with many people, all of whom are asked constantly, Who is missing? It is likely that those left out are groups that previously have not been involved in a planning process. The communications planning stage is the time to determine how to bring them in.

One of the best methods for attracting diverse audiences is to utilize existing social networks for recruitment. Identify a few leaders in each community who will engage in the project personally. These individuals need not be elected or appointed officials; they can be highly regarded social, religious, or neighborhood leaders. This personal touch provides motivation for attending public workshops and keeping people informed and involved through the adoption and implementation processes. Base this recruitment on existing social structures rather than try either to reinvent the process or base it on artificial social structures.

Additionally, recruitment efforts should ensure inclusion of people who may perceive barriers to their being involved. For example, non-native-English speakers may feel intimidated. Depending on the circumstances, strategies for dealing with this group could include hiring translators; hosting workshops and meetings in surroundings the people are likely to find comfortable, such as places of worship; and creating multilingual versions of materials.

Focus groups also can be pivotal in testing messages with different audiences in order to tailor them effectively. Focus group testing has been employed effectively by Louisiana Speaks, Oregon's Big Look, PLANiTULSA, and the Grand Vision in the Grand Traverse region of Michigan. The results revealed that project materials were too complex, filled with planning jargon, and could possibly exclude people with varying levels of education and familiarity with planning issues. The materials were redesigned into visually stimulating publications that were simple in approach, and their key messages were boiled down to be more likely to resonate with a range of audiences. This is apt to have been a major reason why each of these projects had unprecedented numbers of respondents as well as high participation levels among groups that had felt marginalized in the past.

CONCLUSION

We find that an engaging two-way communication campaign is critical to contemporary regional planning. It also must be compelling, interactive, and relevant. In this time of social networking, online information, and interactive communication technologies, the public will accept nothing less. Successfully engaging and communicating with the public must be based on an understanding of community values, because a regional plan that works will reflect the local culture.

Because regional communities are quite diverse, it is important to think about values in terms of the full range of residents. Once rooted in a region's values, a successful engagement campaign focuses on targeted messages built around big ideas and issues that affect people's everyday lives. It also must work with culturally familiar methods and themes. Planning campaigns need to be inclusive and to capitalize on existing community social networks that can bring as many different people and groups as possible into the process.

Engagement should be both fun and meaningful and allow the participants to experiment with real-world tradeoffs. Participation can come through unique events that reflect the style and culture of the local community as well as via social media—Facebook, Twitter, YouTube, and the like—through which ideas and visualizations are shared and feedback is solicited.

Finally, the written plan itself must reflect this layered, participatory approach by introducing new products, such as a vision and a strategic plan, that ultimately create user-friendly, comprehensive resources for a city or region. When done right, everyone will learn new things about their region and about the beliefs they hold most deeply. In our experience, taking the risk to do this properly results in long-lived plans that are at once visionary and effective.

REFERENCES

Burnham Plan Centennial. 2009. Bibliography. http://burnhamplan100.uchicago.edu/learning/bibliography/

Chicago Historical Society. 2005. The electronic encyclopedia of Chicago. Burnham plan. www.encyclopedia.chicagohistory.org/pages/300007.html

City of Dallas. 2006. ForwardDallas! Comprehensive plan vision. Dallas, TX. www.dallascityhall.com/forwardDallas/pdf/Vision.pdf

Envision Utah. n.d. Charting a course for Utah's future: A summary of the Wirthlin Worldwide values research for Envision Utah. www.envisionutah.org/Wirthlin%20Worldwide%20Values%20Research%20Summary.pdf

Noah, Josie. 2009. Louisiana Speaks: A case study examining the use of web technologies to engage residents in the planning process. www.urbaninsight.com/articles/lascasestudy0409.html

Portland Metro. 2040 Growth Concept. http://www.oregonmetro.gov/index.cfm/go/by.web/id=29882/level=3

PLANiTULSA. n.d. www.planitulsa.org

CHAPTER 9

MOVING FORWARD
THE PROMISE OF
MEGAREGIONS AND
HIGH-SPEED RAIL

Robert D. Yaro

The practice of regional planning in city regions in the United States is most closely associated with metropolitan-scale efforts to manage urbanization, urban growth, and change. The evolution of that practice is closely associated with the work of the Regional Plan Association (RPA), the country's oldest metropolitan planning and policy organization. Established in 1922, RPA has developed three regional metropolitan plans and investment strategies and has led advocacy campaigns to support those plans and actions. In the process, RPA created landmark planning documents and procedures that continue to serve as models for U.S. regional planning practice.

Today, with the challenges of climate change, sustainability, and the retrofitting of suburbia, and in the context of enormous global competition for economic activity and prosperity, the United States must once again make regional planning and regional development in metropolitan areas a high priority. As the country embarks on efforts to plan for high-speed rail (HSR), for example, it has the opportunity to transform the metropolitan regions and urban centers that will become the hubs of this system and in the process reshape development patterns in much of the country. Newly elected Republican governors in Florida, Ohio, and Wisconsin, however, have announced that they intend to reject or reconsider federal HSR grants their states may be given. Even with the reset in the program that this will require, it is still anticipated that HSR projects will proceed in the more than 30 other states that already have received or are expected to receive federal HSR funding.

This chapter explores the emergence of what might be regarded in coming years as a new era of regional planning and the implications it could have for regions, megaregions, planners, and the nation. As with today's metropolitan planning and growth management, in the work of RPA we also find precedents for this larger scale of regional planning. Though mostly recognized for its work in the tri-state New York metropolitan region, RPA has also engaged in larger megaregional and national projects.

In the 1930s President Franklin D. Roosevelt asked RPA Chairman Frederic Delano to lead the National Resources Planning Board (NRPB) and to create for the nation the kinds of plans and investment strategies that RPA had established in 1929 in its landmark *Plan for New York and Its Environs*. RPA staff advised the NRPB about developing national infrastructure and economic development strategies, including landmark initiatives such as the 1938 proposal to create the National Toll Road and Free Road System, which was the precursor of the interstate highway system. Later, as part of its *Second Regional Plan*, RPA (1968) developed proposals for high-speed rail and large-scale urban development and resource protection projects for the North Atlantic region, now known as the Northeast Megaregion.

MEGAREGIONS AND HIGH-SPEED RAIL

In 2004, working with other researchers at the University of Pennsylvania and RPA, I began to investigate emerging national development trends and propose solutions to twenty-first-century development, mobility, and sustainability challenges in the United States. One of the initial results of this research was the identification of eleven megaregions—networks of metropolitan areas with linked economies, infrastructure, and natural systems as well as common

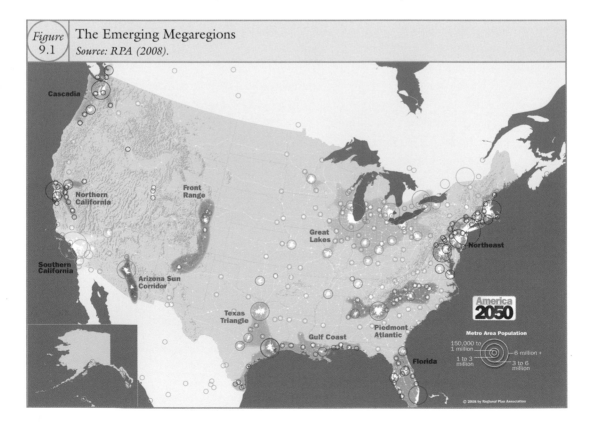

Figure 9.1 The Emerging Megaregions
Source: RPA (2008).

cultural values and histories. In size, they all extended for 300 to 600 miles and each accommodated populations that exceeded, or would soon exceed, 10 million people (figure 9.1).

Collectively, these regions comprise more than 70 percent of the nation's population and economic production and are home to an even larger share of its major research universities, medical centers, and other drivers of the innovation economy. Megaregions are of sufficient size to plan for large-scale infrastructure projects, ecosystem management, and regional economic development across metropolitan areas.

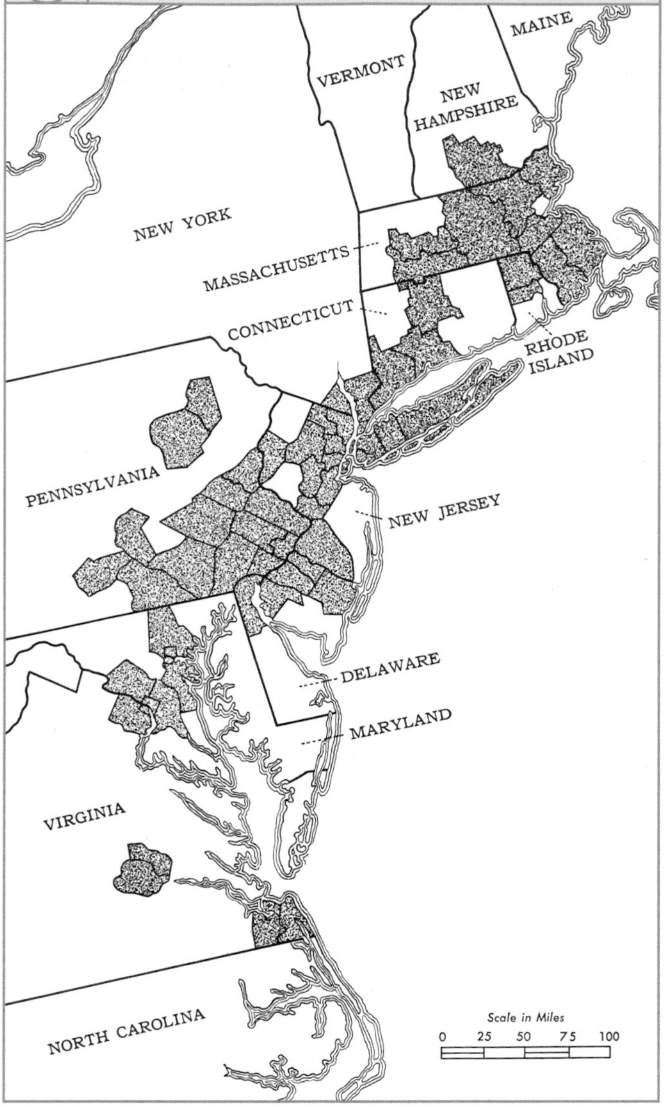

The megaregion concept is not new. Jean Gottman (1961) identified the emergence of what he termed the *Northeast megalopolis* half a century ago (figure 9.2). But the notion that the vast majority of the nation's residents and jobs were located in megaregions—and that these places had become the drivers of the nation's future growth—was a revelation. Since then Richard Florida, Robert Lang, Arthur (Chris) Nelson, and Catherine Ross, among several other researchers, have built upon Gottman's seminal work and contributed their own perspectives on the emergence of megaregions in the United States and elsewhere. Florida (2009), for example, has identified 40 megaregions around the world and has argued that these places are playing the same driving role in the global economy as the U.S. megaregions do here.

Figure 9.2

Gottman's Northeast Megalopolis, 1940–1950
Source: Reproduced by permission of The Century Foundation from Gottman (1961, 20).

In partnership with the Lincoln Institute of Land Policy, in 2005 RPA initiated America 2050—a program to promote national infrastructure and development planning in order to accommodate the nation's expected growth in more functional, livable, and sustainable forms. One particular focus of America 2050 has been national rail planning for both freight and passengers,

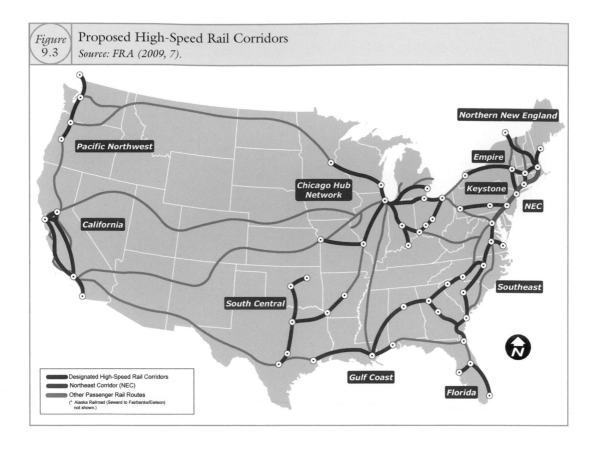

Figure 9.3. Proposed High-Speed Rail Corridors. Source: FRA (2009, 7).

with an emphasis on developing HSR corridors and integrating such rail capabilities with other transportation modes at the megaregion scale. The Federal Railroad Administration (FRA) has proposed HSR corridors in 11 named regions (figure 9.3).

If fully developed, this new mode of transportation could have profound effects, and it has the potential of becoming the mode of choice for intercity travel. While megaregions are too large to be easily traveled by automobile, they are not large enough for easy accessibility by air, and the already highly congested limited-access highways, airports, and airspace in the megaregions are expected to reach crush levels in coming decades. HSR is far more energy efficient than either air or auto travel, so investments in it should be viewed as part of a broader national energy strategy.

If the federal government follows through on its vision for a nationwide network of HSR lines serving the nation's megaregions, this system would provide fast, frequent, reliable, and convenient intercity and commuter rail links among each megaregion's component metropolitan areas and the suburbs in their paths. This could, in turn, create the foundation for new economic synergies between metropolitan areas and among metropolitan centers and second-tier cities, in the process enabling them all to reach their full economic, social, and environmental potential.

Achieving these goals will require original ways of thinking and innovative generation of integrated plans and investments at the megaregional, regional, urban, and station-area scales. It will also require a new level of vision and effectiveness from the nation's regional planning organizations and planners. The development of high-speed rail in megaregions offers a way for regional planning to contribute to the strategic preparation of the United States, its metropolitan regions, and its infrastructure for global economic competitiveness in this century.

LOOKING BACKWARD: INTERSTATE HIGHWAYS

The last time the introduction of a new mode of transportation catalyzed a major transformation in U.S. metropolitan regions was during the mid-twentieth century—in 1956—when the interstate highway system was initiated and then largely completed over the following three decades (figure 9.4).

At the outset, virtually no one—including the nation's regional planners—anticipated the fundamental changes the interstates would promote in the settlement patterns of the nation and its metropolitan regions. In his memoir, *Mandate for Change, 1953–1956*, former president Dwight D. Eisenhower (1963, 650) discussed the impacts that the interstate highway system would have on the nation's urban landscape. "More than any single action by

| Figure 9.4 | Proposed Interregional Highway System, 1939 |
| | *Source: U.S. Bureau of Public Roads (1955).* |

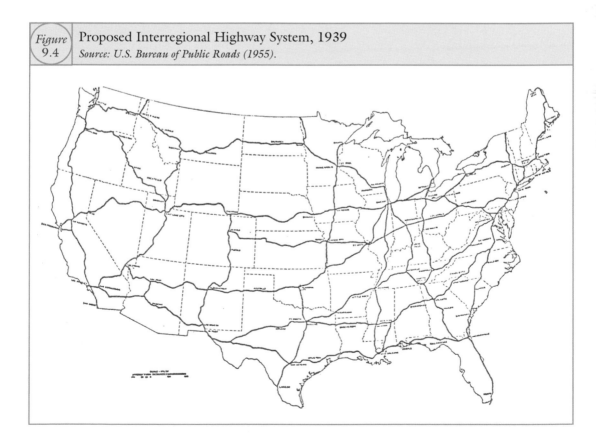

the government since the end of the war, this one would change the face of America. . . . Its impact on the American economy—the jobs it would produce in manufacturing and construction, the rural areas it would open up—was beyond calculation."

Little did he know how prophetic his words would prove to be. The interstates unleashed more than a half-century of low-density, automobile-based metropolitan growth and ushered in what we now know as urban sprawl. It is not clear, however, that President Eisenhower, Congressional leaders of the time, or the federal administrators who were responsible for building the interstates fully understood the extent of the forces they were unleashing with their decision to build the highway system. It is even less apparent that they recognized how difficult it would be to manage it. On 11 September 1957, referring to the administrators of the Federal Highway and Federal Housing Administrations at a national conference in Hartford, Connecticut, Lewis Mumford said that "neither of these administrators had the slightest notion of what they were doing. [If they did, they] would not appear as blithe and cocky" (Weingroff 2006).

The interstates opened up enormous areas of rural land to automobile-based suburban development (figure 9.5). Since 1956 the vast majority of U.S. residents have chosen to live in these places, seeking the detached single-family homes, quality schools and services, low taxes, open space, public safety, and other amenities that the suburbs promised to provide. As suburbia has matured in this country, however, many of the values that initially made these places attractive have vanished. Open land has disappeared, suburban roads have become congested, taxes have escalated, schools and other services have deteriorated, and crime has increased.

For more than one-half century, regional planners have fought rearguard actions to control sprawl and shape metropolitan development in more efficient, less damaging ways. The country's ability to achieve even modest climate and energy goals is now impeded by the decentralized, low-density, automobile-based settlement patterns of its metropolitan areas. Never in history has a settlement pattern consumed more land or energy or produced more greenhouse gas emissions than this one. In only a handful of U.S. metropolitan regions, such as Portland, have planners been able to curtail sprawl effectively and direct growth in more efficient, productive ways.

The interstates also provided a foundation upon which the United States could create enormous wealth and develop new productive capacity. In roughly 50 years, they enabled the country to accommodate twice its population and to expand its GDP dramatically. While the interstates permitted enormous mobility and enabled vast increases in economic growth, in terms of the amount of open land consumed and energy demands they have created the settlement patterns and built forms they promoted have been less satisfactory. Even more striking, the benefits did not accrue to everyone evenly. As we now know, certain communities, particularly those characterized by relatively large percentages

of racial- or ethnic-minority populations and/or low-income households, often
bore the brunt of the social, environmental, and health care costs associated
with highway-enabled sprawl. Central cities found themselves hollowed out and
falling behind, and often they were forced to adopt car-oriented strategies that
only hastened their decline.

What once appeared to be an inexorable flight to low-density communities,
however, now looks far less certain through the lenses provided by the knowledge economy, changing tastes, and growing recognition that key urban nodes
matter much more than we may have realized previously. In many suburbs, such
as those covering New York's Long Island, well-educated young people now
vote with their feet, fleeing these places for the bright lights of the very cities that their parents and grandparents abandoned. An analysis of census data
by CEOs for Cities (2005, 43–44) found that "today's 25- to 34-year-olds are
about 33 percent more likely than persons in other age groups to choose to
live in neighborhoods close to the center of the nation's 50 largest metropolitan areas. In fact, this margin of preference tripled in only 20 years." This same

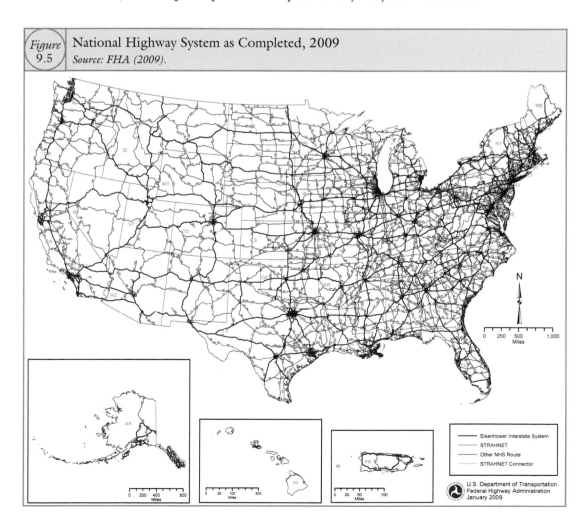

Figure 9.5 National Highway System as Completed, 2009
Source: FHA (2009).

study found that in three of the most densely populated metropolitan regions, 25- to 34-year-olds with college degrees were more than twice as likely to live within three miles of the core of those regions than in other, less-dense regions.

What might have seemed like the right development strategy in the 1950s and 1960s—when energy was cheap, water abundant, and open land a seemingly endless commodity—may not be the right strategy today. The United States is now the world's largest petroleum importer, faces shortages of easily developed land close to metropolitan centers, and has growing concerns about climate change. Much of the suburban fabric was designed for rapid depreciation and replacement over periods of fewer than 20 or 30 years. Therefore, much of this development and the land it occupies can be recycled for better and more intensive uses. But what should those new uses be, and how can we shape more satisfactory patterns of metropolitan development?

A TWENTY-FIRST-CENTURY GROWTH AND DEVELOPMENT AGENDA

Planners in the twenty-first century have inherited a coast-to-coast network of poorly planned metropolitan regions and limited financial resources with which to undertake the big investments in infrastructure and urban development that will be needed to accommodate projected population growth. Despite these challenges, the emergence of megaregions and development of a national HSR system as well as related metropolitan transit systems could provide the next generation of regional planners with a second chance to reshape these places. These investments could create the capacity for increased productivity and growth in GDP that are needed to underpin the next generation of major infrastructure and urban development ventures. Such a transformation could be accomplished in ways that increase the livability, functionality, and competitiveness of megaregions and metropolitan areas. Several trends will make this possible.

- *Population and economic growth.* The United States is virtually alone among present industrial economies in having a population that is exploding. It is predicted to add 130 million new residents—a 33 percent increase over current numbers—by 2050.

- *Changing lifestyles and community preferences.* The Pew Research Center has projected that 82 percent of this growth will result from the arrival of immigrants and their children, many of whom prefer urban to suburban densities and lifestyles (Passel and D'Vera 2008). The other growing segments of the population—including aging Boomers and young GenXers and Millennials—also prefer urban living. As a result, the suburbs are experiencing an exodus of young, well-educated, productive citizens, making those places, as currently configured, unsustainable in the marketplace as well as in virtually every other way.

- *Congested and deteriorating infrastructure.* Most metropolitan areas have exhausted the capacity of their segments of the interstate highway system, and fiscally strapped states in much of the country have virtually stopped even maintaining significant portions of it. Airports, seaports, water and sewer systems, and other major infrastructure systems in many metropolitan areas are reaching the limits of their design lives and capacities.

- *Built-out metropolitan regions.* Arthur C. Nelson (2004) and other observers have noted that to accommodate projected population and economic growth by 2030, the United States will require nearly three-quarters as much new built space—homes, offices, stores, warehouses, and so forth—over the next two decades as has been built over the past four centuries.

Unfortunately, because of the extensive land areas devoted to moving and storing automobiles, most of this country's suburbs have been built out at very low densities and thus have no capacity for additional growth. Unless new forms of suburban transit are built and innovative approaches to more transit- and pedestrian-friendly suburban development are created, these places allow virtually no room for growth. By contrast, New York City, a place that most people considered to have reached its built-out limits decades ago, has added approximately one million residents over the past generation, and it is expected to add an additional million residents by 2030. Ironically, many of these new residents will be the children of people currently living in built-out suburban communities.

Enlarging the scale and creating a new type of intercity and intraregional transportation infrastructure, by themselves, are no guarantee that the outcomes and excesses of the automobile era will not be repeated. The history of transportation infrastructure can be recounted in terms of waves of both concentration and diffusion. Inserting new infrastructure of this scale and intensity will surely have huge impacts on adjacent communities. In fact, if it does not, it will not be accomplishing its purposes.

How can regional planners respond to the opportunities provided by a new federal-level focus on regional planning, sustainability, and HSR to advance a generation of fresh regional plans for metropolitan areas and megaregions in the United States? And how can they integrate planning concerns at the megaregion, metropolitan, and community levels? Dutch planners use the expression "dancing with the scales" to help frame the answers to both of these questions. They mean that planners and policy makers need to address specific issues at the scale most appropriate to each one. Under this concept, for example, planning for traffic at an urban intersection should be addressed at the community scale, while development of a city's housing markets is best handled at the metropolitan scale and HSR configuration requires attention at the scale of the megaregion.

Can we extract lessons from the interstate era to guide us? Do we have the patience and creativity to take advantage of the new land use and transportation relationships emerging from the inception of a national HSR initiative? Can we use them to leverage benefits that will make the future more sustainable for everyone? Megaregional planning for high-speed rail gives us the chance to do it right, to create lasting value and real sustainability. Certainly there are risks, but in the context of on-the-job training for more than a century, planners now have the opportunity of their careers to do regional planning right.

THE EMERGENCE OF HIGH-SPEED RAIL PLANS IN THE UNITED STATES

Japan built the world's first high-speed rail route from Tokyo to Osaka in 1964. France inaugurated its HSR service in 1981 with a Paris-to-Lyon line that became the first link in a continental network of fast trains, which now interconnects much of Europe (figure 9.6). HSR systems have been built or are being developed or planned in more than a dozen industrialized countries in the Middle East and Asia (figure 9.7). Most of these, and those in other countries such as Brazil and Morocco, are being built as integral parts of broader national and regional mobility and economic development and as means to attain climate and energy goals.

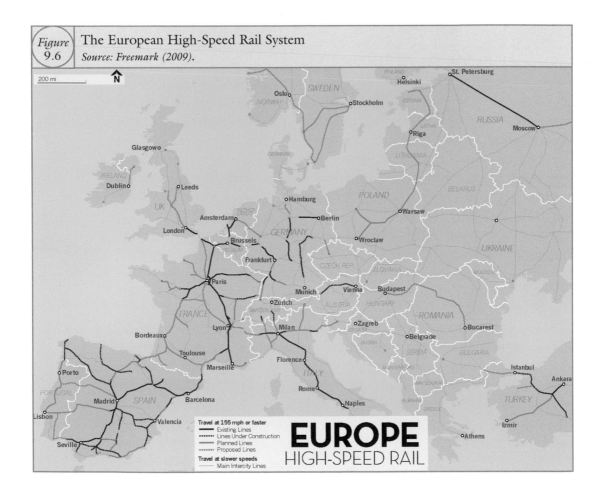

Figure 9.6	The European High-Speed Rail System
	Source: Freemark (2009).

The United States now has the opportunity to learn from the successes and pitfalls in other countries that have already built HSR systems. Researchers at the University of Pennsylvania and America 2050, who have been investigating the factors behind successful Asian and European HSR systems, have concluded that the most successful routes are those that (1) link densely populated cities within 100 to 600 miles of each other; (2) currently are linked by busy air corridors; and (3) have dense networks of transit and transit-oriented development (Todorovich and Hagler 2009).

In the United States, only Amtrak's Acela higher-speed service from Boston through New York to Washington, DC—the Northeast Corridor—even approaches being an HSR line. While the nation once had the world's most extensive passenger rail system, it has declined since the beginning of the interstate era, and it nearly collapsed during the 2000s. President Barack Obama abruptly changed the federal government's outlook on HSR early in 2009, when he insisted that $8.5 billion be included in the American Recovery and Reinvestment Act stimulus bill as a down payment on a national HSR program. Obama outlined his vision for this system on 16 April 2009:

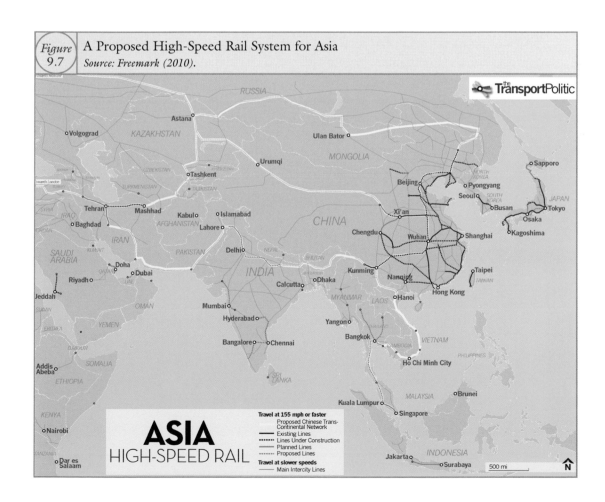

Figure 9.7 A Proposed High-Speed Rail System for Asia
Source: Freemark (2010).

What we're talking about is a vision for high-speed rail in America. Imagine boarding a train in the center of a city. No racing to an airport and across a terminal, no delays, no sitting on the tarmac, no lost luggage, no taking off your shoes. Imagine whisking through towns at speeds over 100 miles an hour, walking only a few steps to public transportation, and ending up just blocks from your destination. Imagine what a great project that would be to rebuild America. (Lee 2009)

Beyond meeting intercity mobility needs, HSR could also serve as a catalyst for the growth and development of megaregions and metropolitan regions in the twenty-first century, much as limited-access highways enabled the sprawling, decentralized U.S. metropolitan regions in the late twentieth century. Due to its centralizing effect, however, HSR also has the potential to promote more compact, efficient, transit-oriented patterns of development at both the megaregion and metropolitan scales. That is, the transportation and economic benefits of HSR are closely associated with networks of widely spaced stations that offer areas of activity concentration that are separated by relatively uncongested corridors. If HSR routes are properly designed and appropriately priced, and if the stations are located in center cities that have well-coordinated strategies for metropolitan transit and land use, HSR can serve a broad range of travel needs, including both intercity and high-speed commuter rail services.

Following its announcement of the HSR program in April 2009, the Obama administration presented its *Vision for High-Speed Rail in America* (FRA 2009), which proposes 10 HSR routes. In the first round of grants, the FRA sifted through more than $50 billion in HSR proposals to award $8 billion to 13 projects in 31 states and the District of Columbia. The administration and most observers saw this funding as a down payment on what ultimately could become a half-trillion-dollar investment. In its first and second grant-making rounds, FRA did not insist that HSR projects be closely coordinated with local transit, land use, and station-area development plans. Consequently, in the two largest funded projects (in Florida and California), HSR corridors are being developed with stations outside urban centers and with poor transit connections to the cities they serve.

The Obama administration's definition of high-speed rail is different from that in other countries. Worldwide, definitions of what qualifies as high-speed range from Amtrak's Acela service (which can reach speeds of 150 mph, but averages 86 mph) to the operating speeds of French, Chinese, and Spanish systems (which average approximately 200 mph). In April 2009, the FRA defined three categories of high-speed rail:

- **HSR Express**—frequent service for distances from 200 to 600 miles, reaching speeds of 150 mph on grade-separated, dedicated rights of way;

- *HSR Regional*—relatively frequent service for distances of between 100 and 500 miles, reaching speeds from 110 to 150 mph on a mix of dedicated and shared tracks; and

- *Emerging HSR*—developing corridors with strong potential for future HSR Express or Regional service, reaching top speeds of 90 to 110 mph mostly on shared tracks.

While not every corridor may require HSR Express service, incremental investments in HSR Regional and Emerging HSR routes can serve important transportation and economic development needs and build ridership for subsequent development of dedicated-track HSR Express routes.

U.S. Secretary of Transportation Raymond LaHood has estimated the total cost for an ambitious HSR program to be more than one-half trillion dollars (Nussbaum 2010). It is clear that this vision cannot be achieved with occasional, modest annual appropriations. Consequently, skepticism is growing about whether a fully developed HSR system will ever be completed in this country. For it to happen, a new dedicated source of funding will be required to complete the Obama administration's HSR vision, but this is part of the larger challenge of finding a new dedicated revenue source for the entire surface transportation program.

Despite the administration's enthusiasm for HSR, it has yet to identify a funding source. For that matter, neither the administration nor Congress has advanced a financing strategy for the other complementary transportation modes needed to make HSR work. This is despite the fact that the vision of high-speed rail for the United States appears to have broad public support. A February 2010 national public opinion survey found that 88 percent of respondents support development of a national HSR system (HNTB 2010). This backing also has been translated into funding commitments at the ballot box. For example, in 2008 California voters approved a $9.95 billion bond issue to build the state's HSR system from San Diego to San Francisco and Sacramento.

As noted earlier, Ohio and Wisconsin have announced plans to drop their HSR projects, and Florida is reconsidering its support for the proposed Tampa-Orlando HSR route. Even so, more than 30 other states plan to proceed with HSR development. If the country does follow through with a robust commitment to HSR, will this and the next generation of regional planners have the foresight to get it right this time? Or will a future Lewis Mumford say about us that we, too, hadn't the faintest notion of what we were doing? Once again, neither Congress nor the White House, nor for that matter the planning profession, has given much thought to this system's potential to reshape the face of U.S. megaregions. In addition, few state-level departments of transportation and HSR authorities deem coordinated regional planning, station-area development, and metropolitan transit planning to be within their purview.

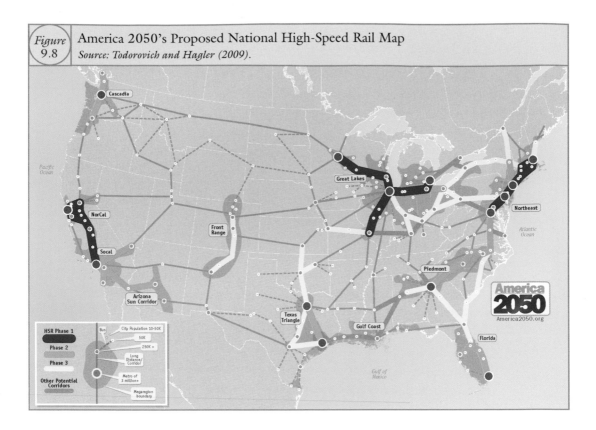

Figure 9.8   America 2050's Proposed National High-Speed Rail Map
Source: Todorovich and Hagler (2009).

But what if we manage to get ahead of the curve this time, anticipating the forces of urbanization that this new mode of transportation can unleash, and shaping them to benefit the long-term public interest (figure 9.8)?

TOWARD A NEW REGIONALISM: HOW HSR CAN PROVIDE A PLATFORM FOR A NEW GENERATION OF REGIONAL PLANS

The emerging HSR system in the United States could provide a superstructure for a new generation of more effective national, megaregional, and regional transportation plans and urban development strategies. In turn these could shape megaregions and metropolitan regions in such a way that they become more compact and efficient in terms of energy and land use, and most of their development would be organized around transit and transit-oriented programs. Experience in completed European and Asian HSR systems indicates that ridership is highest when HSR services interconnect densely populated cities that have fully developed transit systems, and when already strong economic and transportation links exist between cities.

Beyond the Northeast, however, few U.S. cities have large transit systems, so the national commitment to HSR should include a renewed effort to create, strengthen, or expand local and regional transit systems and station areas. To realize fully the potential for mobility and economic development offered by

Grand Central Station, New York
Source: Photograph © RPA.

this vast investment in HSR, the federal government needs to insist that stations be sited in well-situated downtown locations, where they can serve as gateways, magnetic destinations, and catalysts for center-city development and as hubs of expanded metropolitan transit systems.

Experience in Europe and Asia also suggests that, by creating synergies between what are known as "hot" and "cold" places, HSR can lead to opportunities for the redevelopment of underperforming cities and regions. Perhaps the best-documented example is Lille, France, which is situated at the junction of HSR links to Paris, London, and Brussels (Bannister and Berechman 2000; Meade 1994). As a manufacturing nucleus in northern France, Lille was in decline, but by building on its new accessibility to metropolitan hubs across northwestern Europe, it has transformed itself into a successful center for service industries and retail and conference activities.

Lille's transformation required major economic development and urban revitalization investments from the European Union and the French government. In the absence of effective economic development strategies, however, some weak market cities and regions that now have HSR connections to larger hot market cities have lost residents and jobs to more successful places, such as Lille, or have not benefited in the way that it has.

Chia-Lin Chen and Sir Peter Hall (2009) have studied the impact of the higher-speed (125 mph) rail service introduced in England in the 1970s and 1980s on the performance of cities that were brought within one- and two-hour commuting distances of London (figure 9.9). They found that this new accessibility to the capital

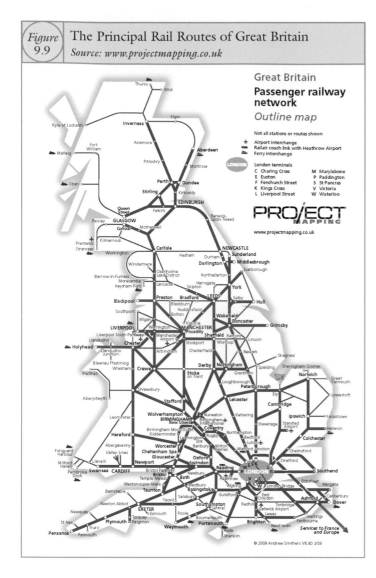

The Principal Rail Routes of Great Britain

Source: www.projectmapping.co.uk

transformed most of these cities, many of which experienced dramatic growth in service sector jobs and a rise in commercial and residential rents as their residents' incomes increased and greater numbers of them commuted into London.

The United Kingdom has made a commitment to developing its HSR system, in part, to integrate the economy and workforce of the former manufacturing belt of the Midlands and northern England with the service economy of London and the southeast (UK Department for Transport 2010). Chen and Hall note, however, that some older industrial cities that are home to high proportions of unskilled workers did not develop effective economic development strategies locally, and thus did not benefit from enhanced rail access (Chen and Hall 2009).

In Asia, South Korea has developed a national economic development strategy centered on its new HSR system. China is organizing a similar strategy around its emerging system, and has specified the goal of strengthening economic ties between its booming coastal cities and those inland that are struggling. These experiences underscore the conclusion that HSR has the potential to promote a new economic geography, though as we in the United States have learned from the development of the interstate highways, our ability to link plans, policies, and investments better at all scales will determine whether we get the results we seek or something else entirely.

By focusing on megaregion-scale economic development strategies, the United States can promote the regeneration of underperforming cities and regions. In the Great Lakes megaregion, for example, an emerging HSR network focusing on a Chicago hub can create new economic connections between it and other hot cities such as Minneapolis, Indianapolis, Columbus, and

Toronto and cold cities such as Milwaukee, St. Louis, Detroit, and Buffalo. Three isolated industrial centers—Cleveland, Youngstown, and Pittsburgh—are exploring the potential for an HSR link to create economic agglomerations among them that currently do not exist.

CASE STUDY: HSR AS THE PLATFORM FOR AN ECONOMIC DEVELOPMENT STRATEGY AT THE MEGAREGION SCALE

In the spring of 2010 a graduate planning studio at the University of Pennsylvania, led by the author and Penn Design School's dean, Marilyn Taylor, proposed that a new HSR system be built in the Northeast Megaregion, which stretches from Boston to Washington, DC. The studio recommended investing $100 billion to develop two new dedicated HSR tracks running the length of the 457-mile corridor. This system's design goals include cutting travel times by half, which would make them 105 minutes from Boston to New York and 90 minutes from New York to Washington. Intercity scheduling would increase from the present two trains per hour to twelve, and passenger capacity would rise from the present rate of fewer than 1,000 to 12,000 passengers per hour. At the same time, the already dense use of the existing Northeast Corridor commuter rail networks would increase in both capacity and reliability.

In September 2010 Amtrak announced its own plans to add two new dedicated HSR tracks running from Boston to Washington in a plan that closely paralleled the principles outlined in the Penn studio, including proposals for new downtown stations in Baltimore and Philadelphia.

The unique economic geography of the northeastern United States makes the region suitable for HSR and for megaregion-scale economic development, mobility, and urban growth strategies. Its economy is driven by five large metropolitan areas—Boston, New York, Philadelphia, Baltimore, and Washington—and a network of smaller urban centers strung like pearls along the current rail corridor. Boston, New York, and Washington are hot regions, with expanding populations, employment, and household incomes. Philadelphia, Baltimore, and smaller cities such as Trenton, New Haven, and Hartford are cold places where the numbers of residents and jobs, like household incomes, are in decline.

The Northeast already claims 90 percent of total U.S. urban rail ridership and 75 percent of national commuter rail passengers. The Penn HSR plan would provide 42 cities that have stations on the proposed HSR system with reliable, frequent service and travel times of less than one hour from one of the Northeast's hot cities. This would create the opportunity to transform the economies of these cold cities, resulting in a new economic geography for the entire Northeast Megaregion (figure 9.10).

This plan would also promote regeneration of central Philadelphia and Baltimore by proposing new HSR stations, along with major new commercial and

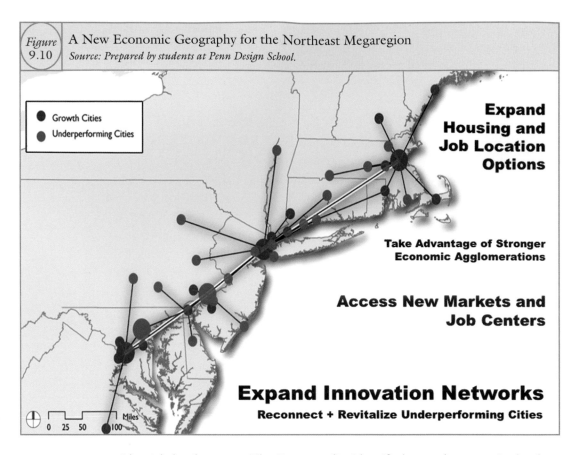

Figure 9.10
A New Economic Geography for the Northeast Megaregion
Source: Prepared by students at Penn Design School.

- Growth Cities
- Underperforming Cities

Expand Housing and Job Location Options

Take Advantage of Stronger Economic Agglomerations

Access New Markets and Job Centers

Expand Innovation Networks
Reconnect + Revitalize Underperforming Cities

Miles
0   25   50   100

residential development. The Penn studio identified several economic development theories that could underpin HSR in this and other megaregions.

- *Urban agglomeration.* In her book *Cities and the Wealth of Nations,* Jane Jacobs (1985) concludes that urban economies are based on agglomerations of skilled workers and firms. Firms are attracted to larger, higher-density centers because they have greater concentrations of skilled workers. Networks of firms in the same industry are attracted to larger centers for the same reason, thus creating specialization, innovation, and industry clusters. A new HSR system in the Northeast, for example, could draw workers from Hartford and Philadelphia into businesses based in Manhattan, and firms in the smaller cities could attract workers from New York's vast labor market.

- *Expanded commutersheds and housing markets.* Compared to existing commutersheds, those with HSR service can encompass much larger areas and incorporate a number of formerly freestanding labor markets. This is especially important to two-worker households, which constitute a large and increasing share in the Northeast. The same principle applies to housing markets, where cities that have been experiencing housing abandonment, such as Philadelphia and Baltimore, can be incorporated into the larger New York and Washington markets, which need relief from shortages and rising prices for housing.

● *Innovation networks.* Of the world's twenty top research universities, the Northeast is home to eight—seven of which are situated in close proximity to proposed HSR stations. This gives the Northeast a unique opportunity to promote collaboration for cutting-edge research (ARWU 2007). Professor Lee Fleming of the Harvard Business School and others have mapped "innovation networks" in the Boston area, finding that scientific and technical innovations are most likely to occur through face-to-face communication among researchers (Fleming and Marx 2006; Goudrais 2010). Concerning invention, Michael Polyani's (1967) work also supports the idea that the requisite tacit knowledge (i.e., concepts that cannot be easily communicated by written or spoken communication) can best be developed and communicated by means of face-to-face interaction. Currently, the vast majority of this kind of interaction in the Northeast occurs within a single metropolitan region, but HSR would make it possible for workers in cities at further distances from each other to share the same opportunities for personal collaboration.

Fabio Casiroli and Vincenzo Donato (2005) of the Politecnico di Milano, investigated travel time impacts of HSR in western Europe. They posited that the longest business trip that could be completed in one day involved four hours of door-to-door travel time each way. When they calculated the extent of the area that could be covered from several European cities in four hours by car, air, conventional rail, and HSR, they found that HSR dramatically expanded opportunities for face-to-face communication (figure 9.11).

The Penn studio conducted a similar analysis for the Northeast, in which they looked at the travel times and numbers of residents and jobs that a traveler could reach from Philadelphia by car, air, and HSR (figure 9.12). The traveler could reach 35.9 million people and 16.5 million jobs by car and 29.7 million people and 13.6 million jobs by air. By the HSR alternative, however, travelers could reach 50.8 million people and 24.3 million jobs—42 and 46 percent more, respectively—than car travel could accommodate.

Despite the presence of dense networks of urban railroads in the Northeast, most post–World War II development has been in automobile-based suburbs and exurbs. RPA's America 2050 program has developed comparative analyses of population and employment densities in Northeast and Sunbelt cities (Todorovich and Hagler 2010). The results show that the Northeast's major regions continue to have far higher concentrations of residents and jobs than their Sunbelt counterparts.

Nevertheless, after four decades of population loss and, in some cases, extensive housing abandonment and commercial decline in inner city and inner ring suburban areas, the Northeast's metropolitan regions also have extensive opportunities for infill and redevelopment. RPA has determined, for example, that virtually all of Long Island's housing needs through 2040 could be accommodated

Figure 9.11	Travel Networks in Europe
	Source: Casiroli and Donato (2005).

Air

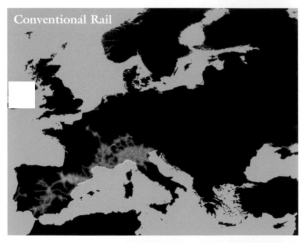

Conventional Rail

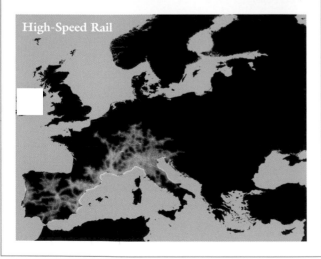

High-Speed Rail

by medium-density infill development on just one-half of the 8,300 acres of surface parking lots and vacant lots that currently lie within walking distance of stations on the Long Island Rail Road system (RPA 2010a). RPA (2010b) has also recently completed suburban infill strategies for the Long Island town of Freeport, along with other transit-accessible communities in New Jersey and Connecticut. They demonstrate the potential to create high-value, mixed-use communities on vacant lots and surface parking areas (figure 9.13).

These reports demonstrate kinds of transit-oriented infill, intensification, and redevelopment opportunities exist throughout the Northeast. Baltimore, Philadelphia, and virtually every older city along the corridor have extensive inventories of vacant and derelict residential and industrial land that could be redeveloped to meet the megaregion's housing and other needs for decades to come. As the consumer preferences of many sectors of the population—including aging Boomers, young and well-educated professionals, and immigrants—shift toward urban living, these trends will be further supported. HSR could be the catalyst, but effective regional and community plans and bold revitalization strategies will be needed to unlock much of this potential, particularly in urban communities presently characterized by extensive dereliction, poverty, and crime.

REFORMING REGIONAL PLANNING THROUGH FEDERAL INCENTIVES

As another form of incentive to participation, the federal government could direct economic development, environmental, infrastructure, affordable housing, and other kinds of discretionary grants to regions that develop plans around HSR and transit investments. The Department of Housing and Urban Development (HUD) and other agencies have already provided a foundation for this effort by stating their intention to focus support on regions that have completed Sustainable Communities Initiative (SCI)–funded plans.

By ramping up and coordinating HSR grants with its new Transportation Investment Generating Economic Recovery (TIGER) and SCI programs, the government could provide powerful incentives for a new generation of comprehensive regional plans and transportation investments. For these efforts to succeed, however, reform of existing metropolitan planning organizations (MPOs) is required to ensure that they represent the regions they serve more broadly and possess the technical capabilities required to take on these new responsibilities. MPOs will need to develop new teeth and increase their public support to ensure that their plans are carried out.

HUD is also using SCI grants to help broaden the MPOs' purview beyond their traditional, narrow transportation focus. The goal of SCI is to fund plans that will integrate transportation issues with concerns regarding affordable housing, climate change, economic development, and land use,

Figure 9.12	Travel Time Analysis for the Northeast
	Source: Prepared by students at Penn Design School.

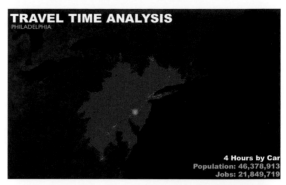

TRAVEL TIME ANALYSIS
PHILADELPHIA

4 Hours by Car
Population: 46,378,913
Jobs: 21,849,719

TRAVEL TIME ANALYSIS
PHILADELPHIA

4 Hours by Car: Heavy Congestion
Population: 35,856,978
Jobs: 16,511,162

TRAVEL TIME ANALYSIS
PHILADELPHIA

4 Hours by Air, then Other Mode
Population: 29,723,077
Jobs: 13,588,854

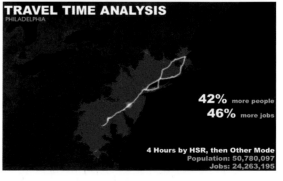

TRAVEL TIME ANALYSIS
PHILADELPHIA

42% more people
46% more jobs

4 Hours by HSR, then Other Mode
Population: 50,780,097
Jobs: 24,263,195

Figure
9.13
Plans for Freeport, New York
Source: RPA (2010b).

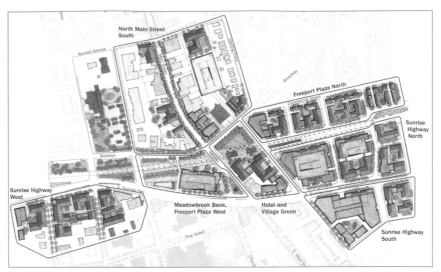

Freeport Downtown Illustrative Plan (Transit-Oriented Development Area)

Freeport Village Green (before)

Freeport Village Green (after)

among others. Coalitions of MPOs could assume this new, larger role at the metropolitan scale by advancing broader civic engagement procedures, employing leadership reflective of each region's diversity, and utilizing professional expertise that encompasses these new mandates. MPOs could partner with civic-led regional planning organizations, such as New York's Regional Plan Association, the Metropolitan Planning Council in Chicago, or the San Francisco Planning + Urban Research Association, to develop and implement these plans.

Presently, this is happening in the Northeast, where new partnerships between the RPA and several cities, counties, and MPOs have joined together in one of HUD's SCI-funded projects to promote transit-oriented development around the expanding commuter rail networks serving New York City, Long Island, Westchester County, and coastal Connecticut. A second SCI project focuses on similar opportunities in the regions of Hartford and nearby Springfield. A proposed intercity rail service will run between Springfield and New Haven.

To build political support, many MPOs will need to expand their boards to include new members from urban and minority communities, business and civic interests, and other constituencies so that they become more representative of the populations they serve. Again, federally funded, incentive-based grants can provide the impetus for these and other reforms.

A new Northeast Corridor Infrastructure and Operations Advisory Commission, established pursuant to the provisions of the Passenger Rail Investment and Improvement Act of 2008, is creating a planning and coordination entity for the region. Its membership includes state transportation commissioners or their delegates from the eight states in the Boston-to-Washington corridor plus the District of Columbia, as well as those from Amtrak and the FRA. It remains to be seen whether this commission will be able to coordinate state investments in commuter rail and transit with those for intercity and high-speed rail services.

Until now, the states and Amtrak have looked at the congested Northeast Corridor as a zero-sum gain, in which improved intercity rail service can be created only at the expense of commuter rail services and vice versa. It also remains to be seen if this new commission will coordinate economic and station-area development strategies in the Northeast with rail investments. Traditionally, state DOTs, FRA, and Amtrak have not paid much attention to these concerns. The RPA-sponsored Business Alliance for Northeast Mobility, a coalition of leading business, civic, and government groups from throughout the corridor, is eager to help the commission make these connections and will advocate for such outcomes.

None of this will succeed, however, unless a new generation of creative and politically astute regional planners can be attracted to the field to lead these plans and administer new regional development programs. As the clout of MPOs and other regional organizations grows, and as opportunities emerge to transform large areas of the country with these plans and investments, thousands of new job opportunities should be created for regional planners in megaregions and metropolitan regions across the country.

CONCLUSION

The United States urgently needs a new, long-range plan for national infrastructure and development because, for the first time in the nation's history, we find ourselves flying blind in the absence of such a strategy. In 1808, the 1860s, 1908, and again in the 1930s, the federal government prepared national infrastructure and growth strategies. Most recently, this happened during the New Deal, when the NRPB promoted national, state, and regional investment strategies for the country's major infrastructure systems. These included the board's 1938 proposal for a national toll road and free road system, which provided the inspiration for what later became President Eisenhower's 1956 National Defense and Interstate Highway System. Today, virtually all of the capacity of these major infrastructure systems has been consumed.

A new national infrastructure strategy is urgently needed to create the capacity in these systems, which the United States will need in coming decades to compete with other nations. This comes at a juncture where, for the first time in more than a century, new competitors are challenging U.S. leadership in the global economy. China, India, Brazil, and other countries are moving ahead with major investments in HSR, urban transit systems, and related economic development strategies. It is becoming clear that we will need effective new action strategies to deal with energy and climate issues if we are to address these growing challenges successfully.

This country has an opportunity to promote an integrated national infrastructure and metropolitan development strategy that will build upon the vision for a nationwide HSR system. Given the current legislative focus on deficit reduction and the partisanship in Washington, getting the Congress to deal with and pass such an effort will not be easy. But in our federal system, even in the absence of leadership at that level, it is possible for states and regions to take the lead from the bottom up on these issues. In fact, in the Cascadia, Great Lakes, Piedmont Atlantic, and Northeast megaregions, among others, governors and mayors are providing this leadership and promoting development of new HSR routes.

The fiscal, global competitiveness, national security, energy, climate, and other challenges presently facing the country could crowd out the longer-term transportation investment strategies. In other periods of national crisis, however, U.S. leaders have risen to the occasion to create new ways to address fundamental problems that were facing the country. In the early 1860s, perhaps the darkest period in U.S. history, President Abraham Lincoln created national development strategies designed to unite the nation and build its economic future by initiating the Transcontinental Railroad, land grant university system, Homestead Act, and other bold initiatives that permanently shaped the nation's future in new and positive directions.

The Obama administration and Congress have the opportunity to provide comparable leadership for the United States in the twenty-first century if they follow through on their initial commitment to building a national high-speed rail network and related investments in urban and regional transit and urban regeneration. The new Congress elected in November 2010 is more conserva-tive than its predecessor, and the new Republican-led House leadership is more skeptical about public spending in general and HSR in particular than the previ-ous Democratic-led House. Nonetheless, these investments would enable eco-nomic growth for decades to come, and in turn create an opportunity for this and the next generations of regional planners to build the plans and institutions needed to ensure more competitive, livable, and sustainable megaregions and metropolitan regions well into the remainder of this century.

REFERENCES

ARWU (Academic Ranking of World Universities). 2007. Academic ranking of world universities, 2007. Shanghai Jiao Tong University. http://www.arwu.org/ARWU2007.jsp

Bannister, David, and Joseph Berechman. 2000. *Transport investment and economic development.* London: UCL Press.

Casiroli, Fabio, and Vincenzo Donato. 2005. *High speed train, organized territory.* Presentation to Conference on Europe of the Cities, Europe of the Regions, Milan, (7 November). www.uic-highspeed2008.com/2005/docs/pres/c1/fabio_casiroli.pdf

CEOs for Cities. 2005. *The young and restless in a knowledge economy.* (December). Washington, DC. www.ceosforcities.org/pagefiles/CEOs_YNR_FINAL.pdf

Chen, Chia-Lin, and Peter Hall. 2009. *The impacts of high-speed trains on British economic geography: A study of the UK's IC125/225 and its effects.* London: University College London.

Eisenhower, Dwight D. 1963. *Mandate for change, 1953–1956.* Garden City, NY: Doubleday.

FHA (Federal Highway Administration). 2009. (January). Washington, DC.

Fleming, Lee, and M. Marx. 2006. Managing creativity in small worlds. *California Management Review* 48(4):6–27.

Florida, Richard. 2009. Mega-regions and high-speed rail. *Atlantic Monthly* (4 May). www.theatlantic .com/national/archive/2009/05/mega-regions-and-high-speed-rail/17006/

FRA (Federal Railroad Administration). 2009. *Vision for high-speed rail in America.* Washington, DC.

Freemark, Yonah. 2009. European high-speed rail expands across the continent with five new line segments. *The Transport Politic.* www.thetransportpolitic.com/2009/12/11/european-high-speed-rail-expands-across-the-continent-with-five-new-line-segments/

———. 2010. China promotes its transcontinental ambitions with massive rail plan. *The Trans-port Politic.* www.thetransportpolitic.com/2010/03/09/china-promotes-its-transcontinental-ambitions-with-massive-rail-plan/

Gottman, Jean. 1961. *Megalopolis: The urbanized seaboard of the United States.* Cambridge, MA: MIT Press.

Goudrais, Elizabeth. 2010. Innovation at the intersection. *Harvard* magazine (December).

HNTB. 2010. America's high-speed rail aspirations remain strong. (18 February). www.hntb.com/news-room/news-release/america%E2%80%99s-high-speed-rail-aspirations-remain-strong

Jacobs, Jane. 1985. *Cities and the wealth of nations.* New York: Random House.

Lee, Jesse. 2009. A vision for high speed rail. Blog (16 April). Washington, DC: White House. www .whitehouse.gov/blog/09/04/16/A-Vision-for-High-Speed-Rail/

Meade, Martin K. 1994. Euralille, the instant city. *Architectural Review* (December).

Nelson, Arthur C. 2004. *Toward a new metropolis: The opportunity to rebuild America.* Washington, DC: Brookings Institution Metropolitan Policy Program.

Nussbaum, Paul. 2010. LaHood sees bright future for high-speed trains in U.S. *Philadelphia Inquirer* (August 11).

Passel, Jeffrey, and D'Vera Cohen. 2008. *U.S. population projections, 2005–2050.* (11 February). Washington, DC: Pew Research Center. http://pewhispanic.org/reports/report.php?ReportID=85

Polanyi, Michael. 1967. *The tacit dimension.* New York: Anchor Books.

RPA (Regional Plan Association). 1929. *Plan for New York and its environs.* New York.

———. 1968. *Second regional plan.* New York.

———. 2008. The emerging megaregions. (America 2050 map). New York. www.america2050.org/images/2050_Map_Megaregions2008_150.png

———. 2010a. *Places to grow: An analysis of the potential for transit-accessible housing and jobs in Long Island's downtowns and station areas.* (January). Garden City, NY: Long Island Index. http://longislandindex.org/fileadmin/Reports_and_Maps/2010_Index/2010_Index.pdf

———. 2010b. *Freeport station area plan master plan.* New York.

Todorovich, Petra, and Yoav Hagler. 2009. *Where high-speed rail works best.* New York: Regional Plan Association.

———. 2010. *High-speed rail in America.* New York: Regional Plan Association.

UK Department for Transport. 2010. *High-speed rail.* White paper. London.

U.S. Bureau of Public Roads. 1955. General location of national system of interstate highways including all additional routes at urban areas designated in September 1955. Washington, DC. www.ajfroggie.com/roads/yellowbook/

Weingroff, Richard F. 2006. The greatest decade 1956–1966: Essential to the national interest. Washington, DC: U.S. Federal Highway Administration. www.fhwa.dot.gov/infrastructure/50interstate.cfm

10 REGIONAL PRACTICE, REGIONAL PROSPECT

Ethan Seltzer and Armando Carbonell

The idea for this book began some years ago as a discussion about what made regional planning different from other kinds of planning, what that meant for practice, and where we go from here. For those engaged in regional planning, or simply convinced that regional planning is an important and distinct form of planning practice, this kind of dialogue is quite common. Although the United States has long been described in terms of its regions—the South, North, East, and West; the Rust, Cotton, Corn, and Borscht Belts, and the list goes on—the story of planning in this country has been written largely as a practice associated with cities, other local units of government, states, and occasionally, the federal government. Regional planning, unlike other kinds of planning, always must both find and defend its place.

This is not accidental. The distribution of powers as put forth in the Constitution offers little to regions. At best, they have been used to make administrative processes easier to manage. At worst, the notion of regional planning has been held up as a fundamental threat to local control and home rule and, in more rhetorical ways, to democracy itself. Regional planning practice in the United States has long tended to focus on the "low-hanging fruit" of coordination and system efficiency. More challenging arenas having to do with comprehensive planning, growth management, sustainability, and resiliency have been relegated largely to aspiration rather than action. Barring either a clear-cut case for efficiency measured in strict financial terms (e.g., regional facilities for wastewater or solid waste management) or to prepare for cataclysmic crises (earthquakes, water shortages, flood control), regional planning has had a difficult time making its case.

As the essays in this book have suggested, however, regional planning is more than just imaginable. In some cases, it is being accomplished, and for purposes inspired by collective aspirations that go beyond marginal improvements in system efficiency. This does not mean that U.S. regional planning has advanced to the point where it can respond consistently to the clear regional basis for economies and ecologies and meet demands for greater sustainability and social justice. It does signal, we believe, a juncture when regional planning may get new attention and respect, and revisiting what makes regional planning different and how planners need to be equipped in order to excel is an important place to start.

In that spirit, three central themes can be distilled from the work presented here. First is the critical task of *defining the region*—the initial necessity for all regional planning practice. Next comes *organizing the region*, because regional planners must go beyond being generalists with a specialty and become organizers with a specialty. The third theme, *sustaining the region*, is accomplished by responding directly to the institutional challenges of sponsoring and acting on regional plans.

DEFINING THE REGION

Regional boundaries can be defined simply and reflect a single attribute or function, or they may be more complex and embody a range of factors. Whether simple or complex, however, the case needs to be made for the actual existence of a region before planning can begin. Most often, regions are defined by a set of overlapping attributes and concerns. This usually means that the centers of regions are easy to identify and their outer edges are much more indistinct, or "fuzzy." In contrast, the jurisdictions through which planning typically occurs—cities, townships, parishes, and counties—have exact boundaries that demarcate the territory within which their authority resides. Whereas these jurisdictions are able to proceed with a clear sense of where their territory lies and what powers they hold, with their planning authority intact and unquestioned, regions must first negotiate their boundaries, authorities, and purpose.

Regions, then, must always fend for themselves. While there is only one city in every city and one state in every state, there may be many regions crossing through every city and state. In fact, every place is likely contributing to several different "regions"—bioregion, economic region, cultural region, political region, etc. Defining the region is critically important for regional planning. This is the only way to create direct links among the territory, the purposes for planning, and the planning itself. In regional planning, nothing is assumed. By defining the region, we articulate what we are planning *for*. Territory clarifies the purposes and scope of regional planning because it is described with respect to function and encapsulates purpose.

This is, in fact, why regional planning, or at least memorable and effective regional planning, happens so rarely: Defining a region directly interferes with existing conceptions about both territory and power. At least at the outset, regional planning cannot help but be regarded as a challenge to the ways that boundaries have been defined, disputed, and settled. With those boundaries come powers that will not be ceded willingly, even in the face of fact and impeccable logic.

Making the case for a region is at once a first and a critical step in any regional planning exercise. It has to be done in a compelling manner, a lesson that is reflected in the work presented in this book. Kathryn Foster states forthrightly, "regional planning means planning for shared space." That is, by definition regions are composites of many features, concerns, and authorities, and enlisting them all is at the heart of the art of regional planning. Timothy Beatley's "green regionalism" explicitly calls for a "nested" geography of territories and purposes. In his formulation, defining the green region establishes the actual ecology and building blocks of ecological function and recovery as sharing the same frame for planning and action as political divisions. He argues that the region is the essential scale for which planning for sustainability and understanding and defining the green region constitute the first step.

Two other chapters—those by Gerrit-Jan Knaap and Rebecca Lewis and by Manuel Pastor and Chris Benner—point to the metropolitan region as an important scale for planning and action. To Knapp and Lewis, this is true for the purposes of growth management, while Pastor and Benner find it so in terms of advancing social justice and conditions of equity in society. In both cases, planning begins by reframing issues at a metropolitan scale. They also agree that the necessity of working at this scale is complicated notably by the lack of capable institutions that can match it. Pastor and Benner explicitly note that planners working at the regional scale must become comfortable with fuzzy boundaries, reaffirming the notion that defining the region remains a difficult and ongoing task.

ORGANIZING THE REGION

In defining a region, creating a regional plan, and acting on the results, planners have to intervene in pre-existing agreements concerning who will do what and who controls what. Thus, in some ways, the role of the planner is similar to that of a community organizer. We use the term *community* all the time, but the existence of communities—particularly regional communities—is far from certain. Further, even when any type of community exists, its capacity to affect decisions and to exercise power over its fate is never something that can be taken for granted. Like a community organizer, the regional planner needs to make shared interests apparent and help to articulate them in ways that make regional planning an asset rather than a threat in serving a range of local and regional goals. Regional planning is akin to an ongoing conversation, and regional planners need to become adept at recognizing what makes their contributions vital, acceptable, and respected.

However, this does not mean that regional planning is merely an accretion of local desires or that it lacks explicit purposes. For regional planners, the metaphor of organizing is presented both to suggest an outcome (shared objectives and desires) as well as a style. As Pastor and Benner note, regional planners need to proceed with humility. Similarly, Foster calls for planners to seek the common threads that enable boundary-crossing planning and action to occur. John Fregonese and C. J. Gabbe outline a planning process that begins with an examination of commonly held regional values, and Robert Yaro's megaregions are posited as becoming loci for common cause in the country's struggle for global competitiveness. Regional planners have to be adept at "dancing with scales," able to interact successfully across boundaries and to envision the fundamental interconnectedness of our world.

Again, regional planning calls for clear purposes articulated in concert with the way in which the region is defined. Organizing the region to act on those purposes requires acknowledging the needs and concerns of local and other jurisdictional interests, but it cannot be limited to the strictly local. Indeed, it can serve to mediate effectively between local interests (not in my backyard) and the needs of society at large. The art of regional planning, like the art of community organizing, is to understand the widest possible range of interests in the broadest possible context. In this way, regional planners can begin the hard work of creating, nurturing, and stewarding the community that is necessary for making and implementing regional plans.

Both the definition of the region and activation of the regional community provide the foundation for regional planning. The engagement of planners with the region has to occur before the planning begins, however, and it must continue after the plan has been completed. To some degree, this ongoing engagement of planners, plans, and planning is implied in typical descriptions of planning processes. After a plan is made, adopted, and implemented, presumably feedback loops will be created to inform decision makers about the efficacy of the plans and the need for adjustments or even new plans.

This kind of feedback is rarely present at the local level, and if it is, often it falls within the province of some other set of actors on a local stage. Once the plan is done, regional planning and planners cannot disengage because the existence of the region and the community of interests sharing common concerns advanced through regional plans require consistent and careful tending. Deborah and Frank Popper, for example, remind us that though we may have wanted the "frontier" to close, it never really did. Frontier planning and development in the United States is, as they note, an ongoing challenge and responsibility. In this sense, regional planning incorporates stewardship for the plan as a key role for regional planners.

SUSTAINING THE REGION

Many of the book's chapters identify the lack of effective regional institutions as a huge stumbling block to sustained regional planning. Create a city plan, and the city is there to implement it. Create a regional plan, and the locus of responsibility for action and for enforcing mutual accountability become hard to identify and, in some cases, envision. Almost all of the preceding chapters address the necessity for capable, empowered institutions to act on the outcomes of regional planning in a manner that reflects the regional project and prospect. Whether they discuss agencies that will be able and willing to make metropolitan plans work, the creation of a new commission for frontier planning and development, Ian McHarg's effort to plan by maintaining regard for global ecosystems, or simply reaching agreement on mutually accountable roles and responsibilities across boundaries, the authors cannot overemphasize the crucial role of effective regional institutions.

It is certainly attractive to believe that networked and voluntary associations can serve as hosts for regional planning and action. As the work presented in this book makes clear, however, bringing about real change through these networks is a struggle, and it is difficult to find encouragement in the results to date. Change, after all, requires putting what is known and comfortable at risk. This is no small task under any circumstances, but it is doubly difficult in the contested territories addressed by regional planning. Case studies in the chapters by Beatley, Foster, and Knaap and Lewis all suggest that this approach is getting a good look. Perhaps in time its efficacy will be proven.

Some of the most effective examples of regional planning have depended on the intervention of more senior levels of government. Regional planning can more easily take hold when a state or the federal government requires planning or enables it with the presentation of incentives and the prospect of new investment. The old idea that regions are part of a whole, and regional planning is a means by which to articulate or reframe what a region contributes to something larger, is clearly implied.

Engaging the states and the federal government in generating regional responses with the ability to make real change is attractive for all the reasons already stated, however this task is difficult and the outcome is far from certain. One only has to look at the real challenges faced by major federally inspired, large landscape preservation efforts, such as those for the New Jersey Pinelands, Lake Tahoe, and the Columbia River Gorge, to recognize that although federal intervention can start things off, by itself it cannot cause the efforts to succeed. In the end, local action over time is what actually ratifies regional plans and determines their success or failure.

This is not to say that regional implementation is impossible. As Janice Morphet (2011) notes in her review of the spatial planning experience in Great Britain, what once was viewed as a limited policy exercise at the regional level has now become a more active engagement in guiding capital investment decisions and actual project management. The realm of regional planning, particularly in the context of complex, multijurisdictional lifestyles and the specter of climate change, has expanded, at least in the European context, to broader operational realms, just as it has in the U.S. metropolitan regions visited by Fregonese and Gabbe, Knaap and Lewis, and Yaro.

As Foster makes clear, regional planning means that units with decision-making power need to contribute some of that power to regional efforts. In her view, the regional effort requires greater responsibility to be vested in one or more of central, local, and/or nongovernmental authorities. There is no other option. In this environment, and echoing Pastor and Benner's call for "humble" planners, Foster identifies the greatest capacity necessary for regional planners as being a "deep appreciation for interconnectedness in an interdependent world."

Interestingly, Stefanie Duhr, Claire Colomb, and Vincent Nadin (2010) echo this last point in their examination of European spatial planning. In the European context, *transboundary cooperation* is the term applied to the European Union–scale spatial planning experience. They point to the need for regional planners to have the ability to understand the "spatial position" from which they work and its connections to the broader European Union. They also note that planners often unconsciously proceed with an understanding of how the jurisdiction they represent fits into its national context. Working at the regional—here European—scale, however, requires a more conscious and critical understanding of place and connection.

In sum, regional planning differs from local or state planning by requiring the identification of territory as a first step, by the roles that planners need to play in creating and stewarding regional communities, and by the need to anticipate and explicitly address the institutional context for getting things done. Regional planning is unusual in that the contextual basis for the kind of planning assumed for jurisdictions with authority over territory must be discovered or created for the region.

This is both a tremendous challenge and a huge opportunity. Regional planning done well is possibly the truest expression of the democratic principal of self-rule. No regional plan can succeed without the consent of those who occupy and constitute the region. However, making effective regional plans requires securing the consent of the governed early on. To do otherwise is to relegate regional plans to that oft-sited shelf where plans go, never again to see the light of day.

TOWARD A REGION ETHIC

We believe that the challenges facing our nation and world—climate change and the threat of ecological collapse; the goal of sustainability; inequities from uneven development; and looming shortages of energy, water, and materials, to name a few—will increase the need to create useful regional plans. We do not believe that this means doing away with the methods and means that we have chosen traditionally to carry out planning in this country, however. To the contrary, as regional planners we are well aware of the strong hold that local interests and perspectives have on planning in the United States. For many, imagining or imaging the region is more elusive than visualizing the neighborhood or city. Citizens of this country like government close to home and their own representatives, even while they voice distrust in larger units of government and someone else's representatives. As famously stated by Tip O'Neill, the late representative from Massachusetts, "All politics is local." To that we would add, "Most affections are, too."

Still, planners cannot avoid confronting the known, serious deficiencies in the ways that land use, urban form, and resource use and management have unfolded over the past 100 years. So, what's next? For starters, we'd like to build on an old idea that helped to make the modern concept of sustainability possible. Decades ago, Aldo Leopold (1966) advanced the notion of a "land ethic." As he noted, an ethic defines what is and is not socially acceptable, the relationships and the ways that individuals and communities view their individual purposes in relation to other individuals and communities. Leopold's concern was with land, and more specifically with what he regarded as a willingness to overlook and overrun fundamental relationships that are needed to sustain life, including our own.

In response, he proposed that it was time for humankind to embrace a land ethic to complement other ethical principles in society, especially those associated with economic relationships. Leopold stated his land ethic in simple terms: "A thing is right when it tends to preserve the integrity, stability, and beauty of the biotic community. It is wrong when it tends otherwise" (Leopold 1966, 240).

This ethical principle suggests that human communities need to create a "golden rule" for engagement with the biotic or natural landscape. To Leopold it was inconceivable for people to consider themselves to be at arm's length or separate from the ecology of the natural world. He saw the human community as intimately intertwined with the natural world and the fate of both as inseparable.

The contemporary notion of sustainability presents us with a similar reframing of perspectives. Though Leopold focused largely on bringing the biotic community into better focus in the course of human affairs, sustainable development looks in several directions, calling for a new appreciation of our choices' impacts on the environment, on each other, and on future generations.

Today, sustainability is no more certain or easy than when Leopold was writing. As during his time, today we are faced with remaking relationships in an environment that privileges old ways of thinking and acting. If our challenges are regional in scope, then we must empower a regional planning that is capable of supporting big changes. Can it be made strong enough to attain sustainability for everyone, and not merely create islands of sustainability for the few? Or will it take some sort of cataclysmic crisis to reframe for all time our understanding of the world and our role in it?

For us, as for Leopold, the challenge is to make relationships in a new way. Leopold proposed a land ethic rather than a new land department or set of codes for land use because real change capable of overcoming the inertia of existing relationships without inflicting harm on huge numbers of people and landscapes must begin with a change in outlook, not simply a change in the rules. As we have identified in this book, just as real and important roles exist for extant jurisdictions to play in the emergence of a regionally conceived sustainable world, new institutional relationships are also crucial. The first step is to understand better the task before us in context. The way that our society articulates that context will be through its understanding and use of ethics.

Consider, for example, the familiar "three *E*s," the "triple bottom line" formulation for sustainability in its simplest form: environment, economy, and equity. In this construct, sustainable development results from the interaction of our goals and desires for a vital economy, a healthy environment, and a society characterized by justice for all. Decisions are seen as being enmeshed in all three dimensions. It is impossible to speak only of environment or economy or equity when making choices or defining goals for the future. In a sense, this formulation of sustainable development is a statement of ethics. Fully accounting for impacts in all three realms is the only path to real sustainability, or even to understand whether something done in the name of sustainability can be considered to be so ethically.

Because the future we will experience will be the sum of myriad individual actions and incremental choices, our grandest plans and aims can be undone by the most mundane decisions and actions made and taken over time. Leopold challenged us to rethink our role in the ecology of the landscapes we inhabit. Similarly, regional planning is being asked to take on a range of issues that require us to reconsider our roles in the context of the regions in which we live. The future of regional planning lies in making this context for our lives and choices more useful for achieving the goals of sustainability. We think that the path toward the future for regional planning begins with the call for a "region ethic" that will advance the sustainability of the regions we inhabit and on which our existence depends.

As an ethic, this is all about relationships and conditioning choices. To present sustainability or even regional growth management in softer, more equivocal terms would be to relegate regional planning to the same marginal role in which it often finds itself today. Recasting regional planning as an ethical pursuit makes its true purposes transparent in a constructive way. It is not about jurisdiction, size, or number, but rather about relationships, as ethical principles must be, and more specifically, about relationships between people and place, people and each other, and people and the choices we all make.

For regional planning, this suggests that the task is concerned less with the exercise of jurisdiction and more with the recognition of needs, compatibility, and true equality. The core vision here is of a form of habitation of regions that recognizes that to live in both society and an ecology rooted in place requires limitations for everyone. We coexist in the truest and broadest sense. Regional planning is the best means to mediate relationships between the scales native to the systems that sustain us and the institutional scales through which we exercise power in our society.

For regional planners, embracing the region ethic is based on a clear commitment to advancing sustainability and a recognition of the time needed for it to succeed. Regional planners are presented with specific technical tasks, but they exist in relation to higher and broader aims that the planners must consciously articulate and share if they, and regional planning, are to succeed.

As with Leopold's land ethic, the region ethic is a call to recognize the central interdependencies that make our inhabitation of cities and landscapes possible. As Frederick Steiner notes in chapter 2, this was at the heart of Ian McHarg's seminal observations and his life's work, although today McHarg would probably understand this as an even more complex and integrated endeavor than was the case when *Design with Nature* was first published in 1969.

Regional planning, sometimes seen as art and other times as science, is probably best viewed as craft that is honed and understood through practice and reflection. The chapters in *Regional Planning in America* suggest that the coming generations of regional planners will need to be: able to understand local issues in a regional and global context; adept at defining planning regions based on functional planning problems; capable of reaching across boundaries to assess, identify, and act on common cause; and able to navigate the currents of power and to create the lasting relationships and institutions that are needed to perform and implement plans. Persistence should be included as a requisite character trait, for we must be in this for the long haul.

We are optimistic about the future role for regional planning in the United States. It faces enormous challenges, but both the demands for an effective regional planning brought about by the issues we face and the trends pointing to more vigorous and sustained experimentation to find ways to accomplish it suggest that we are likely to see more, not less, regional activity in the coming decades. Helping U.S. regional planning to evolve in the next century will reward the best efforts of planning practitioners, educators, and researchers. Making the region ethic a tool for practice is, perhaps, the first step.

REFERENCES

Duhr, Stefanie, Claire Colomb, and Vincent Nadin. 2010. *European spatial planning and territorial cooperation*. London: Routledge.

Leopold, Aldo. 1966. *A Sand County Almanac*. New York: Oxford University Press.

Morphet, Janice. 2011. *Effective practice in spatial planning*. London: Routledge.

ACKNOWLEDGMENTS

We are grateful to the authors of these chapters for their enthusiastic embrace of the challenge we set for them and ourselves: to assess the current state of regional planning in the United States and chart its possible future course. Starting with their presentations at a discussion session at the Lincoln Institute of Land Policy in June 2010 through the final review of the artfully produced text and graphics, they have been unstinting in their efforts. We also thank Gil Kelley, former planning director in Portland, Oregon, and Professor Robert Fishman of the University of Michigan for participating in the discussion and helping to shape the final message.

Gregory K. Ingram, president of the Lincoln Institute, has provided strong and unwavering support for this effort and for advancing the role of regional planning in general. We thank him and the Institute for sponsoring the contributors' research, the discussion session, and this publication. The staff who have been especially critical to this entire project include Lisa Cloutier, senior program manager in the Department of Planning and Urban Form, and Ann LeRoyer, senior editor and director of publications. We also have enjoyed working with book designer Peter Blaiwas and editor Brian Hotchkiss of Vern Associates, and thank them for crafting a book that we hope will have a long shelf life.

Further, Ethan and Armando thank their respective wives, Melanie and Jean, for their support and forbearance.

— Ethan Seltzer and Armando Carbonell

CONTRIBUTORS

Editors

Armando Carbonell
Senior Fellow and Chair
Department of Planning and Urban Form
Lincoln Institute of Land Policy
Cambridge, Massachusetts

Ethan Seltzer
Professor
Toulan School of Urban Studies
and Planning
College of Urban and Public Affairs
Portland State University, Oregon

Authors

Timothy Beatley
Teresa Heinz Professor of Sustainable
Communities
School of Architecture
University of Virginia, Charlottesville

Chris Benner
Chair
Community Development Graduate Group
Associate Professor
Community and Regional Development
Human and Community Development
Department
University of California, Davis

Kathryn A. Foster
Director
University at Buffalo Regional Institute
The State University of New York, Buffalo

John Fregonese
President
Fregonese Associates
Portland, Oregon

C. J. Gabbe
Project Manager
Fregonese Associates
Portland, Oregon

Gerrit-Jan Knaap
Executive Director and Professor
of Urban Studies and Planning
National Center for Smart Growth
Research and Education
University of Maryland, College Park

Rebecca Lewis
Research Assistant
National Center for Smart Growth
Research and Education
University of Maryland, College Park

Manuel Pastor
Professor
American Studies and Ethnicity
Director
Program for Environmental
and Regional Equity
University of Southern California,
Los Angeles

Deborah E. Popper
Professor of Geography
College of Staten Island and
Graduate Center/City University of New York
Staten Island, New York

Frank J. Popper
Professor
Bloustein School of Planning
and Public Policy
Rutgers University
New Brunswick, New Jersey

Frederick Steiner
Dean and Henry M. Rockwell Chair
in Architecture
School of Architecture
The University of Texas at Austin

Robert D. Yaro
President
Regional Plan Association
New York, New York

INDEX

ABOUT THE LINCOLN INSTITUTE OF LAND POLICY

The Lincoln Institute of Land Policy is a private operating foundation whose mission is to improve the quality of public debate and decisions in the areas of land policy and land-related taxation in the United States and around the world. The Institute's goals are to integrate theory and practice to better shape land policy and to provide a nonpartisan forum for discussion of the multi-disciplinary forces that influence public policy. This focus on land derives from the Institute's founding objective—to address the links between land policy and social and economic progress—that was identified and analyzed by political economist and author Henry George.

The work of the Institute is organized in three departments: Valuation and Taxation, Planning and Urban Form, and International Studies. We seek to inform decision making through education, research, demonstration projects, and the dissemination of information through publications, our Web site, and other media. Our programs bring together scholars, practitioners, public officials, policy advisers, and involved citizens in a collegial learning environment. The Institute does not take a particular point of view, but rather serves as a catalyst to facilitate analysis and discussion of land use and taxation issues—to make a difference today and to help policy makers plan for tomorrow.

The Lincoln Institute of Land Policy is an equal opportunity institution.

L LINCOLN INSTITUTE
OF LAND POLICY

113 Brattle Street
Cambridge, MA 02138-3400 USA

Phone: 1-617-661-3016 or 1-800-526-3873
Fax: 1-617-661-7235 or 1-800-526-3944
E-mail: help@lincolninst.edu
Web: www.lincolninst.edu